[illegible]ector

Illustration: Anna Backhausen

Story & Raster: Sophie Schönhammer

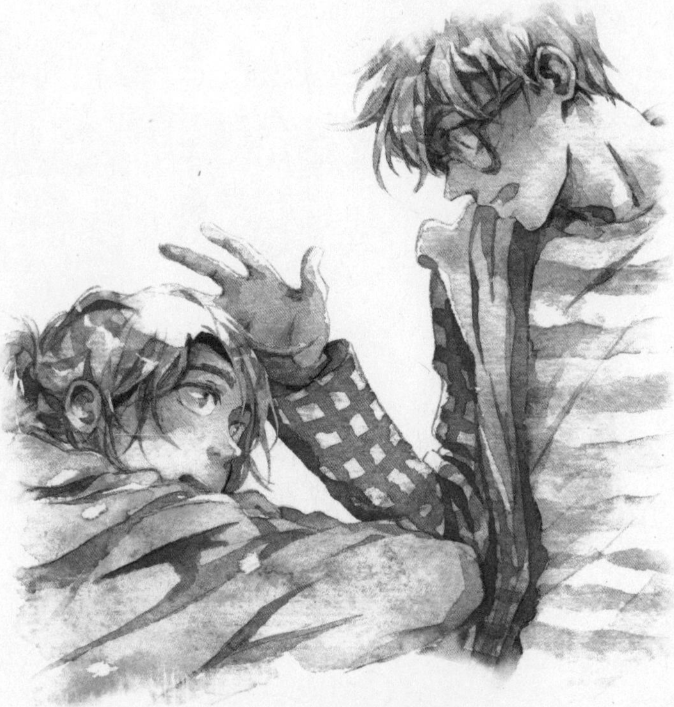

TOKYOPOP®

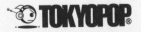

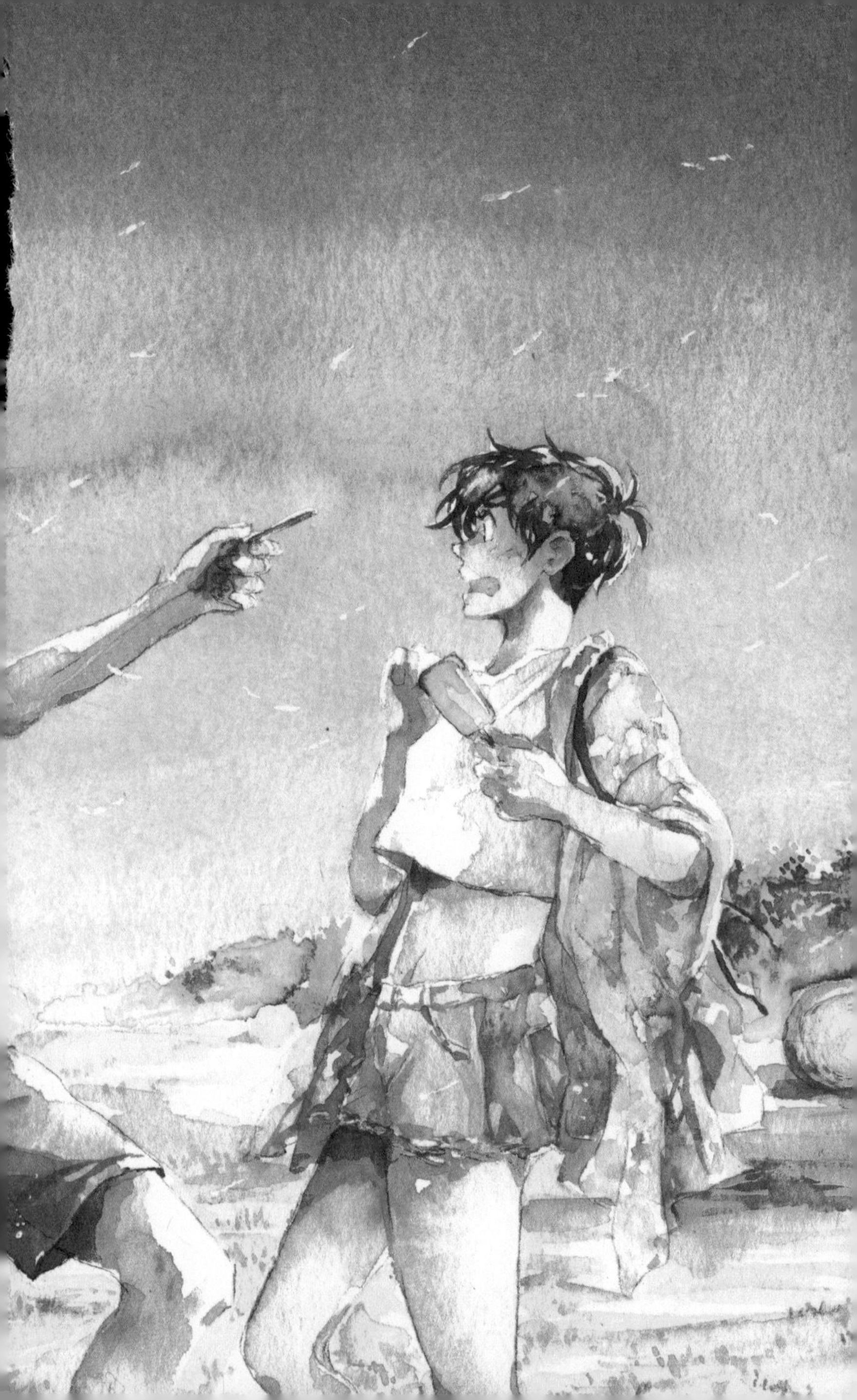

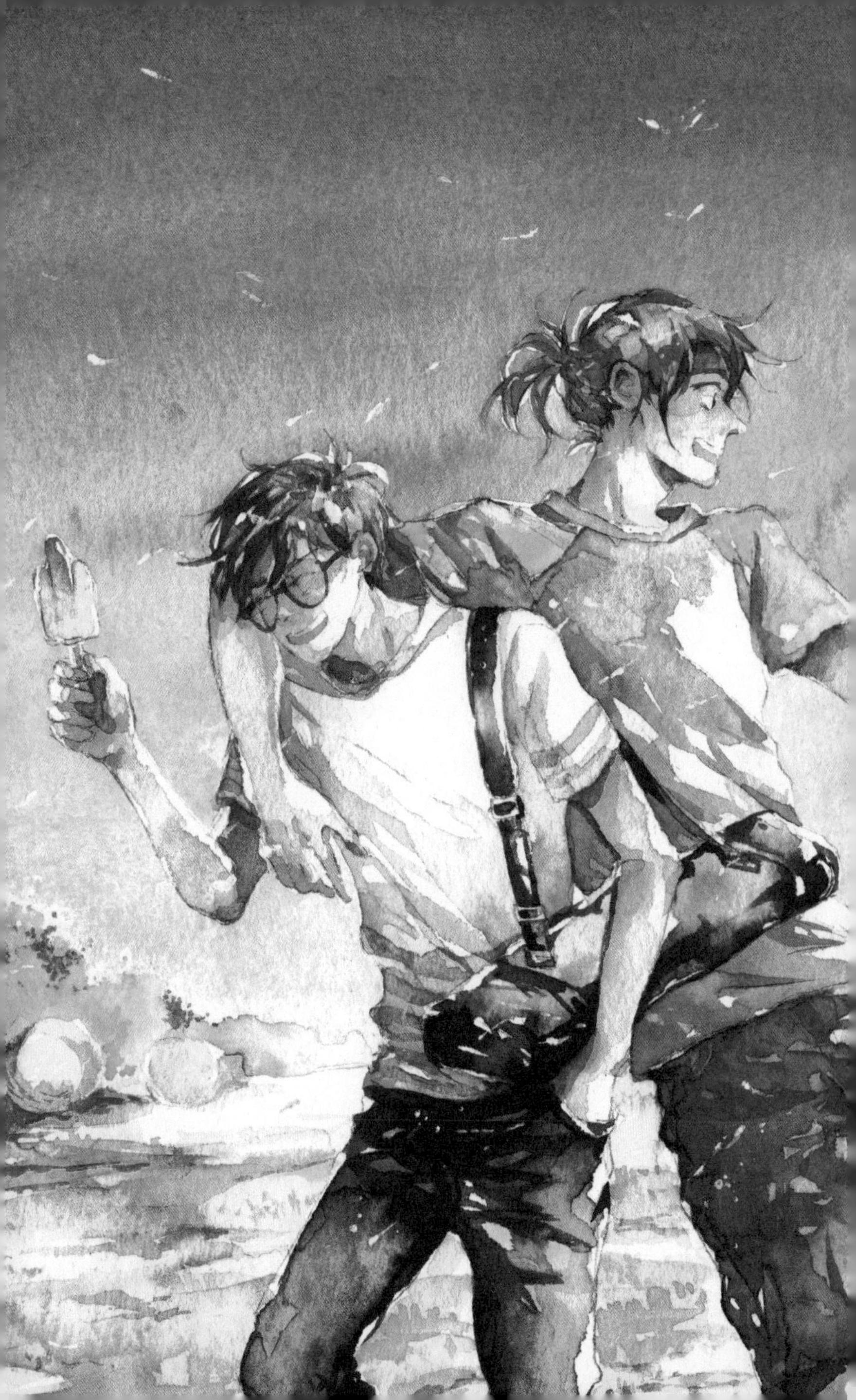

CONTENTS

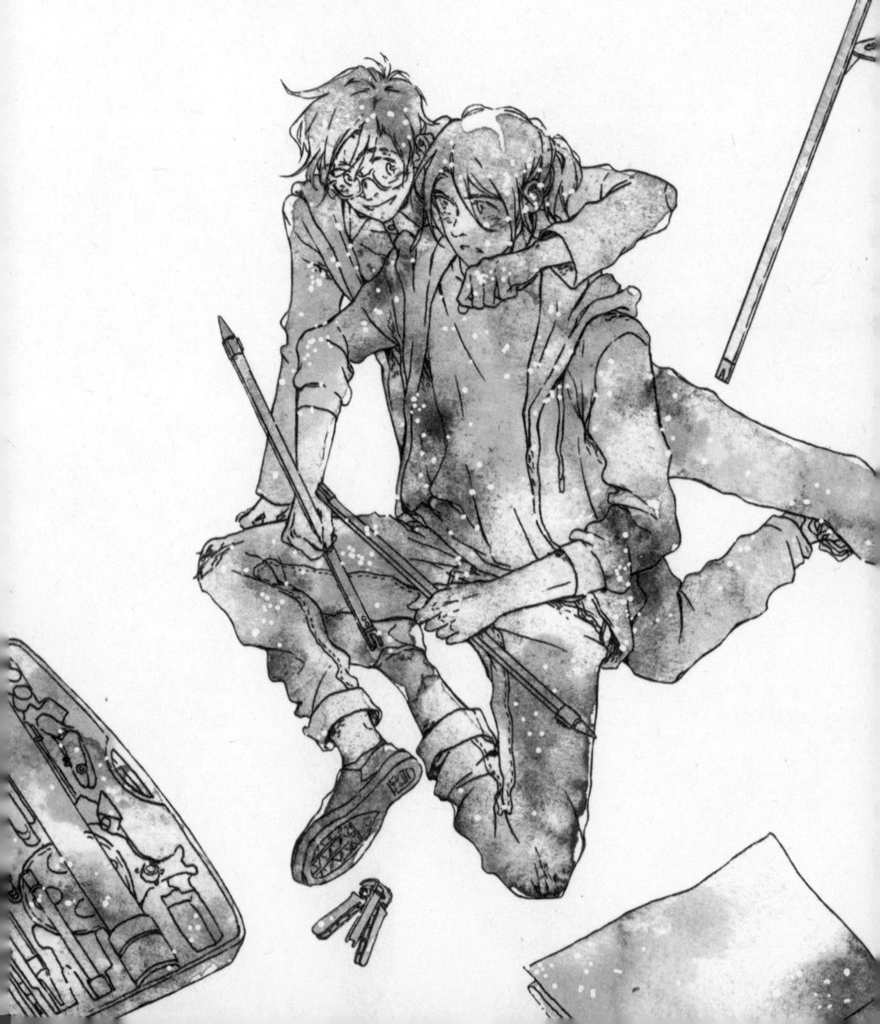

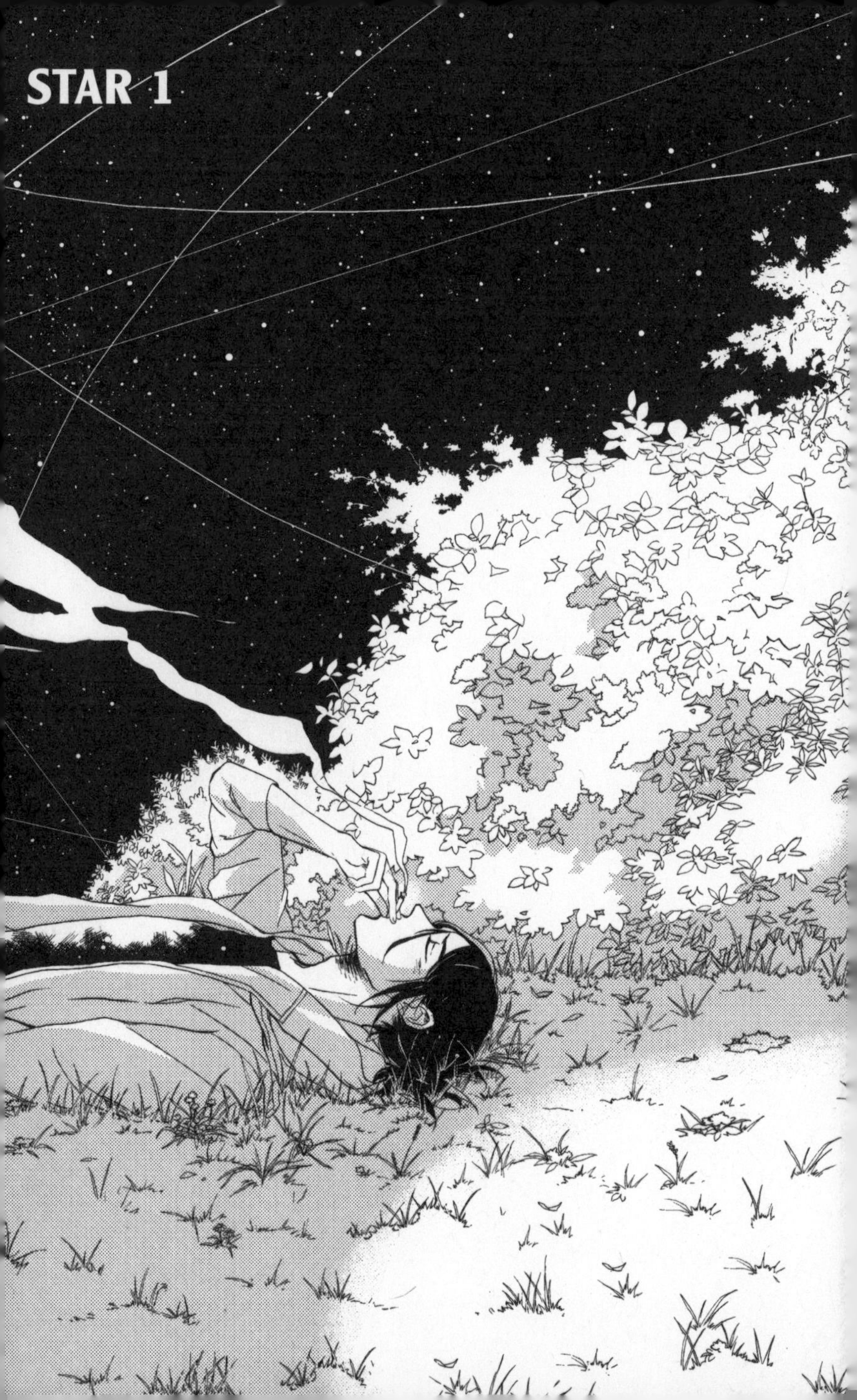
STAR 1

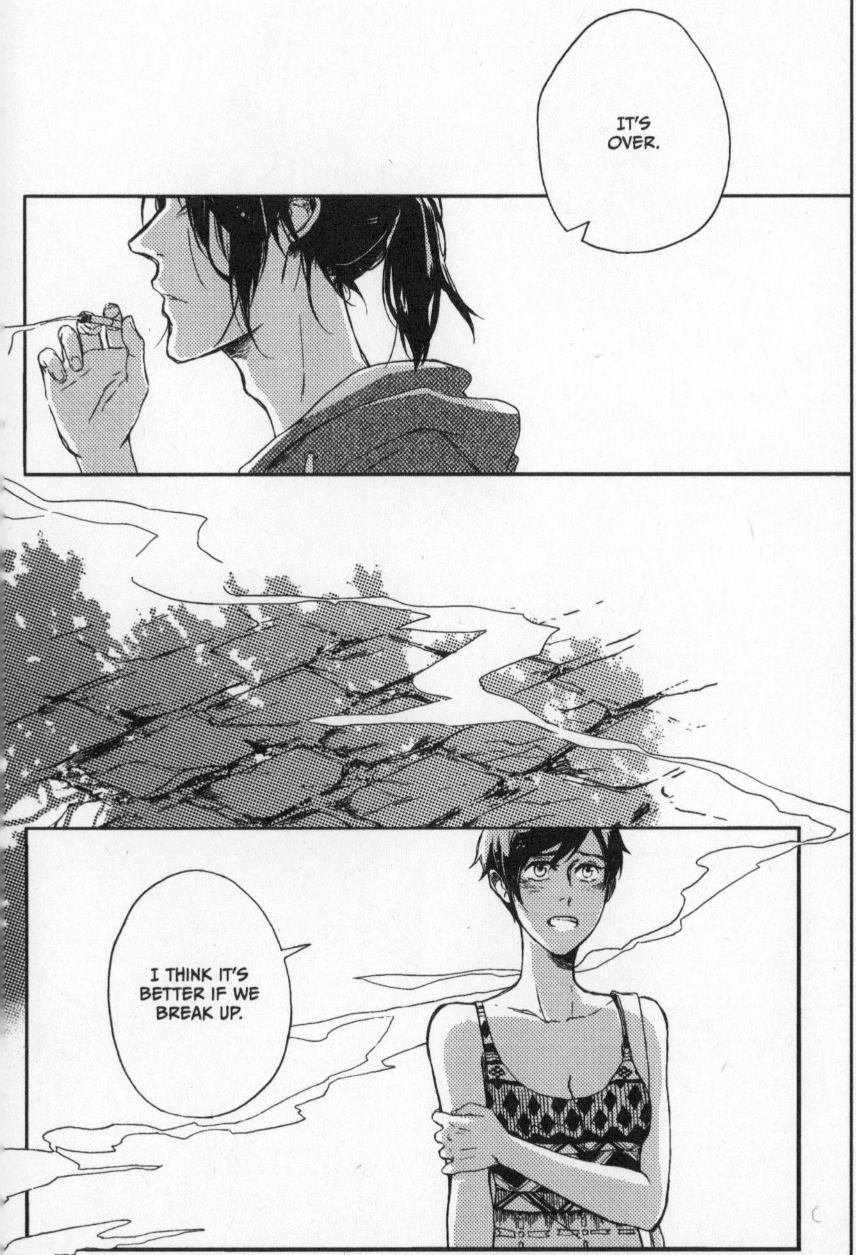
IT'S OVER.
I THINK IT'S BETTER IF WE BREAK UP.

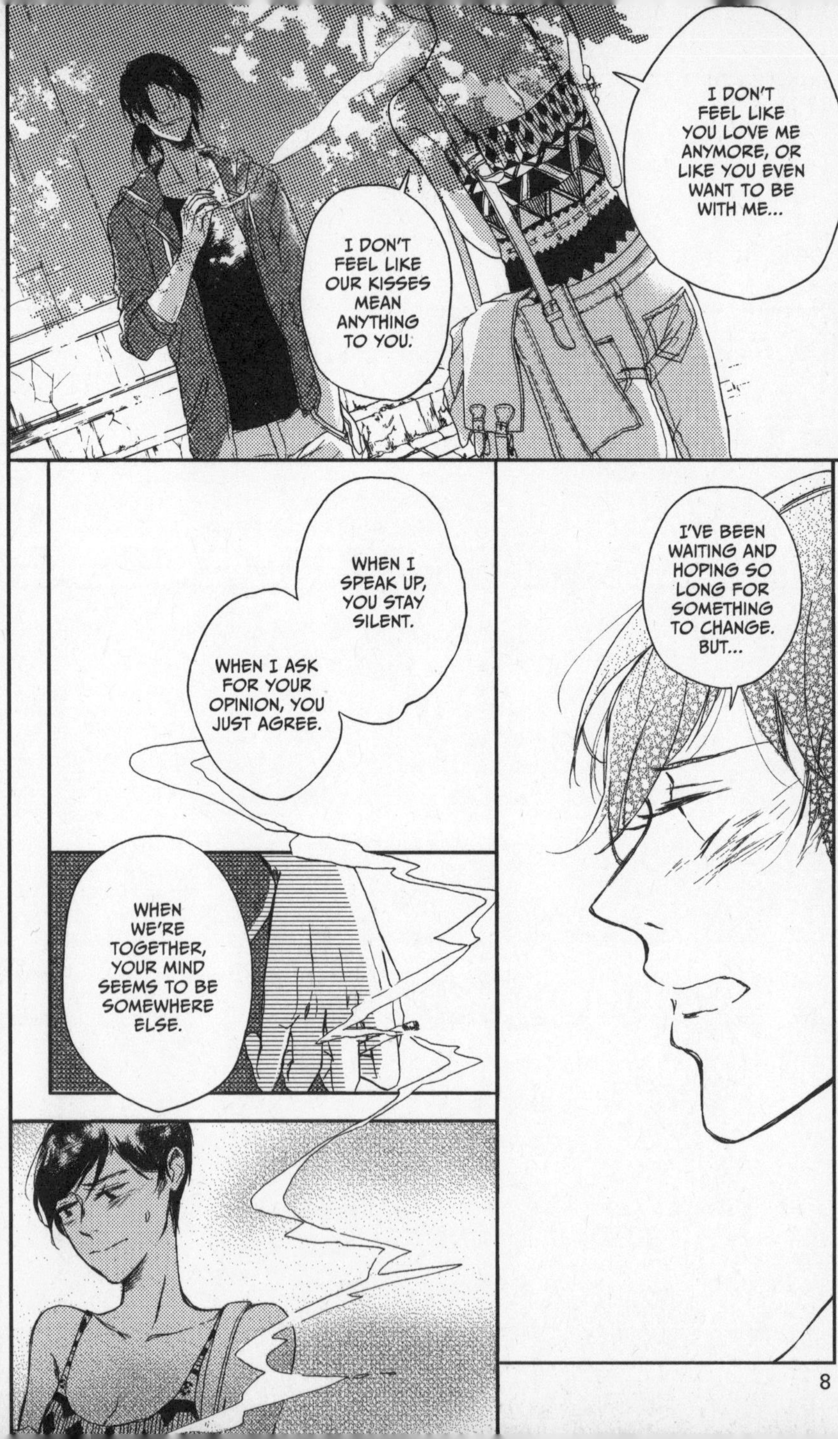
I DON'T FEEL LIKE YOU LOVE ME ANYMORE, OR LIKE YOU EVEN WANT TO BE WITH ME...
I DON'T FEEL LIKE OUR KISSES MEAN ANYTHING TO YOU.
I'VE BEEN WAITING AND HOPING SO LONG FOR SOMETHING TO CHANGE. BUT...
WHEN I SPEAK UP, YOU STAY SILENT.
WHEN I ASK FOR YOUR OPINION, YOU JUST AGREE.
WHEN WE'RE TOGETHER, YOUR MIND SEEMS TO BE SOMEWHERE ELSE.

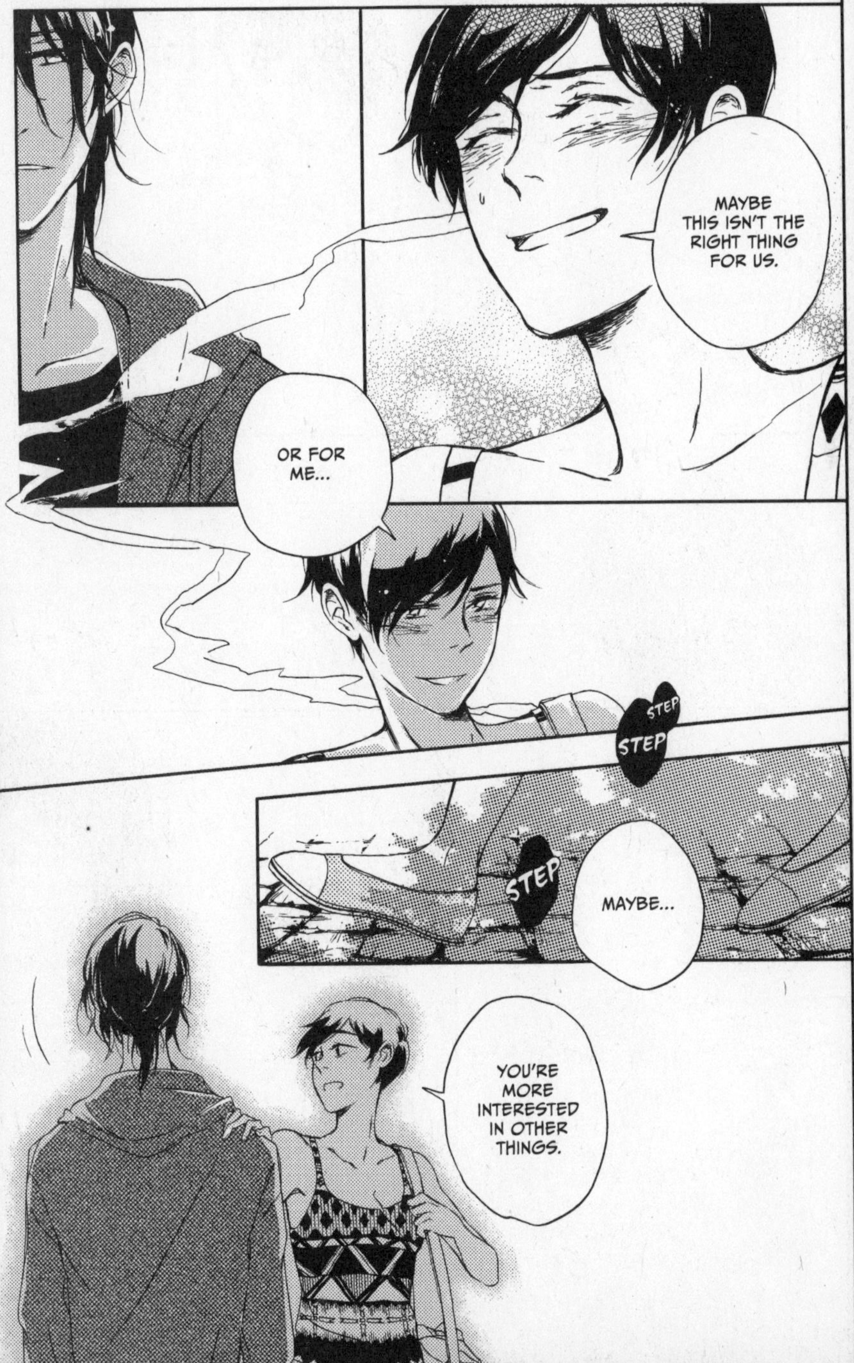
MAYBE THIS ISN'T THE RIGHT THING FOR US.
OR FOR ME...
STEP
STEP
STEP
MAYBE...
YOU'RE MORE INTERESTED IN OTHER THINGS.

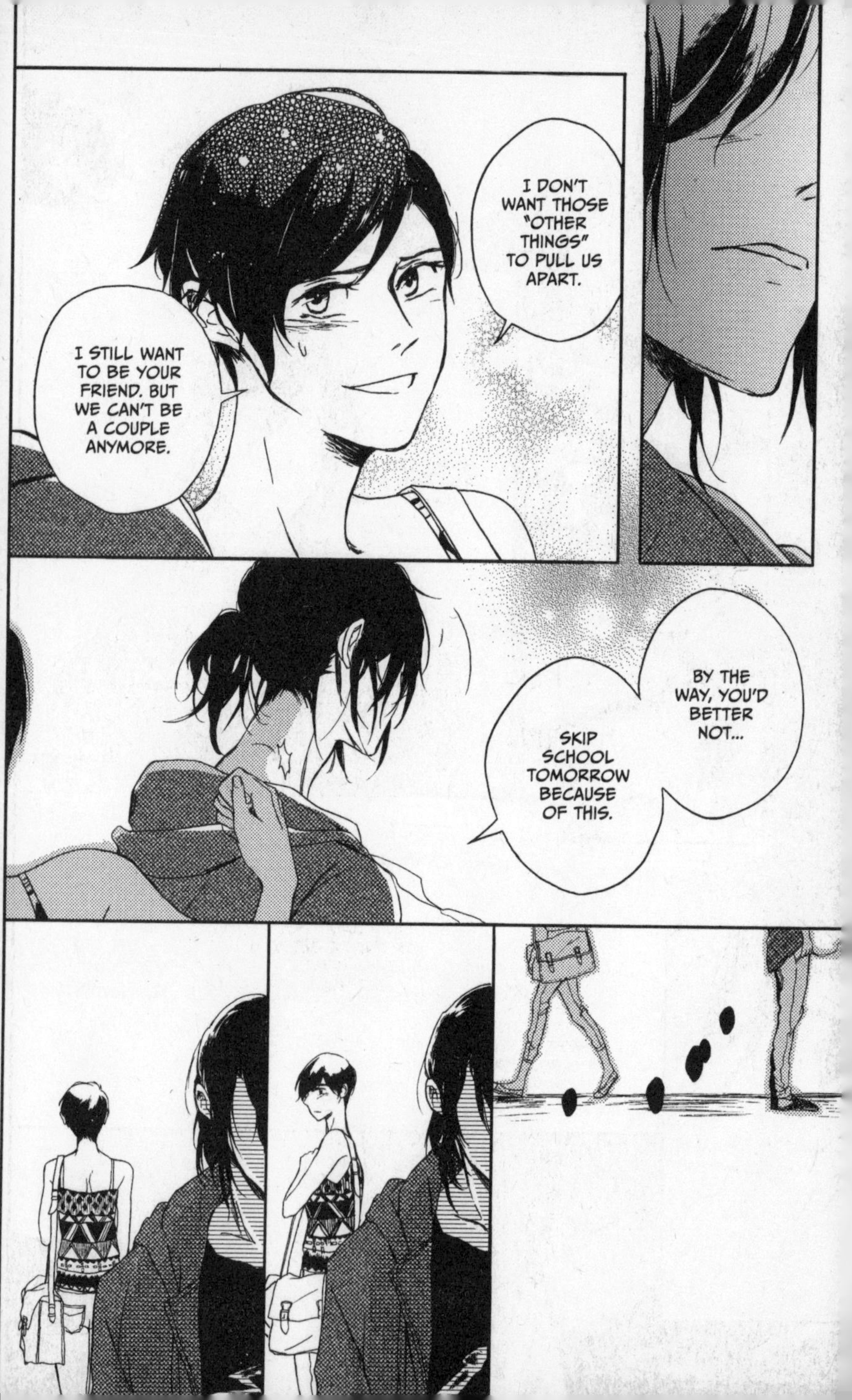
I DON'T WANT THOSE "OTHER THINGS" TO PULL US APART.
I STILL WANT TO BE YOUR FRIEND. BUT WE CAN'T BE A COUPLE ANYMORE.
BY THE WAY, YOU'D BETTER NOT...
SKIP SCHOOL TOMORROW BECAUSE OF THIS.

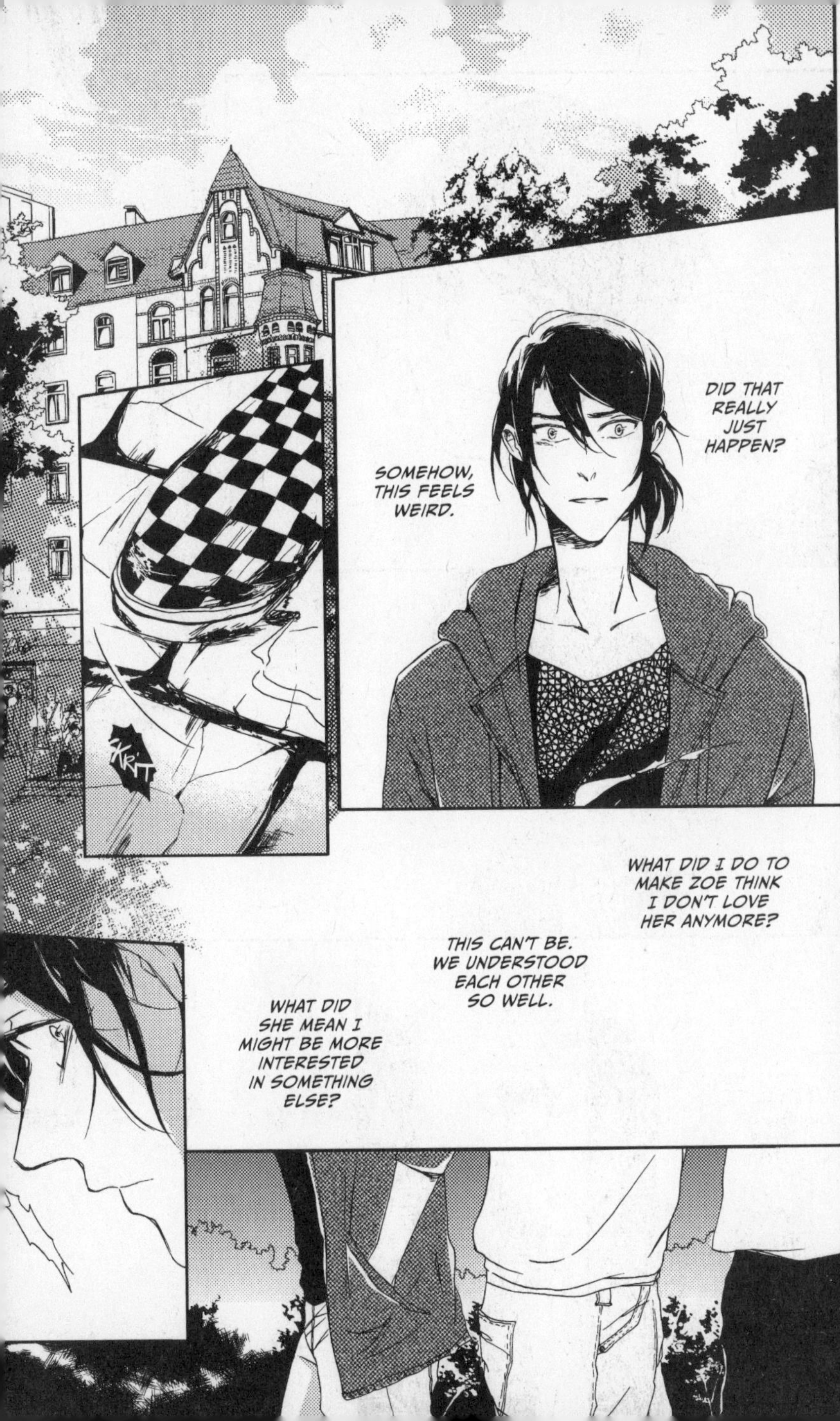
DID THAT REALLY JUST HAPPEN?
SOMEHOW, THIS FEELS WEIRD.
SKRIT
WHAT DID I DO TO MAKE ZOE THINK I DON'T LOVE HER ANYMORE?
THIS CAN'T BE. WE UNDERSTOOD EACH OTHER SO WELL.
WHAT DID SHE MEAN I MIGHT BE MORE INTERESTED IN SOMETHING ELSE?

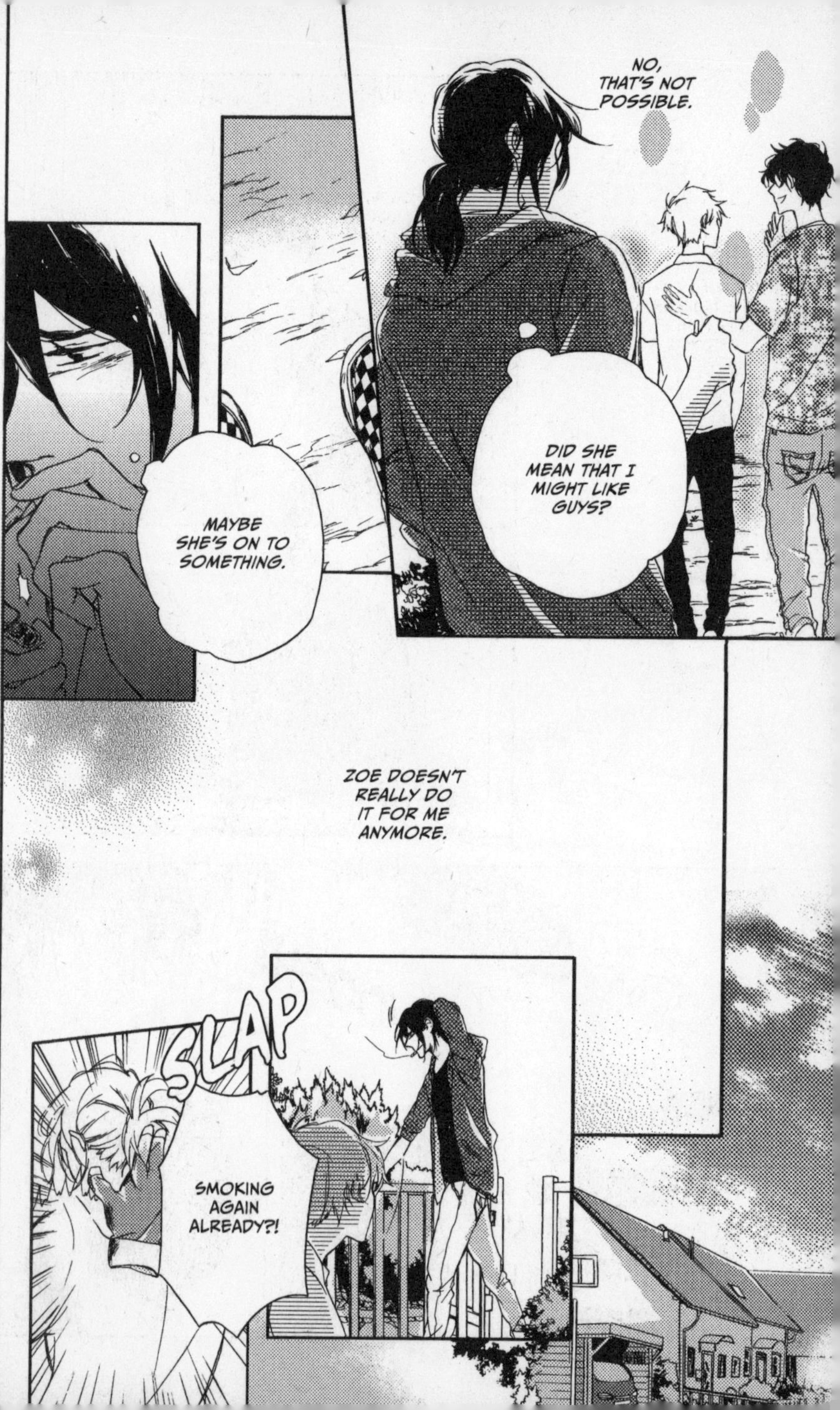
NO, THAT'S NOT POSSIBLE.
DID SHE MEAN THAT I MIGHT LIKE GUYS?
MAYBE SHE'S ON TO SOMETHING.
ZOE DOESN'T REALLY DO IT FOR ME ANYMORE.
SLAP
SMOKING AGAIN ALREADY?!

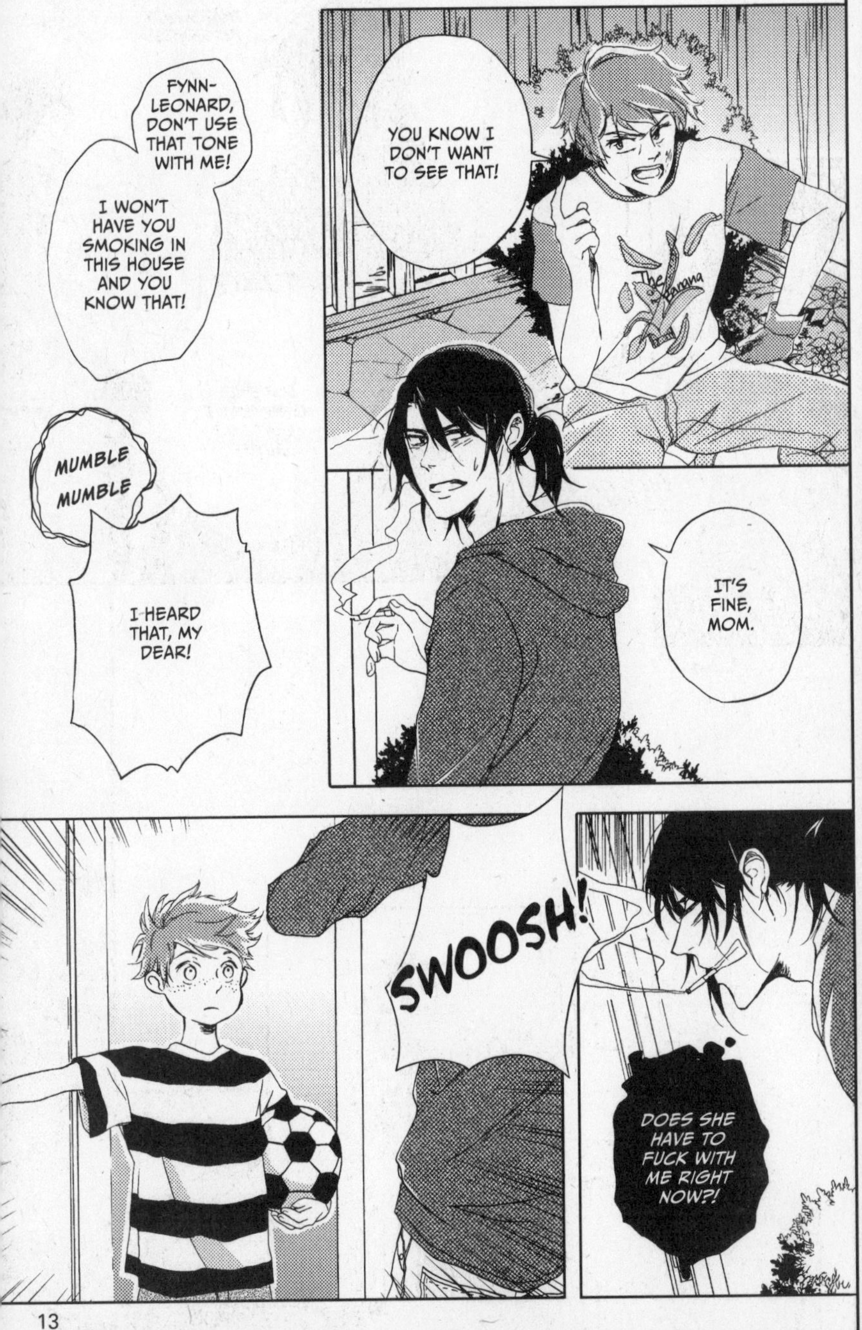
YOU KNOW I DON'T WANT TO SEE THAT!
IT'S FINE, MOM.
FYNN-LEONARD, DON'T USE THAT TONE WITH ME!
I WON'T HAVE YOU SMOKING IN THIS HOUSE AND YOU KNOW THAT!
MUMBLE MUMBLE
I HEARD THAT, MY DEAR!
DOES SHE HAVE TO FUCK WITH ME RIGHT NOW?!
SWOOSH!

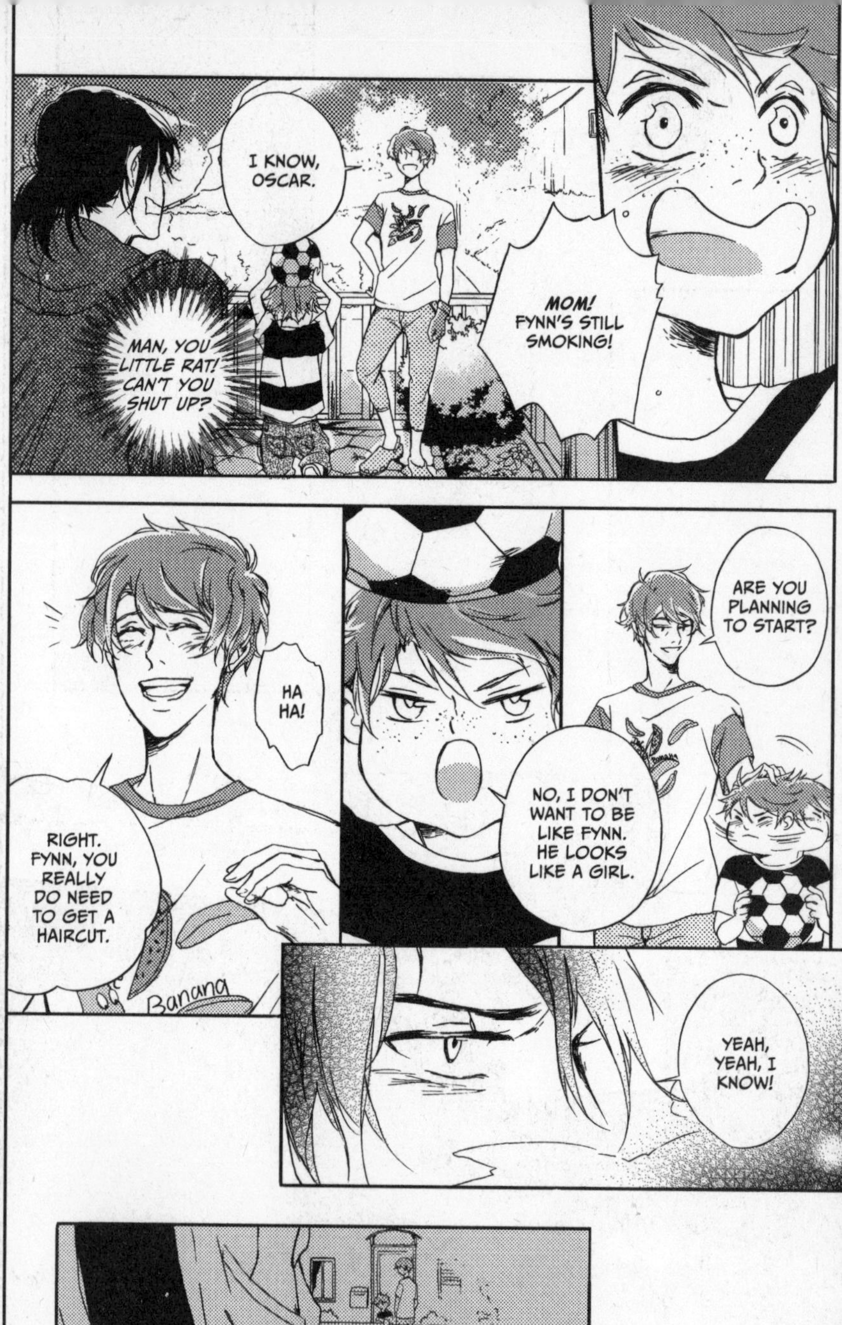
MOM! FYNN'S STILL SMOKING!
I KNOW, OSCAR.
MAN, YOU LITTLE RAT! CAN'T YOU SHUT UP?
ARE YOU PLANNING TO START?
NO, I DON'T WANT TO BE LIKE FYNN. HE LOOKS LIKE A GIRL.
HA HA!
RIGHT. FYNN, YOU REALLY DO NEED TO GET A HAIRCUT.
Banana
YEAH, YEAH, I KNOW!

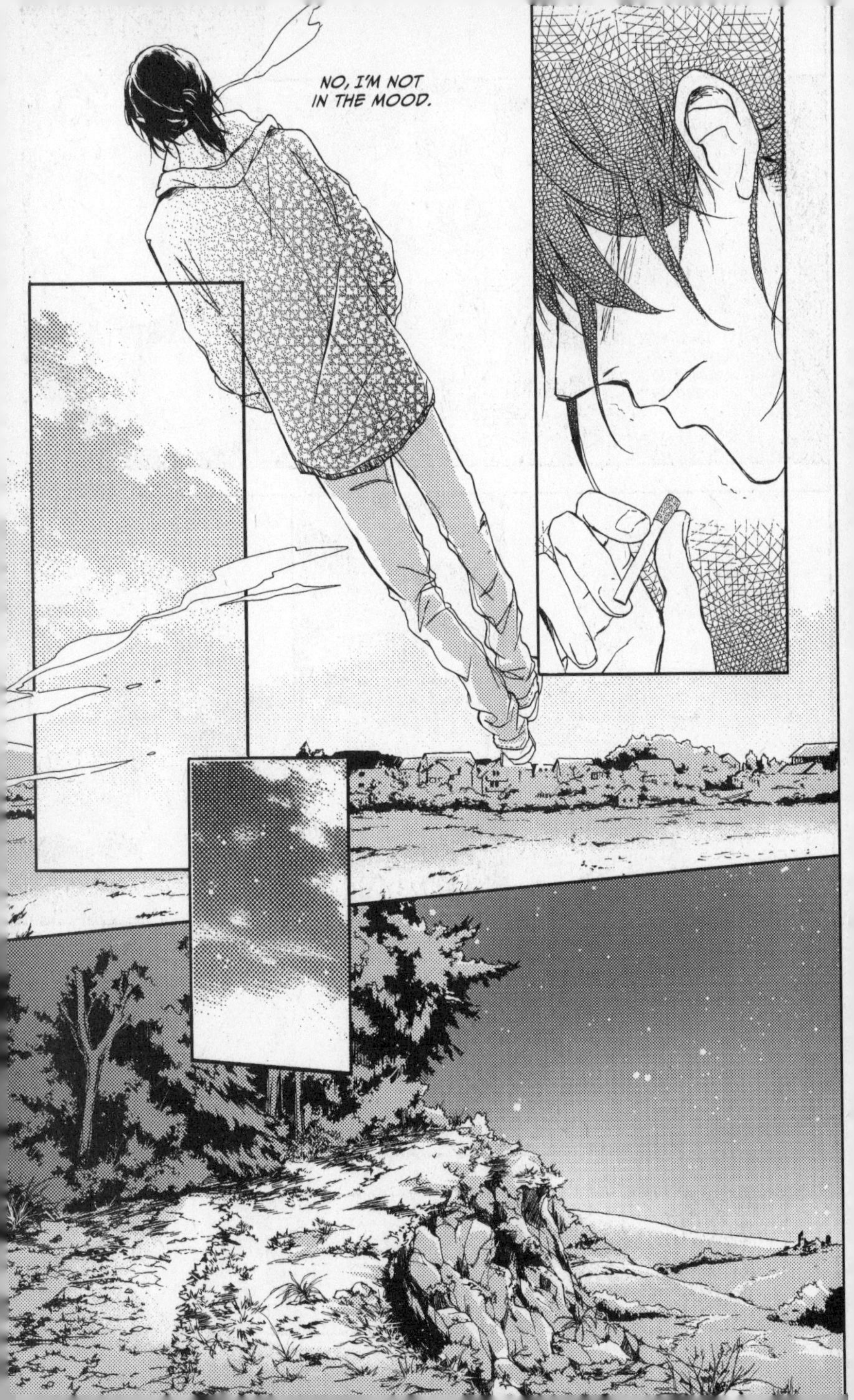
NO, I'M NOT IN THE MOOD.

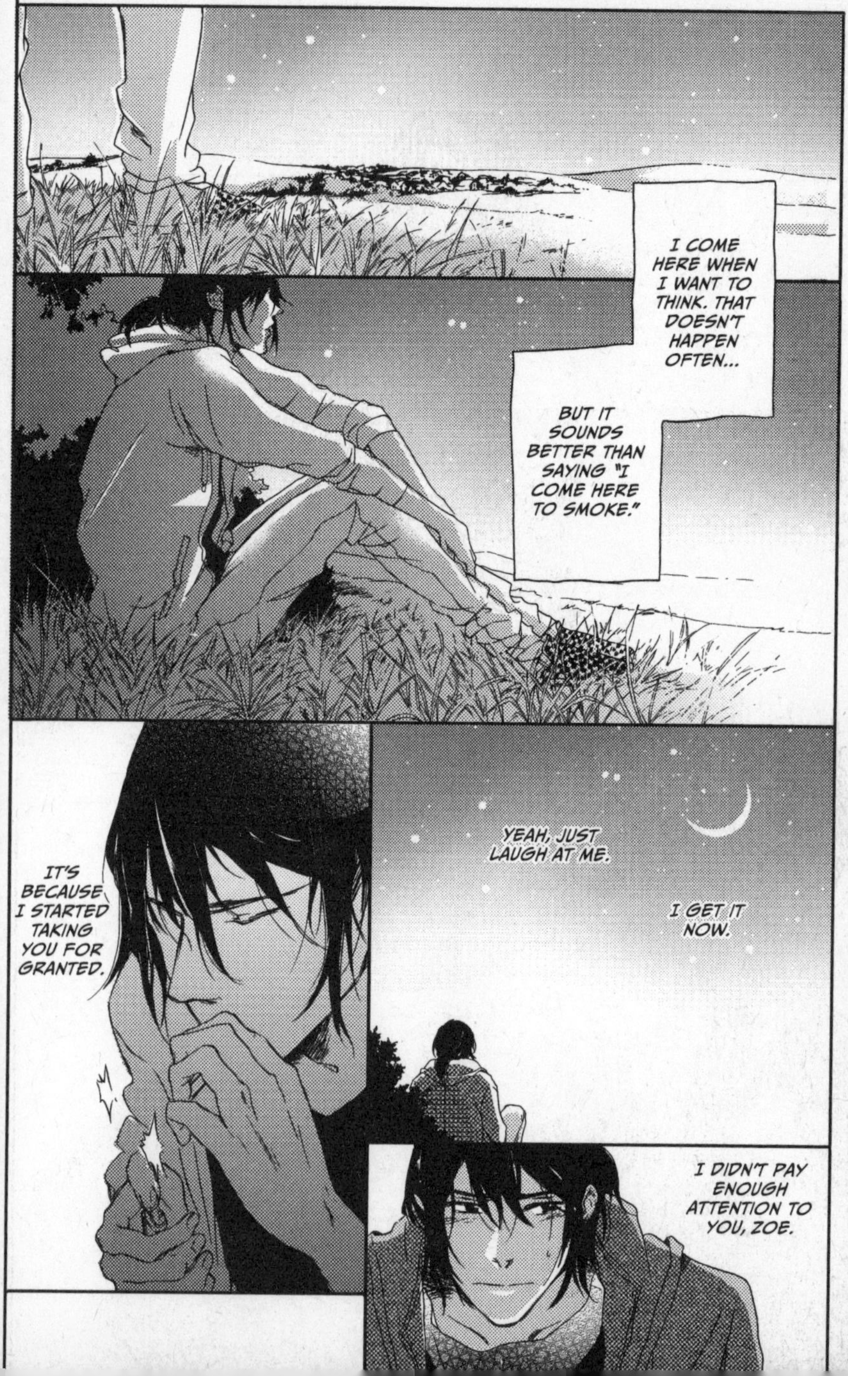
I COME HERE WHEN I WANT TO THINK. THAT DOESN'T HAPPEN OFTEN...
BUT IT SOUNDS BETTER THAN SAYING "I COME HERE TO SMOKE."
YEAH, JUST LAUGH AT ME.
I GET IT NOW.
I DIDN'T PAY ENOUGH ATTENTION TO YOU, ZOE.
IT'S BECAUSE I STARTED TAKING YOU FOR GRANTED.

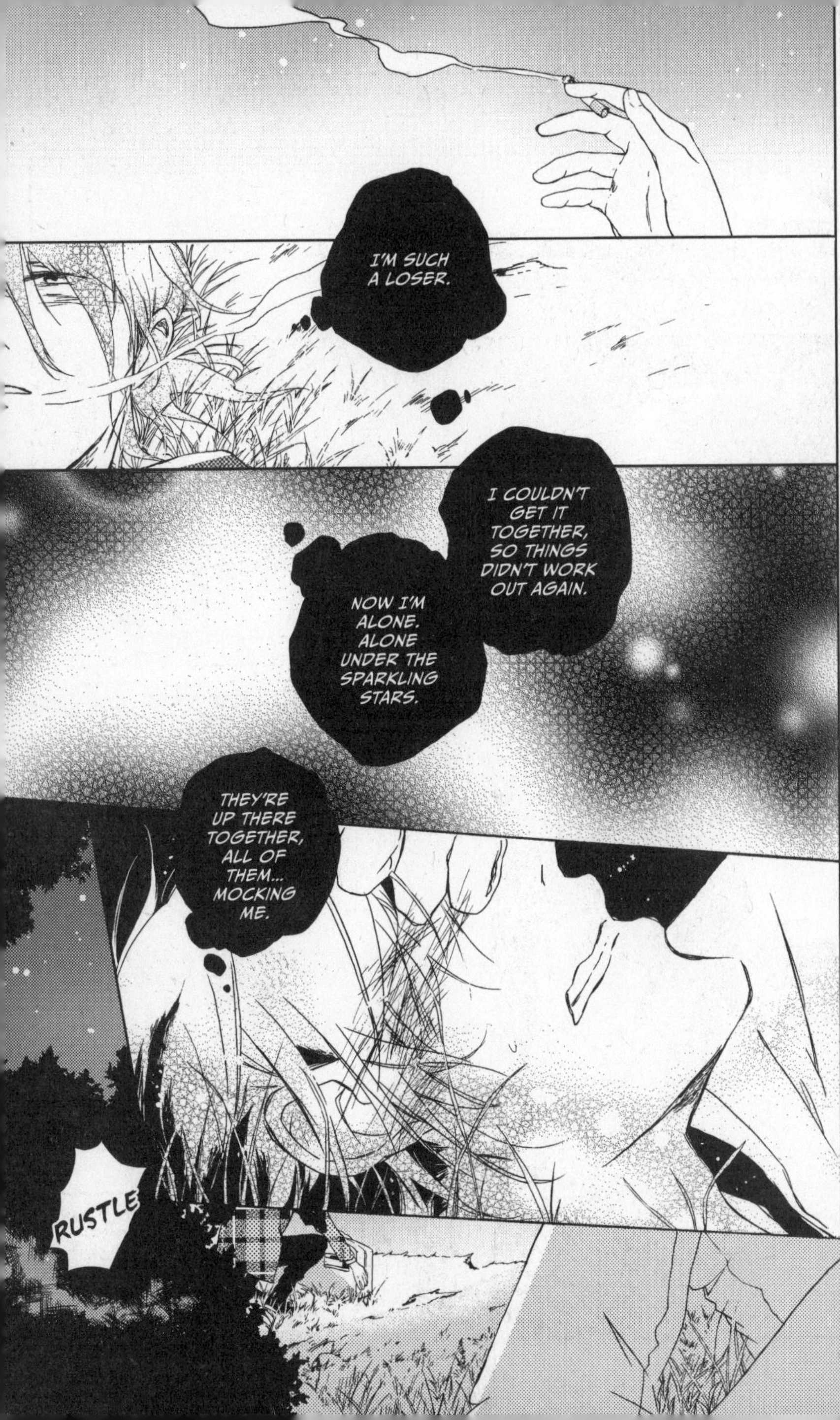
I'M SUCH A LOSER.
I COULDN'T GET IT TOGETHER, SO THINGS DIDN'T WORK OUT AGAIN.
NOW I'M ALONE. ALONE UNDER THE SPARKLING STARS.
THEY'RE UP THERE TOGETHER, ALL OF THEM... MOCKING ME.
RUSTLE

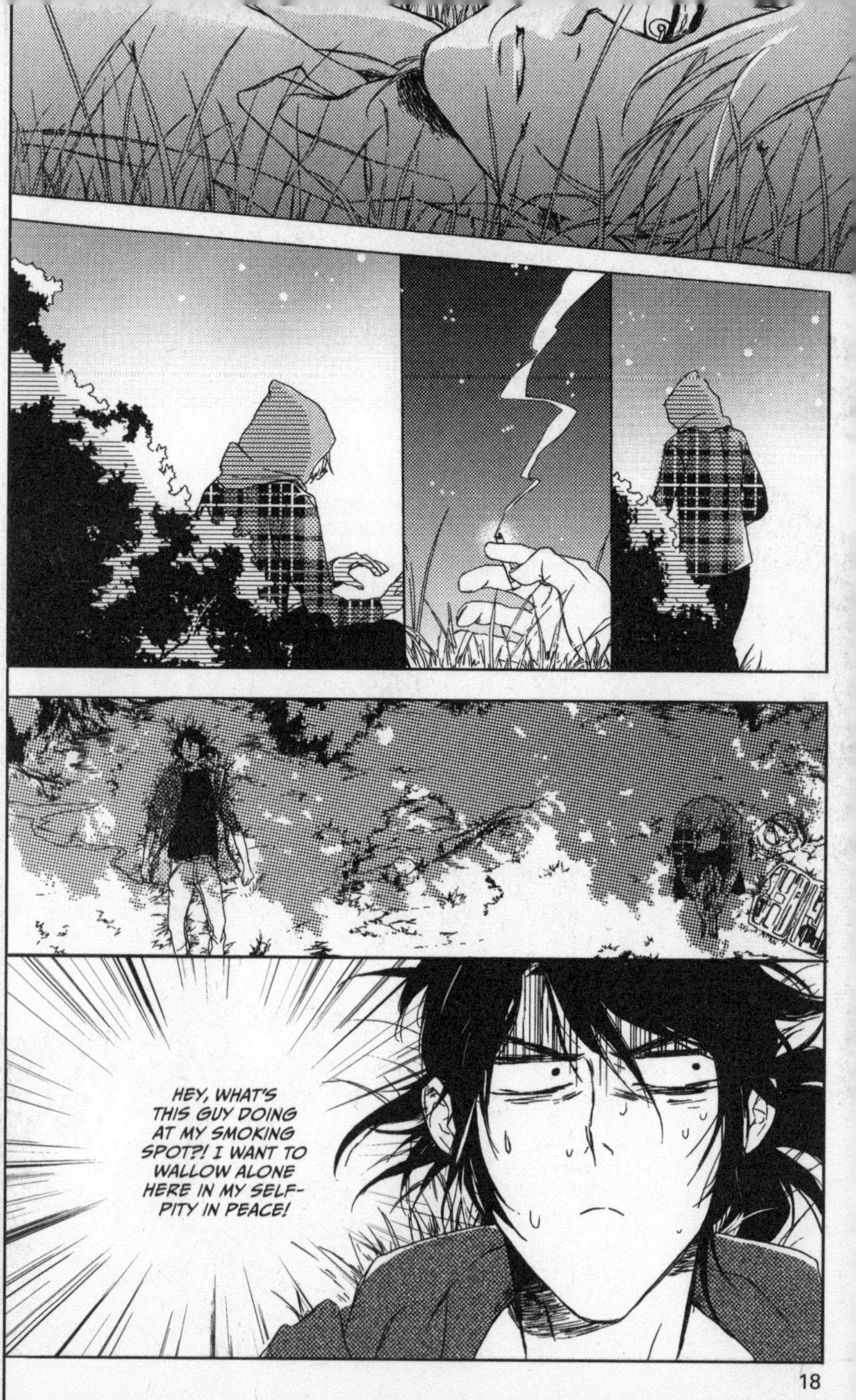
HEY, WHAT'S THIS GUY DOING AT MY SMOKING SPOT?! I WANT TO WALLOW ALONE HERE IN MY SELF-PITY IN PEACE!

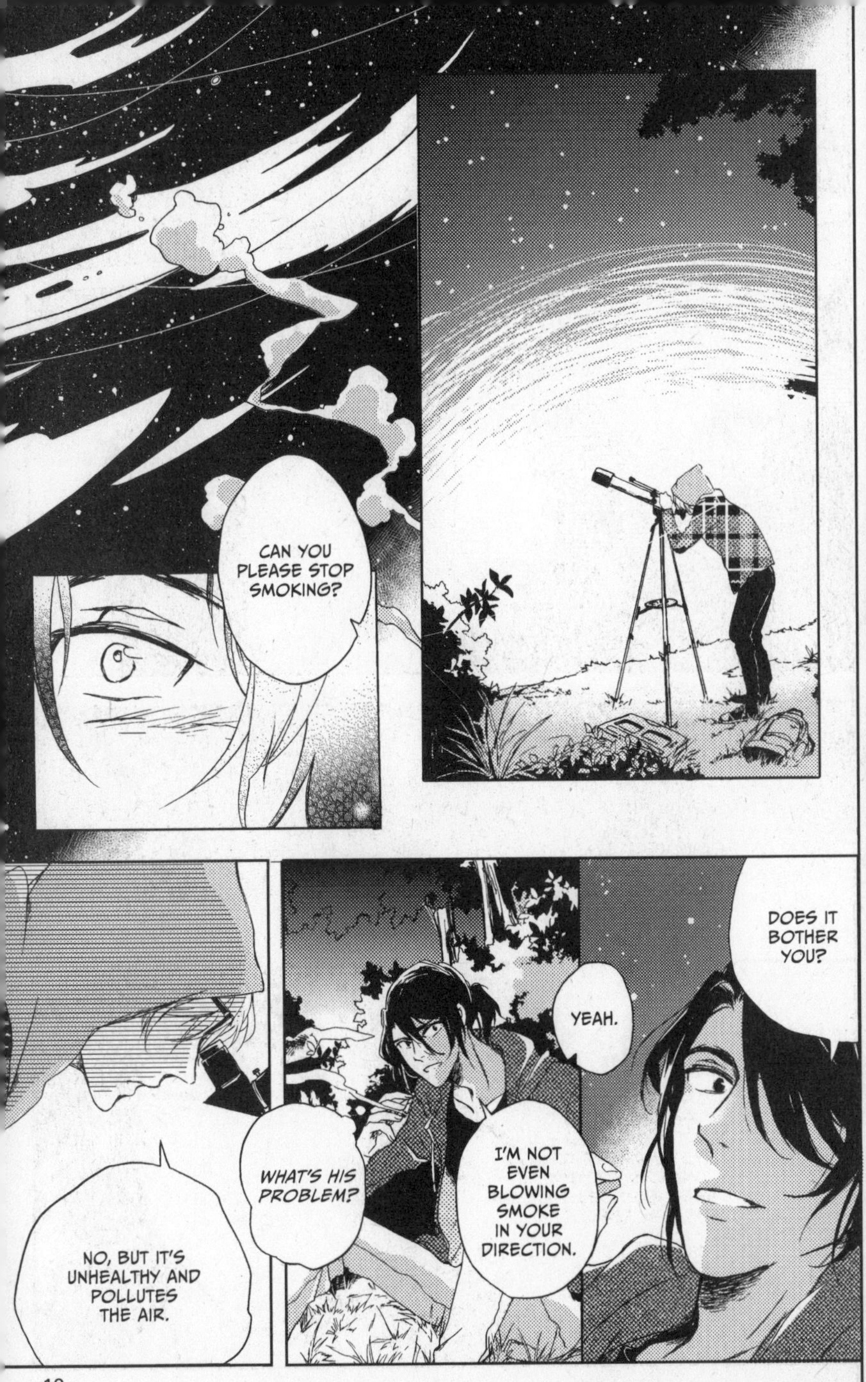
CAN YOU PLEASE STOP SMOKING?
DOES IT BOTHER YOU?
YEAH.
I'M NOT EVEN BLOWING SMOKE IN YOUR DIRECTION.
WHAT'S HIS PROBLEM?
NO, BUT IT'S UNHEALTHY AND POLLUTES THE AIR.

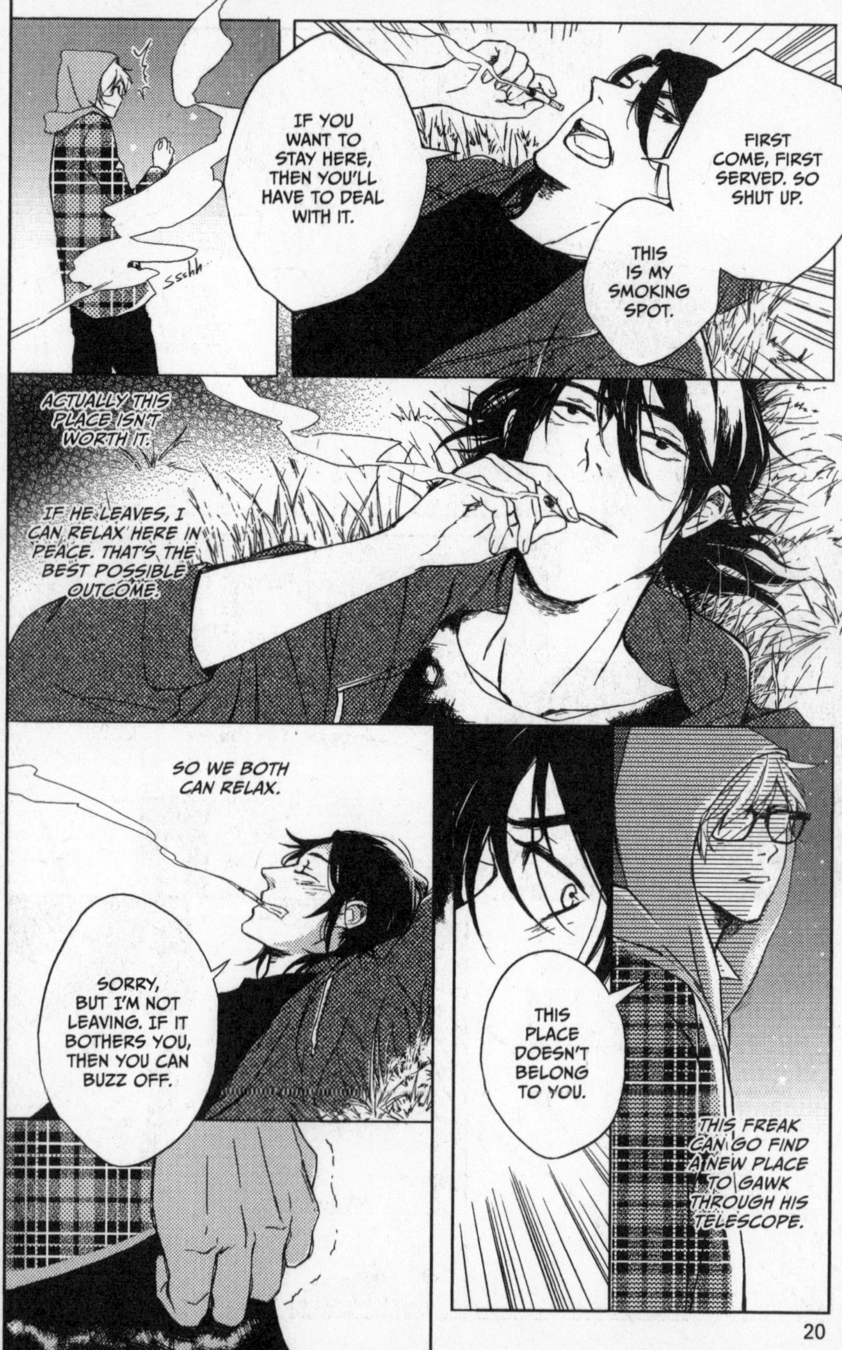
FIRST COME, FIRST SERVED. SO SHUT UP.
THIS IS MY SMOKING SPOT.
IF YOU WANT TO STAY HERE, THEN YOU'LL HAVE TO DEAL WITH IT.
SSSHH...
ACTUALLY THIS PLACE ISN'T WORTH IT.
IF HE LEAVES, I CAN RELAX HERE IN PEACE. THAT'S THE BEST POSSIBLE OUTCOME.
THIS PLACE DOESN'T BELONG TO YOU.
THIS FREAK CAN GO FIND A NEW PLACE TO GAWK THROUGH HIS TELESCOPE.
SO WE BOTH CAN RELAX.
SORRY, BUT I'M NOT LEAVING. IF IT BOTHERS YOU, THEN YOU CAN BUZZ OFF.

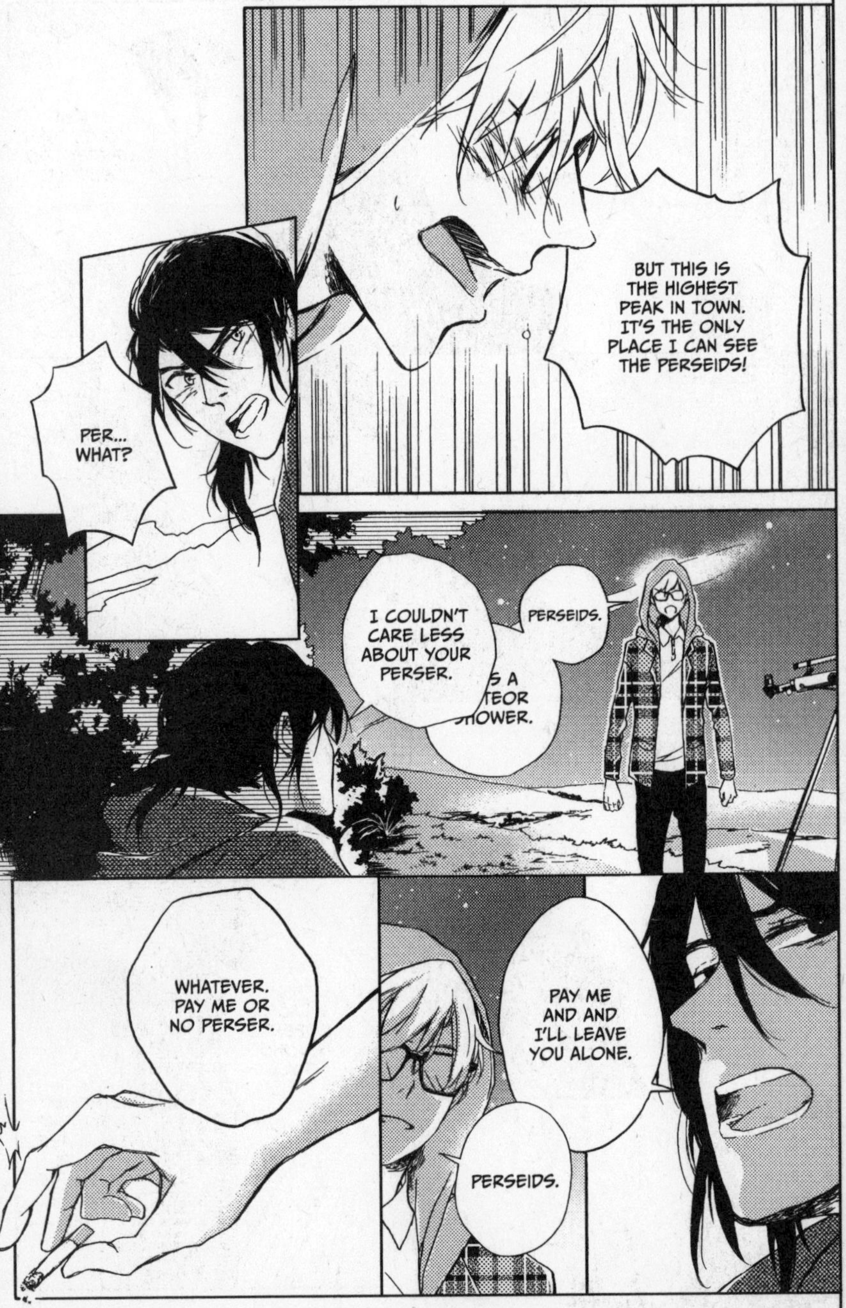
BUT THIS IS THE HIGHEST PEAK IN TOWN. IT'S THE ONLY PLACE I CAN SEE THE PERSEIDS!
PER... WHAT?
PERSEIDS.
S A TEOR SHOWER.
I COULDN'T CARE LESS ABOUT YOUR PERSER.
PAY ME AND AND I'LL LEAVE YOU ALONE.
PERSEIDS.
WHATEVER. PAY ME OR NO PERSER.

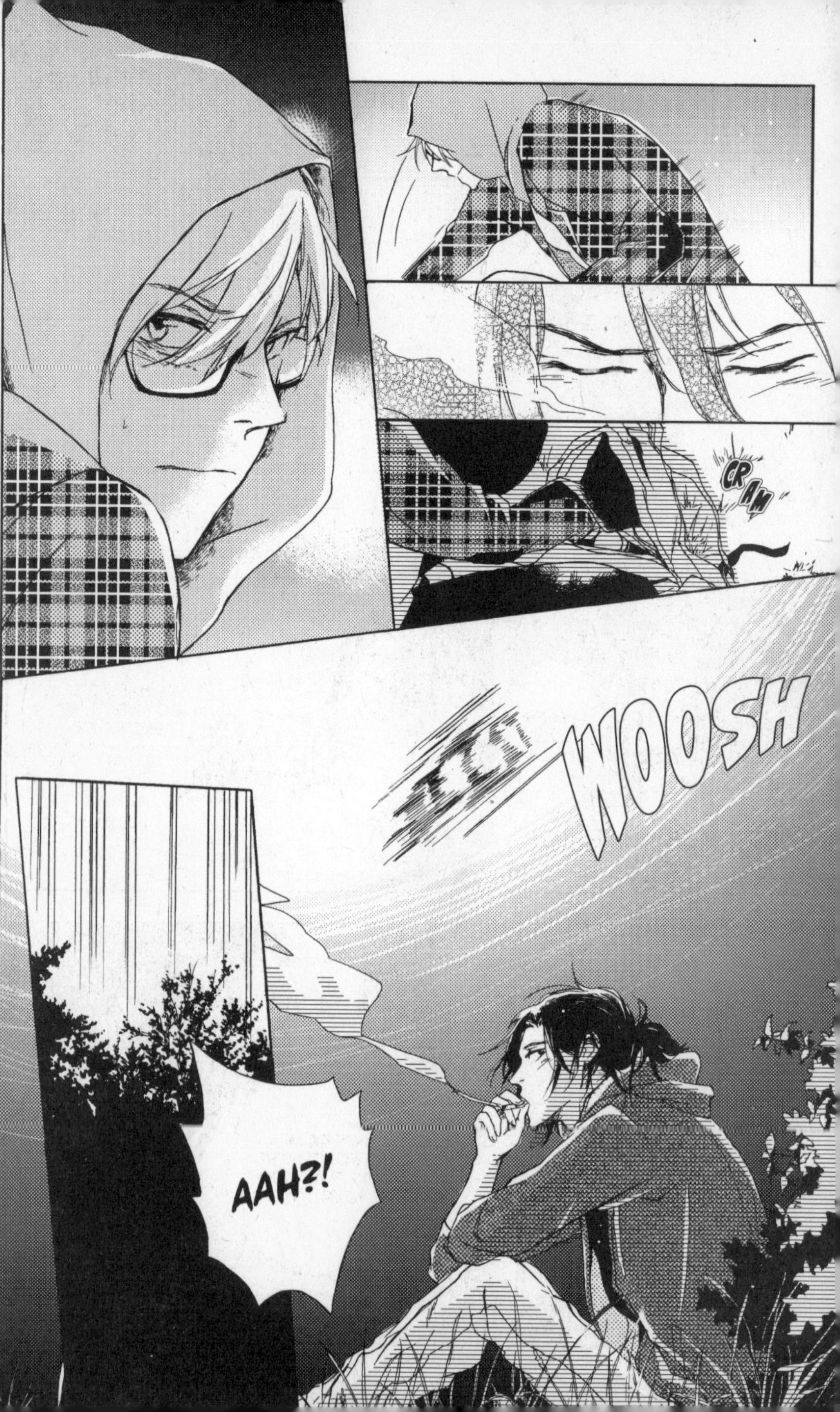
CRAM
WOOSH
AAH?!

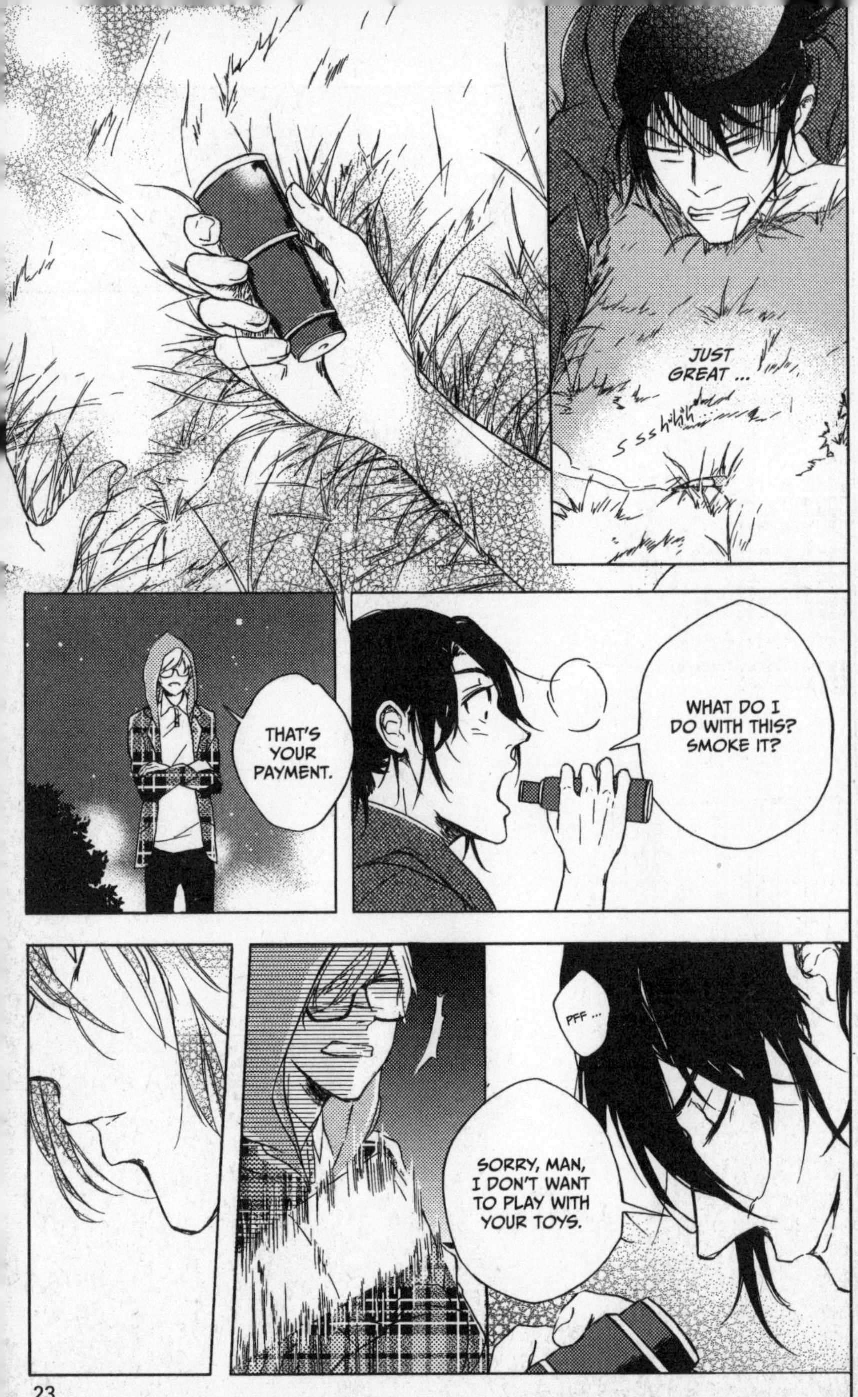
JUST GREAT ...
WHAT DO I DO WITH THIS? SMOKE IT?
THAT'S YOUR PAYMENT.
PFF ...
SORRY, MAN, I DON'T WANT TO PLAY WITH YOUR TOYS.

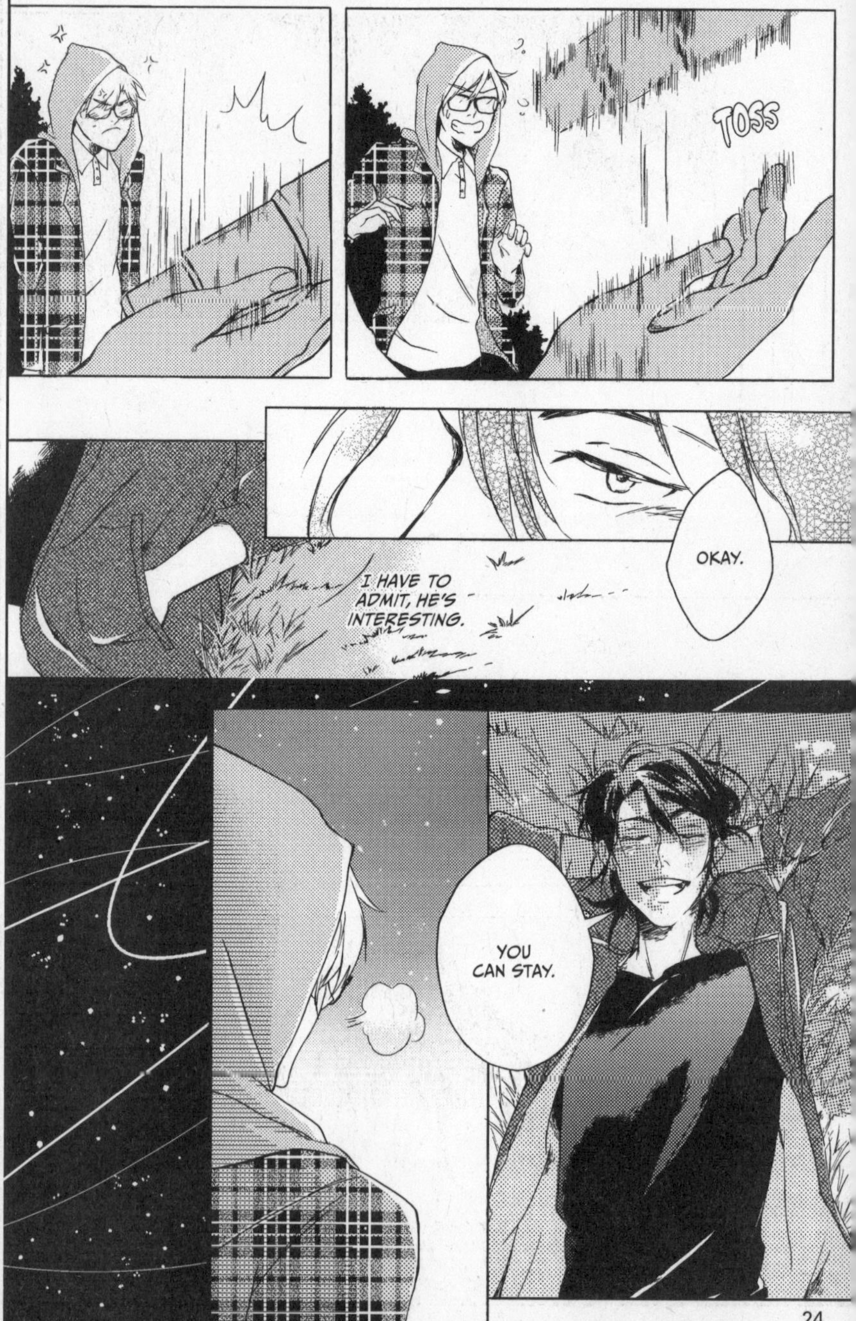
TOSS
OKAY.
I HAVE TO ADMIT, HE'S INTERESTING.
YOU CAN STAY.

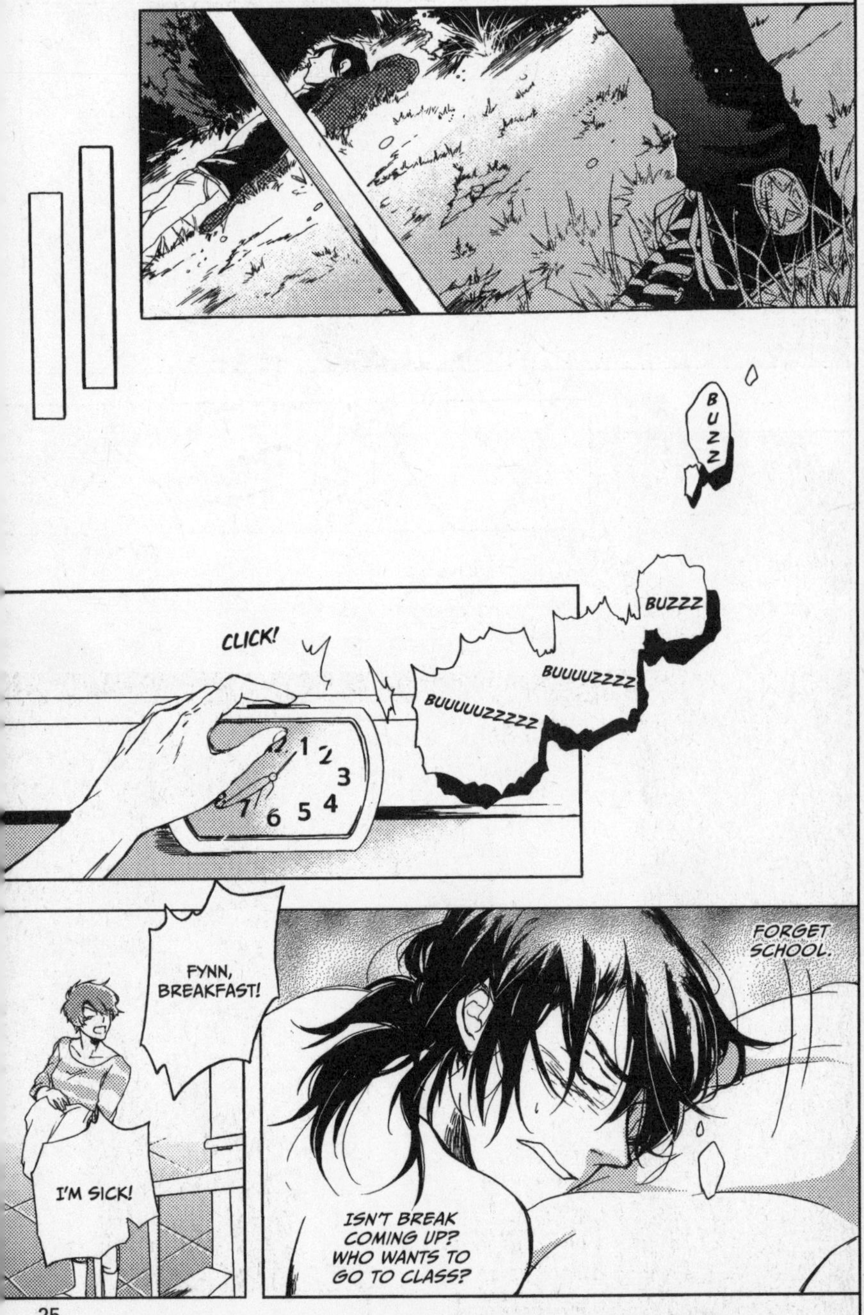
B U Z Z
BUZZZ
BUUUUZZZZ
BUUUUUZZZZZ
CLICK!
FORGET SCHOOL.
ISN'T BREAK COMING UP? WHO WANTS TO GO TO CLASS?
FYNN, BREAKFAST!
I'M SICK!

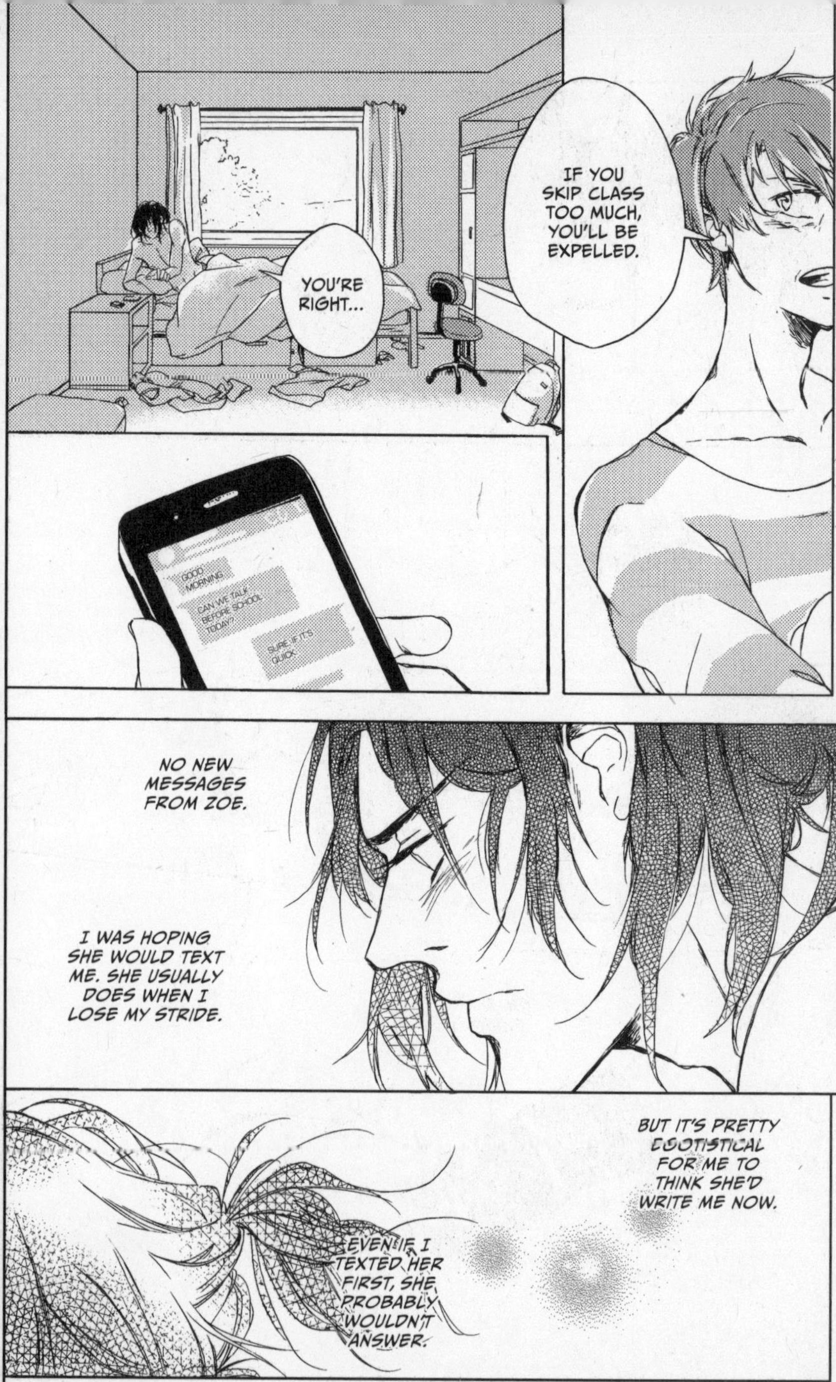
IF YOU SKIP CLASS TOO MUCH, YOU'LL BE EXPELLED.
YOU'RE RIGHT...
GOOD MORNING
CAN WE TALK BEFORE SCHOOL TODAY?
SURE IF IT'S QUICK
NO NEW MESSAGES FROM ZOE.
I WAS HOPING SHE WOULD TEXT ME. SHE USUALLY DOES WHEN I LOSE MY STRIDE.
BUT IT'S PRETTY EGOTISTICAL FOR ME TO THINK SHE'D WRITE ME NOW.
EVEN IF I TEXTED HER FIRST, SHE PROBABLY WOULDN'T ANSWER.

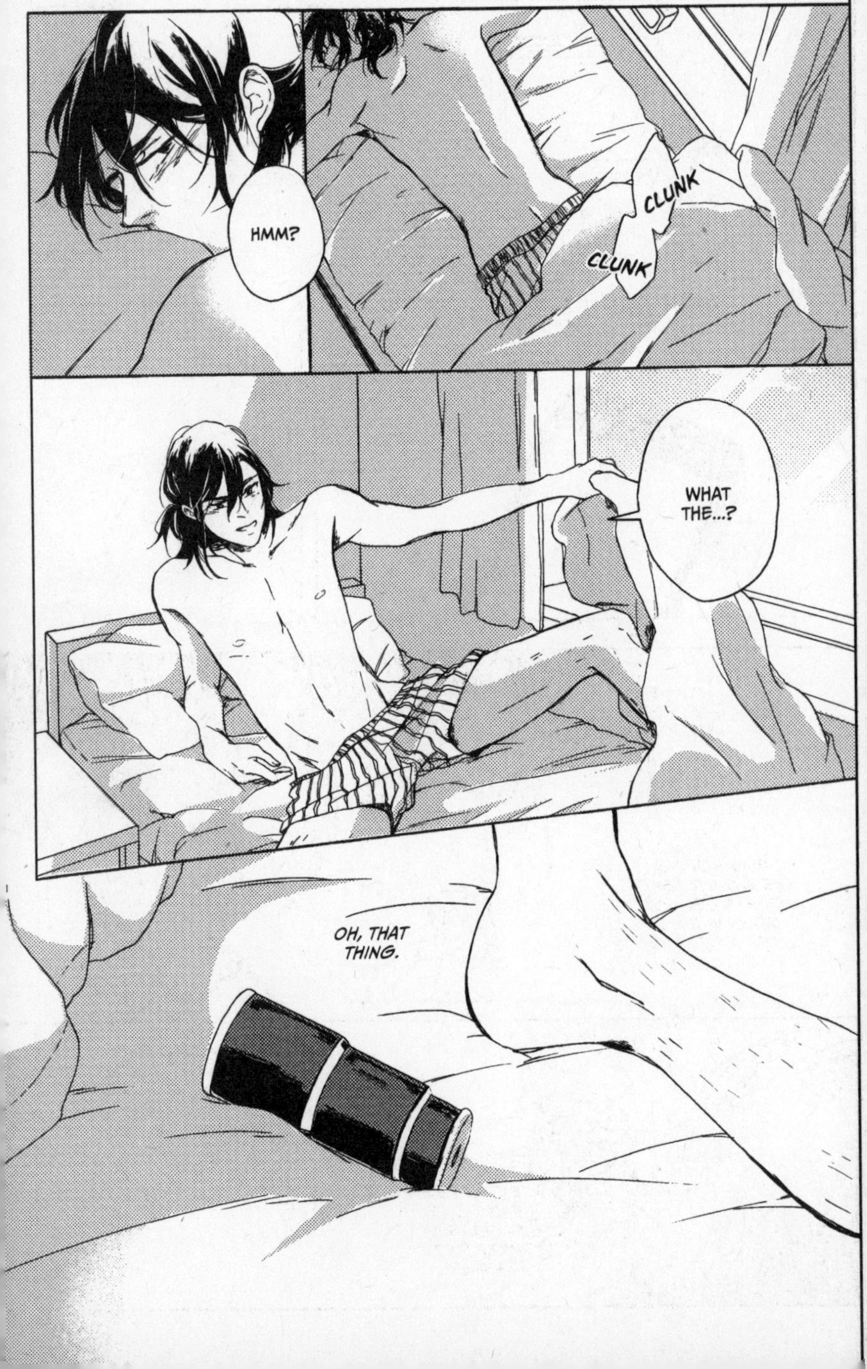
CLUNK
CLUNK
HMM?
WHAT THE...?
OH, THAT THING.

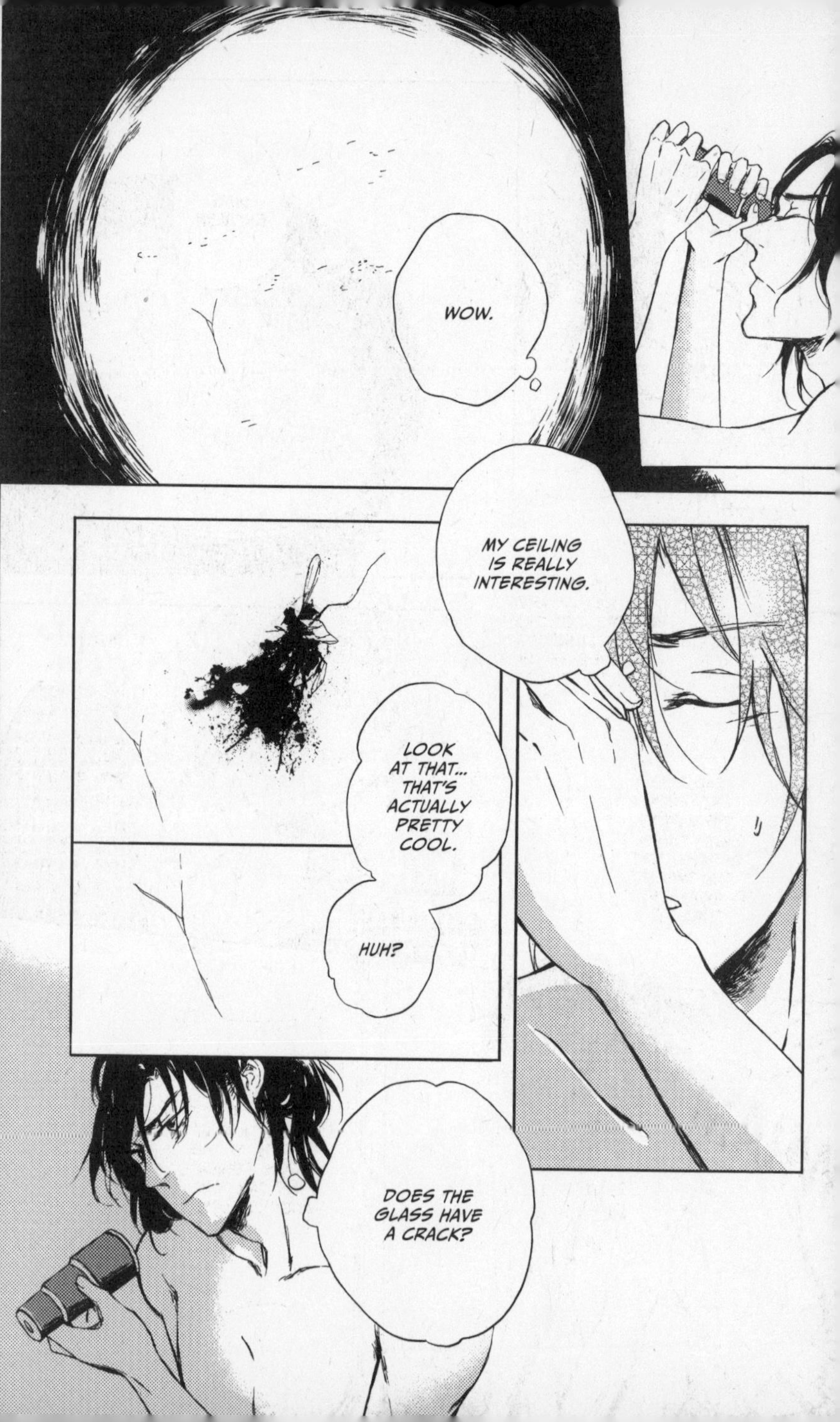
WOW.
MY CEILING IS REALLY INTERESTING.
LOOK AT THAT... THAT'S ACTUALLY PRETTY COOL.
HUH?
DOES THE GLASS HAVE A CRACK?

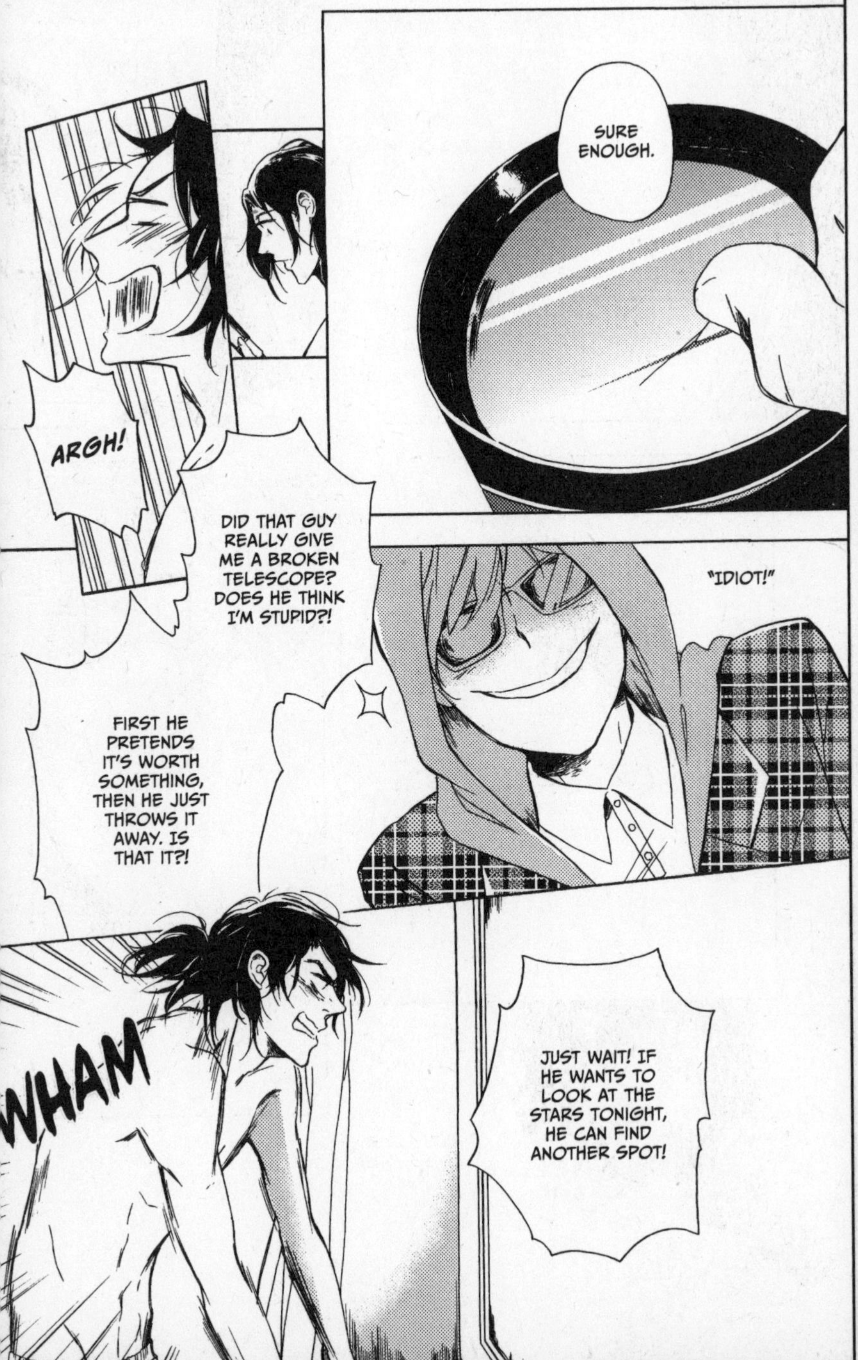
SURE ENOUGH.
ARGH!
DID THAT GUY REALLY GIVE ME A BROKEN TELESCOPE? DOES HE THINK I'M STUPID?!
"IDIOT!"
FIRST HE PRETENDS IT'S WORTH SOMETHING, THEN HE JUST THROWS IT AWAY. IS THAT IT?!
JUST WAIT! IF HE WANTS TO LOOK AT THE STARS TONIGHT, HE CAN FIND ANOTHER SPOT!
WHAM

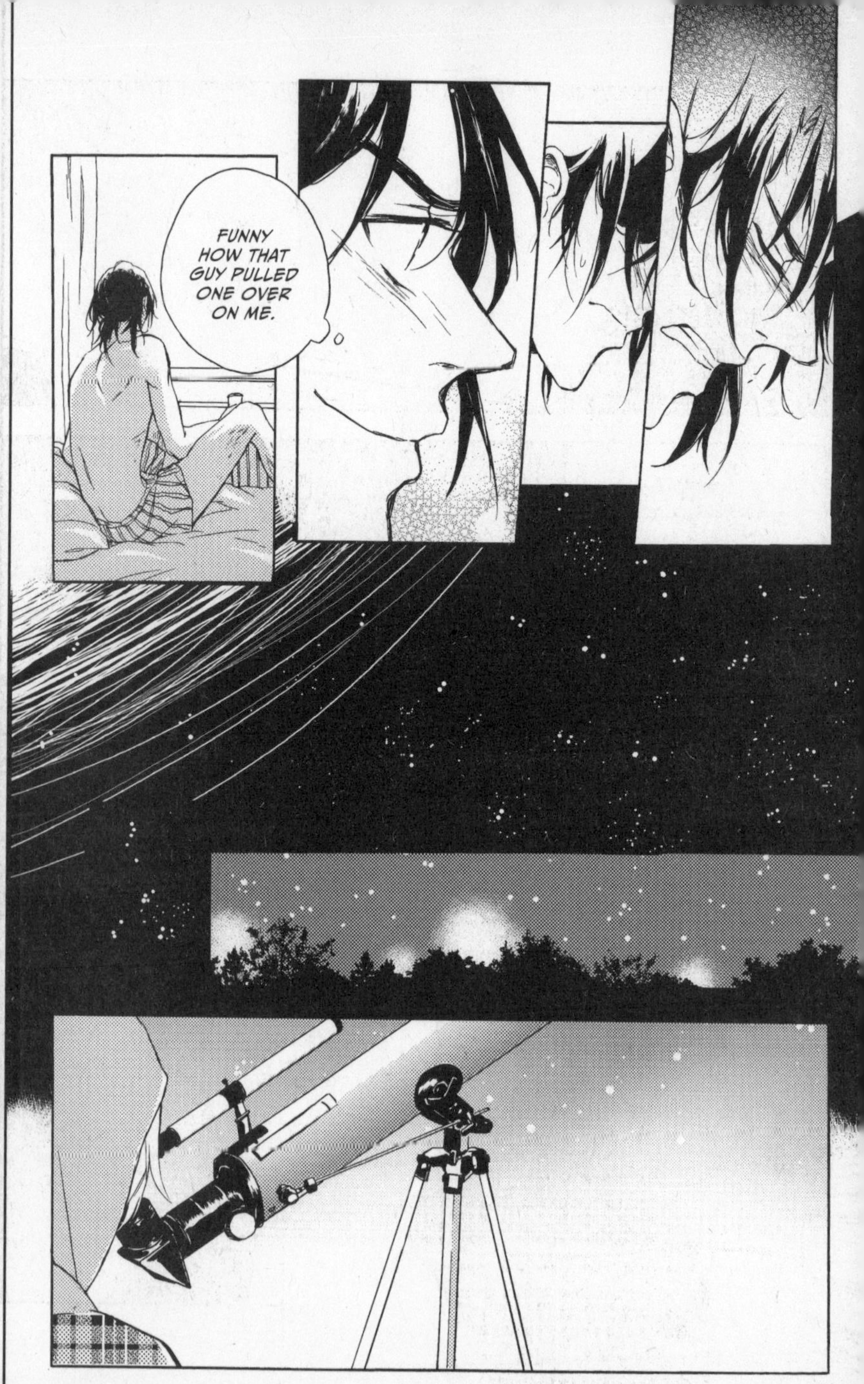
FUNNY HOW THAT GUY PULLED ONE OVER ON ME.

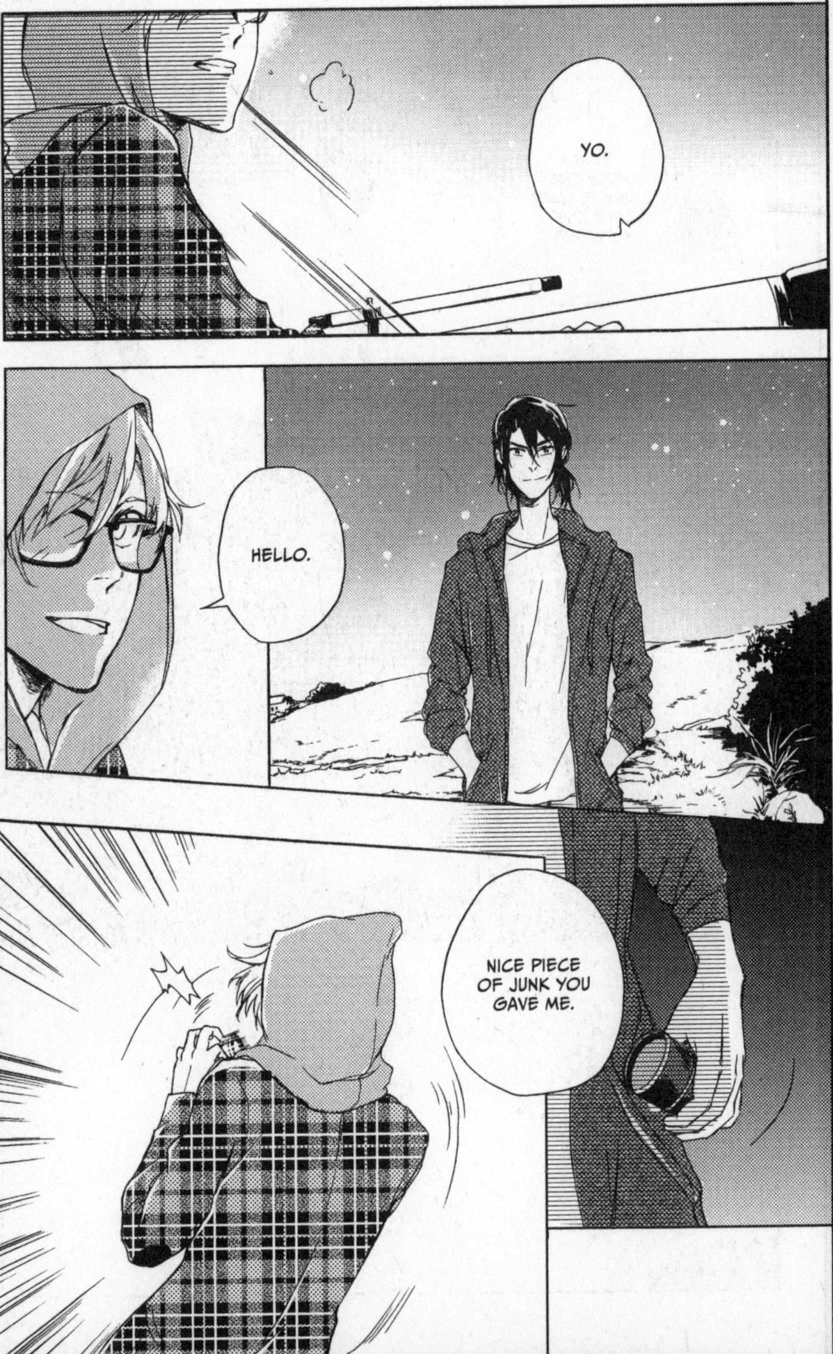
YO.
HELLO.
NICE PIECE OF JUNK YOU GAVE ME.

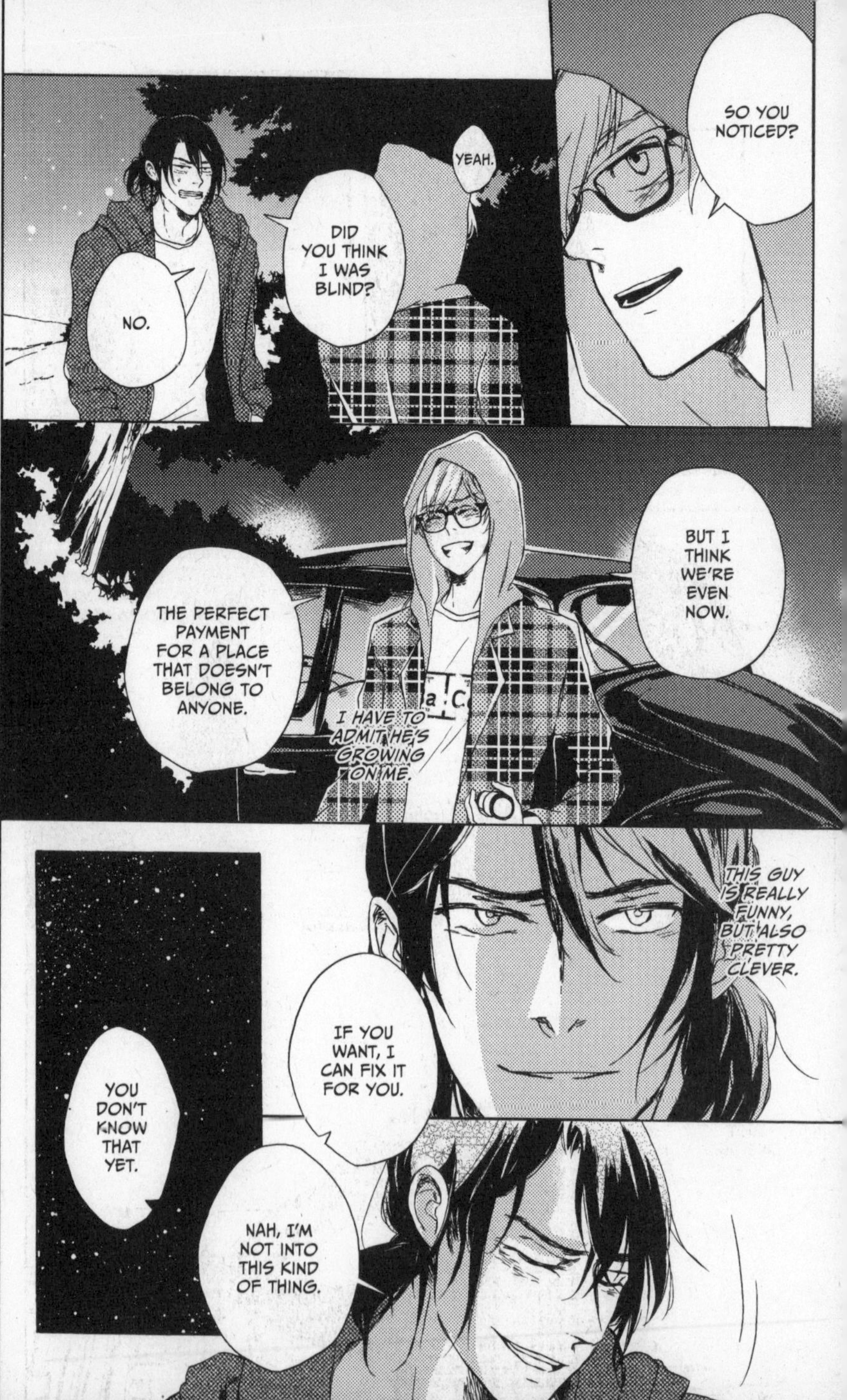
SO YOU NOTICED?
YEAH.
DID YOU THINK I WAS BLIND?
NO.
BUT I THINK WE'RE EVEN NOW.
THE PERFECT PAYMENT FOR A PLACE THAT DOESN'T BELONG TO ANYONE.
I HAVE TO ADMIT HE'S GROWING ON ME.
THIS GUY IS REALLY FUNNY, BUT ALSO PRETTY CLEVER.
IF YOU WANT, I CAN FIX IT FOR YOU.
NAH, I'M NOT INTO THIS KIND OF THING.
YOU DON'T KNOW THAT YET.

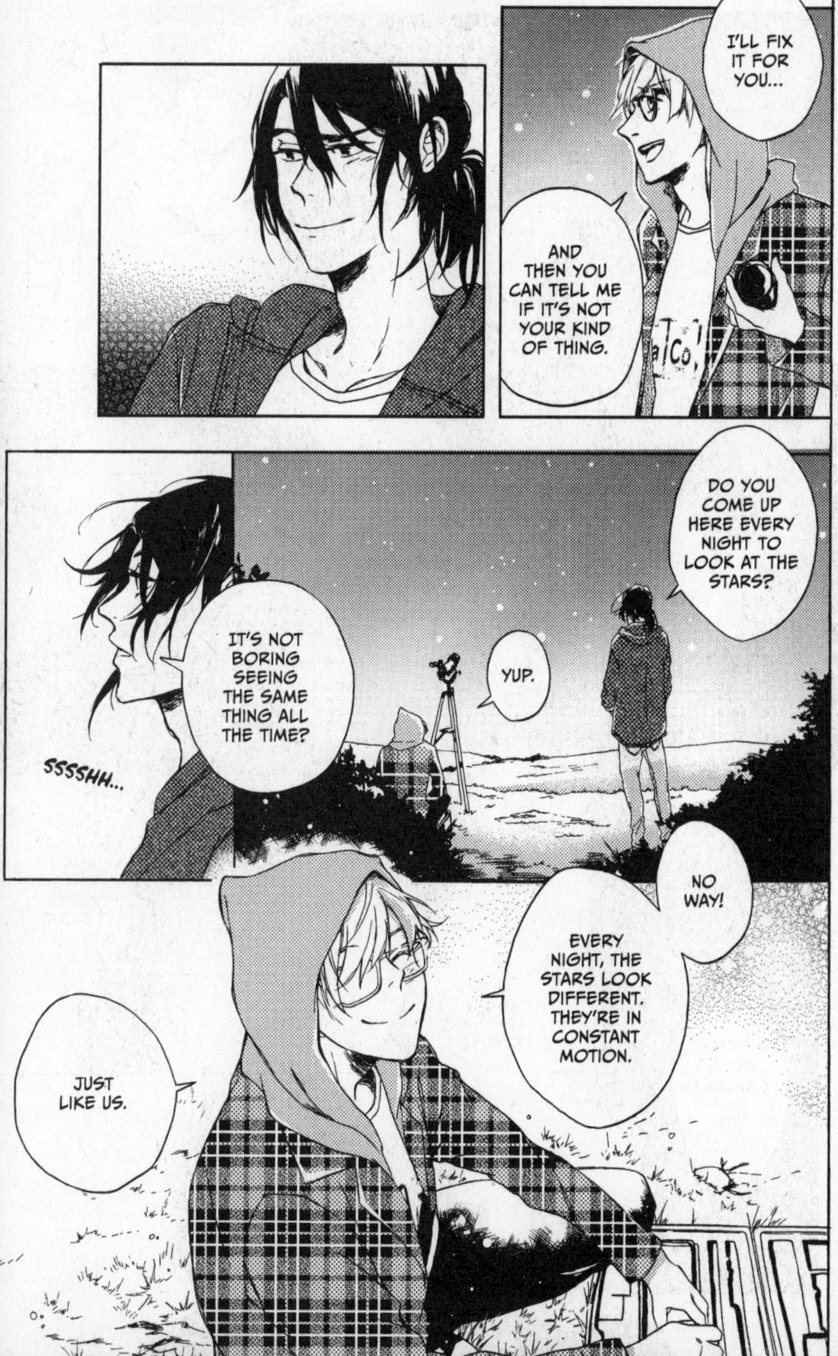
I'LL FIX IT FOR YOU...
AND THEN YOU CAN TELL ME IF IT'S NOT YOUR KIND OF THING.
DO YOU COME UP HERE EVERY NIGHT TO LOOK AT THE STARS?
YUP.
IT'S NOT BORING SEEING THE SAME THING ALL THE TIME?
SSSSHH...
NO WAY!
EVERY NIGHT, THE STARS LOOK DIFFERENT. THEY'RE IN CONSTANT MOTION.
JUST LIKE US.

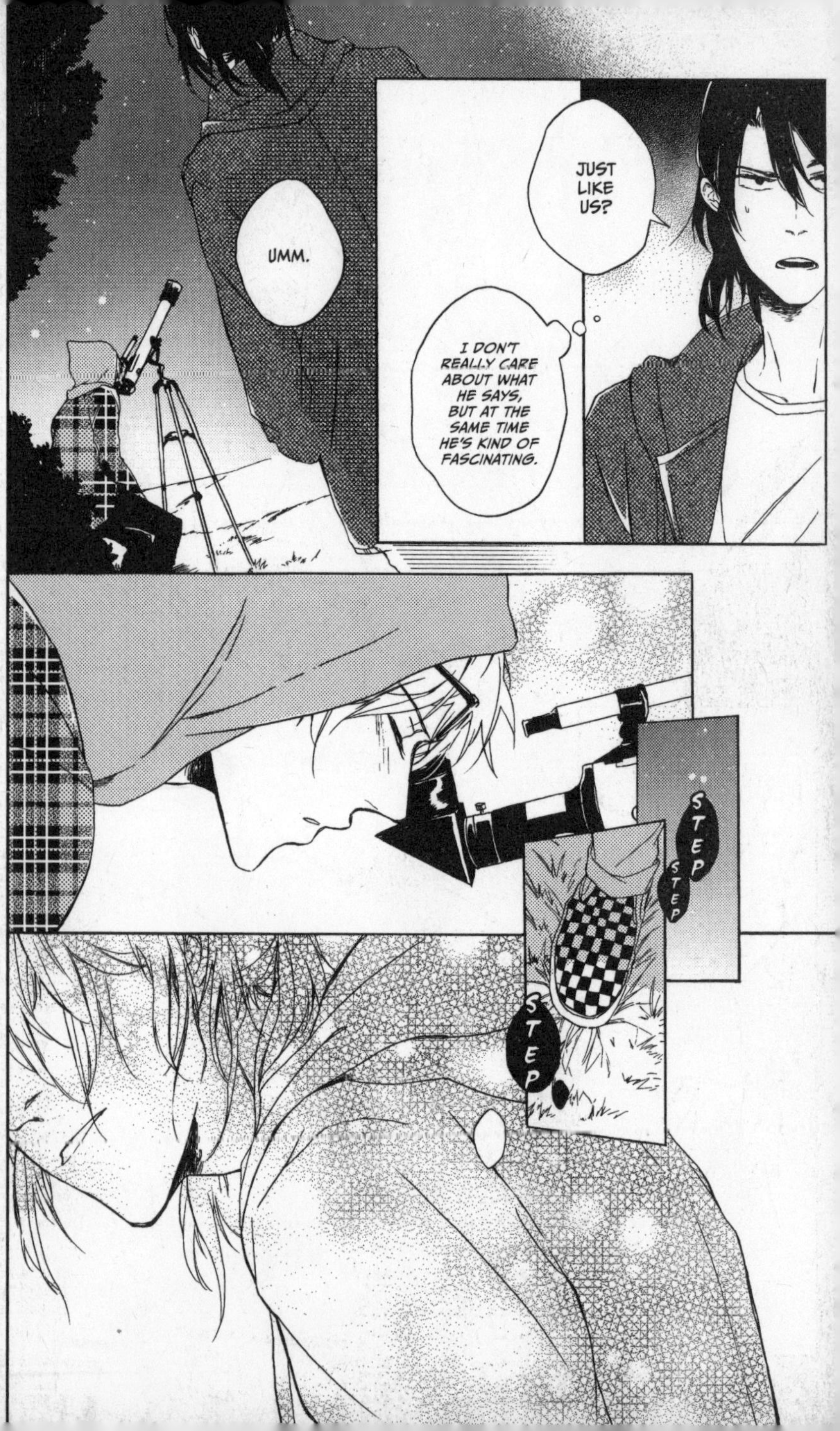
JUST LIKE US?
I DON'T REALLY CARE ABOUT WHAT HE SAYS, BUT AT THE SAME TIME HE'S KIND OF FASCINATING.
UMM.
STEP
STEP
STEP

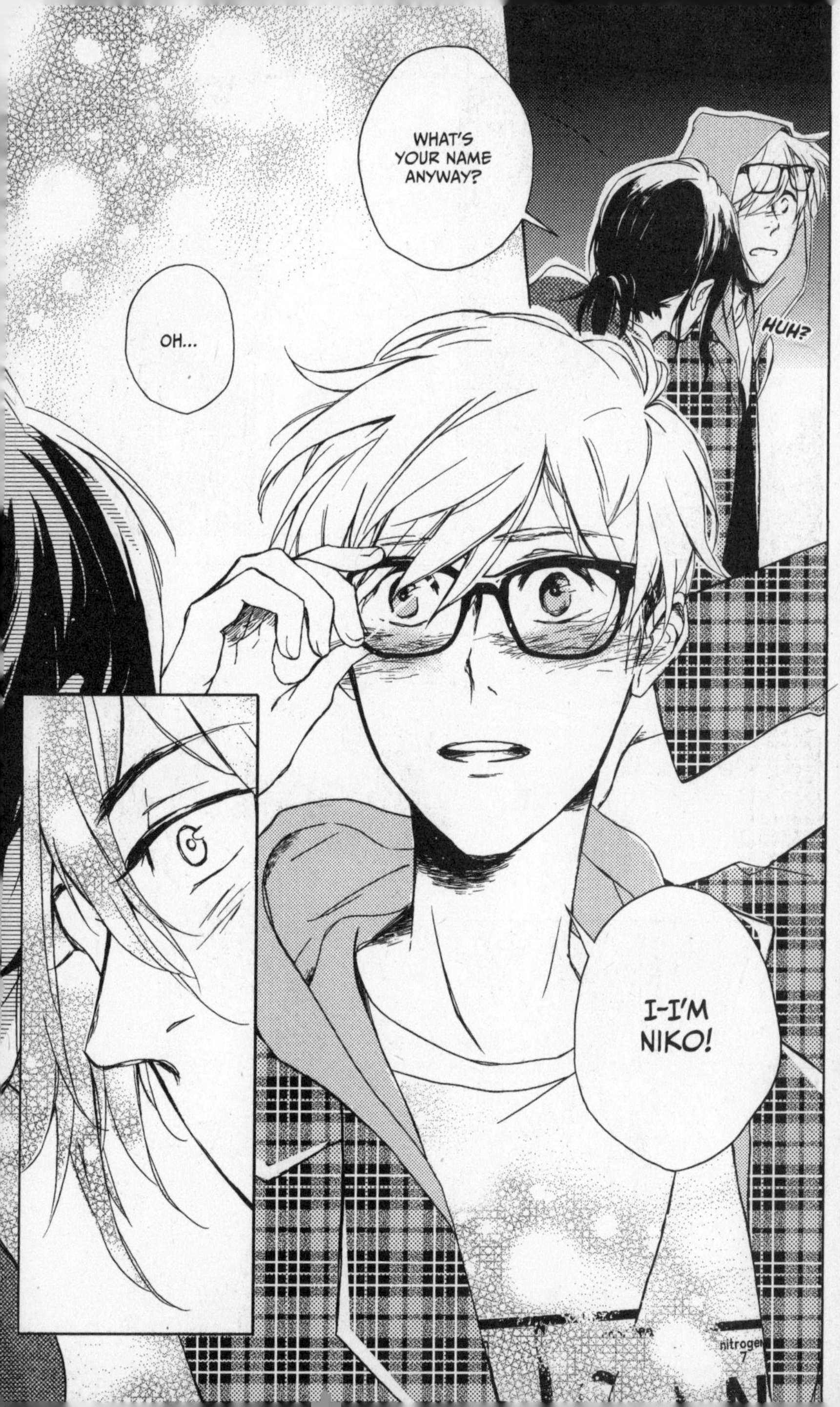
WHAT'S YOUR NAME ANYWAY?
HUH?
OH...
I-I'M NIKO!
nitrogen
7

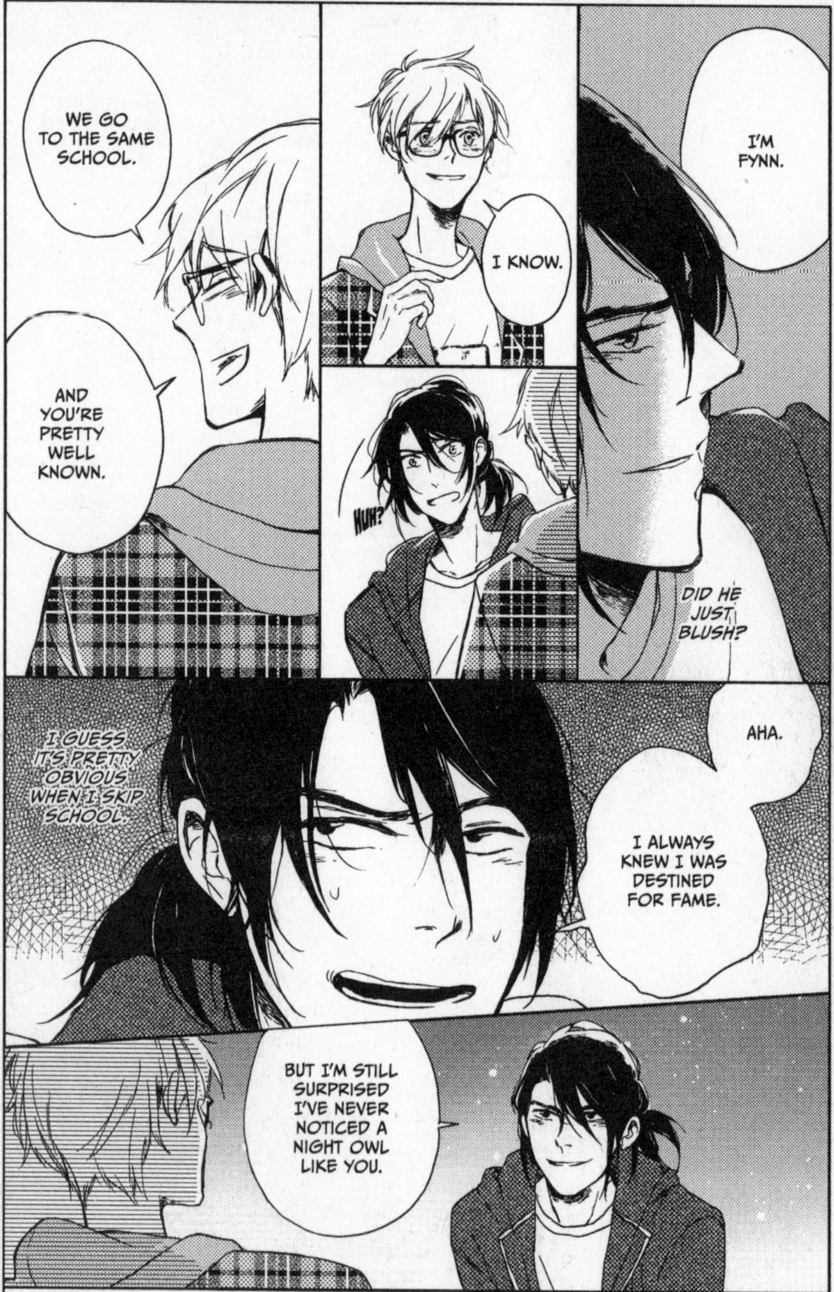
I'M FYNN.
DID HE JUST BLUSH?
I KNOW.
HUH?
WE GO TO THE SAME SCHOOL.
AND YOU'RE PRETTY WELL KNOWN.
AHA.
I ALWAYS KNEW I WAS DESTINED FOR FAME.
I GUESS IT'S PRETTY OBVIOUS WHEN I SKIP SCHOOL.
BUT I'M STILL SURPRISED I'VE NEVER NOTICED A NIGHT OWL LIKE YOU.

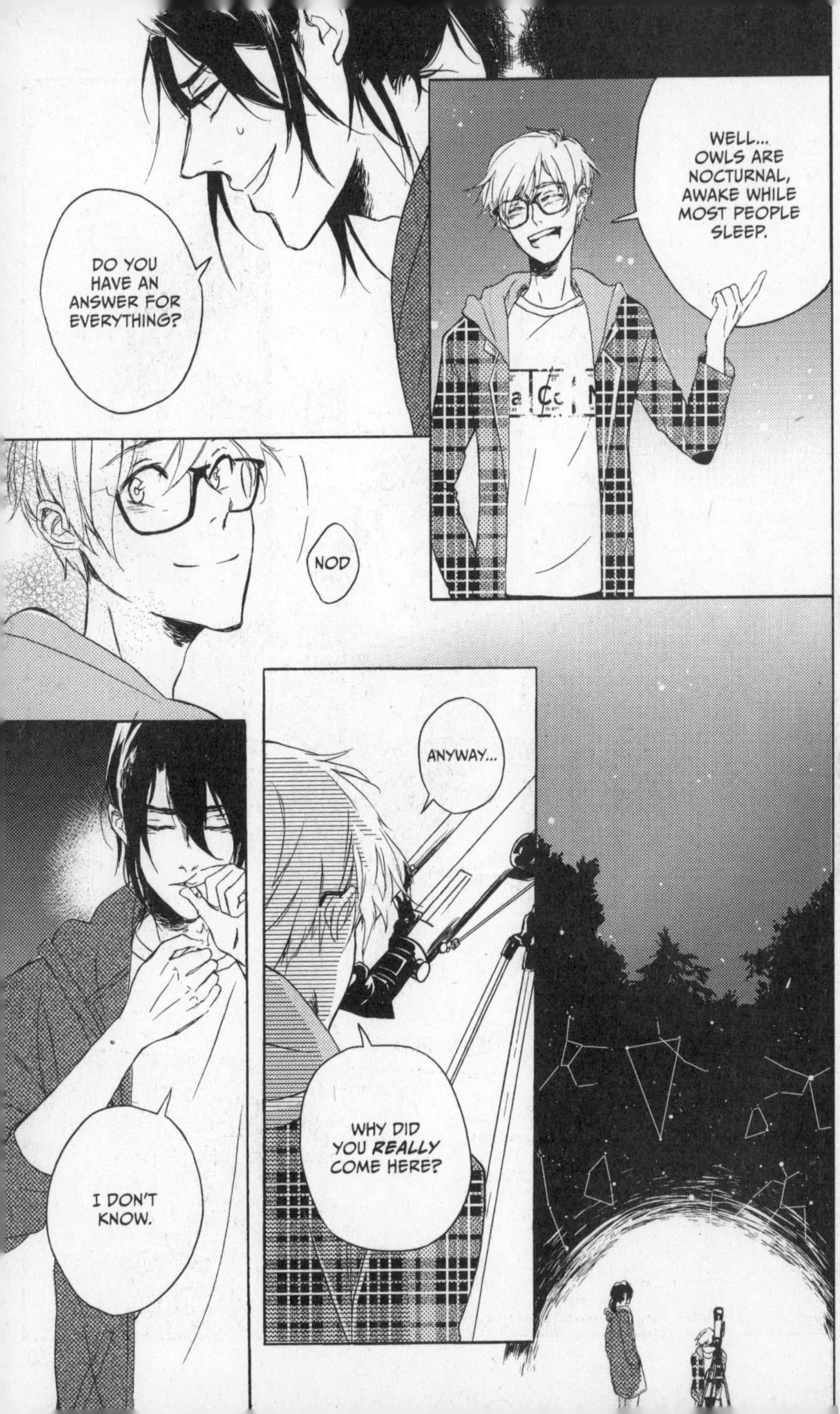
WELL... OWLS ARE NOCTURNAL, AWAKE WHILE MOST PEOPLE SLEEP.
DO YOU HAVE AN ANSWER FOR EVERYTHING?
NOD
ANYWAY...
WHY DID YOU *REALLY* COME HERE?
I DON'T KNOW.

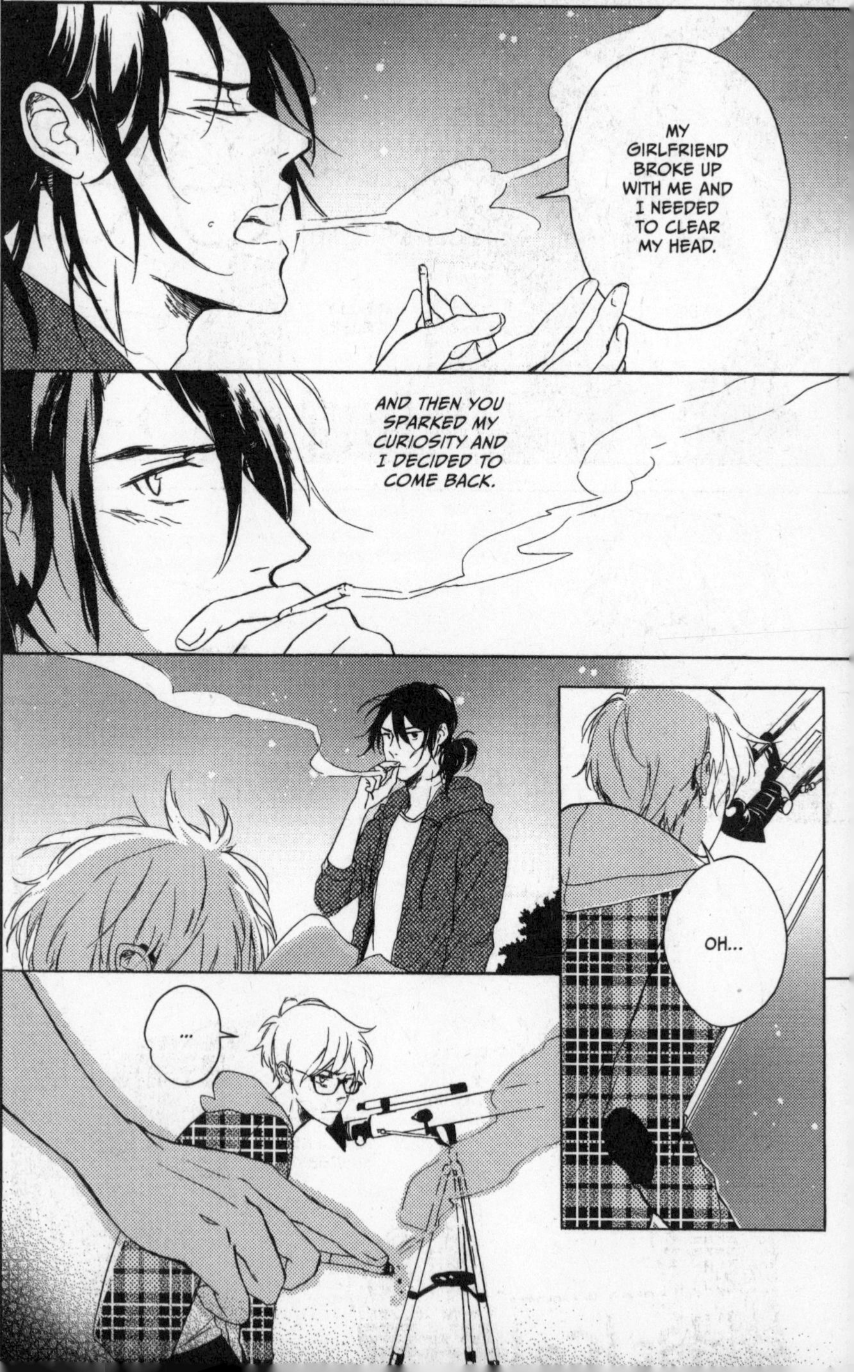
MY GIRLFRIEND BROKE UP WITH ME AND I NEEDED TO CLEAR MY HEAD.
AND THEN YOU SPARKED MY CURIOSITY AND I DECIDED TO COME BACK.
OH...
...

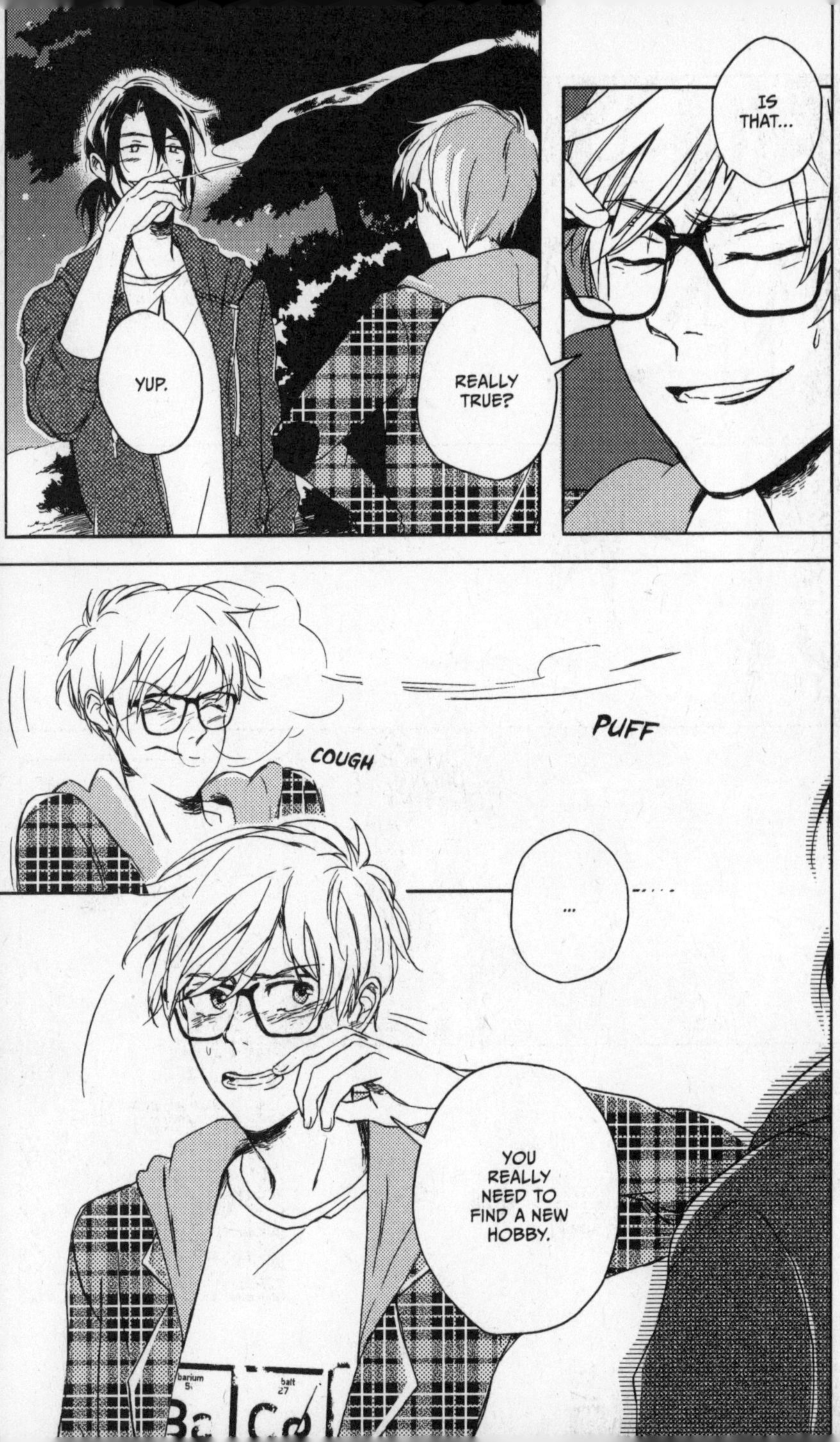
IS THAT...
REALLY TRUE?
YUP.
PUFF
COUGH
...
YOU REALLY NEED TO FIND A NEW HOBBY.

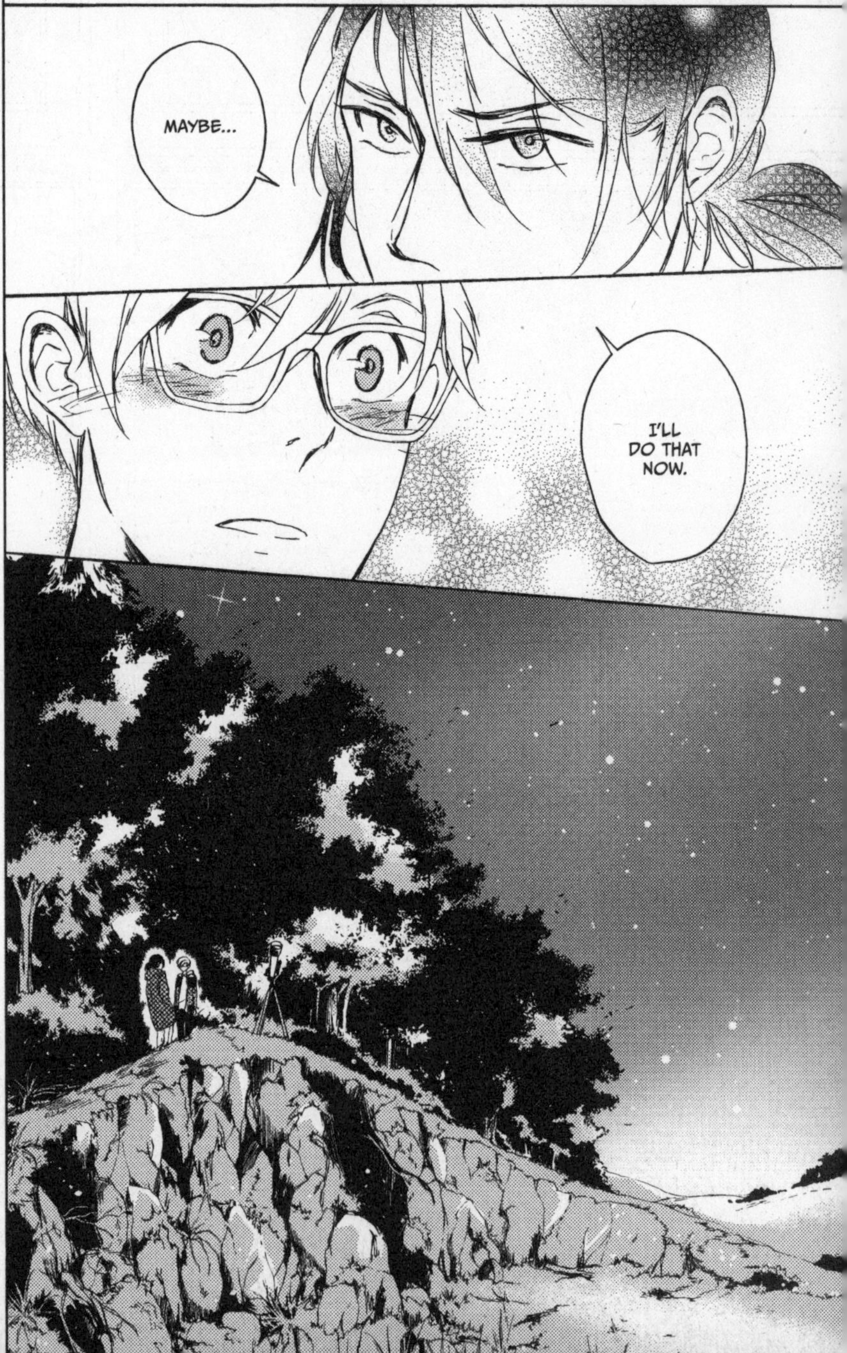
MAYBE...
I'LL DO THAT NOW.

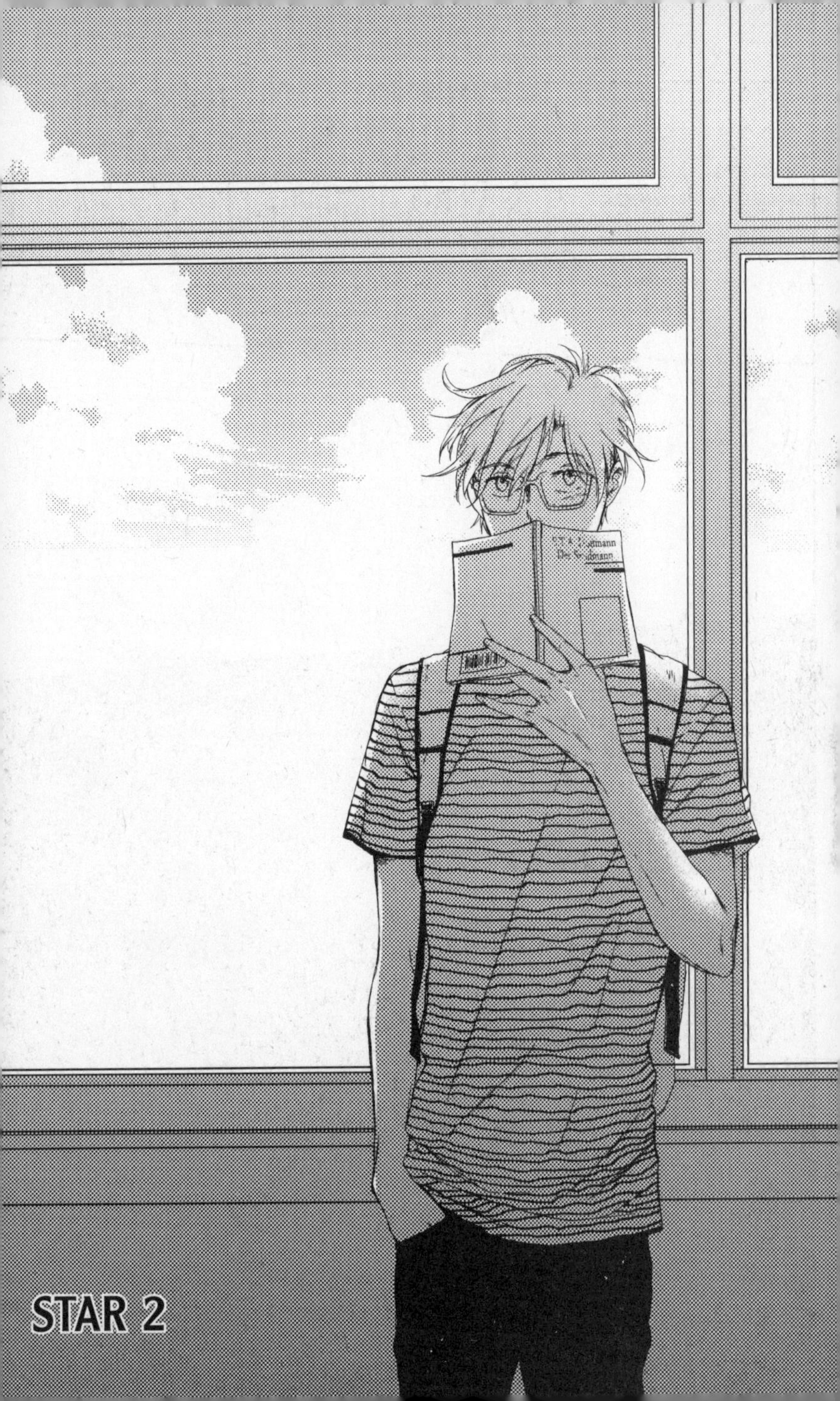
STAR 2

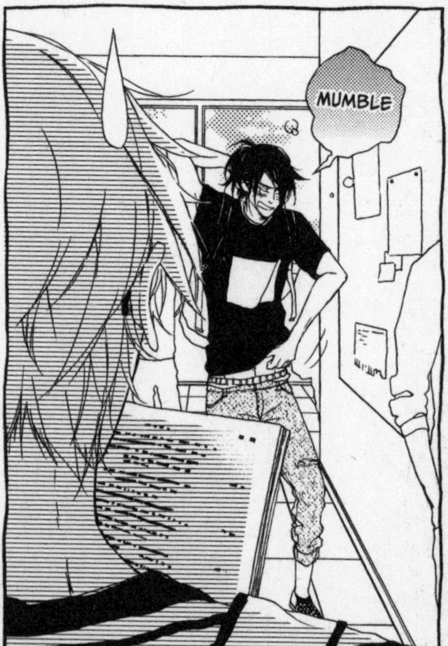
MUMBLE

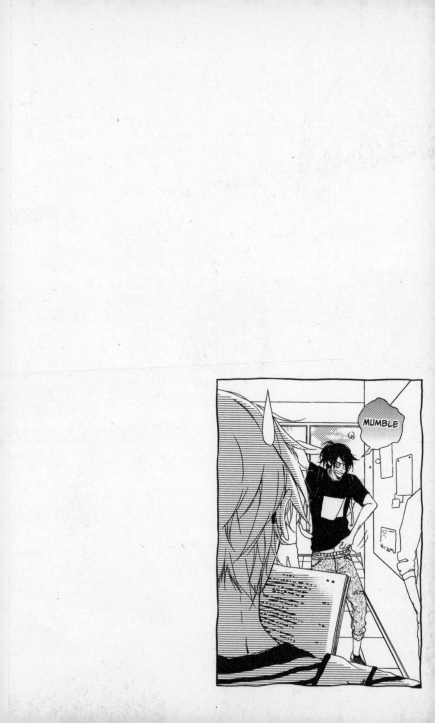

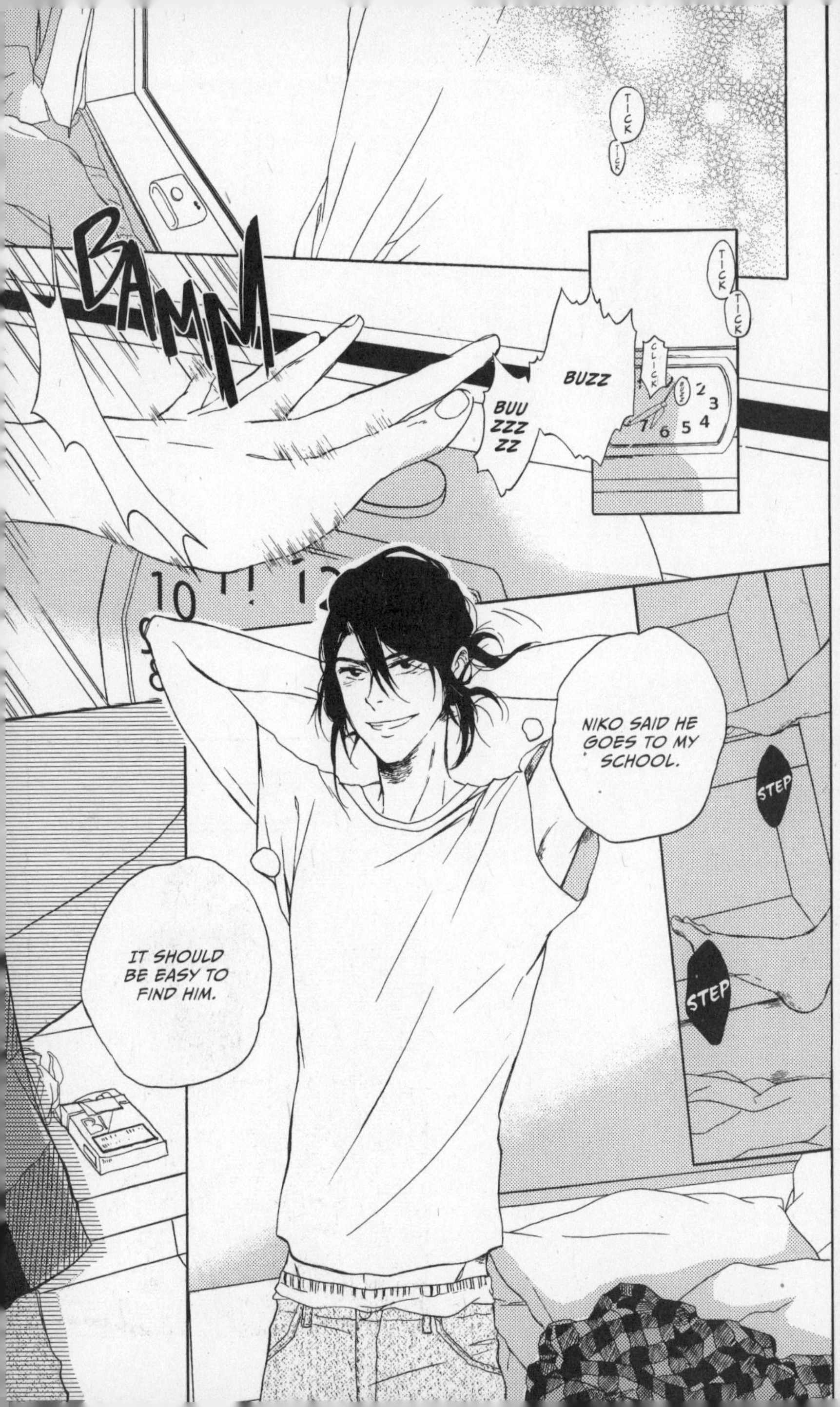

TICK TICK
TICK TICK
CLICK
BUZZ
BUZZ
BUU ZZZ ZZ
BAMM
NIKO SAID HE GOES TO MY SCHOOL.
STEP
STEP
IT SHOULD BE EASY TO FIND HIM.

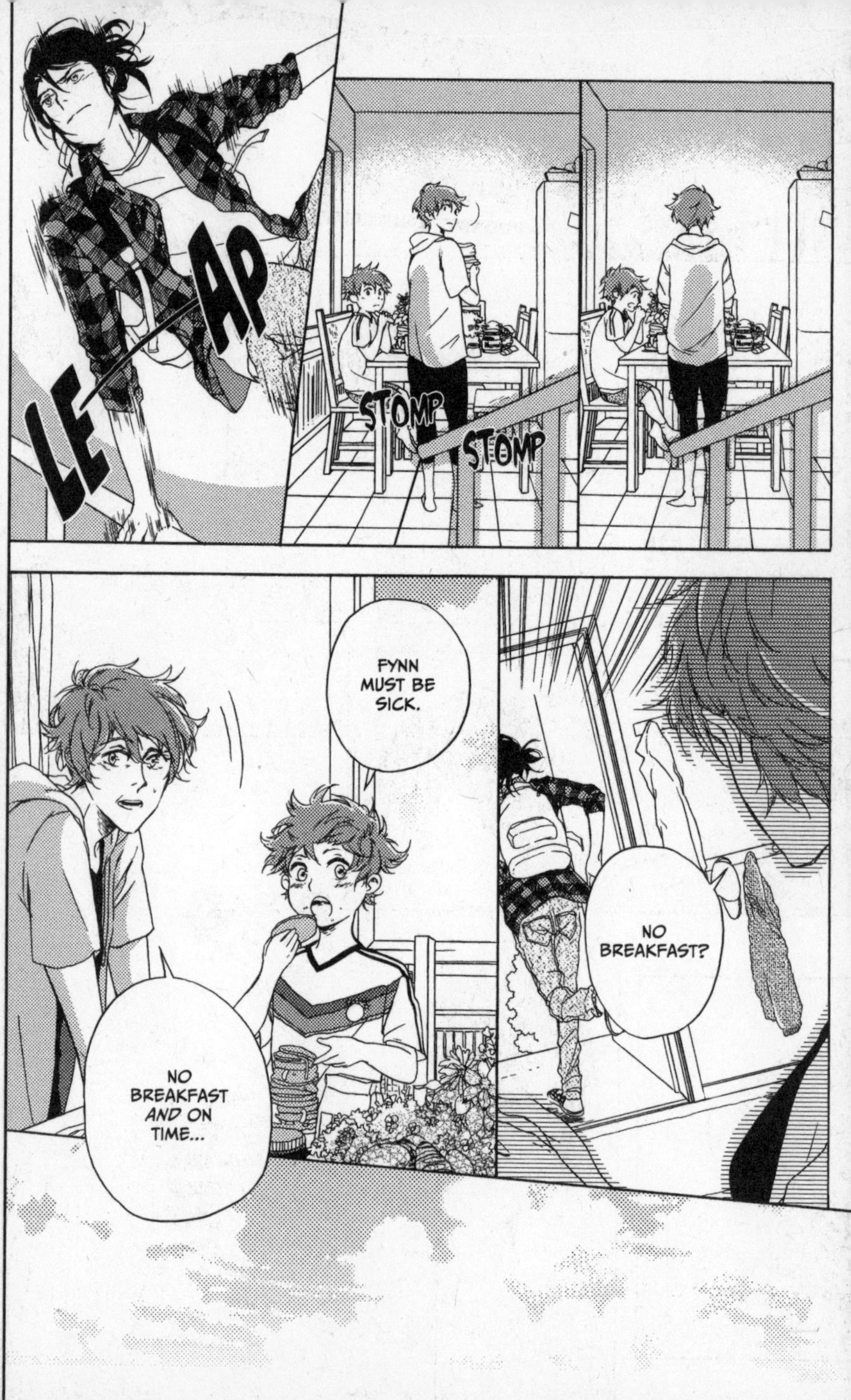
STOMP
STOMP
LE
AP
NO BREAKFAST?
FYNN MUST BE SICK.
NO BREAKFAST AND ON TIME...

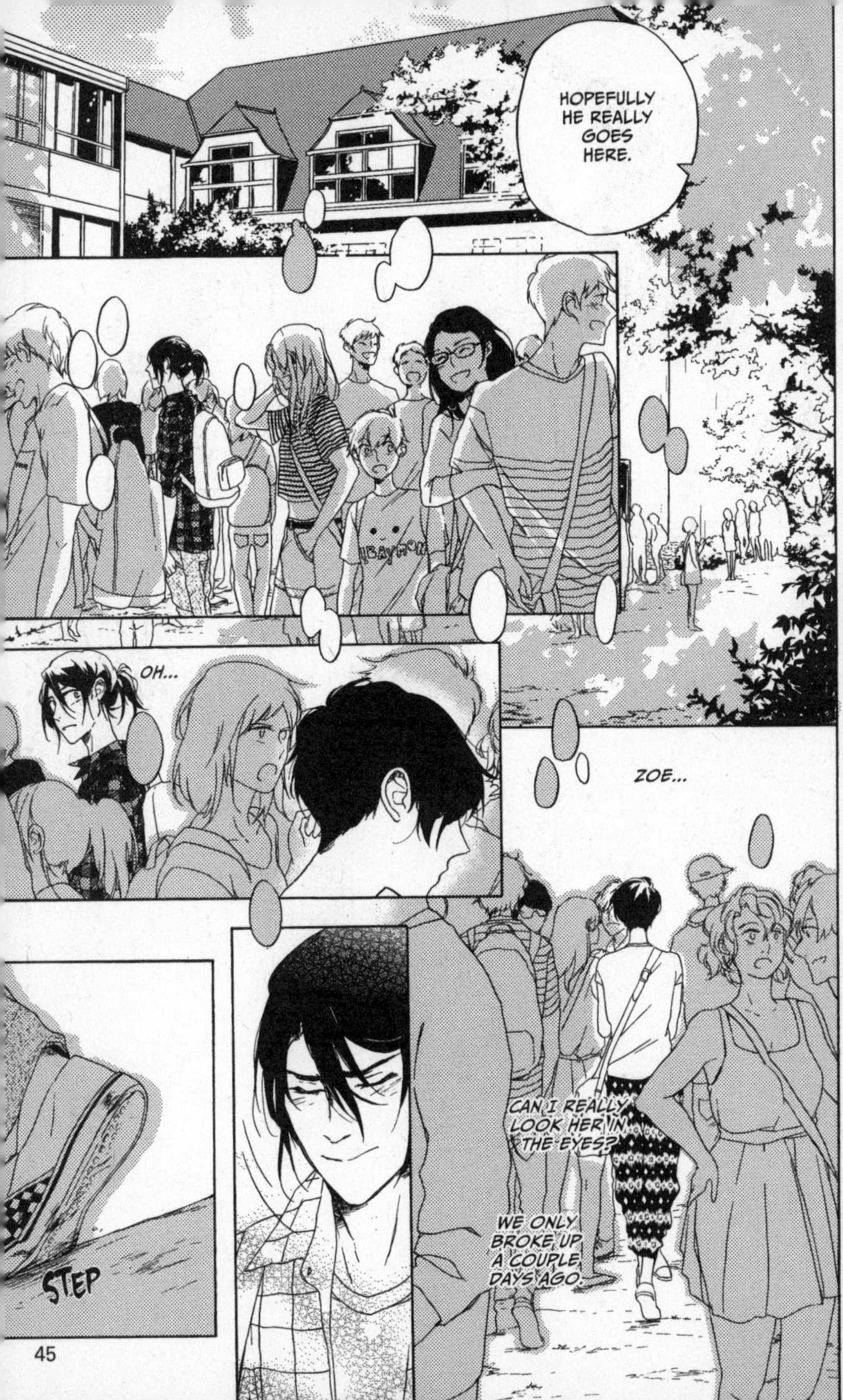
HOPEFULLY HE REALLY GOES HERE.
ZOE...
CAN I REALLY LOOK HER IN THE EYES?
WE ONLY BROKE UP A COUPLE DAYS AGO.
OH...
STEP

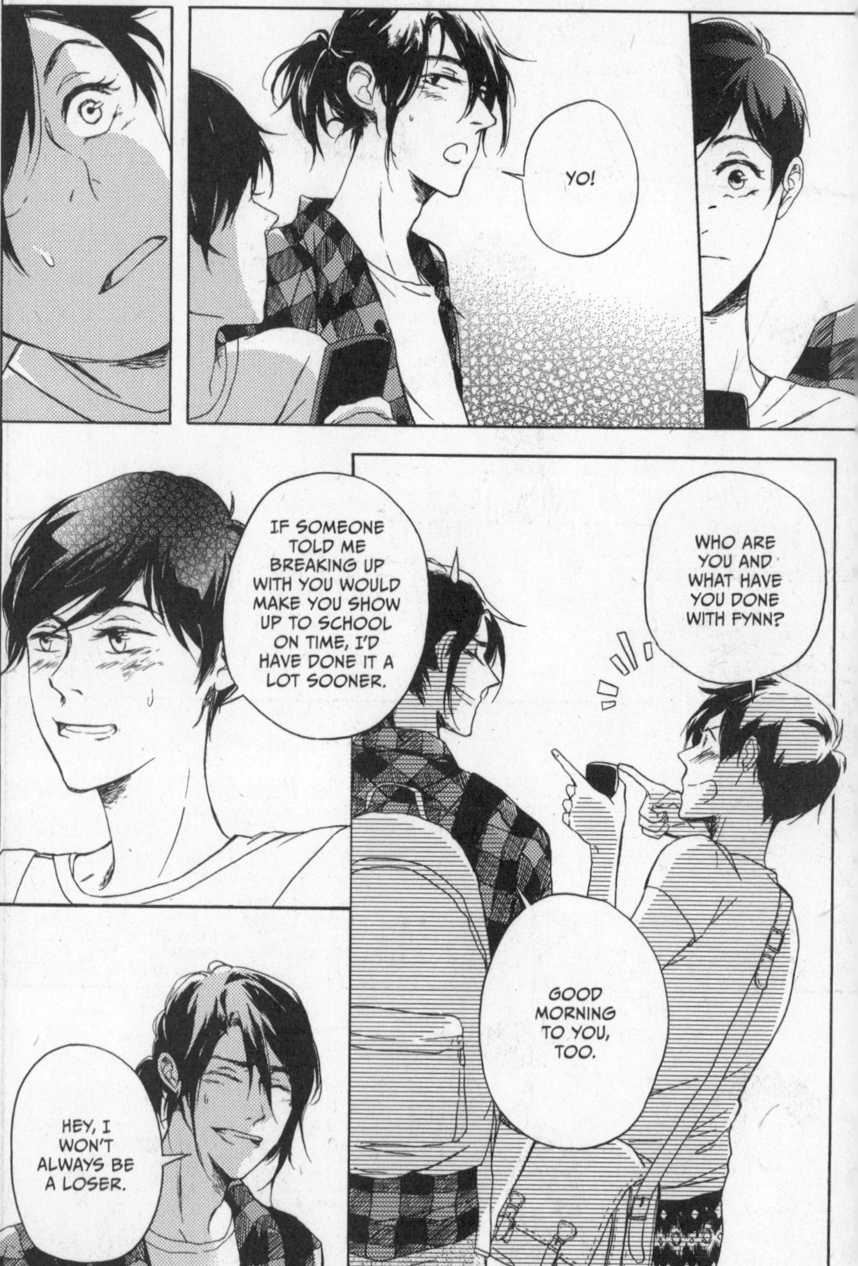
YO!
WHO ARE YOU AND WHAT HAVE YOU DONE WITH FYNN?
GOOD MORNING TO YOU, TOO.
IF SOMEONE TOLD ME BREAKING UP WITH YOU WOULD MAKE YOU SHOW UP TO SCHOOL ON TIME, I'D HAVE DONE IT A LOT SOONER.
HEY, I WON'T ALWAYS BE A LOSER.

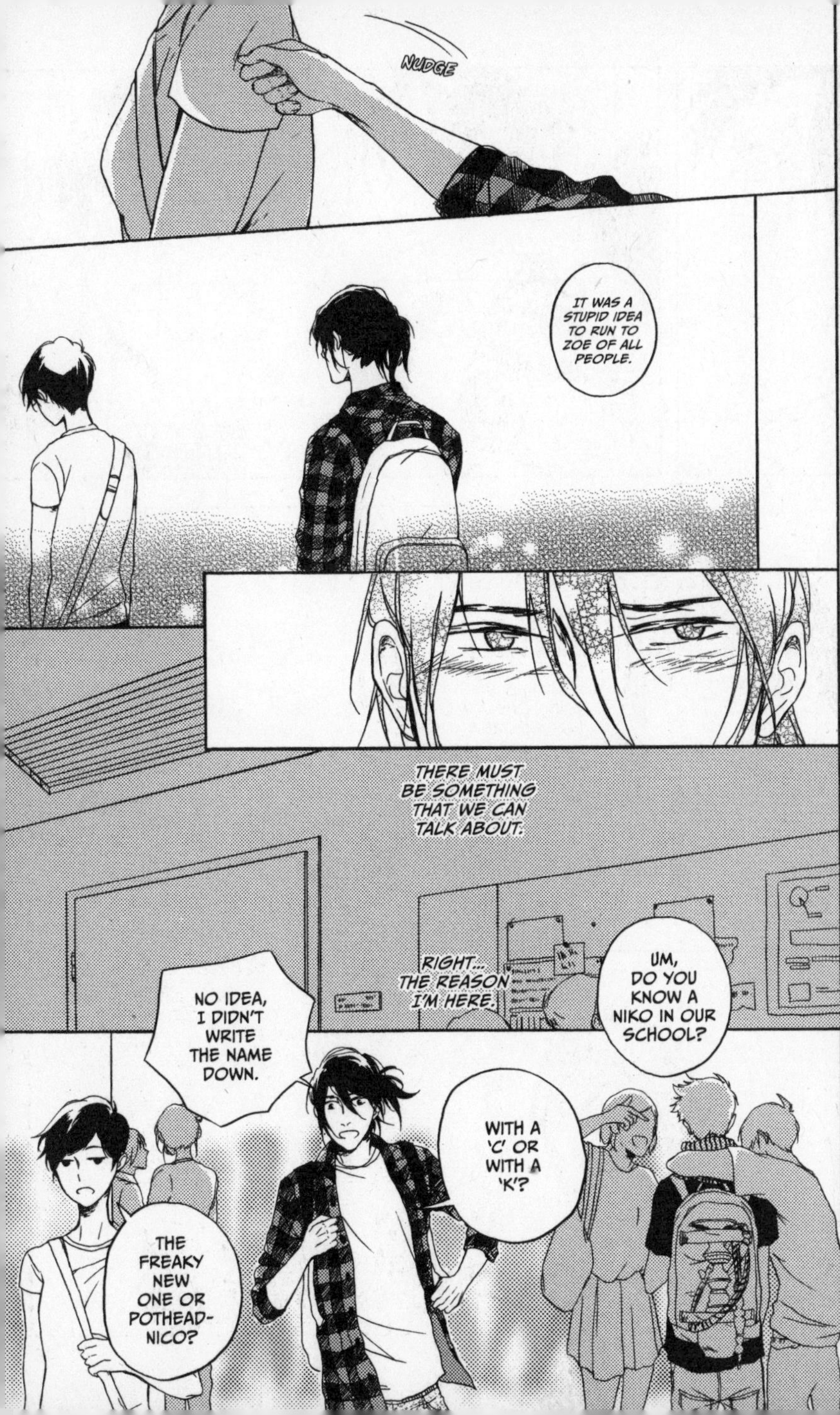
NUDGE
IT WAS A STUPID IDEA TO RUN TO ZOE OF ALL PEOPLE.
THERE MUST BE SOMETHING THAT WE CAN TALK ABOUT.
RIGHT... THE REASON I'M HERE.
UM, DO YOU KNOW A NIKO IN OUR SCHOOL?
WITH A 'C' OR WITH A 'K'?
NO IDEA, I DIDN'T WRITE THE NAME DOWN.
THE FREAKY NEW ONE OR POTHEAD-NICO?

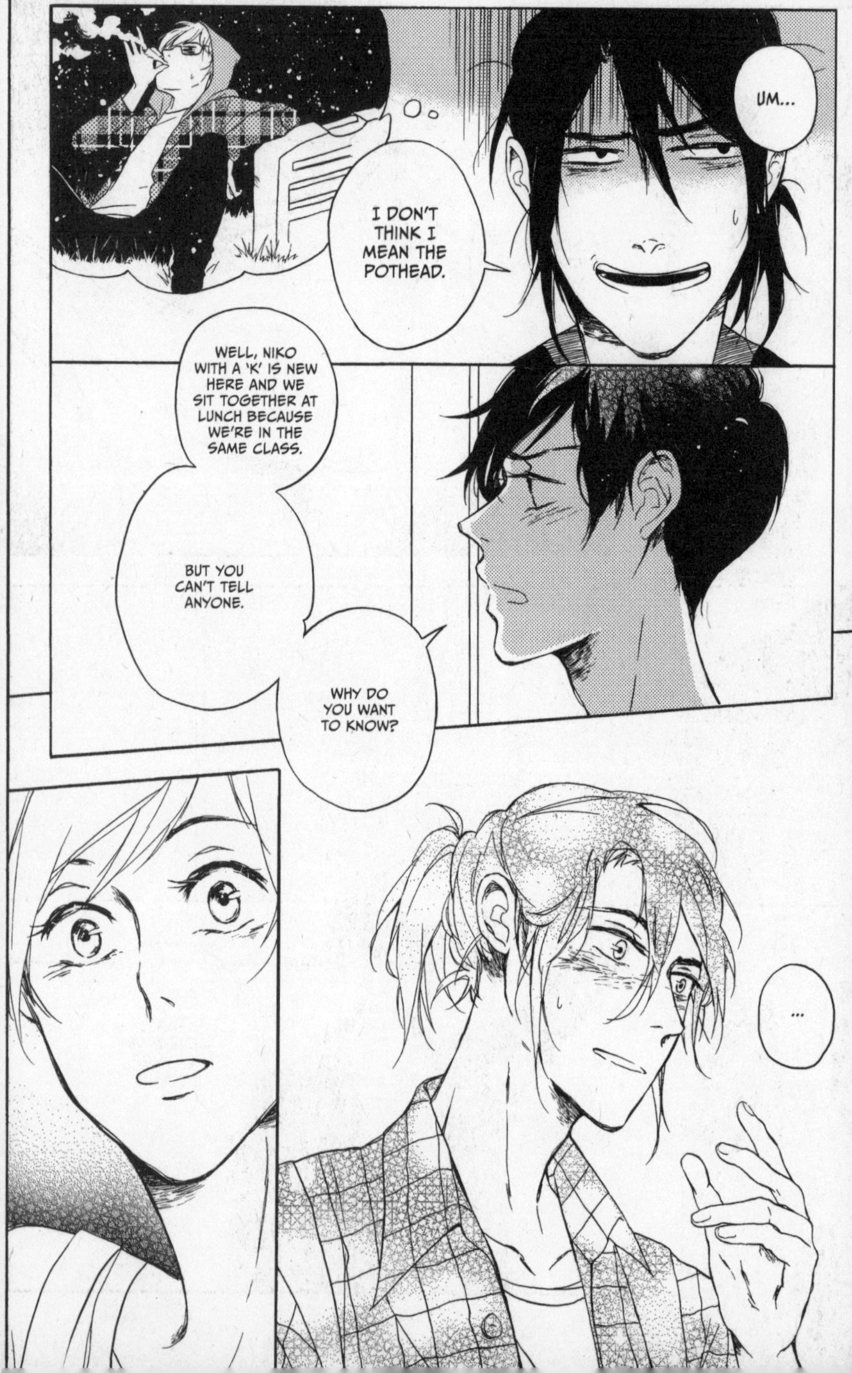
UM...
I DON'T THINK I MEAN THE POTHEAD.
WELL, NIKO WITH A 'K' IS NEW HERE AND WE SIT TOGETHER AT LUNCH BECAUSE WE'RE IN THE SAME CLASS.
BUT YOU CAN'T TELL ANYONE.
WHY DO YOU WANT TO KNOW?
...

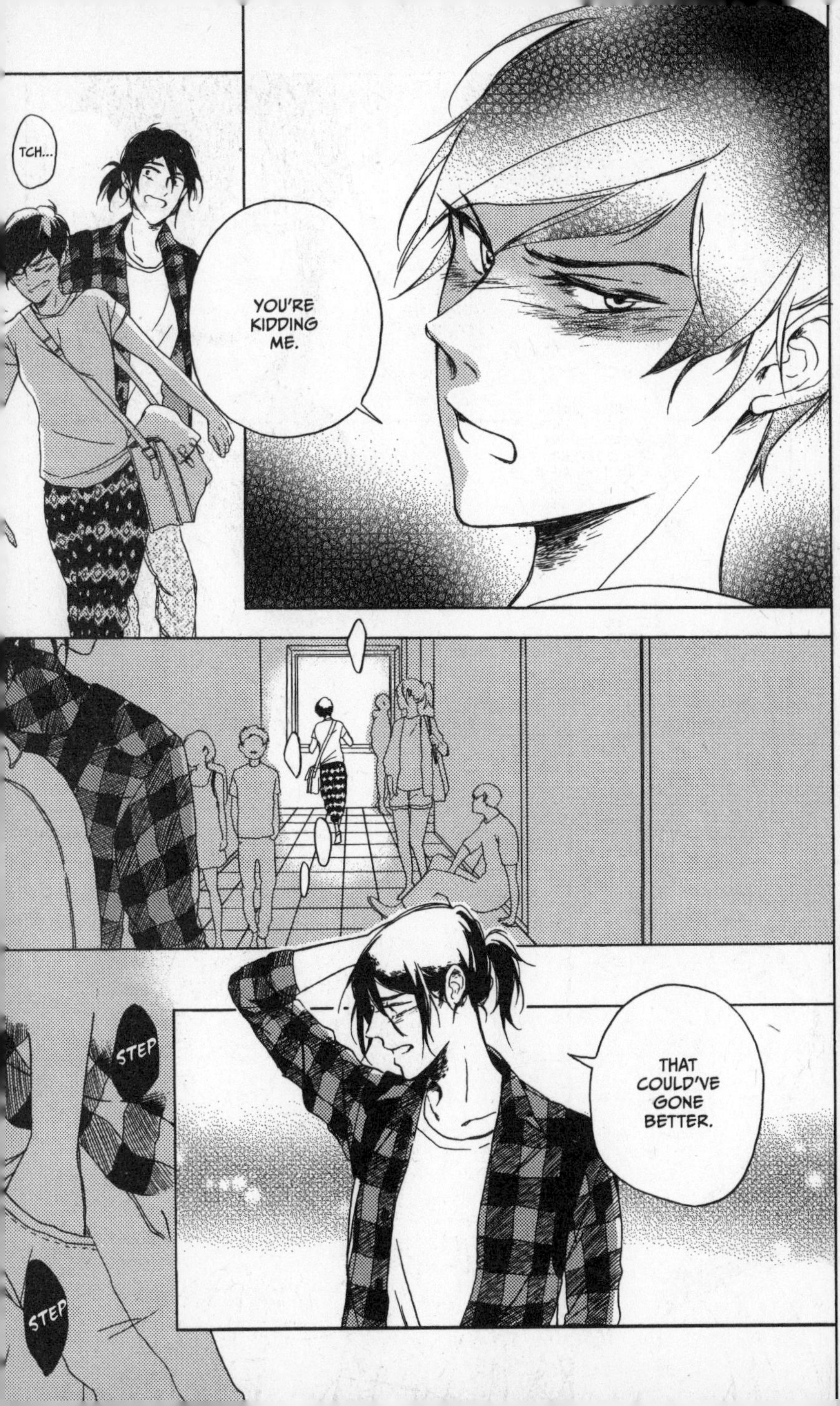
YOU'RE KIDDING ME.
TCH...
THAT COULD'VE GONE BETTER.
STEP
STEP

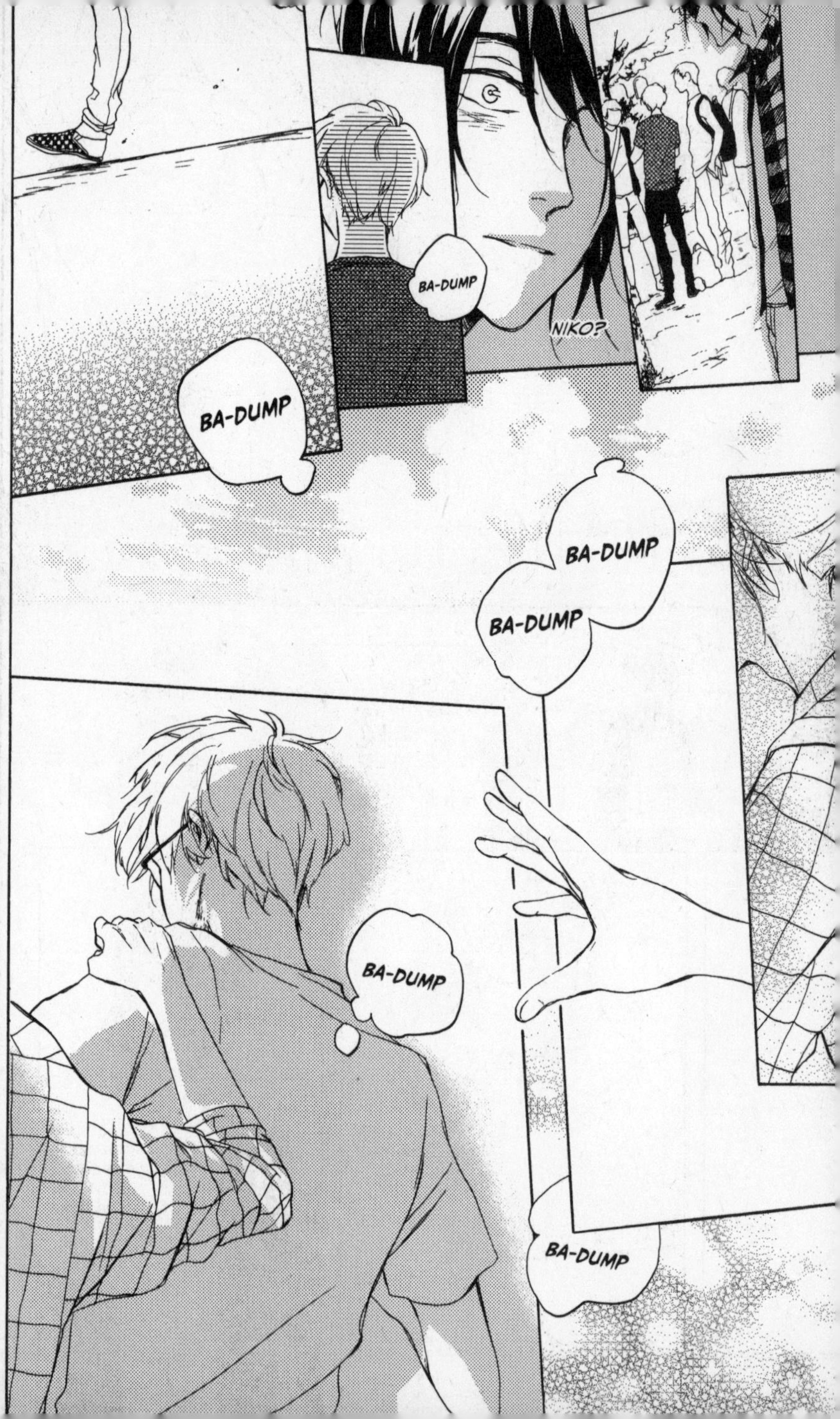
NIKO?
BA-DUMP
BA-DUMP
BA-DUMP
BA-DUMP
BA-DUMP
BA-DUMP

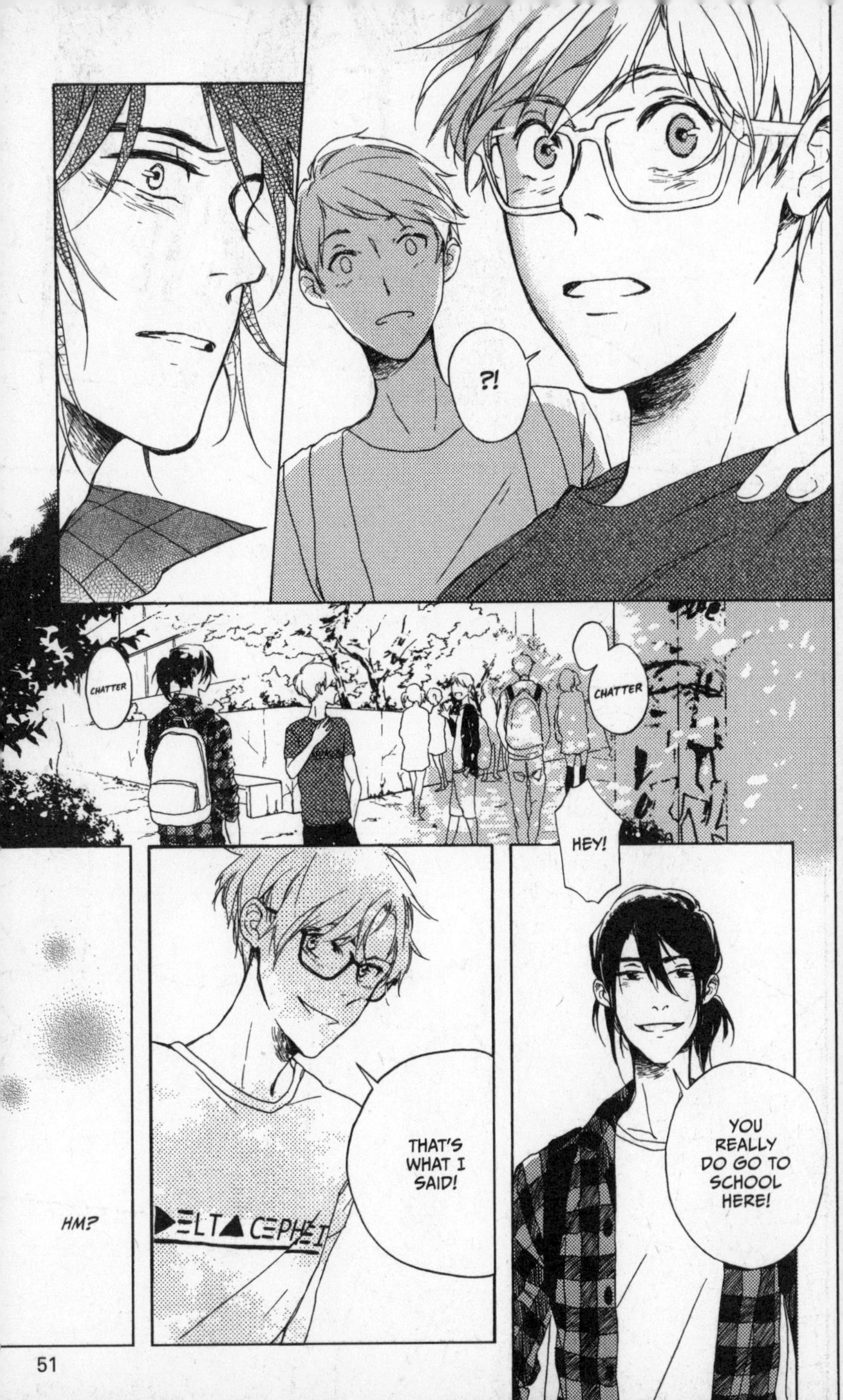
?!
CHATTER
CHATTER
HEY!
YOU REALLY DO GO TO SCHOOL HERE!
THAT'S WHAT I SAID!
HM?

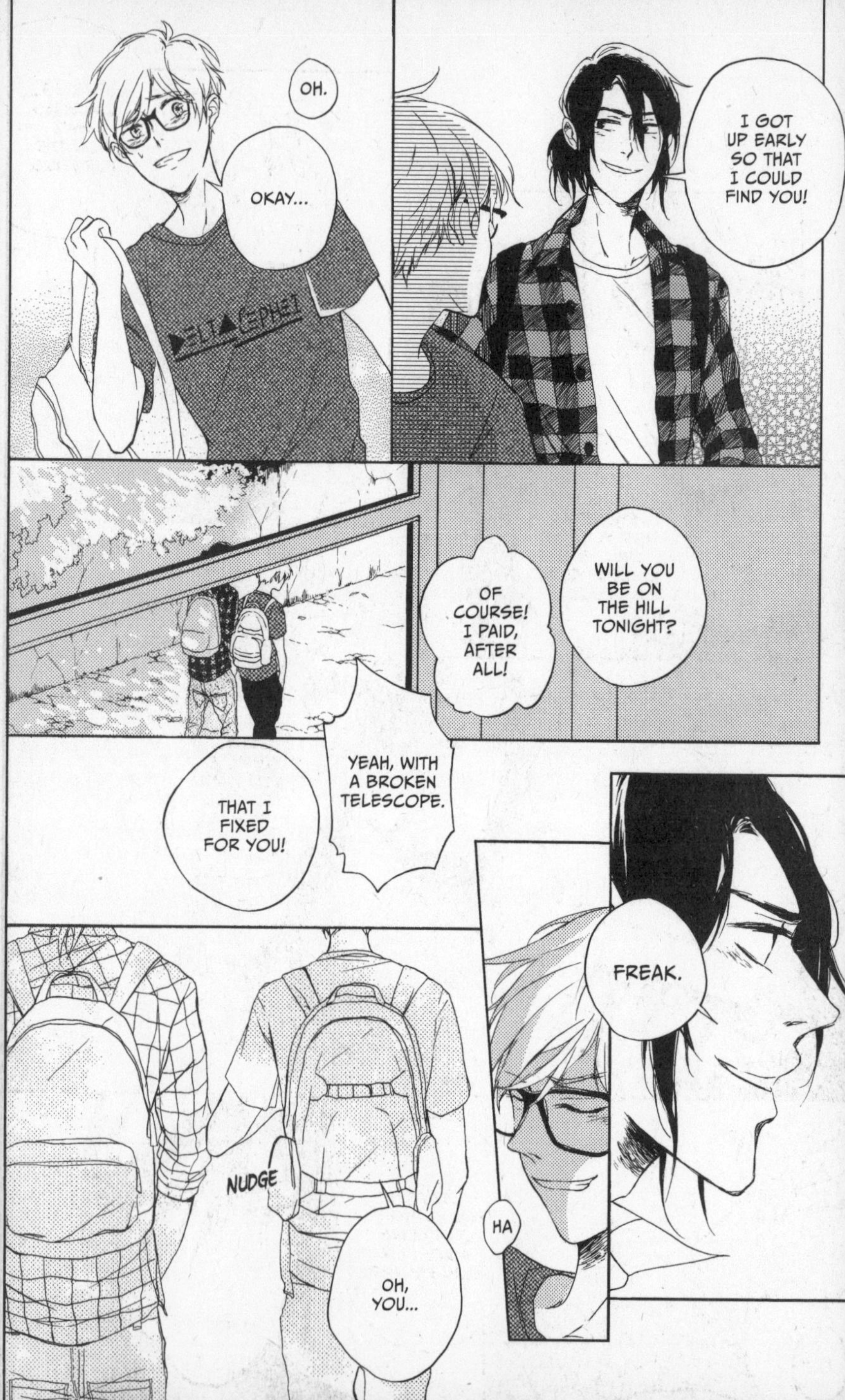
I GOT UP EARLY SO THAT I COULD FIND YOU!
OH.
OKAY...
WILL YOU BE ON THE HILL TONIGHT?
OF COURSE! I PAID, AFTER ALL!
YEAH, WITH A BROKEN TELESCOPE.
THAT I FIXED FOR YOU!
FREAK.
HA
NUDGE
OH, YOU...

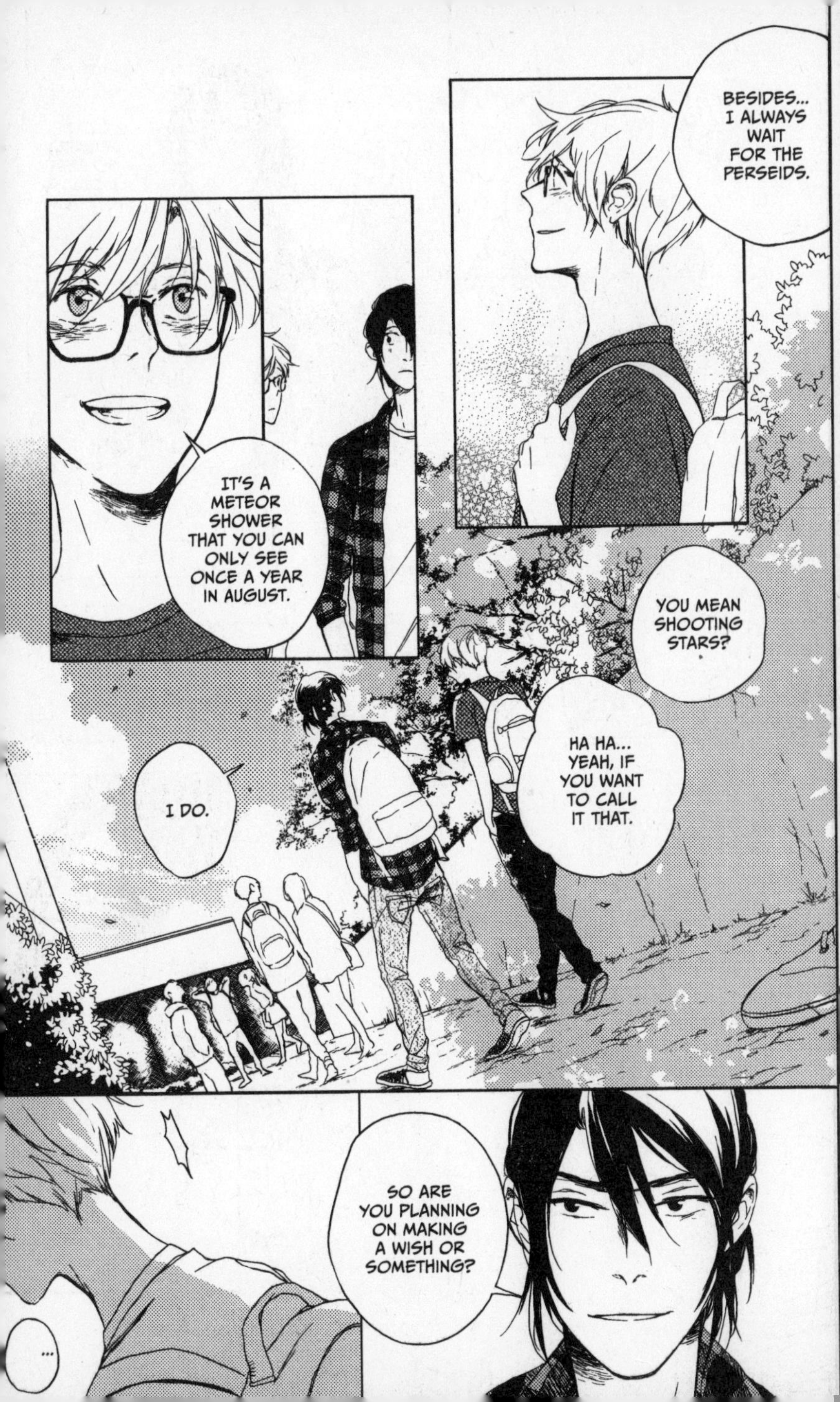
BESIDES... I ALWAYS WAIT FOR THE PERSEIDS.
IT'S A METEOR SHOWER THAT YOU CAN ONLY SEE ONCE A YEAR IN AUGUST.
YOU MEAN SHOOTING STARS?
HA HA... YEAH, IF YOU WANT TO CALL IT THAT.
I DO.
SO ARE YOU PLANNING ON MAKING A WISH OR SOMETHING?
...

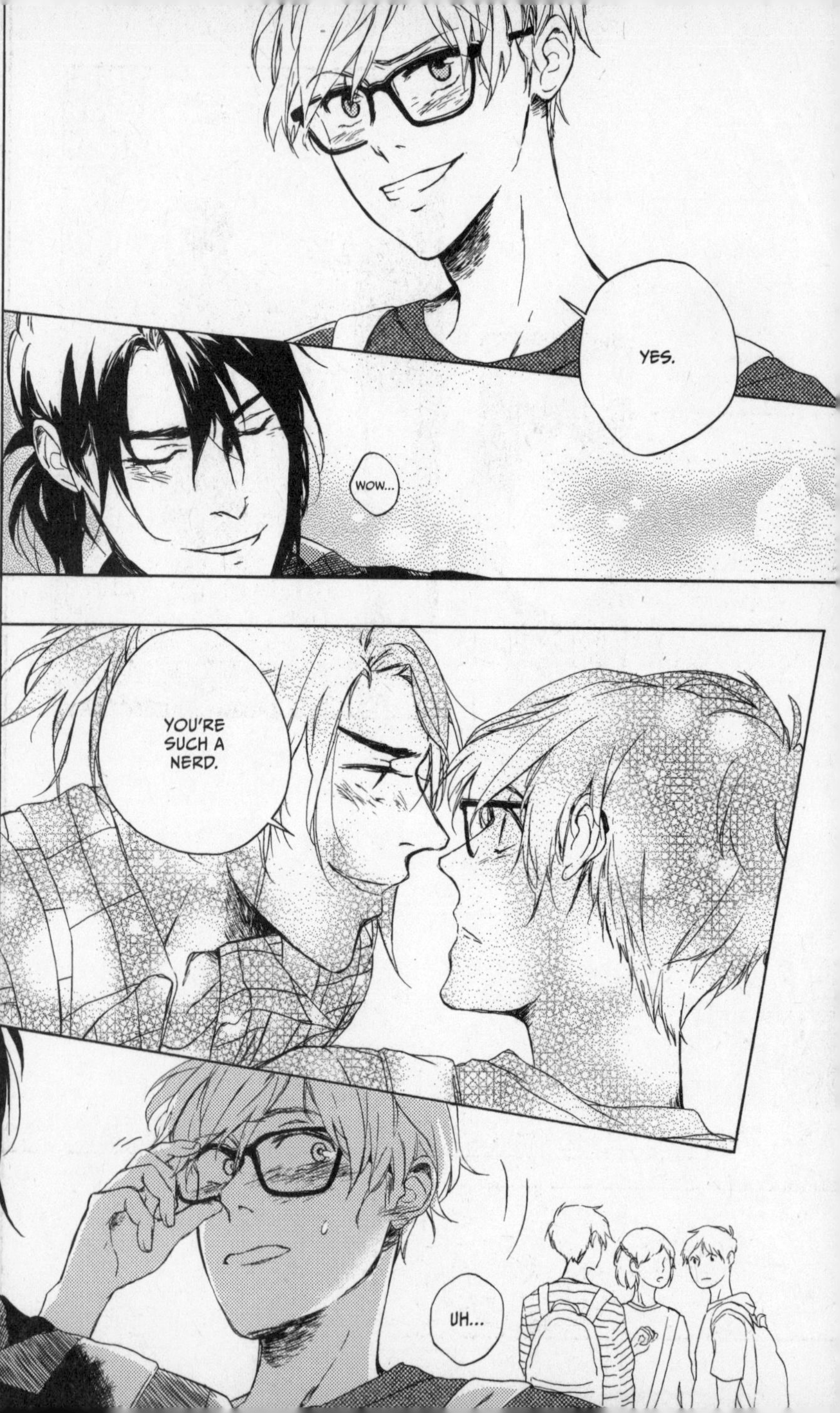
YES.
WOW...
YOU'RE SUCH A NERD.
UH...

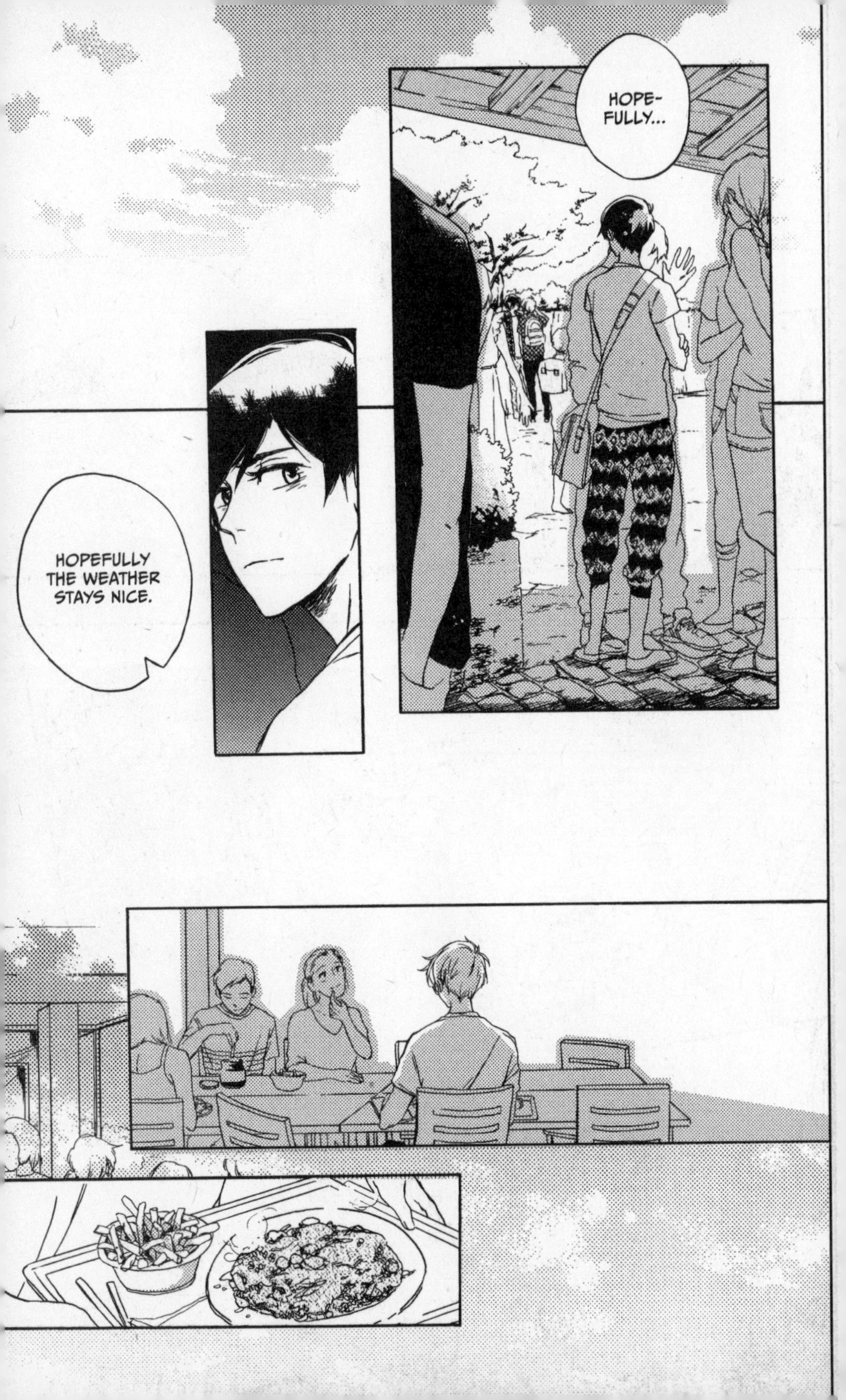
HOPE-
FULLY...
HOPEFULLY
THE WEATHER
STAYS NICE.

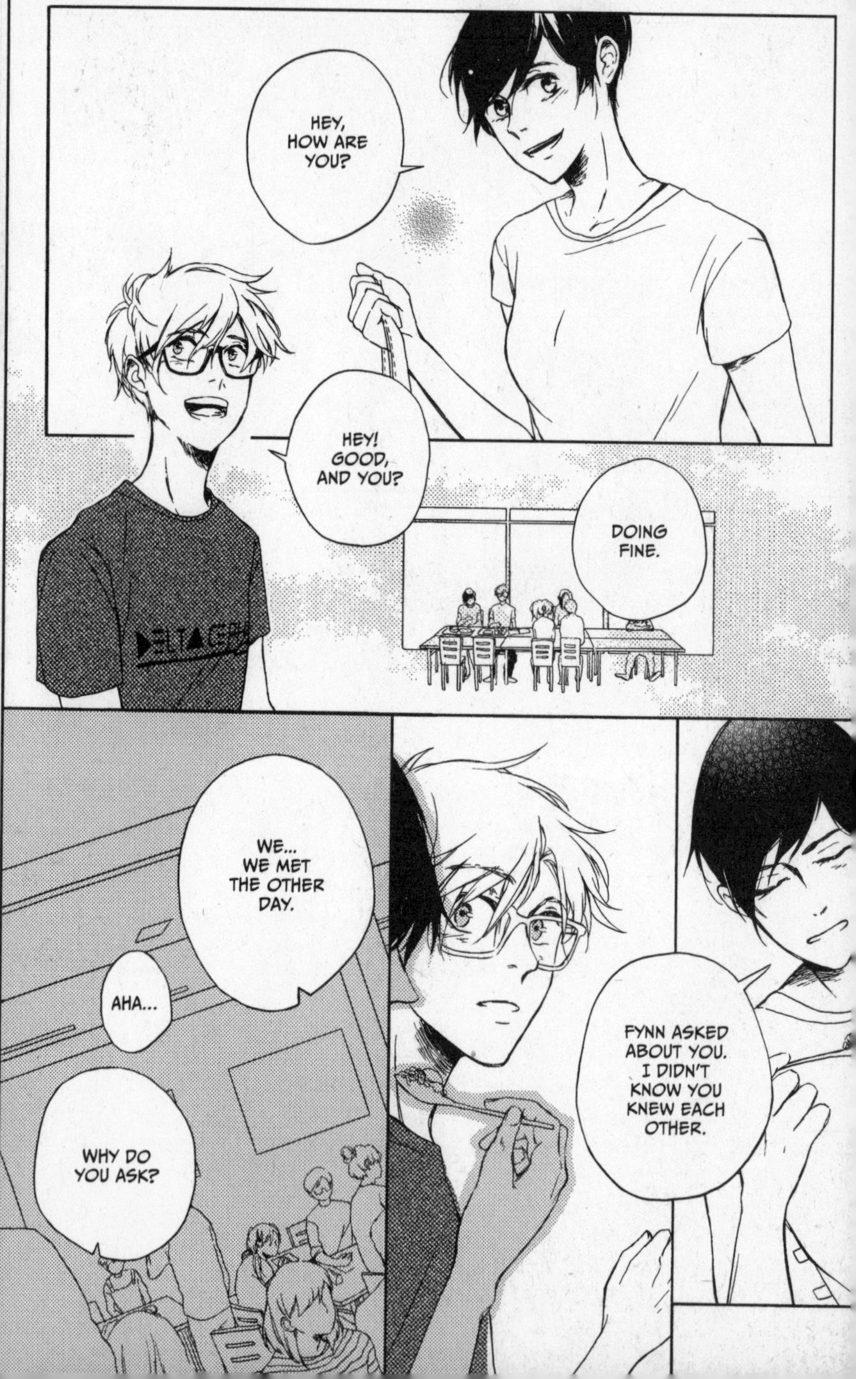
HEY, HOW ARE YOU?
HEY! GOOD, AND YOU?
DOING FINE.
FYNN ASKED ABOUT YOU. I DIDN'T KNOW YOU KNEW EACH OTHER.
WE... WE MET THE OTHER DAY.
AHA...
WHY DO YOU ASK?

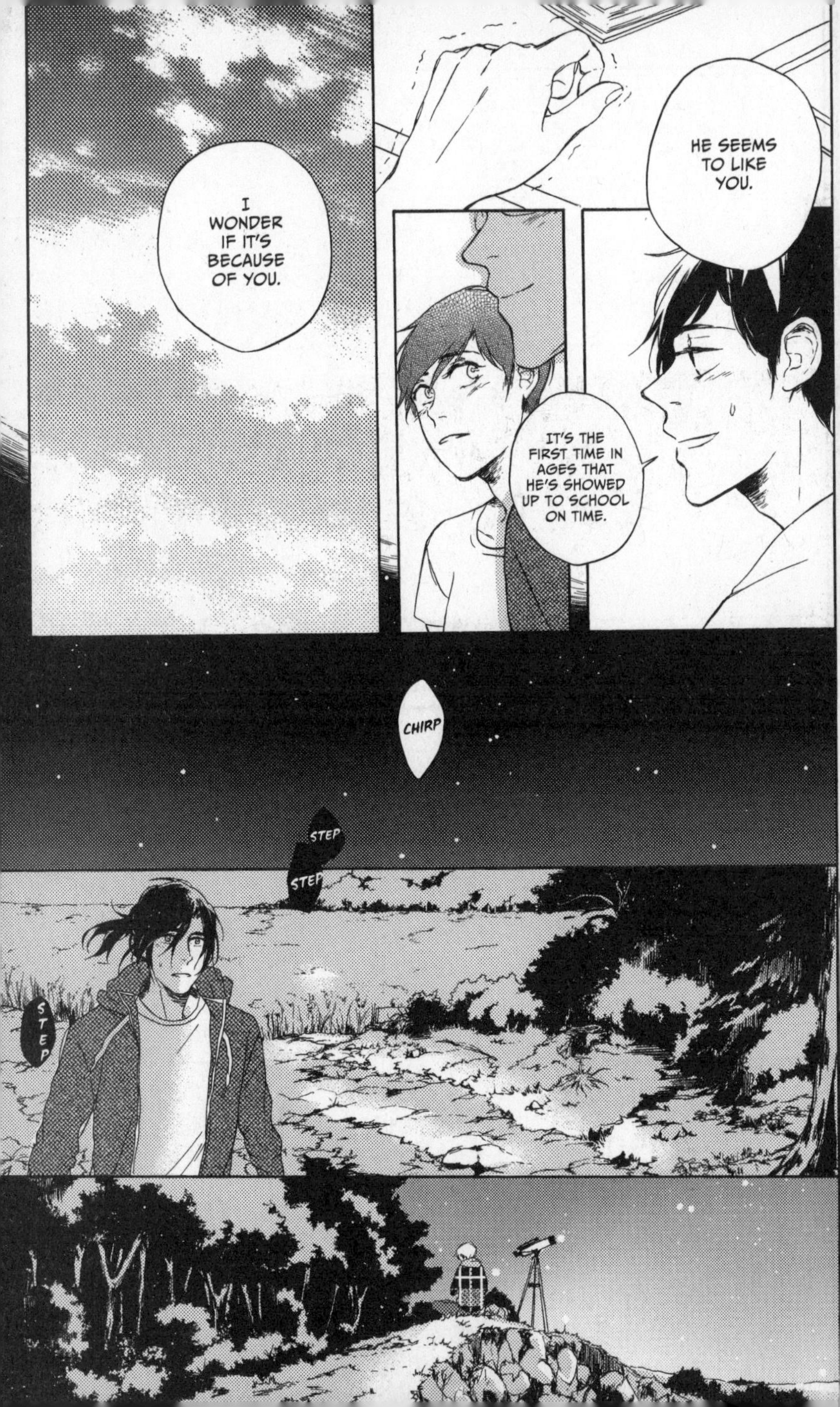
HE SEEMS TO LIKE YOU.
IT'S THE FIRST TIME IN AGES THAT HE'S SHOWED UP TO SCHOOL ON TIME.
I WONDER IF IT'S BECAUSE OF YOU.
CHIRP
STEP
STEP
STEP

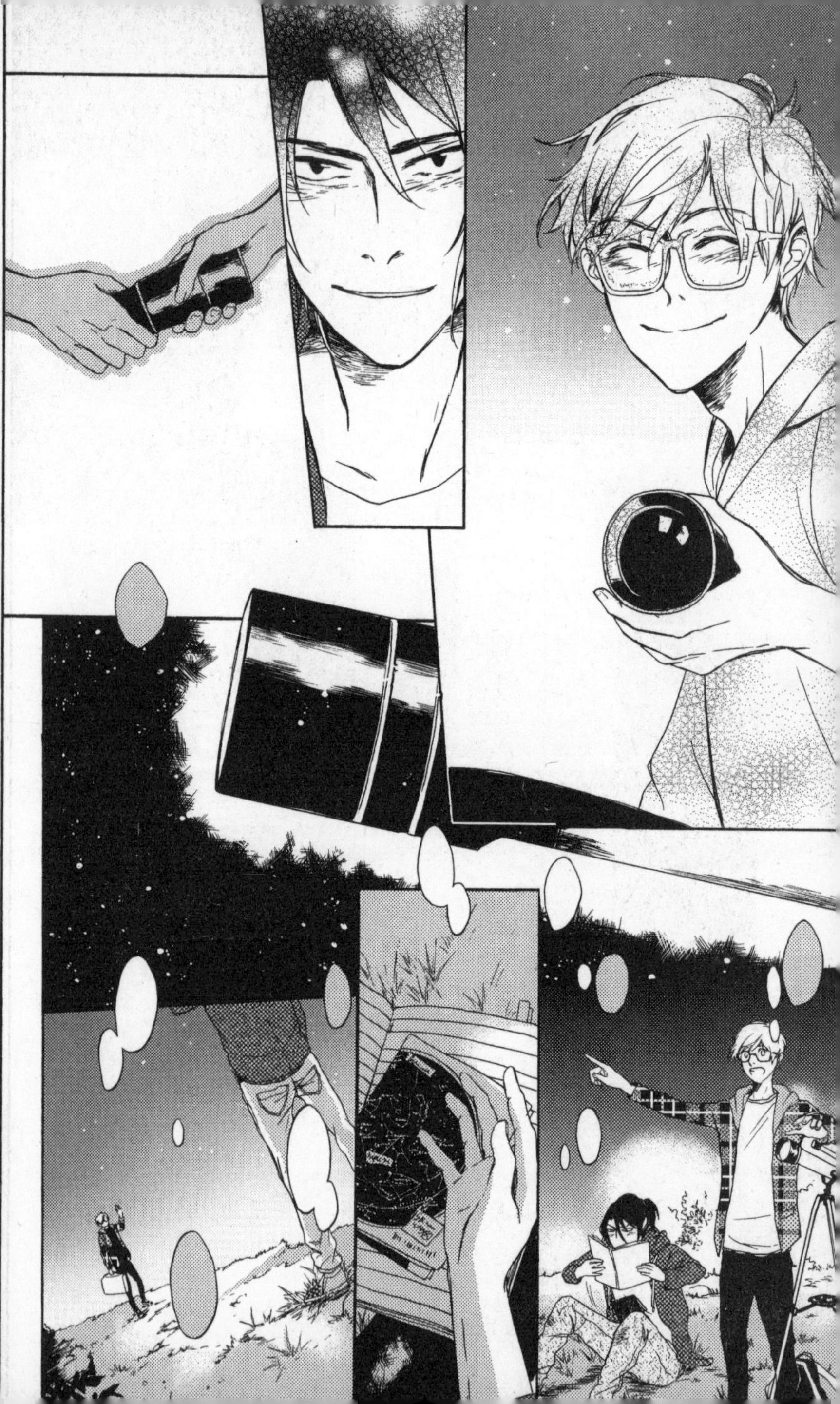

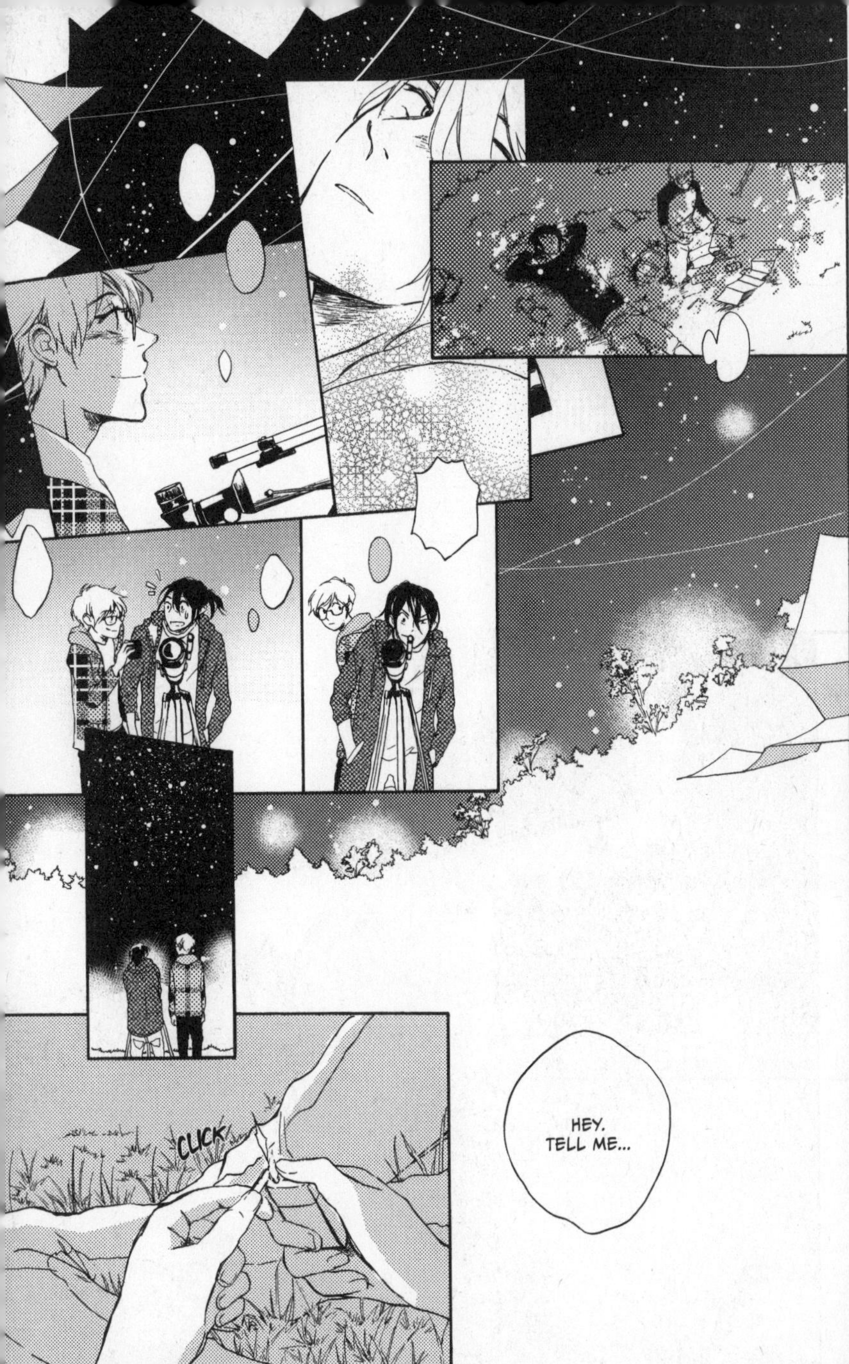
CLICK
HEY.
TELL ME...

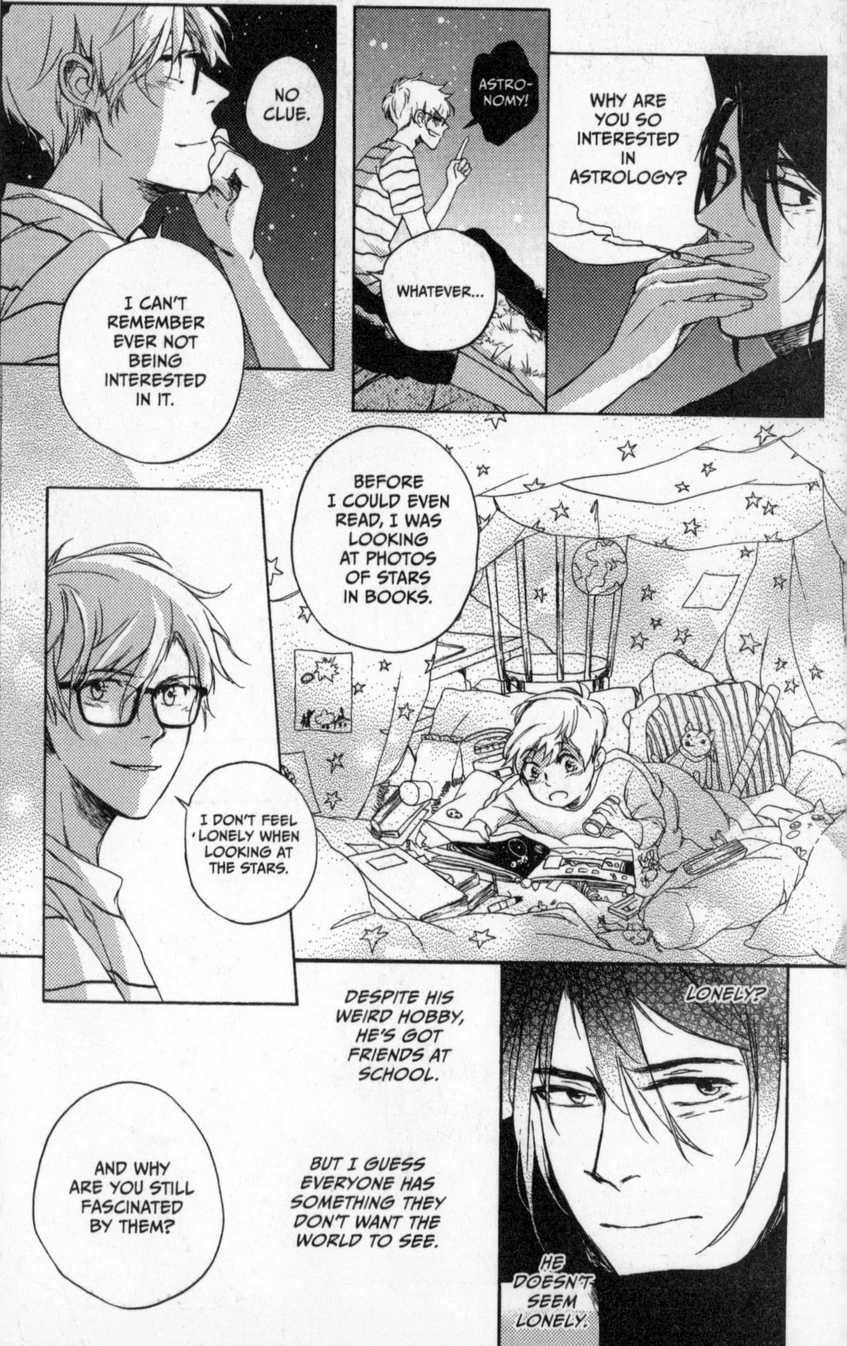
WHY ARE YOU SO INTERESTED IN ASTROLOGY?
ASTRO-NOMY!
WHATEVER...
NO CLUE.
I CAN'T REMEMBER EVER NOT BEING INTERESTED IN IT.
BEFORE I COULD EVEN READ, I WAS LOOKING AT PHOTOS OF STARS IN BOOKS.
I DON'T FEEL LONELY WHEN LOOKING AT THE STARS.
LONELY?
HE DOESN'T SEEM LONELY.
DESPITE HIS WEIRD HOBBY, HE'S GOT FRIENDS AT SCHOOL.
BUT I GUESS EVERYONE HAS SOMETHING THEY DON'T WANT THE WORLD TO SEE.
AND WHY ARE YOU STILL FASCINATED BY THEM?

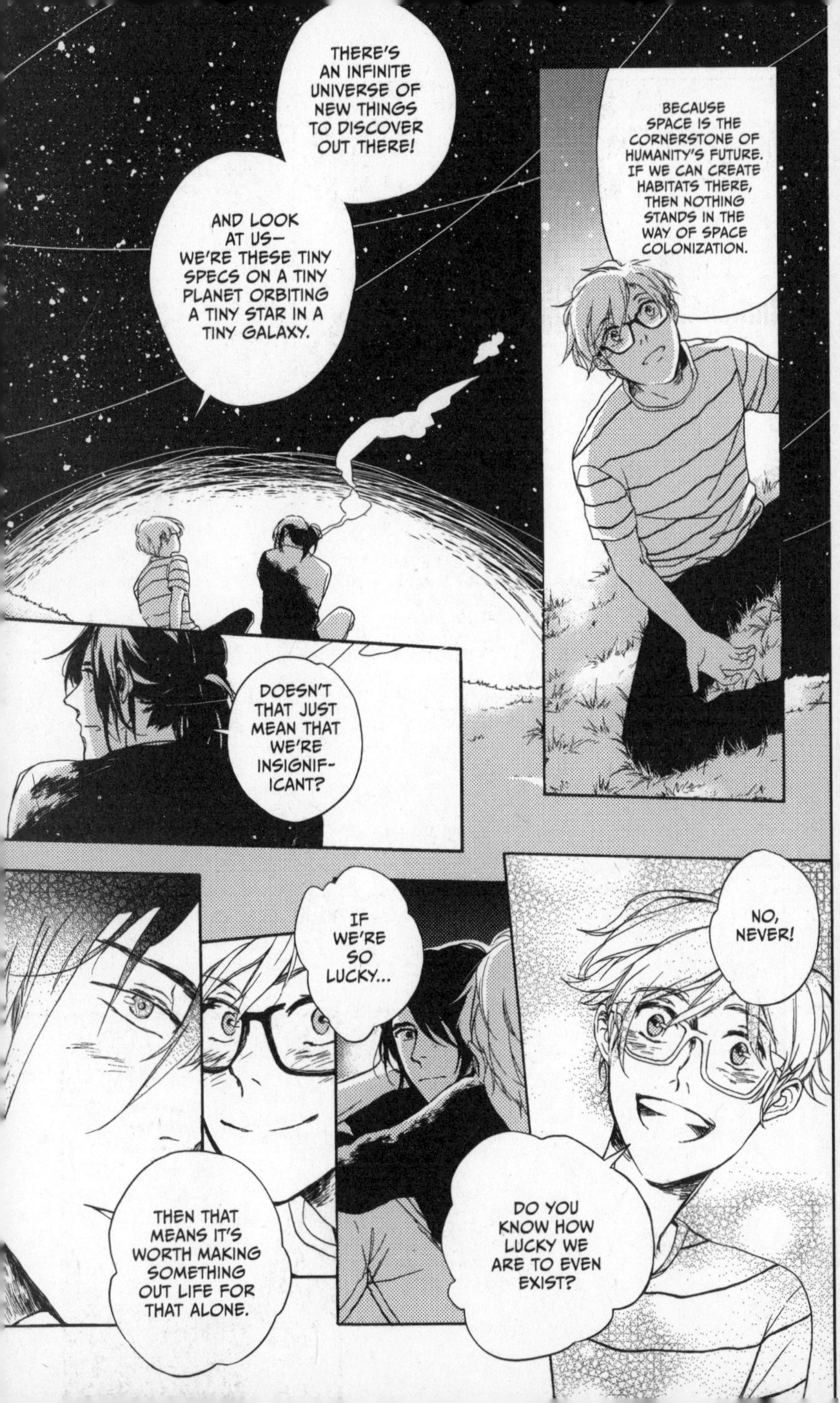
BECAUSE SPACE IS THE CORNERSTONE OF HUMANITY'S FUTURE. IF WE CAN CREATE HABITATS THERE, THEN NOTHING STANDS IN THE WAY OF SPACE COLONIZATION.
THERE'S AN INFINITE UNIVERSE OF NEW THINGS TO DISCOVER OUT THERE!
AND LOOK AT US— WE'RE THESE TINY SPECS ON A TINY PLANET ORBITING A TINY STAR IN A TINY GALAXY.
DOESN'T THAT JUST MEAN THAT WE'RE INSIGNIF-ICANT?
NO, NEVER!
DO YOU KNOW HOW LUCKY WE ARE TO EVEN EXIST?
IF WE'RE SO LUCKY...
THEN THAT MEANS IT'S WORTH MAKING SOMETHING OUT LIFE FOR THAT ALONE.

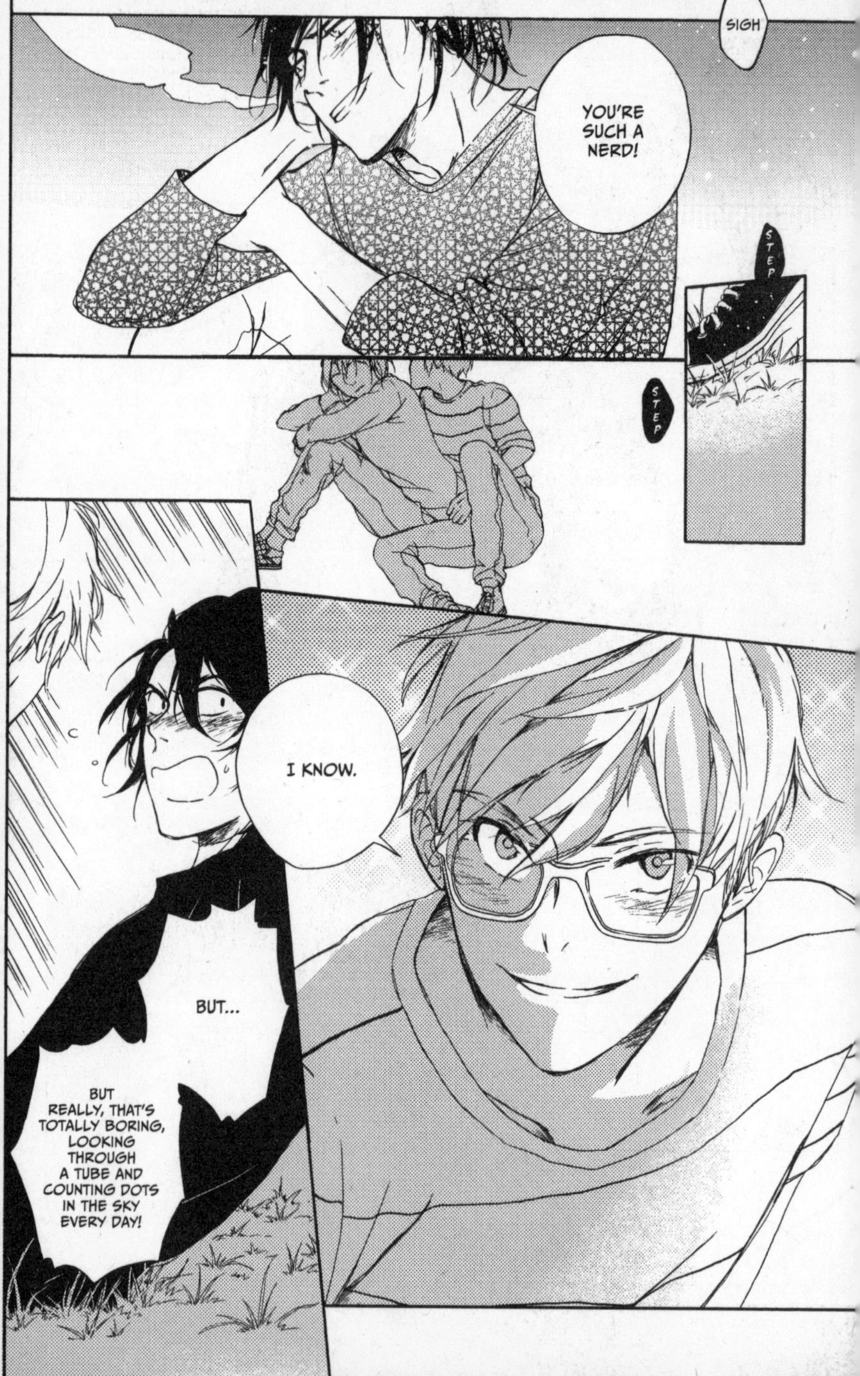
SIGH
YOU'RE SUCH A NERD!
STEP
STEP
I KNOW.
BUT...
BUT REALLY, THAT'S TOTALLY BORING, LOOKING THROUGH A TUBE AND COUNTING DOTS IN THE SKY EVERY DAY!

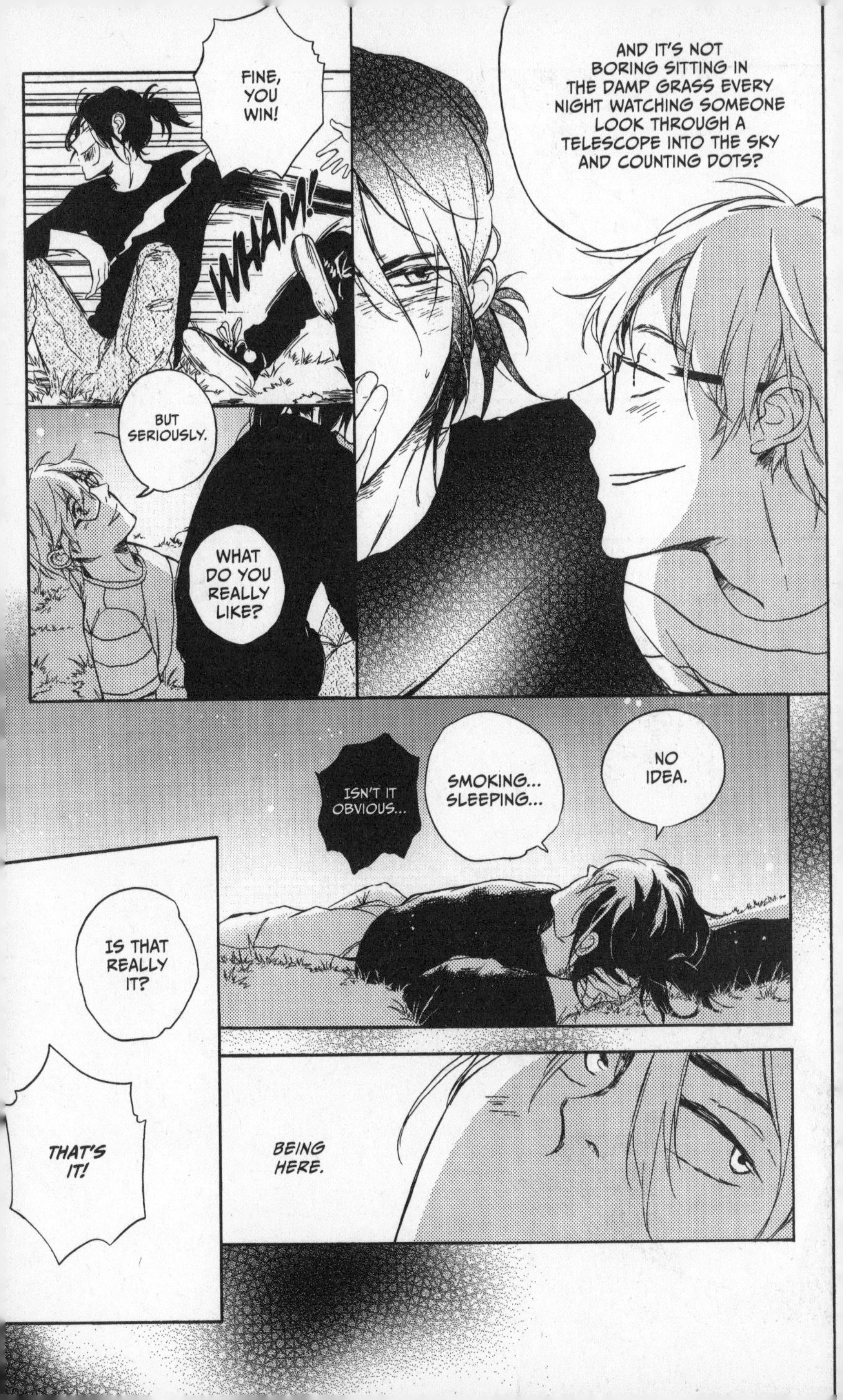
AND IT'S NOT BORING SITTING IN THE DAMP GRASS EVERY NIGHT WATCHING SOMEONE LOOK THROUGH A TELESCOPE INTO THE SKY AND COUNTING DOTS?
FINE, YOU WIN!
WHAM!
BUT SERIOUSLY.
WHAT DO YOU REALLY LIKE?
NO IDEA.
SMOKING... SLEEPING...
ISN'T IT OBVIOUS...
IS THAT REALLY IT?
BEING HERE.
THAT'S IT!

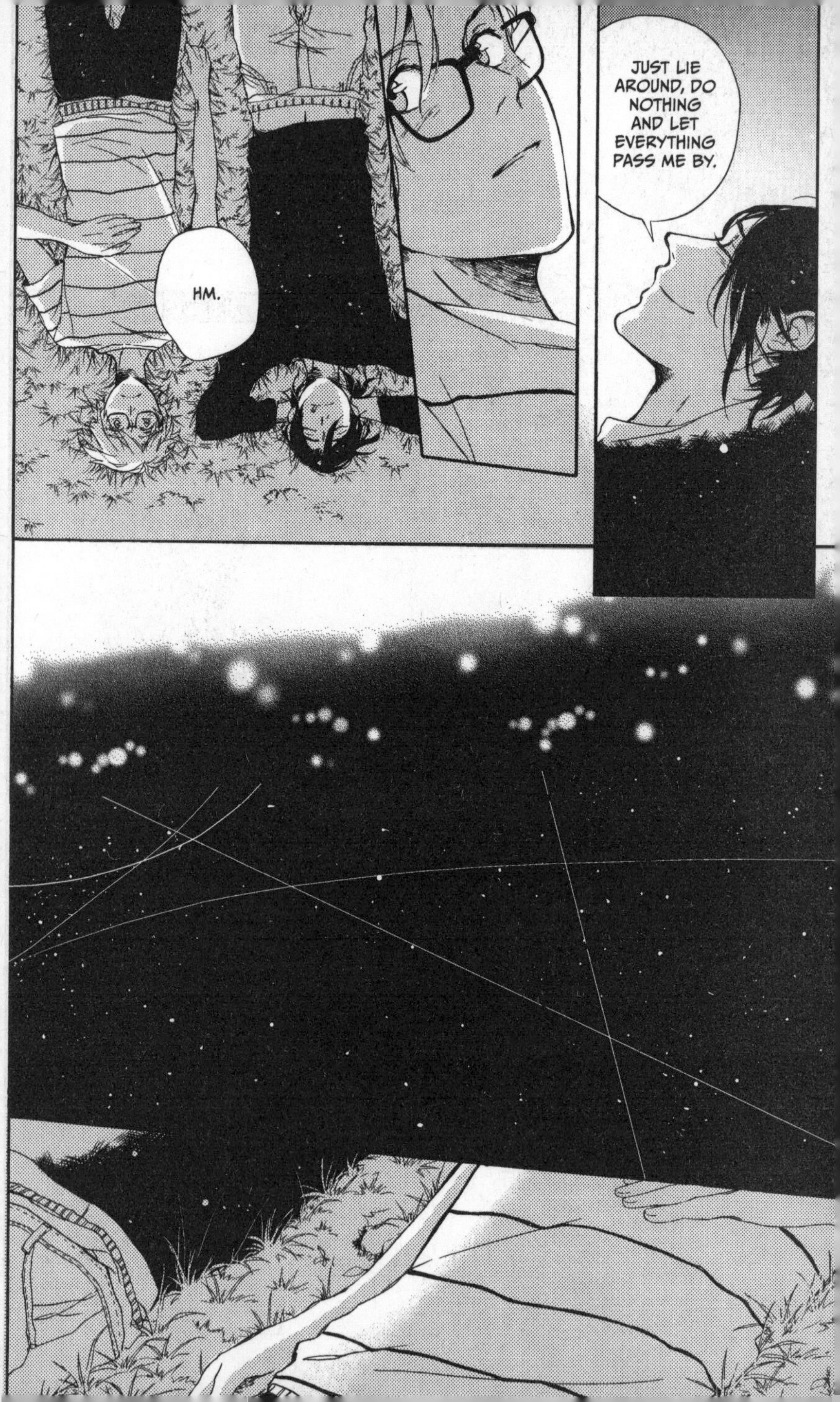
JUST LIE AROUND, DO NOTHING AND LET EVERYTHING PASS ME BY.
HM.

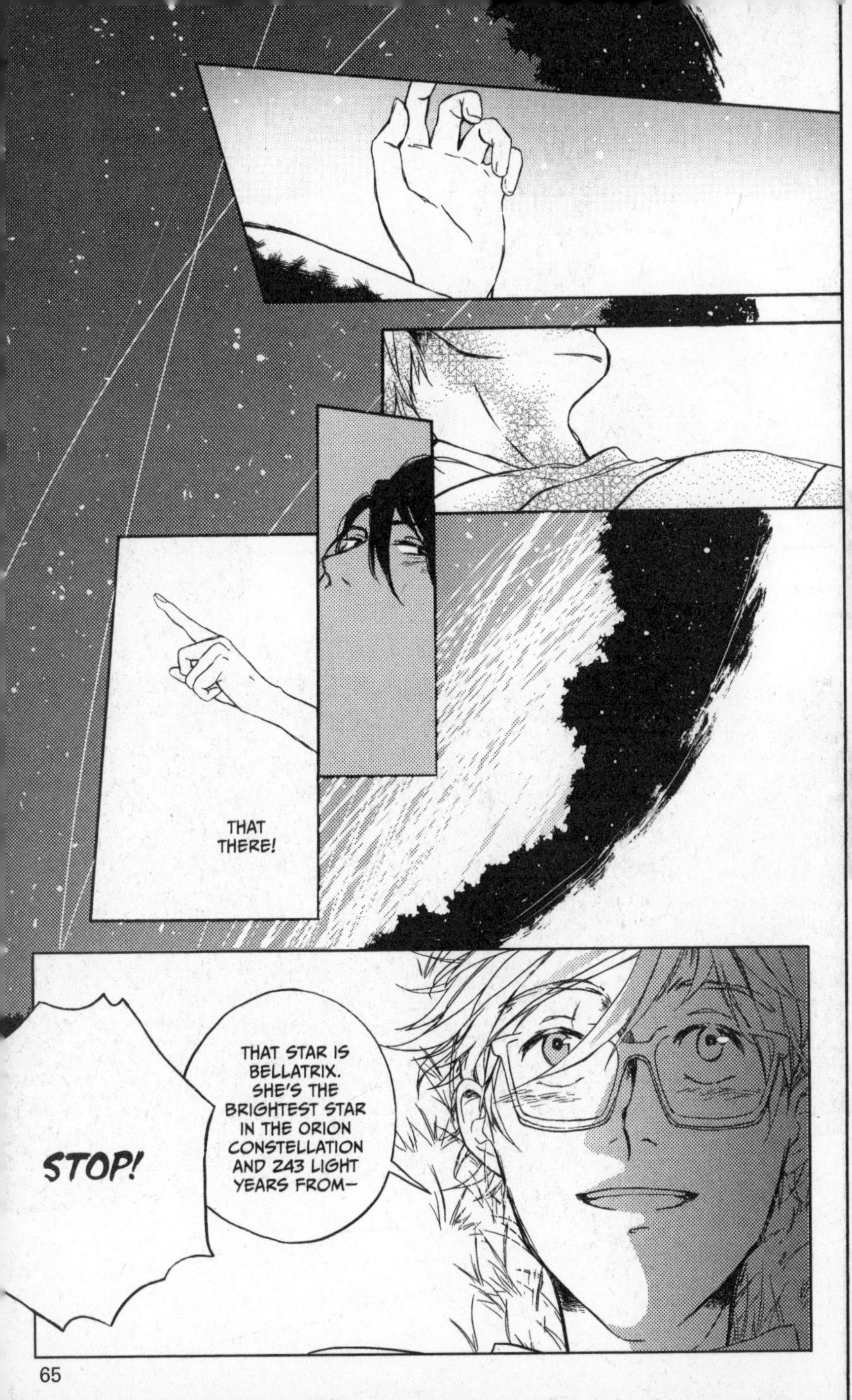
THAT THERE!
THAT STAR IS BELLATRIX. SHE'S THE BRIGHTEST STAR IN THE ORION CONSTELLATION AND 243 LIGHT YEARS FROM—
STOP!

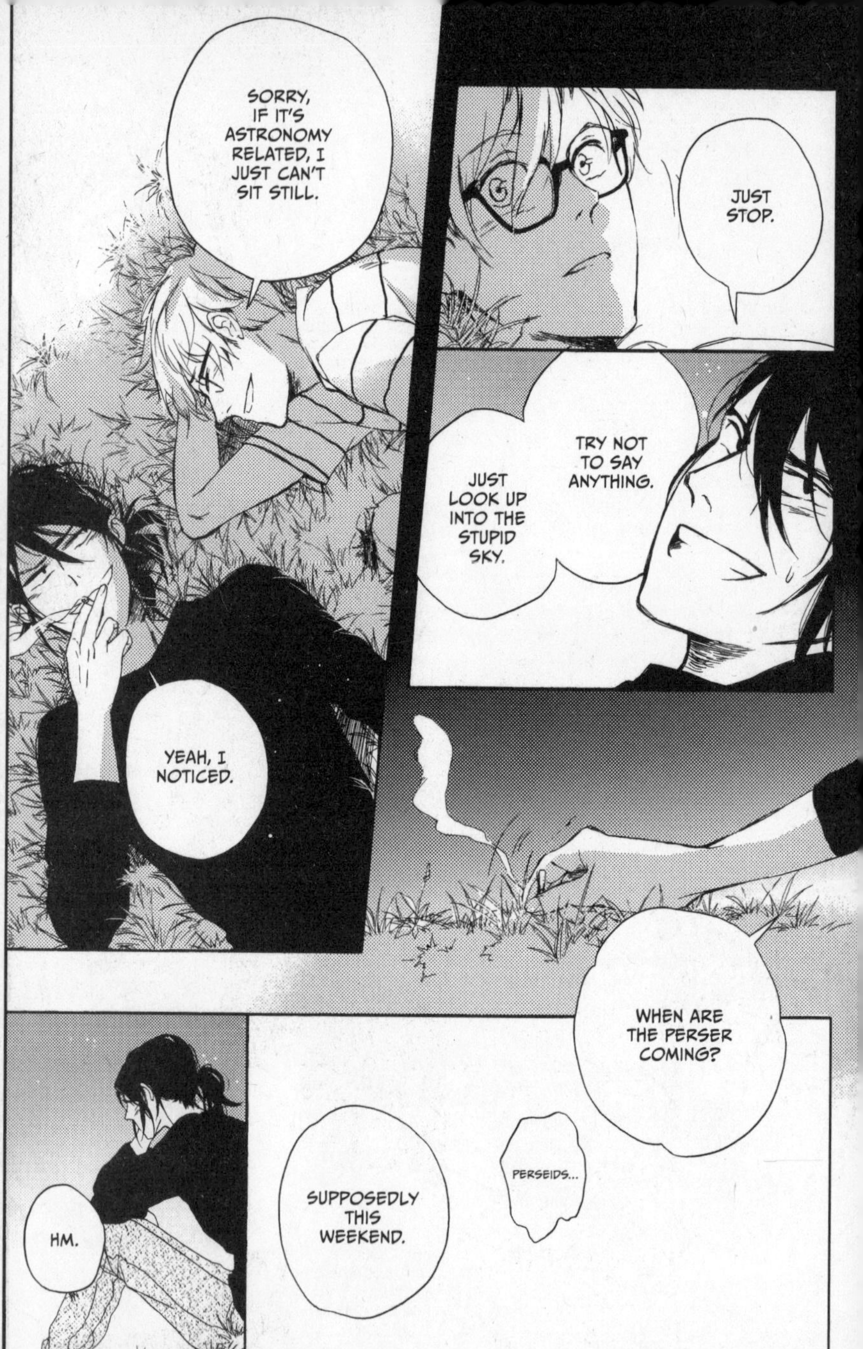
JUST STOP.
TRY NOT TO SAY ANYTHING.
JUST LOOK UP INTO THE STUPID SKY.
SORRY, IF IT'S ASTRONOMY RELATED, I JUST CAN'T SIT STILL.
YEAH, I NOTICED.
WHEN ARE THE PERSER COMING?
PERSEIDS...
SUPPOSEDLY THIS WEEKEND.
HM.

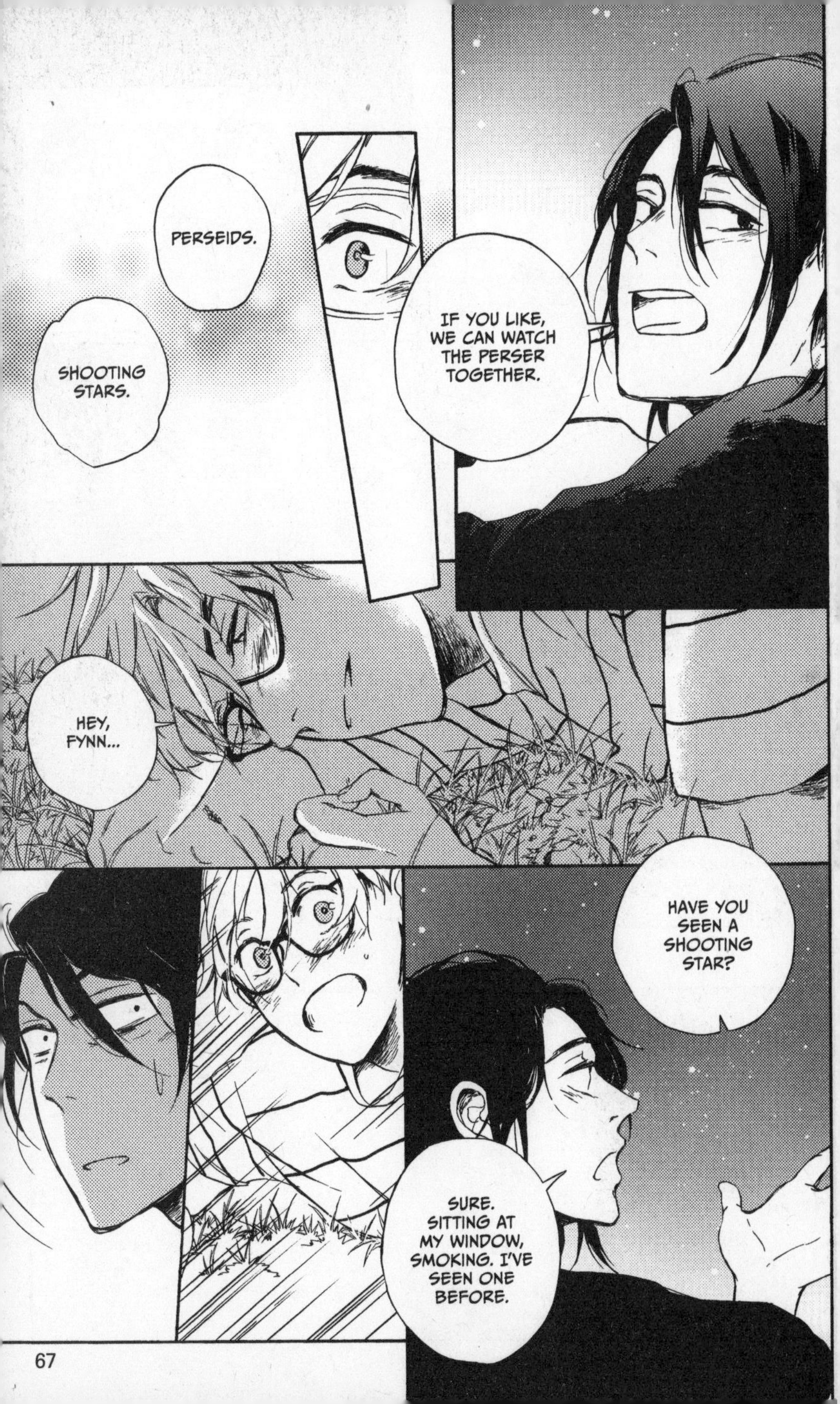
IF YOU LIKE, WE CAN WATCH THE PERSER TOGETHER.
PERSEIDS.
SHOOTING STARS.
HEY, FYNN...
HAVE YOU SEEN A SHOOTING STAR?
SURE. SITTING AT MY WINDOW, SMOKING. I'VE SEEN ONE BEFORE.

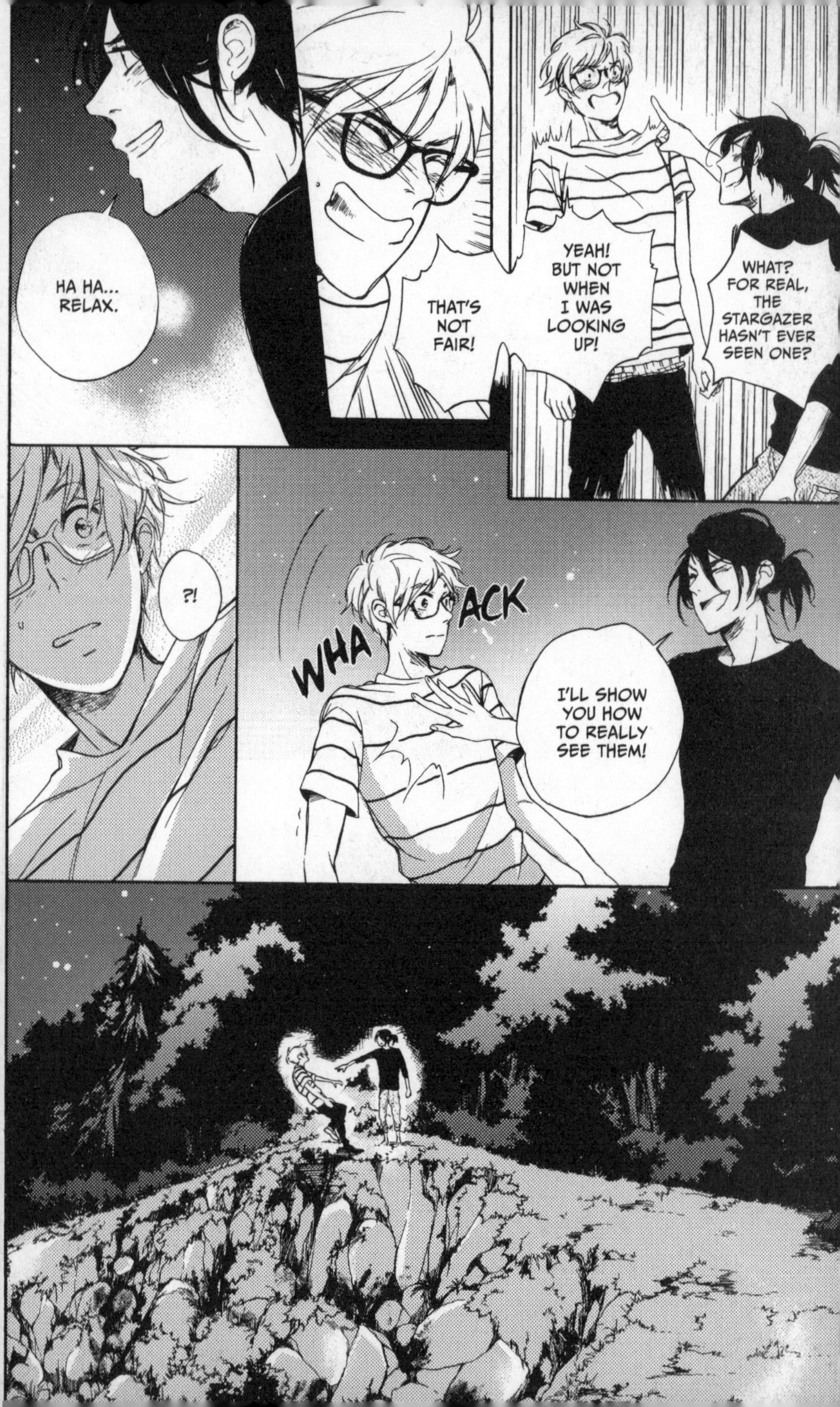
WHAT? FOR REAL, THE STARGAZER HASN'T EVER SEEN ONE?
YEAH! BUT NOT WHEN I WAS LOOKING UP!
THAT'S NOT FAIR!
HA HA... RELAX.
WHA ACK
I'LL SHOW YOU HOW TO REALLY SEE THEM!
?!

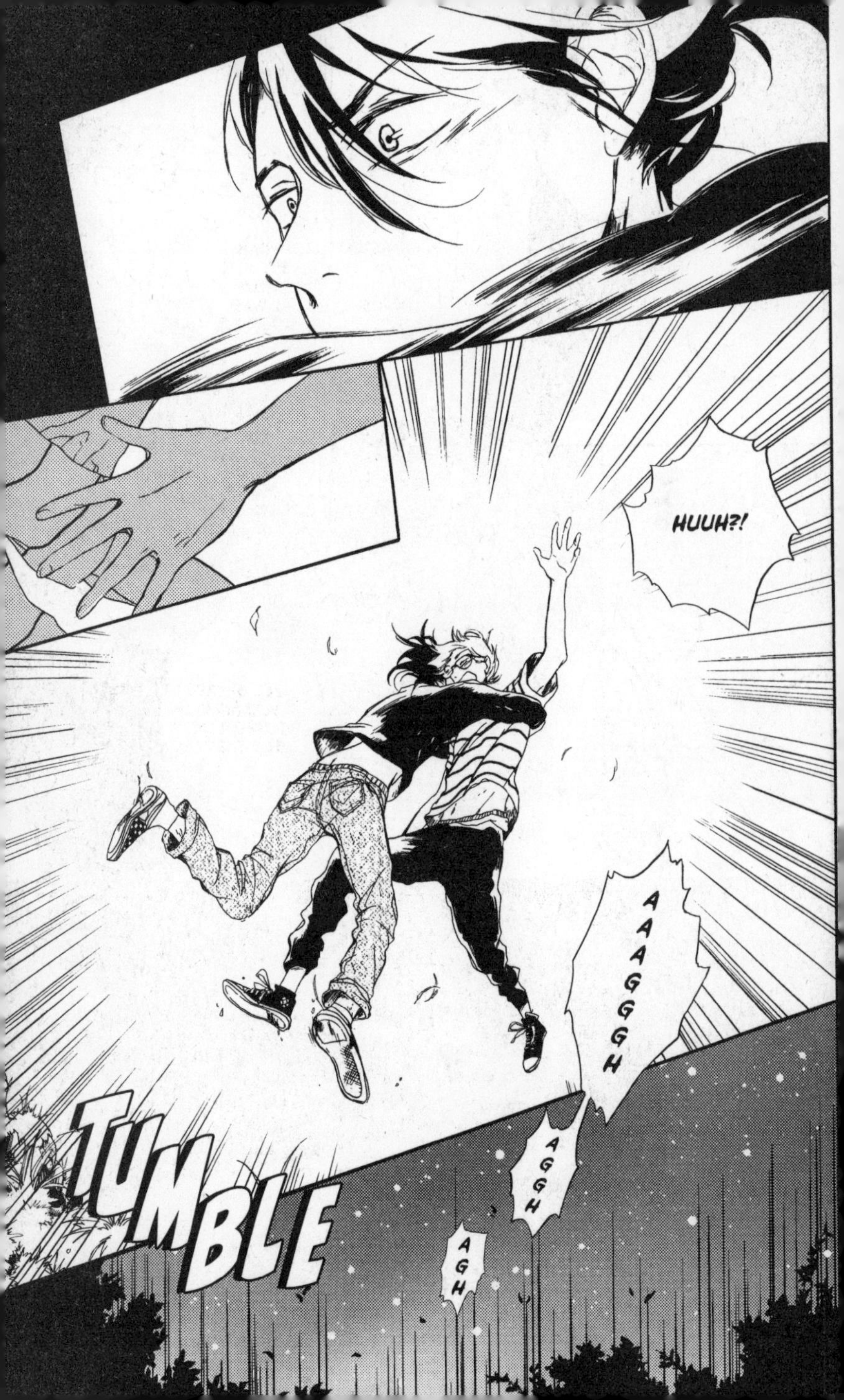
HUUH?!
AAAAGGGH
AGGH
AGH
TUMBLE

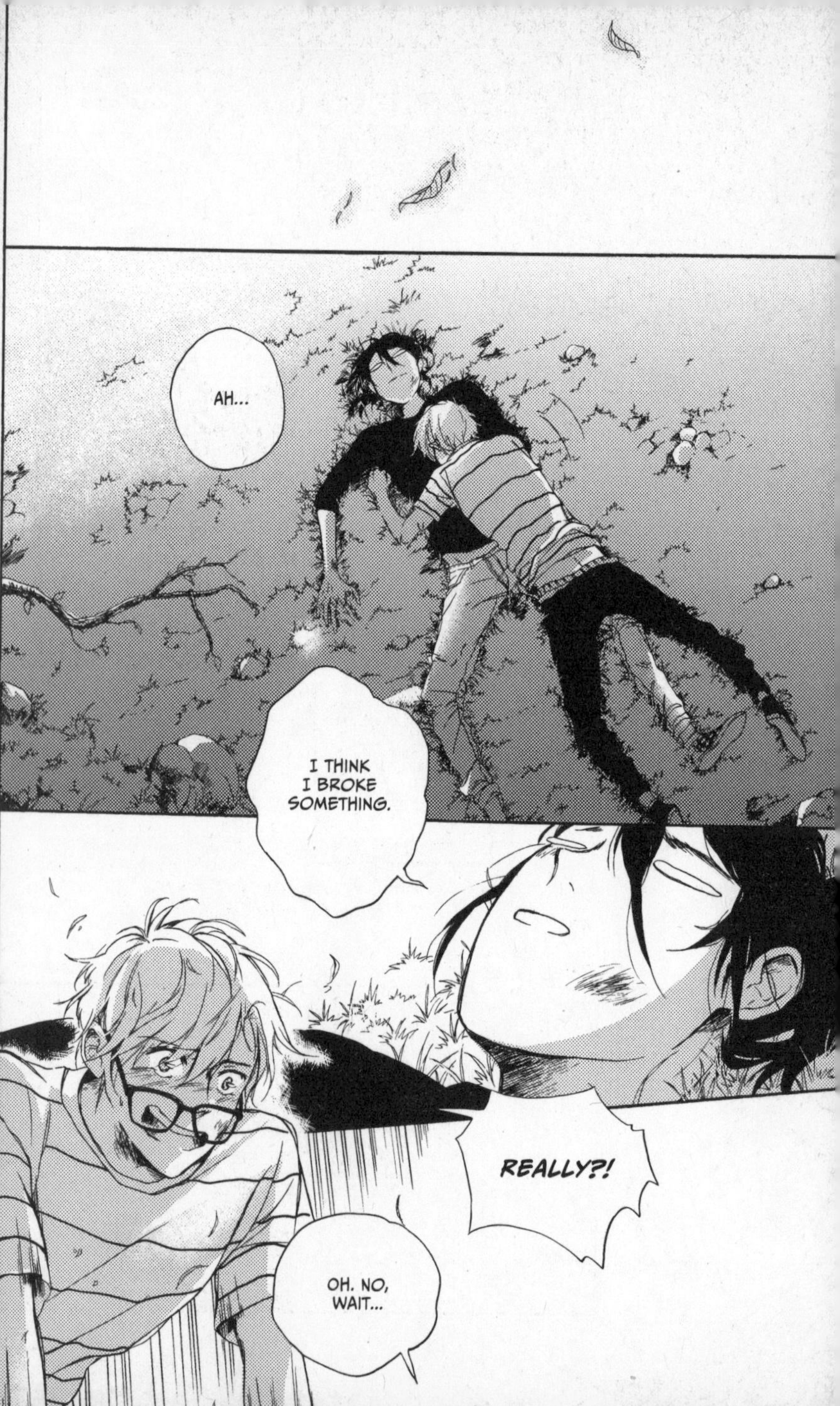
AH...
I THINK I BROKE SOMETHING.
REALLY?!
OH. NO, WAIT...

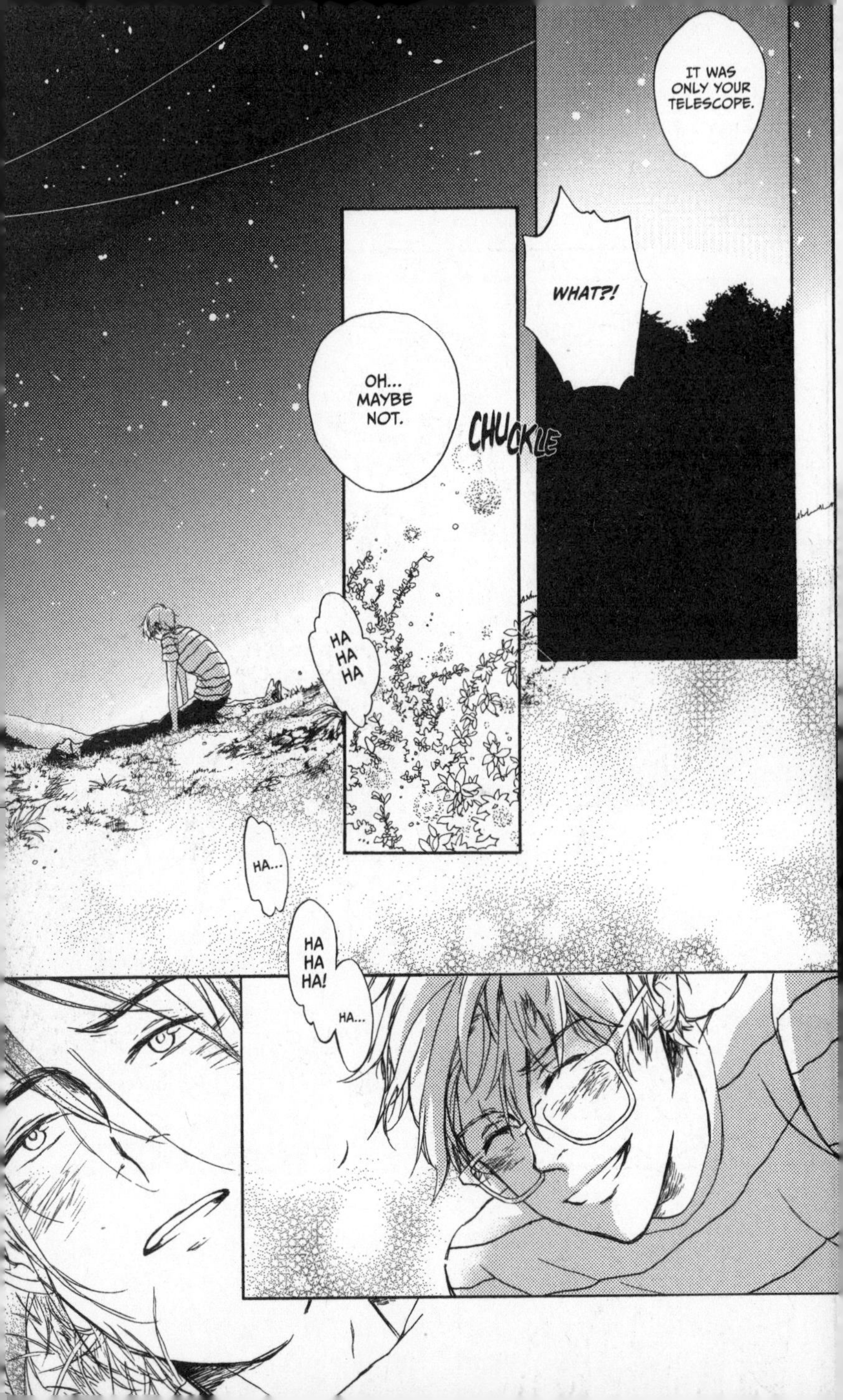
IT WAS ONLY YOUR TELESCOPE.
WHAT?!
OH... MAYBE NOT.
CHUCKLE
HA HA HA
HA...
HA HA HA!
HA...

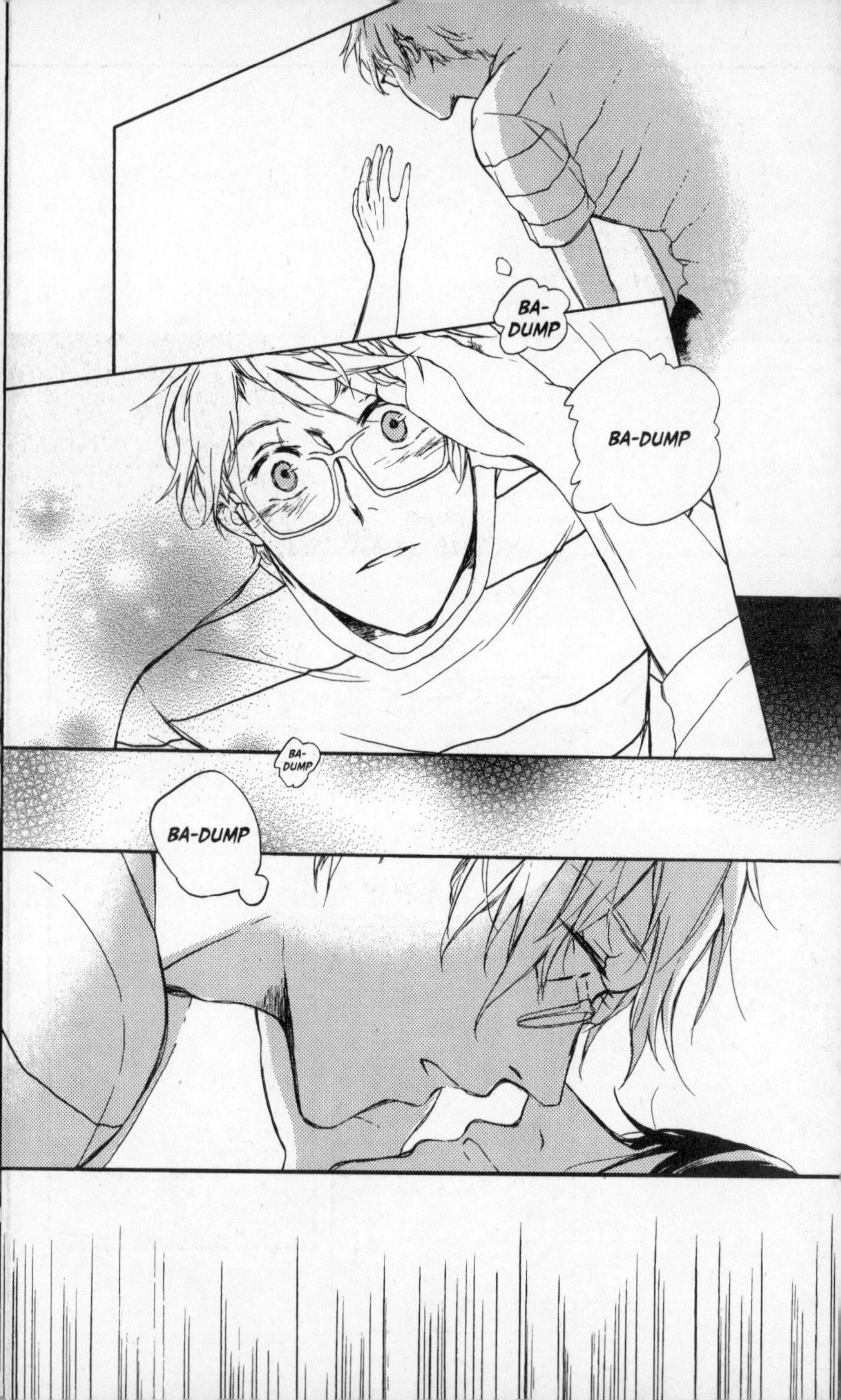
BA-
DUMP
BA-DUMP
BA-
DUMP
BA-DUMP

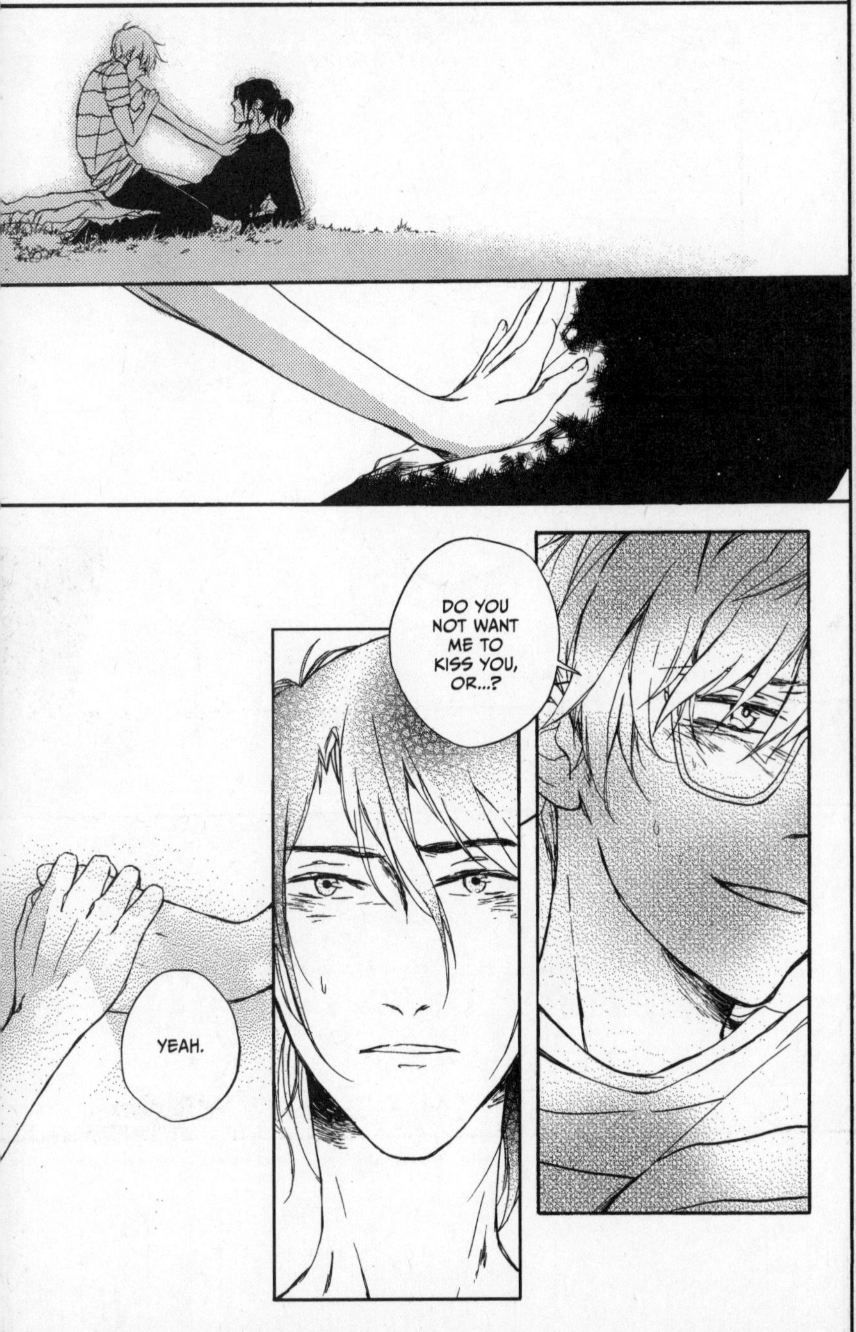
DO YOU NOT WANT ME TO KISS YOU, OR...?
YEAH.

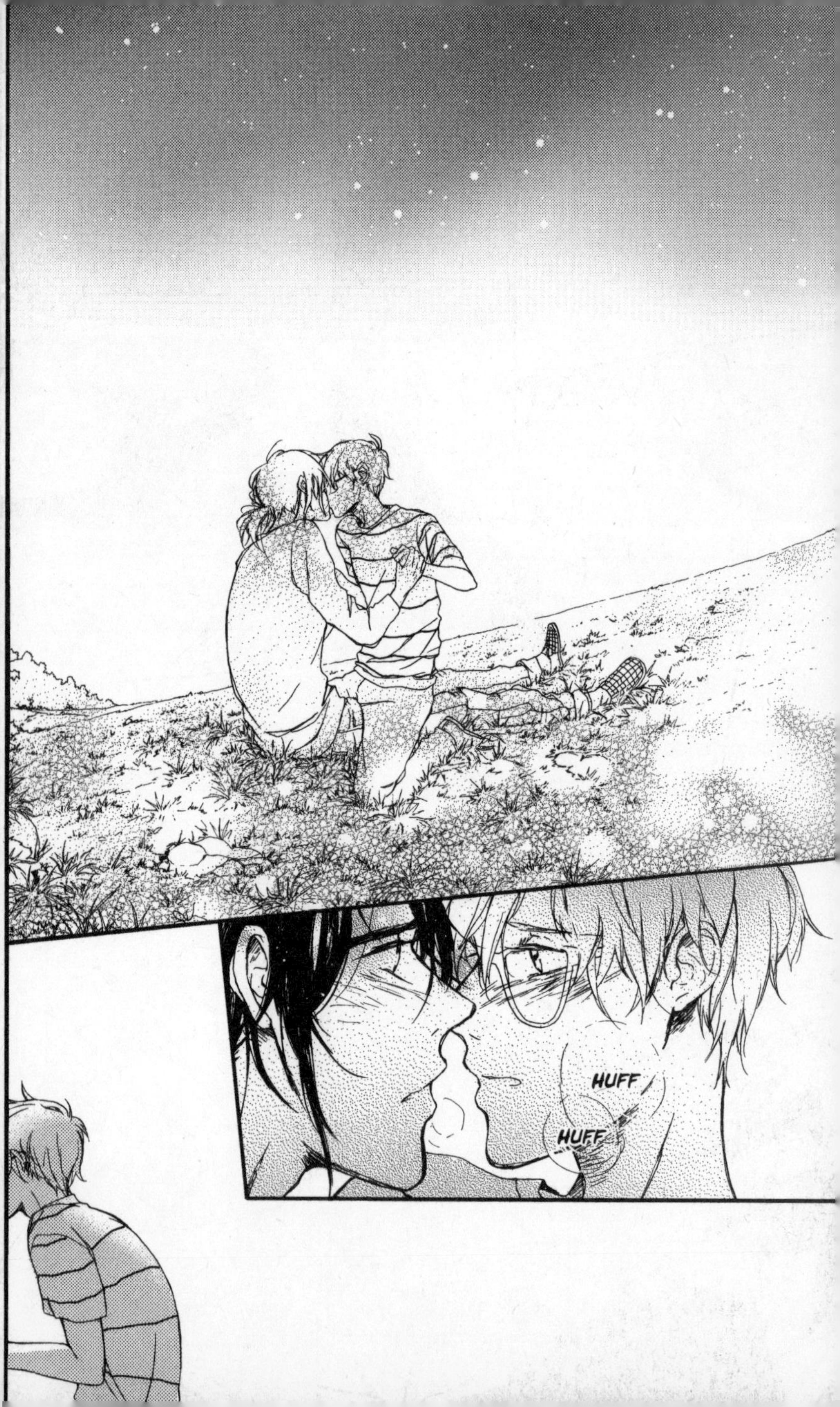
HUFF
HUFF

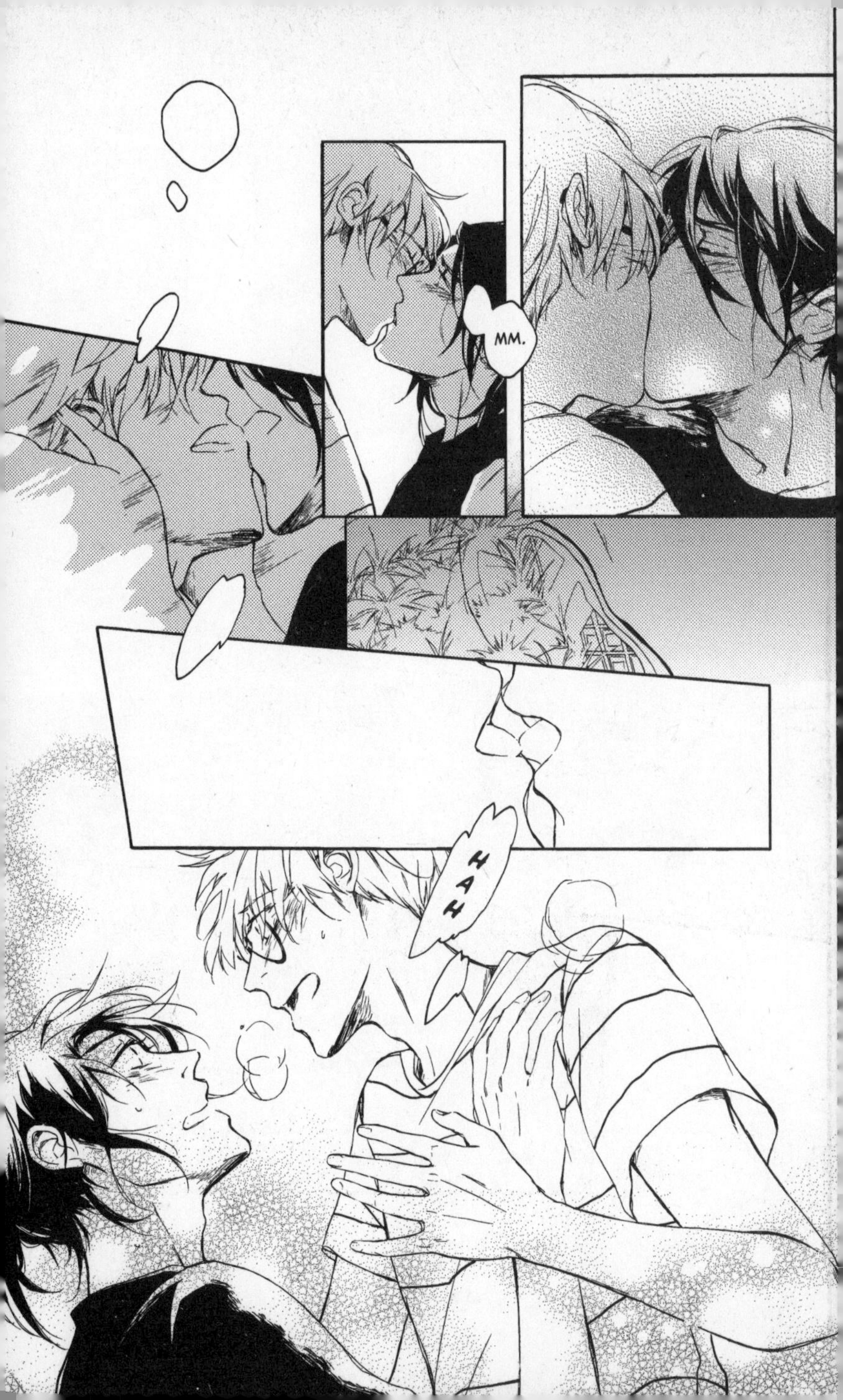
MM.
HAH

HAH

HAAH

STAR 3

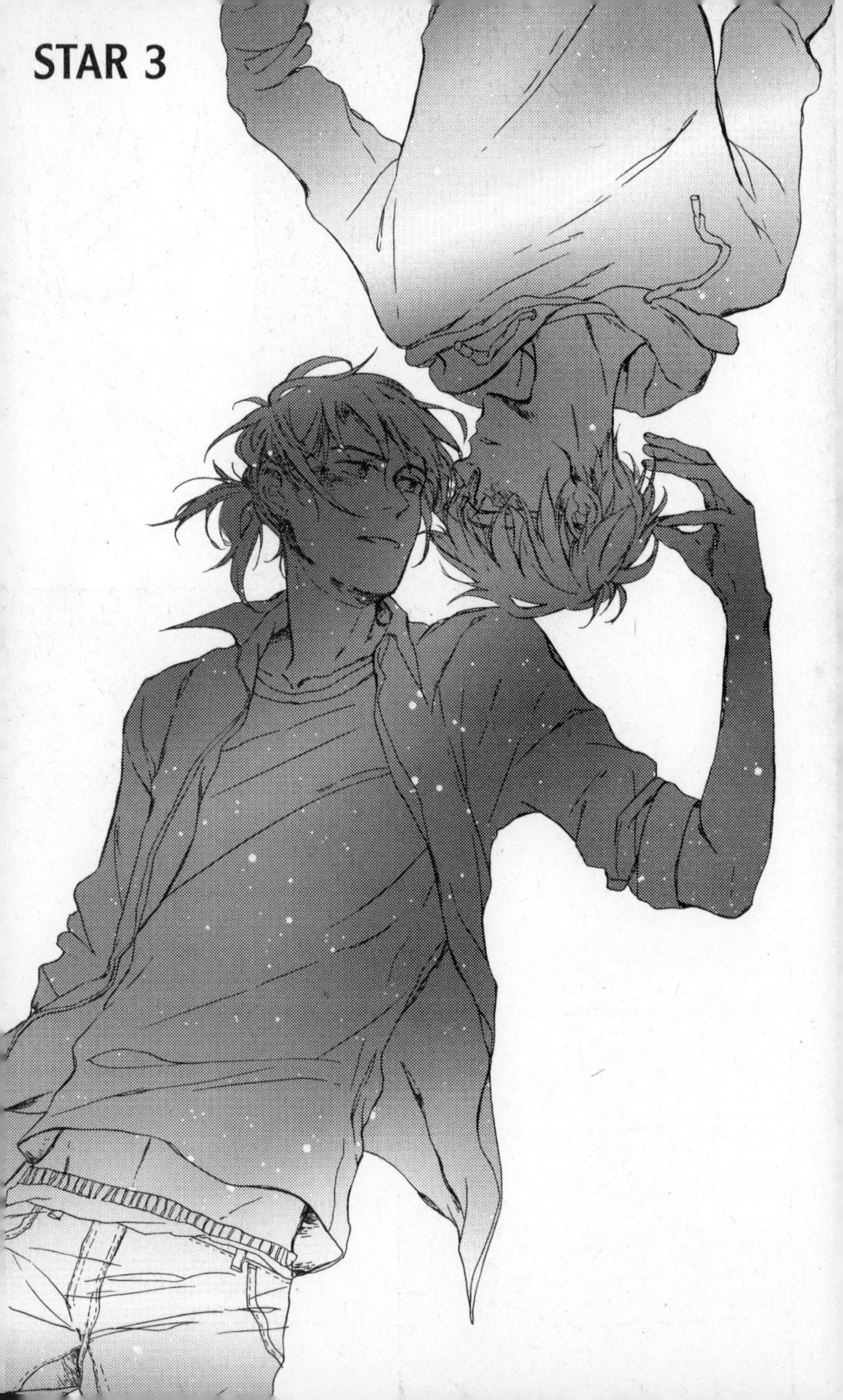

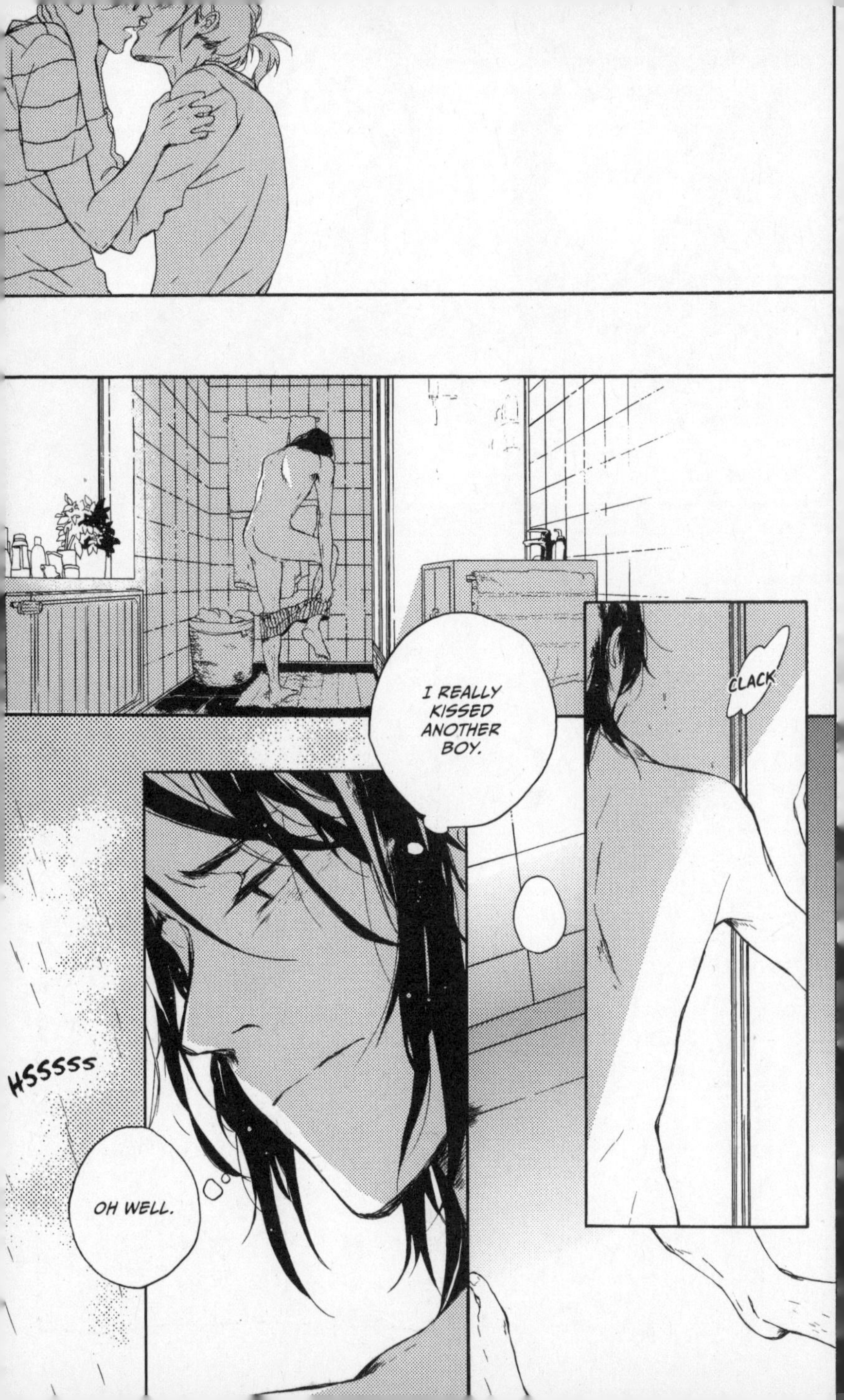
CLACK
I REALLY KISSED ANOTHER BOY.
HSSSSS
OH WELL.

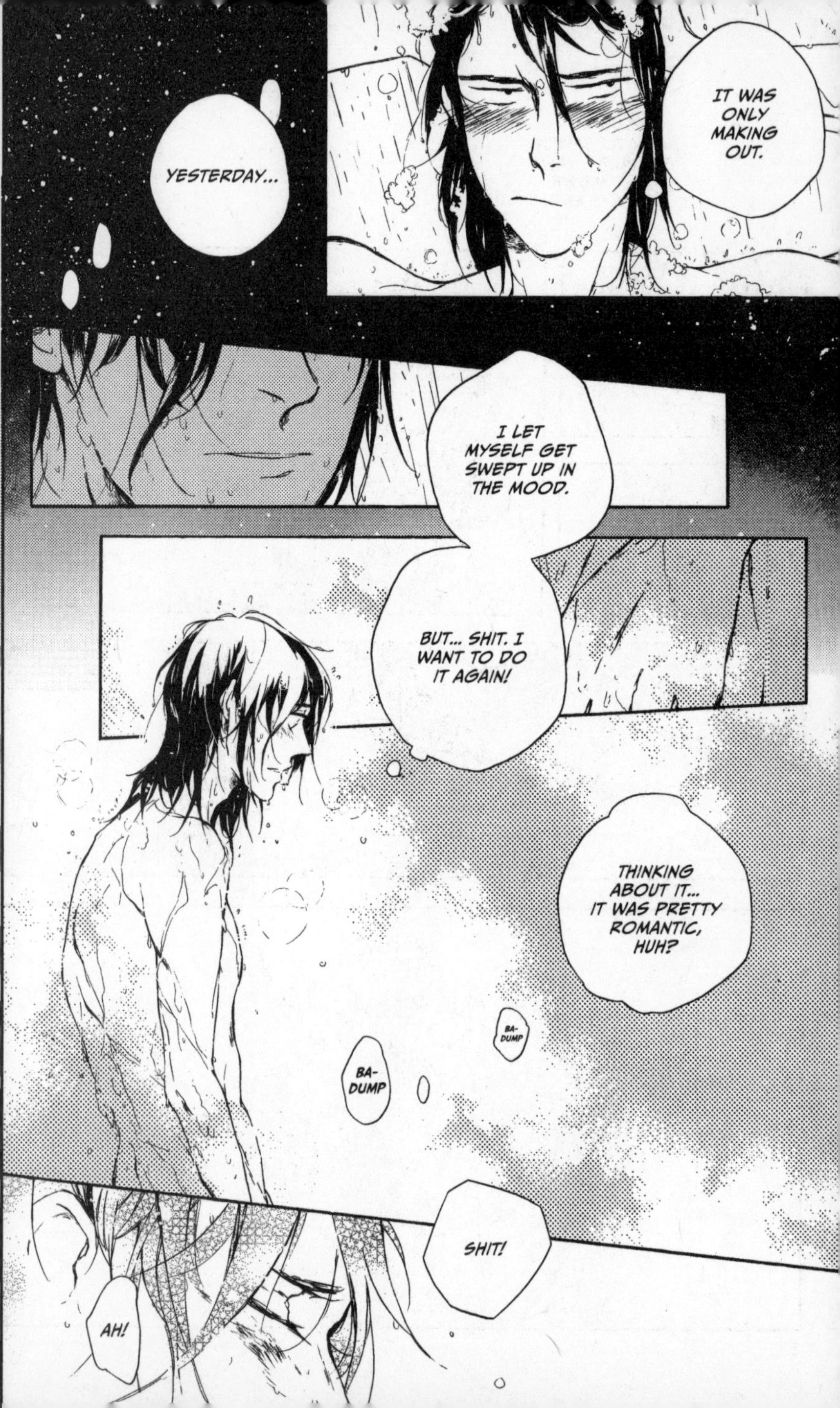
IT WAS ONLY MAKING OUT.
YESTERDAY...
I LET MYSELF GET SWEPT UP IN THE MOOD.
BUT... SHIT. I WANT TO DO IT AGAIN!
THINKING ABOUT IT... IT WAS PRETTY ROMANTIC, HUH?
BA-DUMP
BA-DUMP
SHIT!
AH!

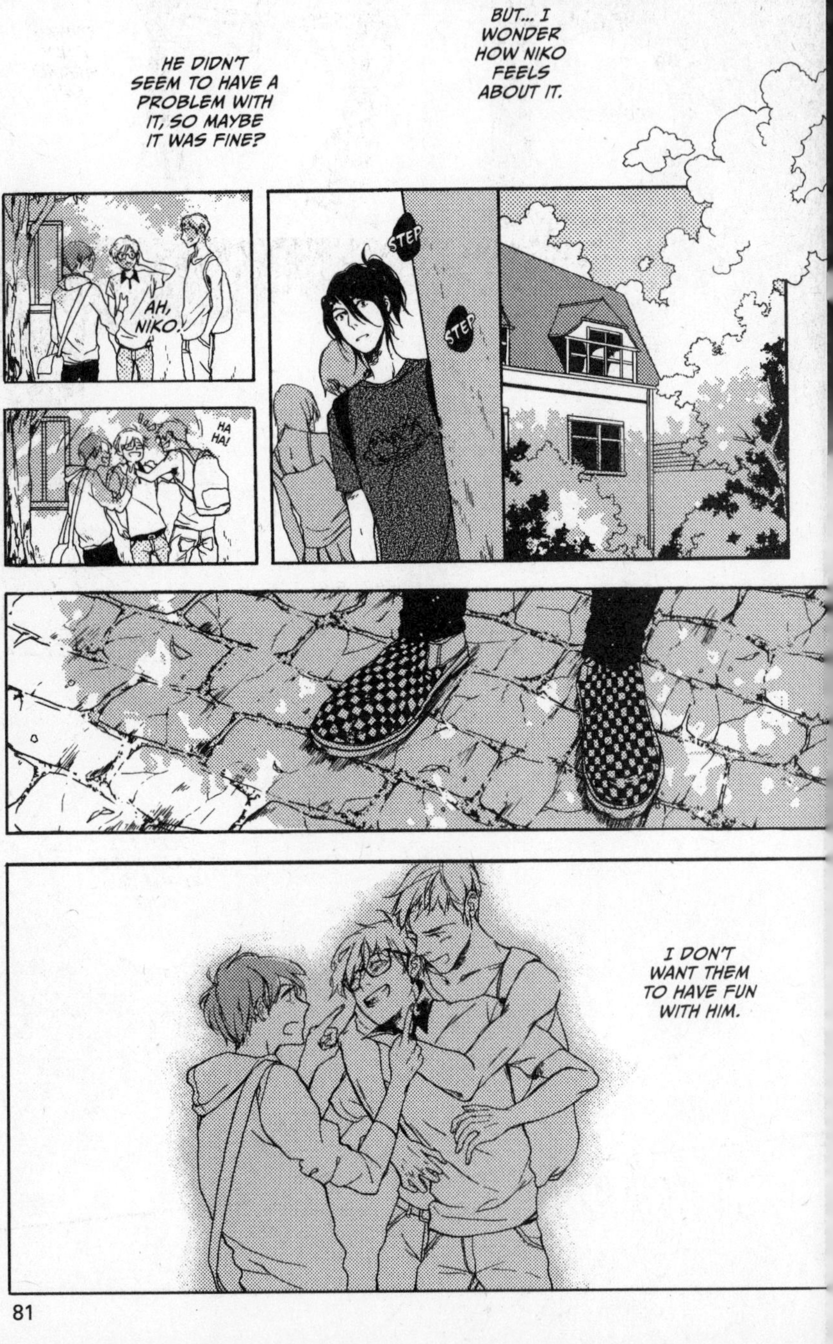
HE DIDN'T SEEM TO HAVE A PROBLEM WITH IT, SO MAYBE IT WAS FINE?
BUT... I WONDER HOW NIKO FEELS ABOUT IT.
STEP
STEP
AH, NIKO.
HA HA!
I DON'T WANT THEM TO HAVE FUN WITH HIM.

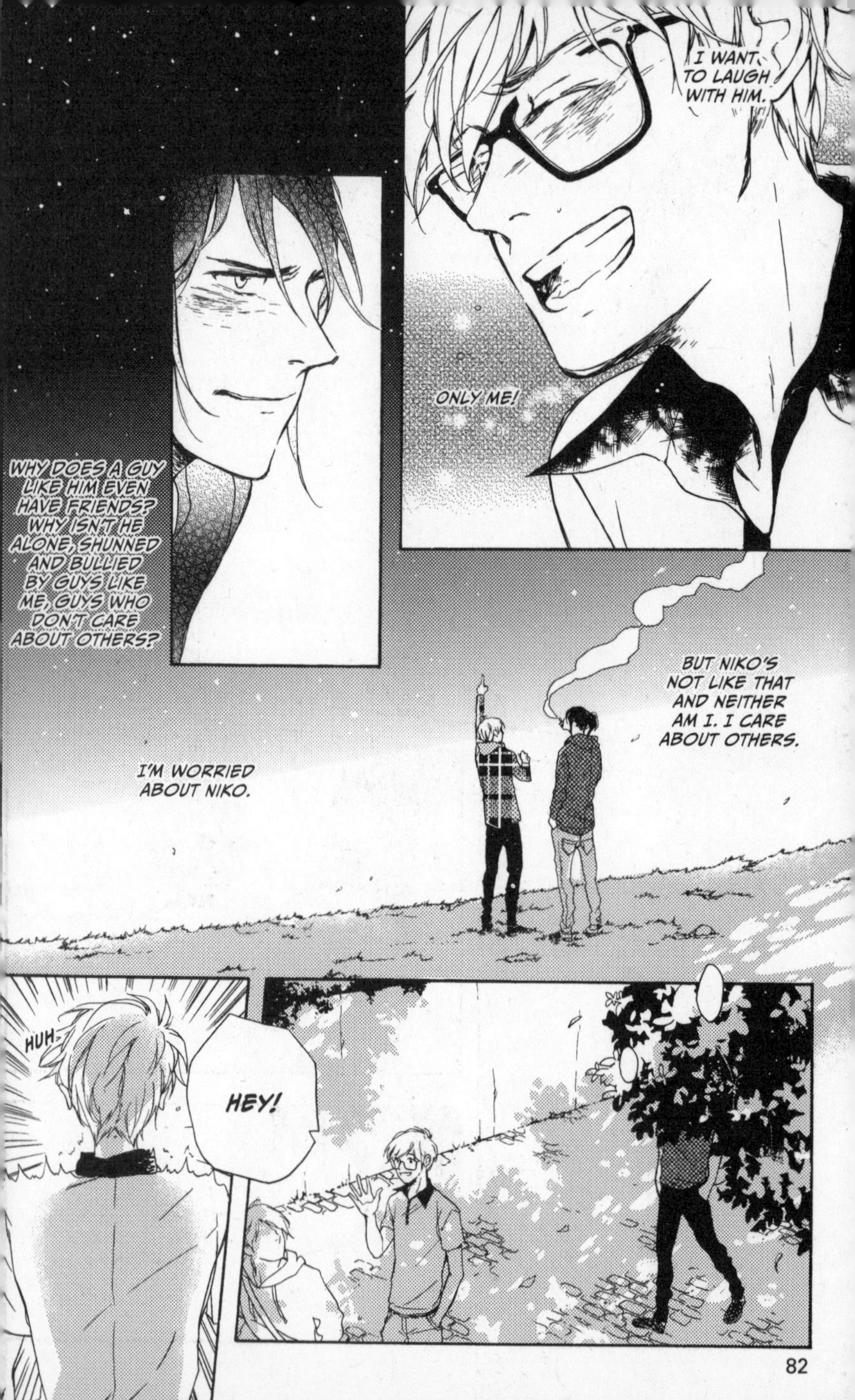
I WANT TO LAUGH WITH HIM.
ONLY ME!
WHY DOES A GUY LIKE HIM EVEN HAVE FRIENDS? WHY ISN'T HE ALONE, SHUNNED AND BULLIED BY GUYS LIKE ME, GUYS WHO DON'T CARE ABOUT OTHERS?
BUT NIKO'S NOT LIKE THAT AND NEITHER AM I. I CARE ABOUT OTHERS.
I'M WORRIED ABOUT NIKO.
HEY!
HUH

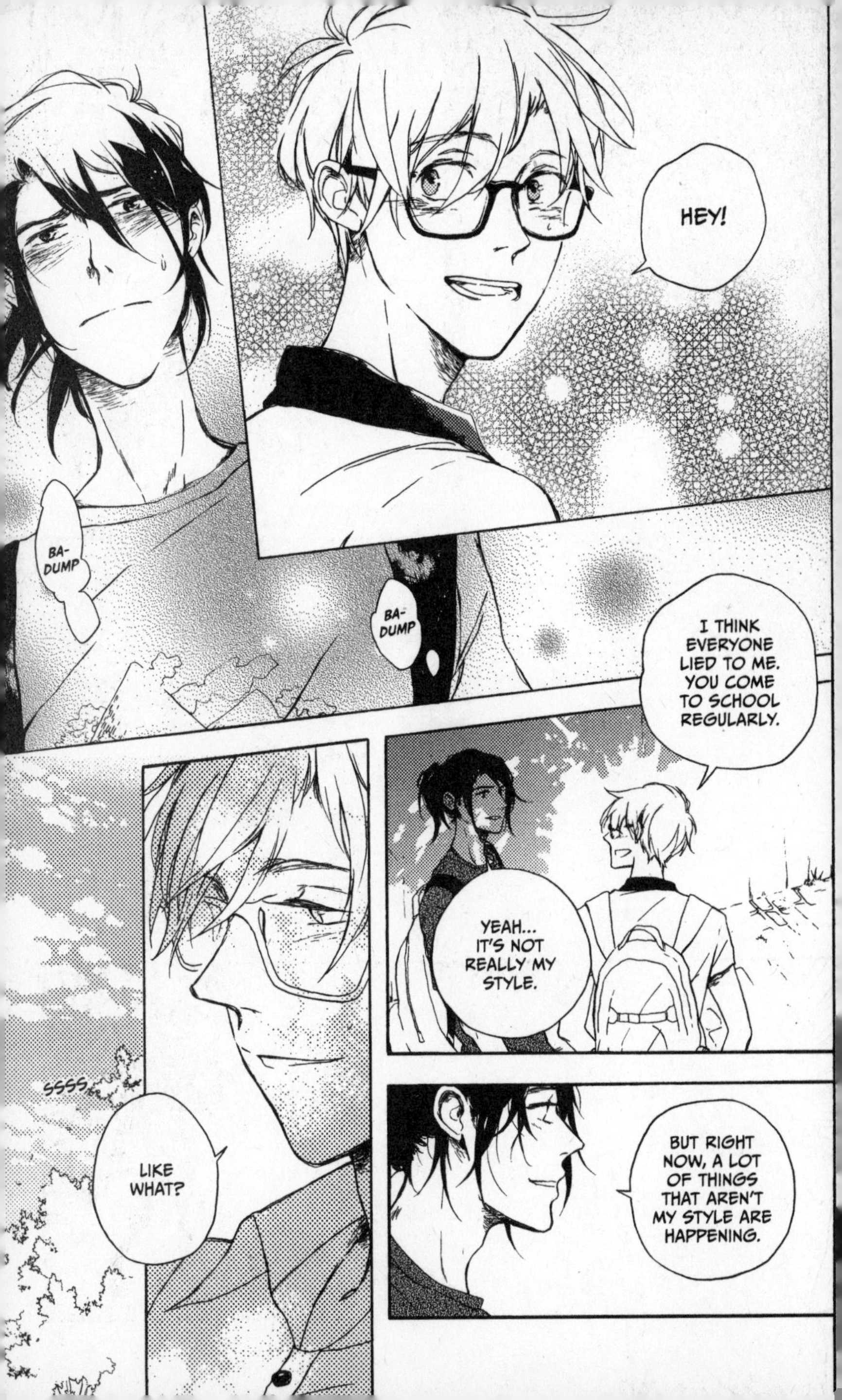
HEY!
BA-DUMP
BA-DUMP
I THINK EVERYONE LIED TO ME. YOU COME TO SCHOOL REGULARLY.
YEAH... IT'S NOT REALLY MY STYLE.
BUT RIGHT NOW, A LOT OF THINGS THAT AREN'T MY STYLE ARE HAPPENING.
SSSS
LIKE WHAT?

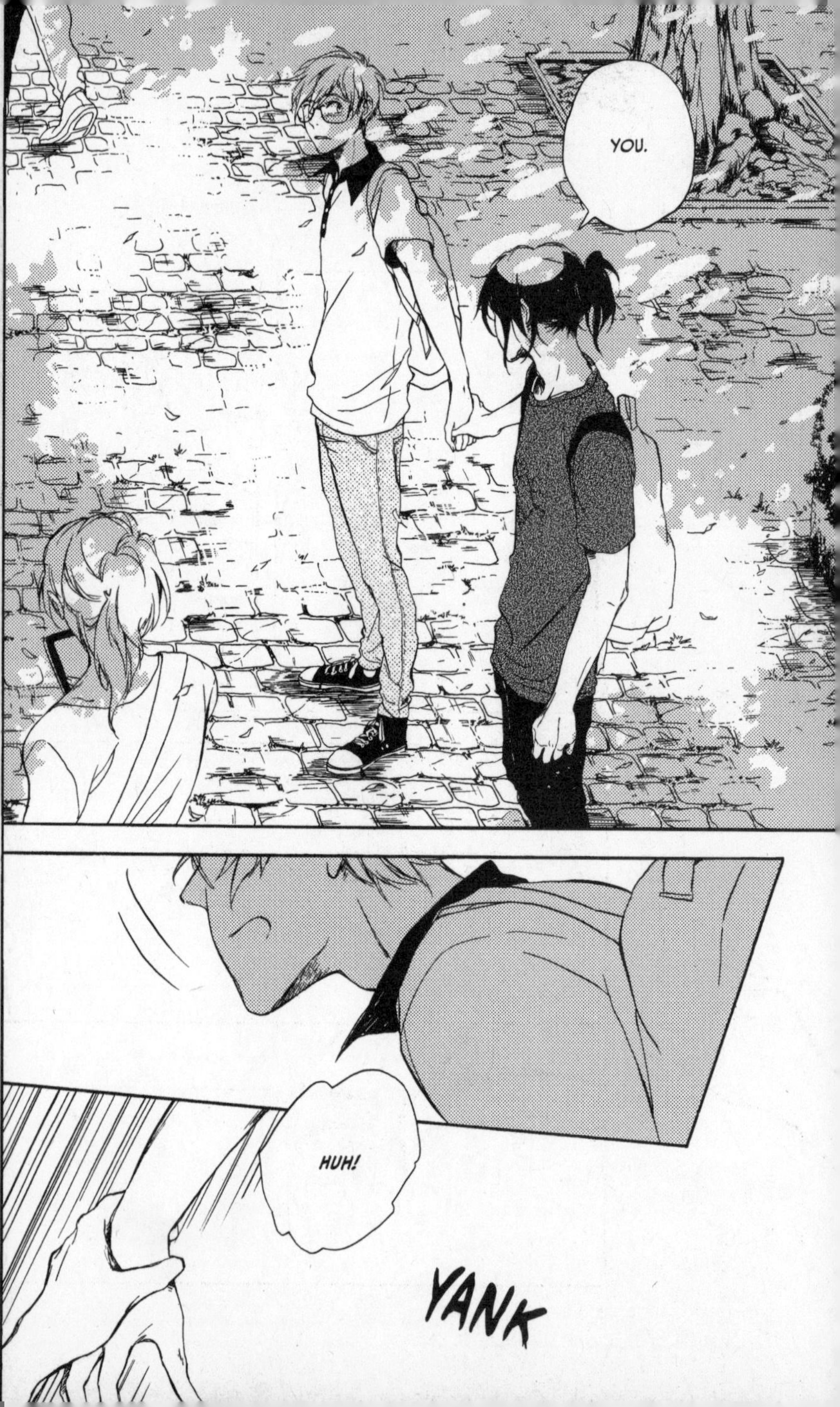
YOU.
HUH!
YANK

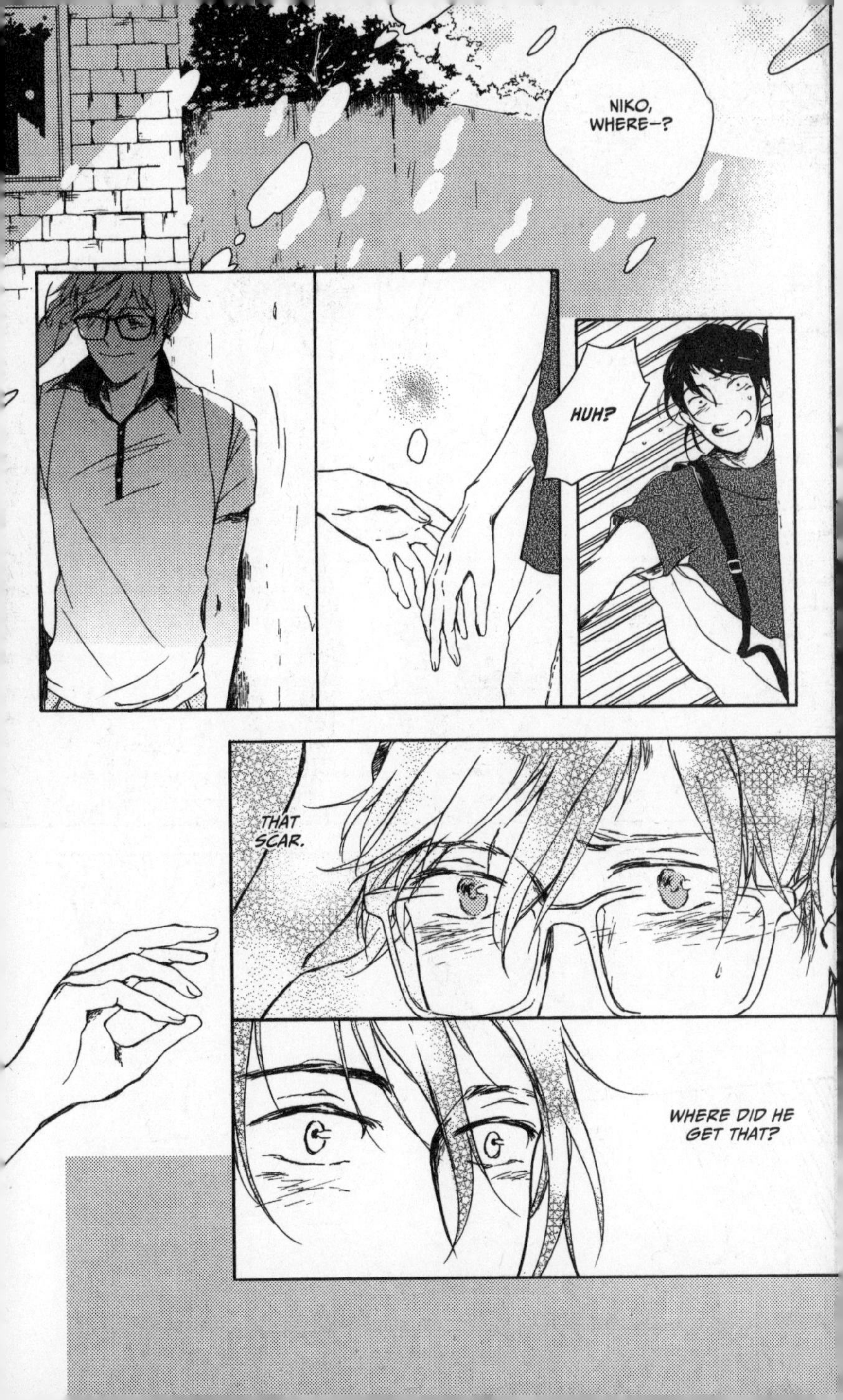
NIKO, WHERE–?
HUH?
THAT SCAR.
WHERE DID HE GET THAT?

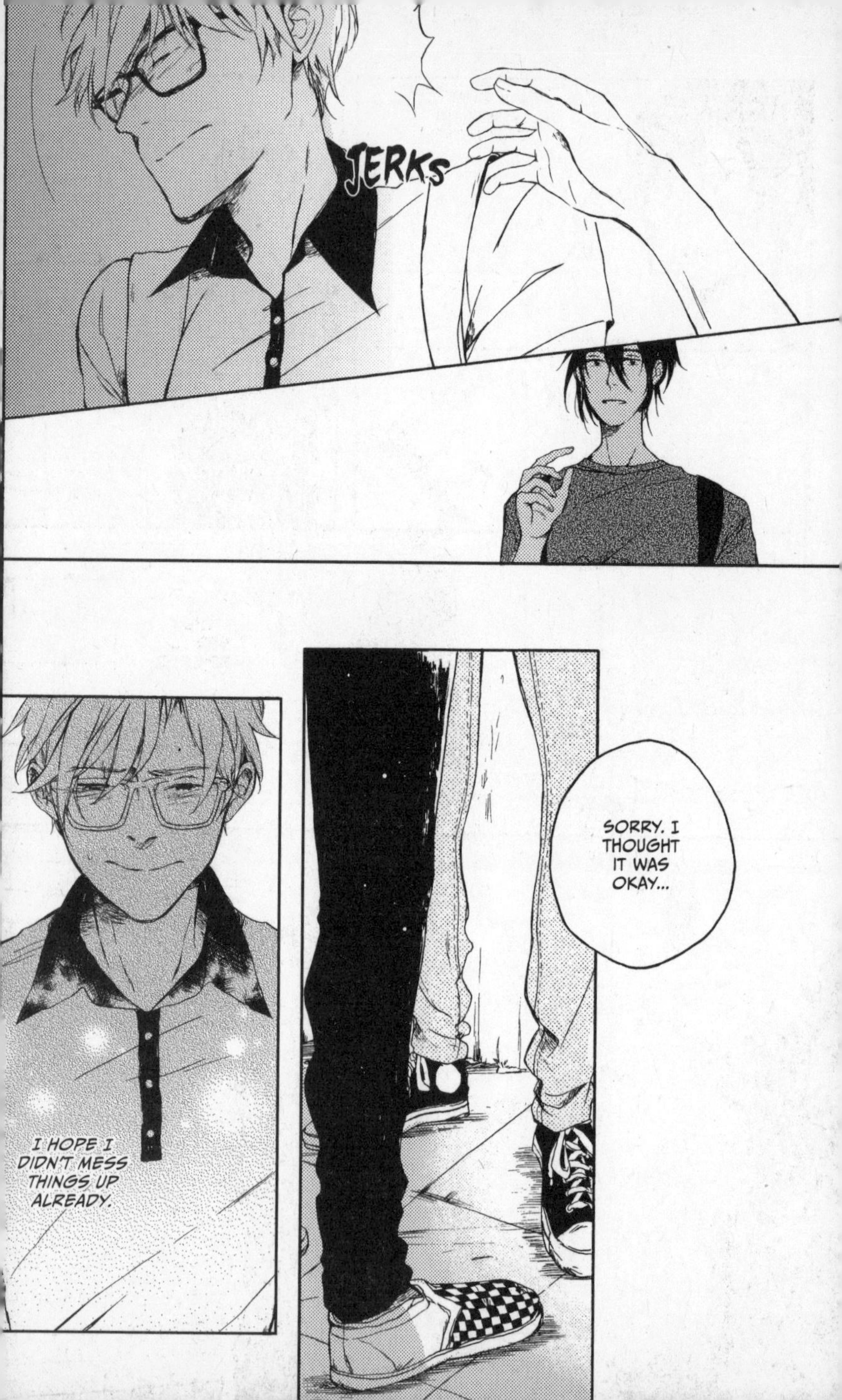
JERKS
SORRY. I THOUGHT IT WAS OKAY...
I HOPE I DIDN'T MESS THINGS UP ALREADY.

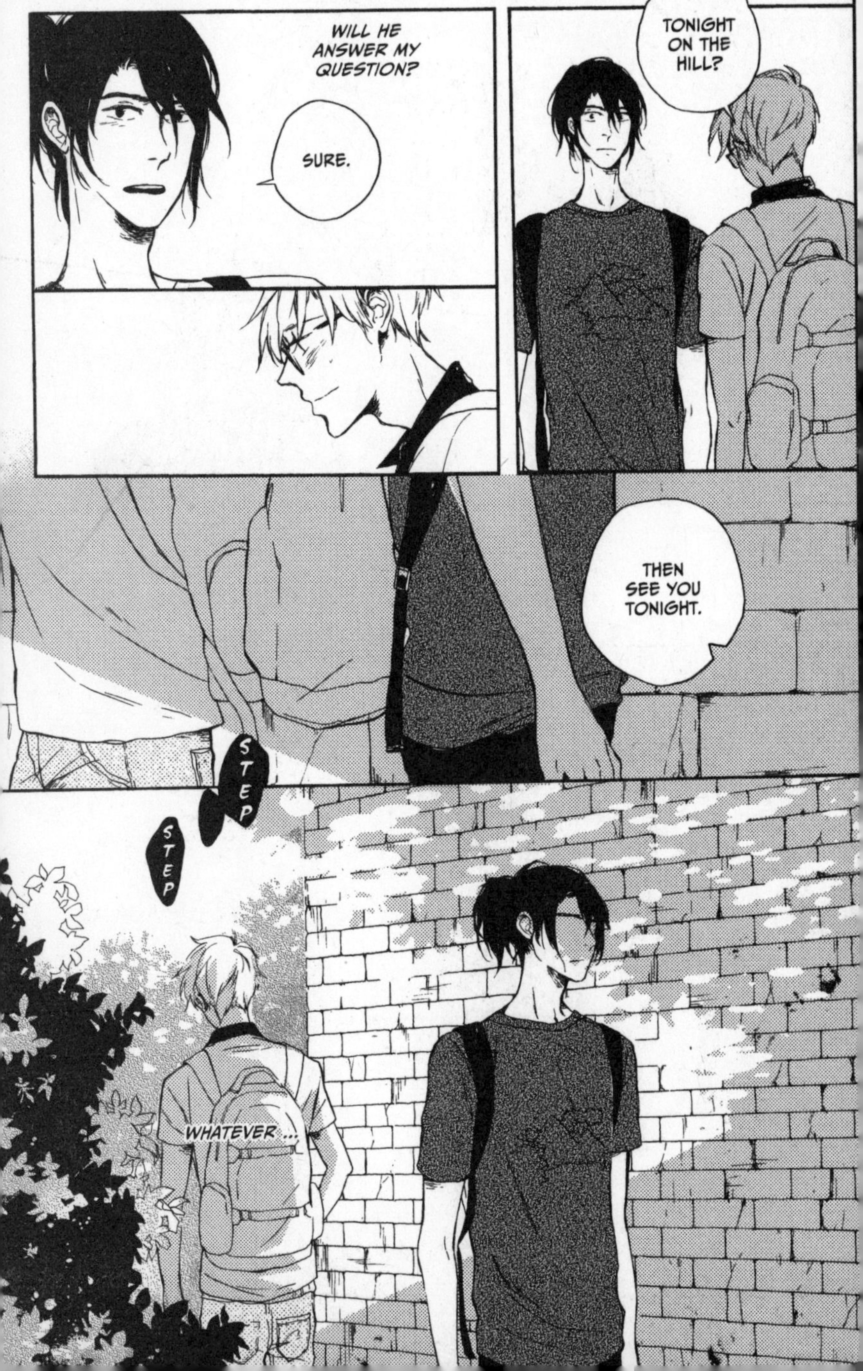
TONIGHT ON THE HILL?
WILL HE ANSWER MY QUESTION?
SURE.
THEN SEE YOU TONIGHT.
STEP
STEP
WHATEVER ...

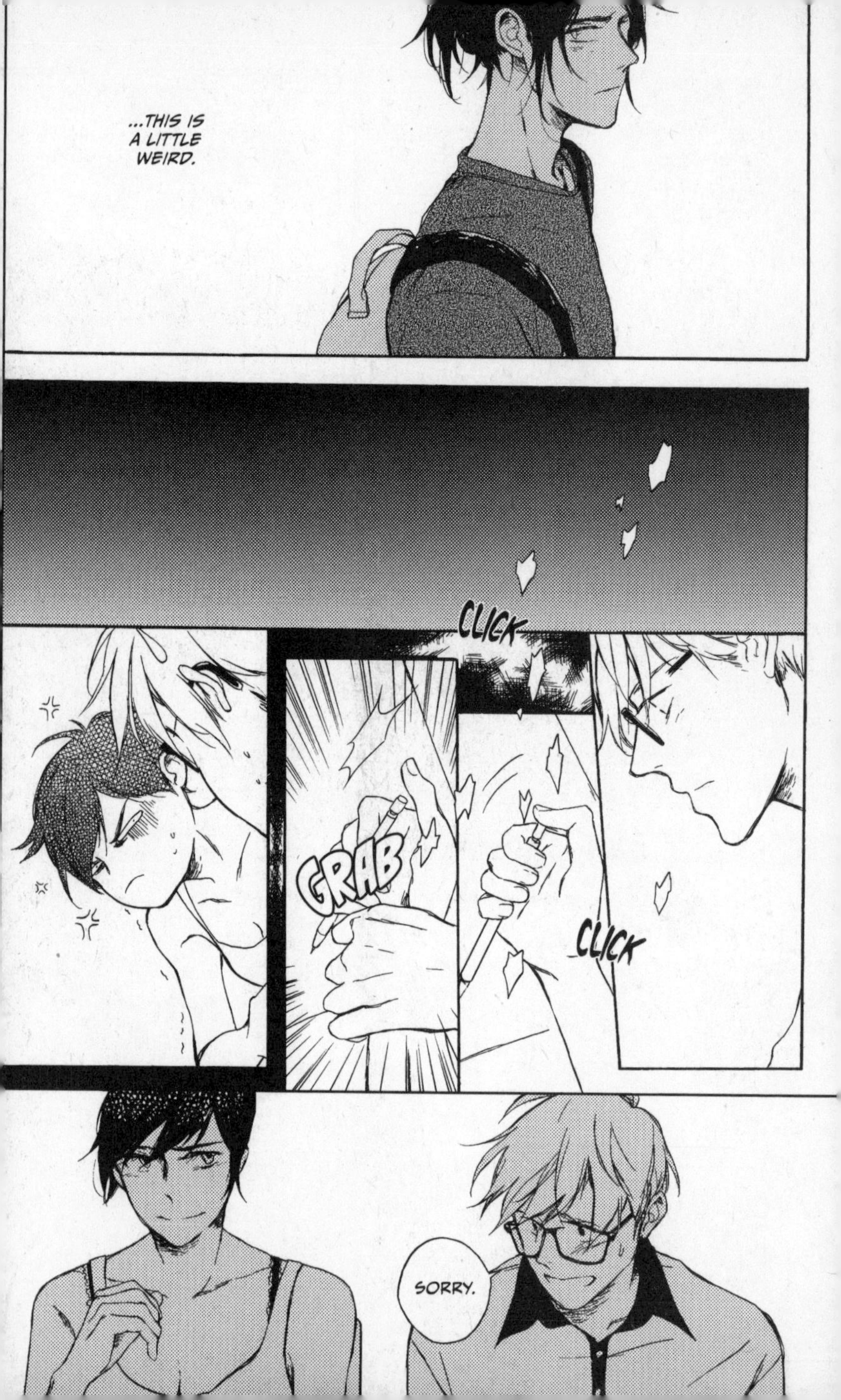
...THIS IS A LITTLE WEIRD.
CLICK
CLICK
GRAB
SORRY.

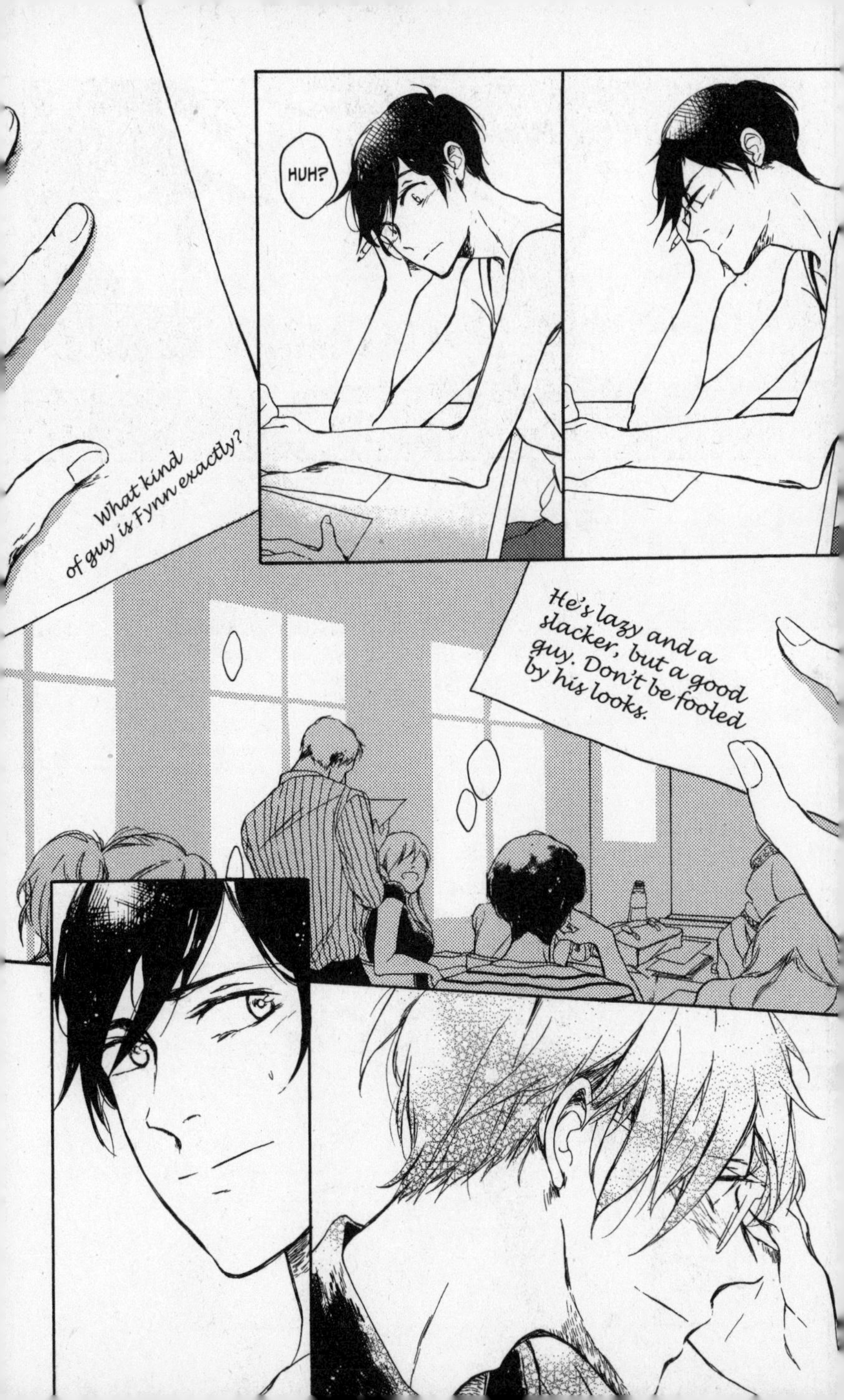
HUH?
What kind of guy is Fynn exactly?
He's lazy and a slacker, but a good guy. Don't be fooled by his looks.

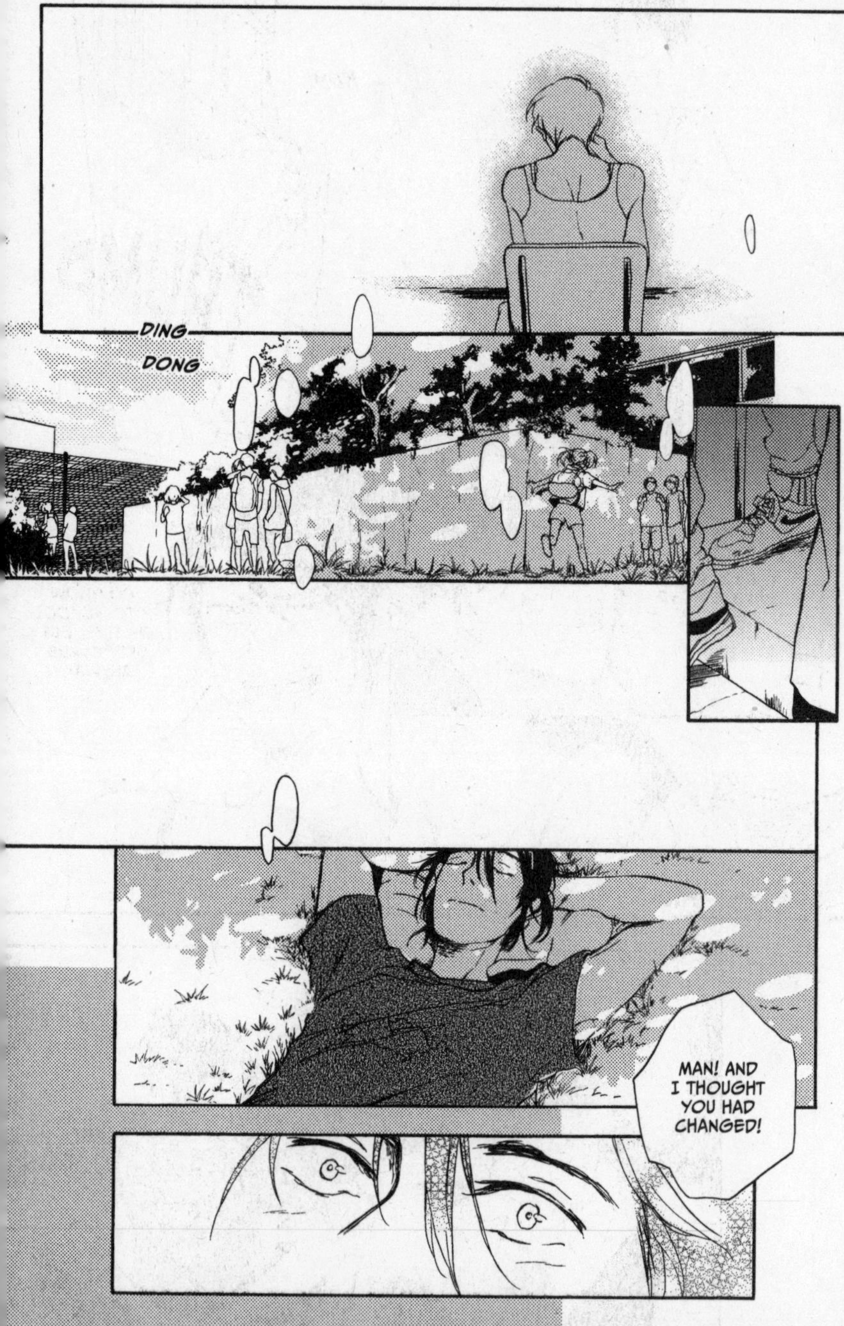
DING DONG
MAN! AND I THOUGHT YOU HAD CHANGED!

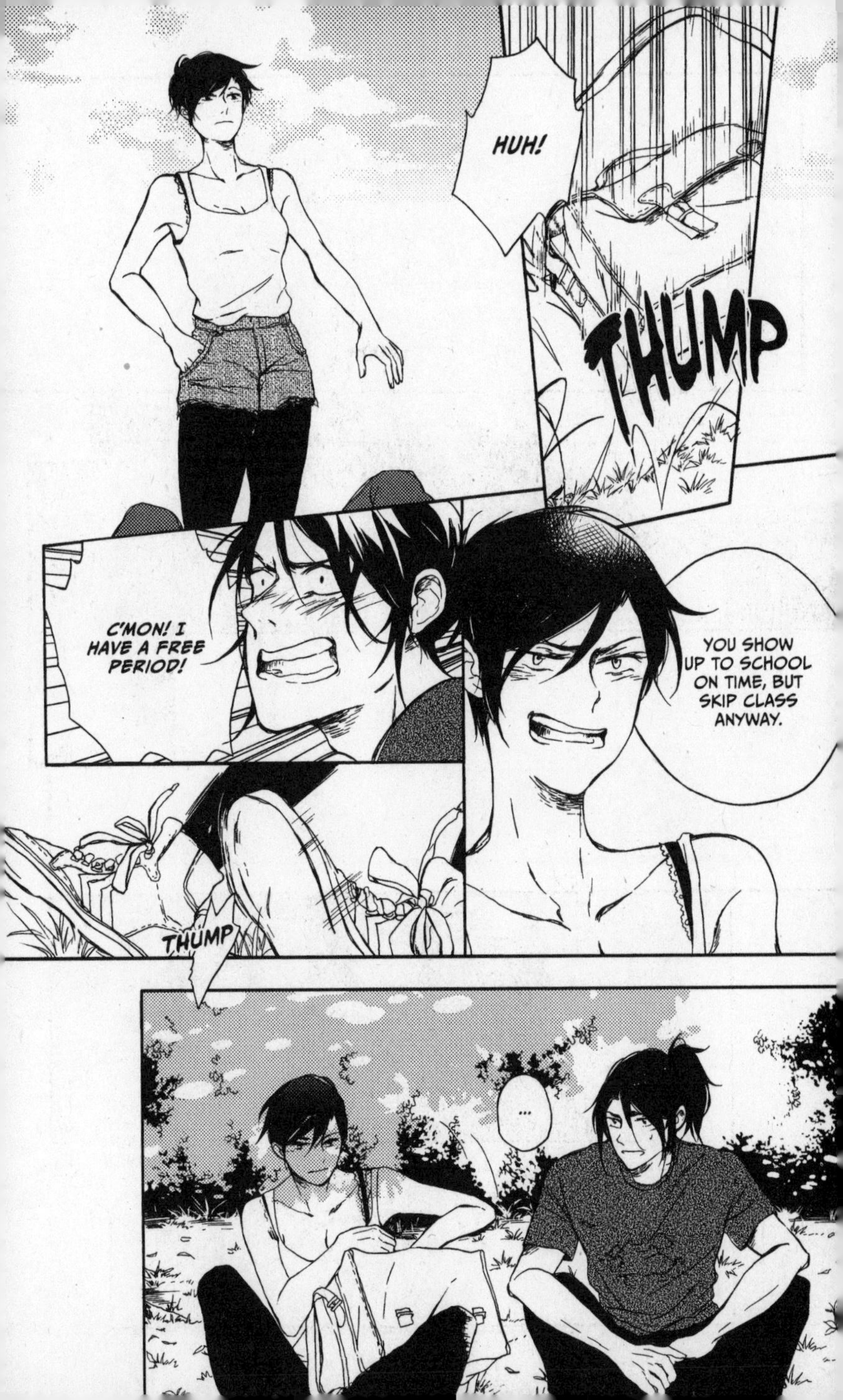
HUH!
THUMP
YOU SHOW UP TO SCHOOL ON TIME, BUT SKIP CLASS ANYWAY.
C'MON! I HAVE A FREE PERIOD!
THUMP
...

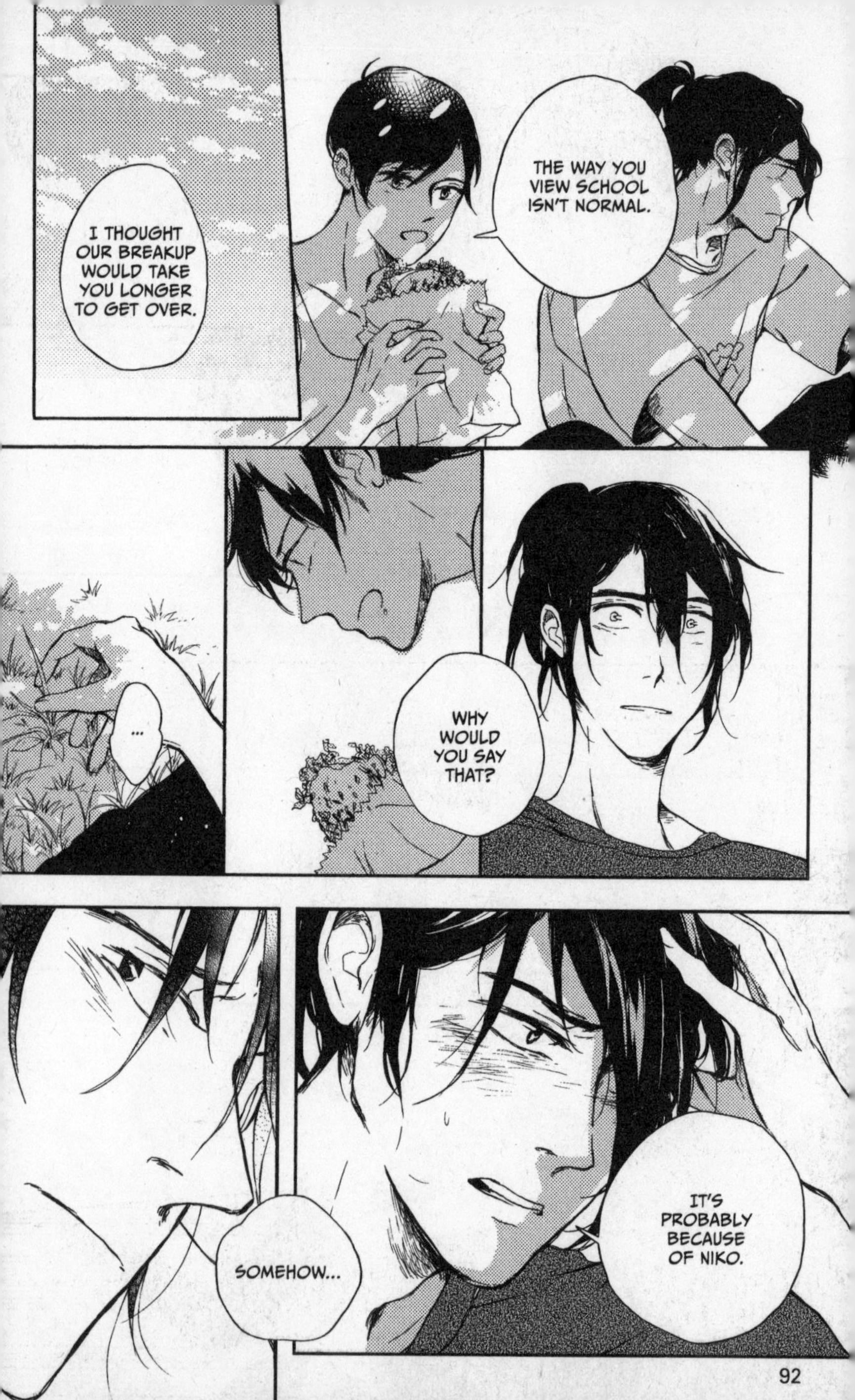
THE WAY YOU VIEW SCHOOL ISN'T NORMAL.
I THOUGHT OUR BREAKUP WOULD TAKE YOU LONGER TO GET OVER.
WHY WOULD YOU SAY THAT?
...
IT'S PROBABLY BECAUSE OF NIKO.
SOMEHOW...

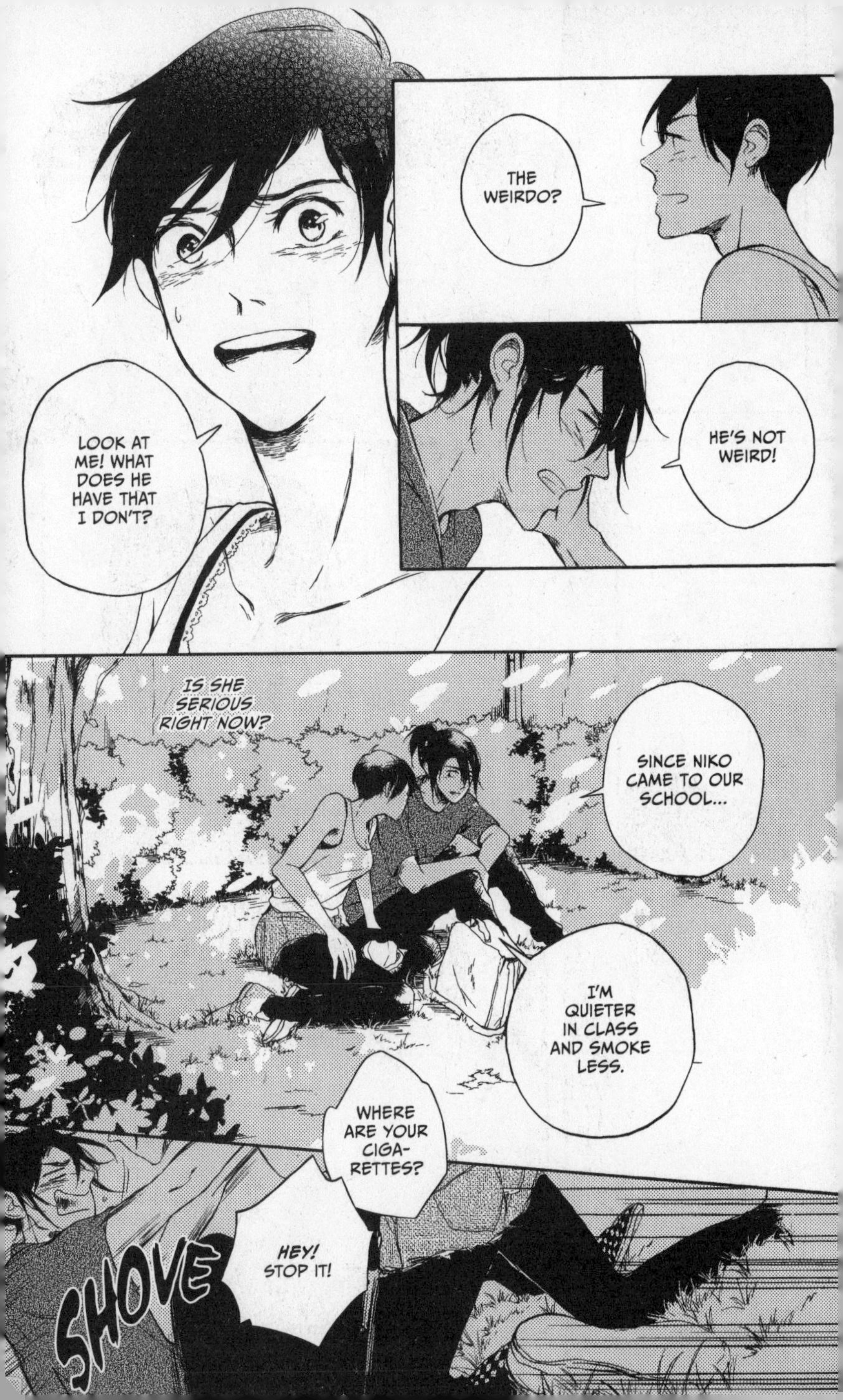
THE WEIRDO?
HE'S NOT WEIRD!
LOOK AT ME! WHAT DOES HE HAVE THAT I DON'T?
SINCE NIKO CAME TO OUR SCHOOL...
I'M QUIETER IN CLASS AND SMOKE LESS.
IS SHE SERIOUS RIGHT NOW?
WHERE ARE YOUR CIGA-RETTES?
HEY! STOP IT!
SHOVE

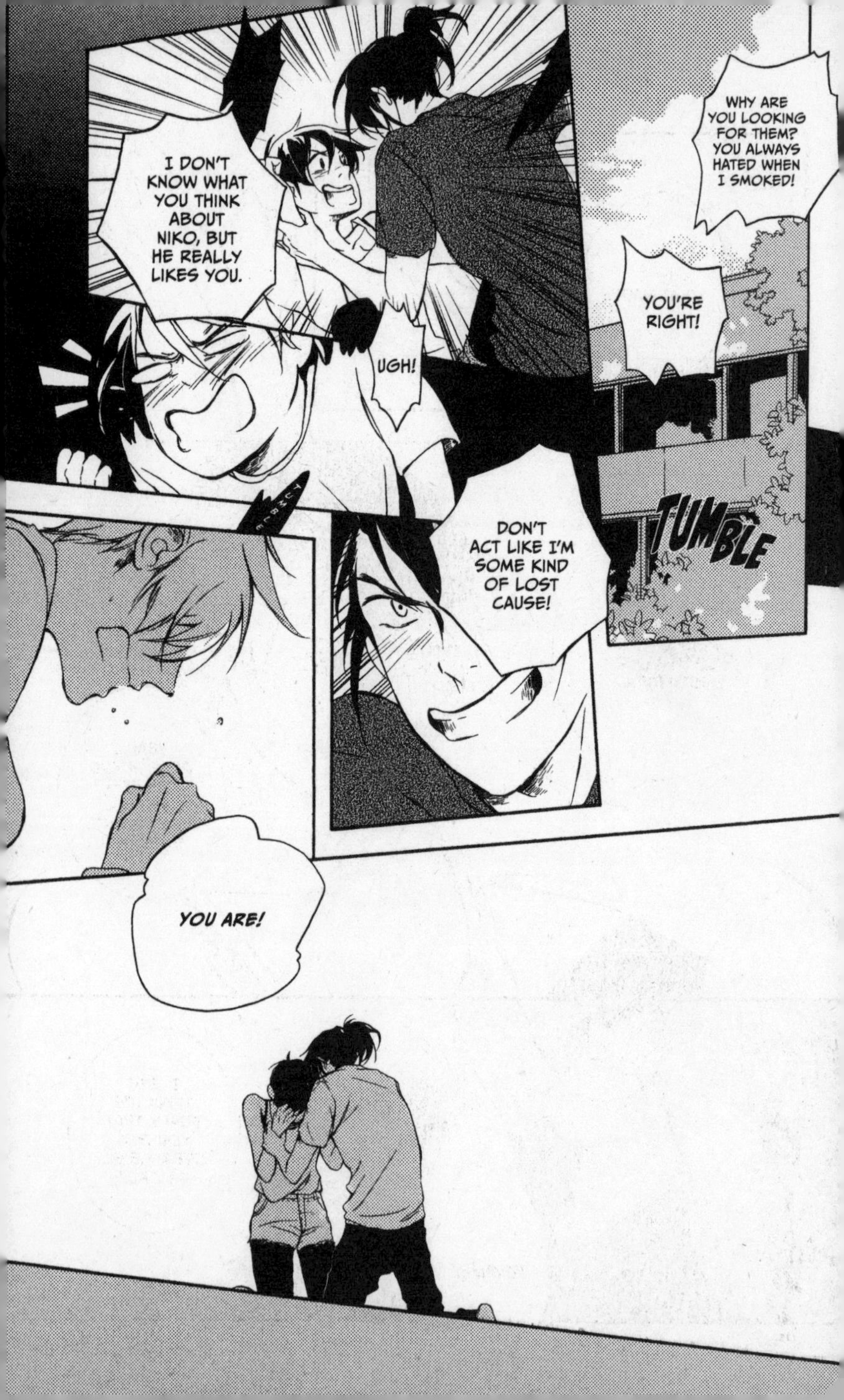
WHY ARE YOU LOOKING FOR THEM? YOU ALWAYS HATED WHEN I SMOKED!
YOU'RE RIGHT!
TUMBLE
I DON'T KNOW WHAT YOU THINK ABOUT NIKO, BUT HE REALLY LIKES YOU.
UGH!
TUMBLE
DON'T ACT LIKE I'M SOME KIND OF LOST CAUSE!
YOU ARE!

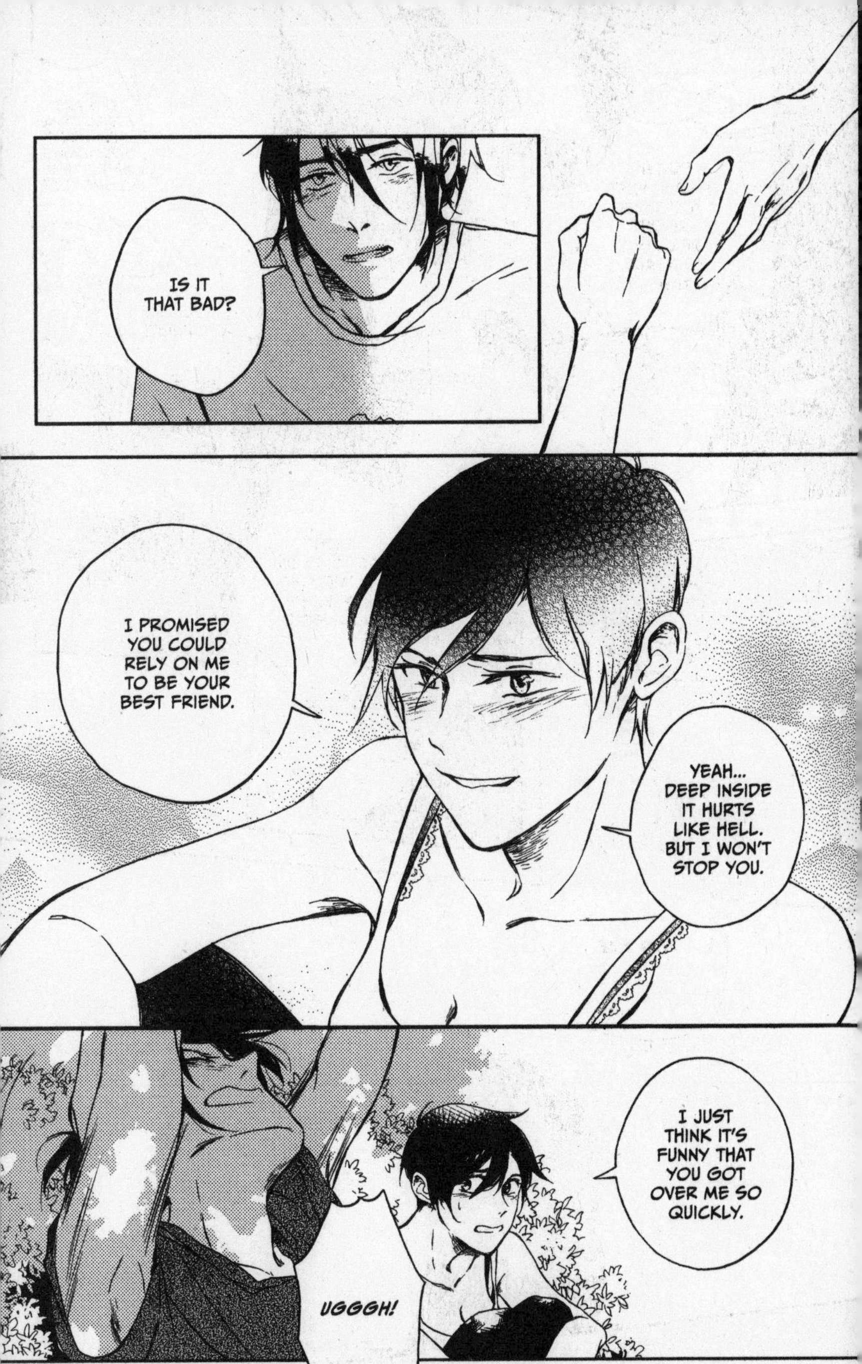
IS IT THAT BAD?
YEAH... DEEP INSIDE IT HURTS LIKE HELL. BUT I WON'T STOP YOU.
I PROMISED YOU COULD RELY ON ME TO BE YOUR BEST FRIEND.
I JUST THINK IT'S FUNNY THAT YOU GOT OVER ME SO QUICKLY.
UGGGH!

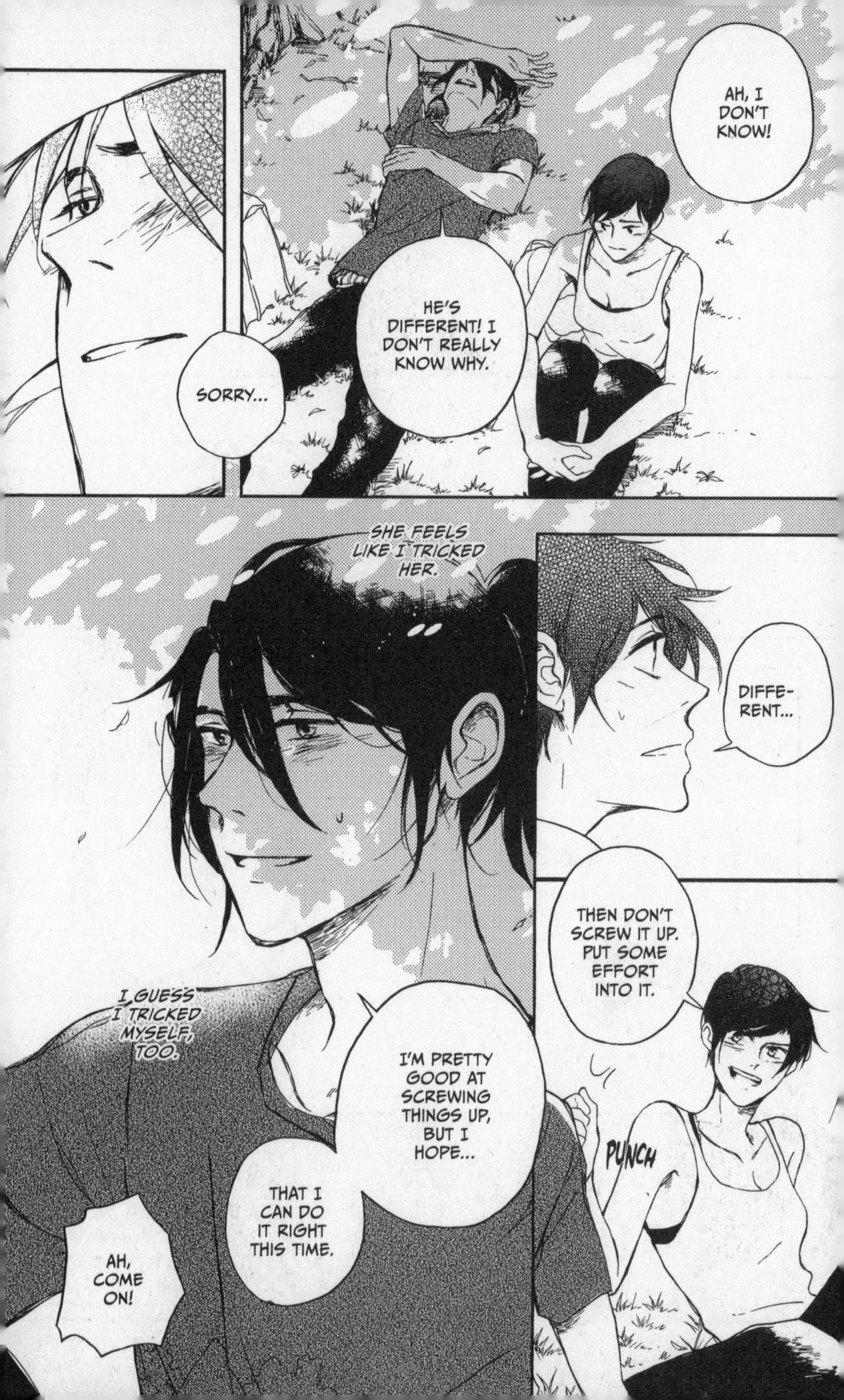
AH, I DON'T KNOW!
HE'S DIFFERENT! I DON'T REALLY KNOW WHY.
SORRY...
DIFFE-RENT...
THEN DON'T SCREW IT UP. PUT SOME EFFORT INTO IT.
PUNCH
SHE FEELS LIKE I TRICKED HER.
I'M PRETTY GOOD AT SCREWING THINGS UP, BUT I HOPE...
THAT I CAN DO IT RIGHT THIS TIME.
I GUESS I TRICKED MYSELF, TOO.
AH, COME ON!

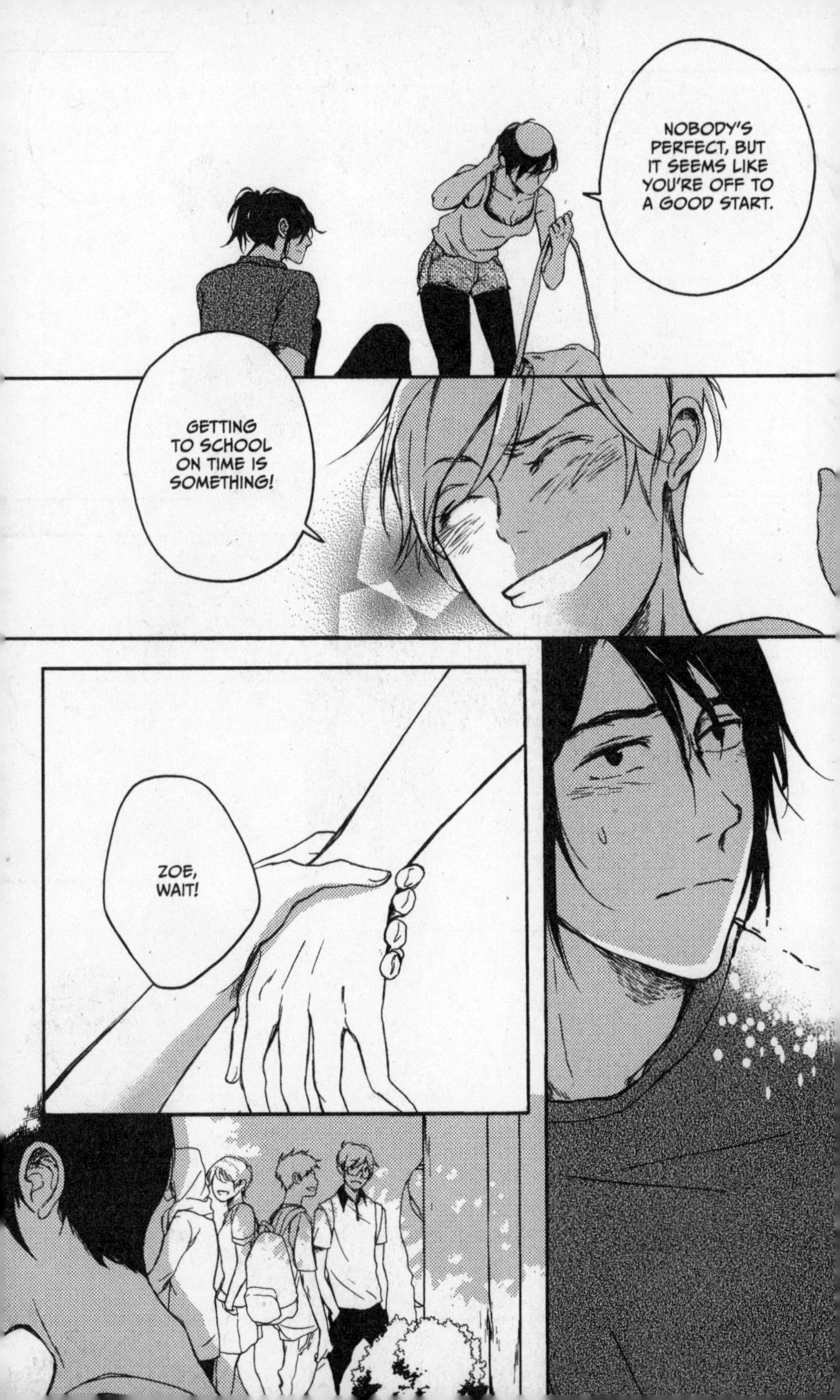
NOBODY'S PERFECT, BUT IT SEEMS LIKE YOU'RE OFF TO A GOOD START.
GETTING TO SCHOOL ON TIME IS SOMETHING!
ZOE, WAIT!

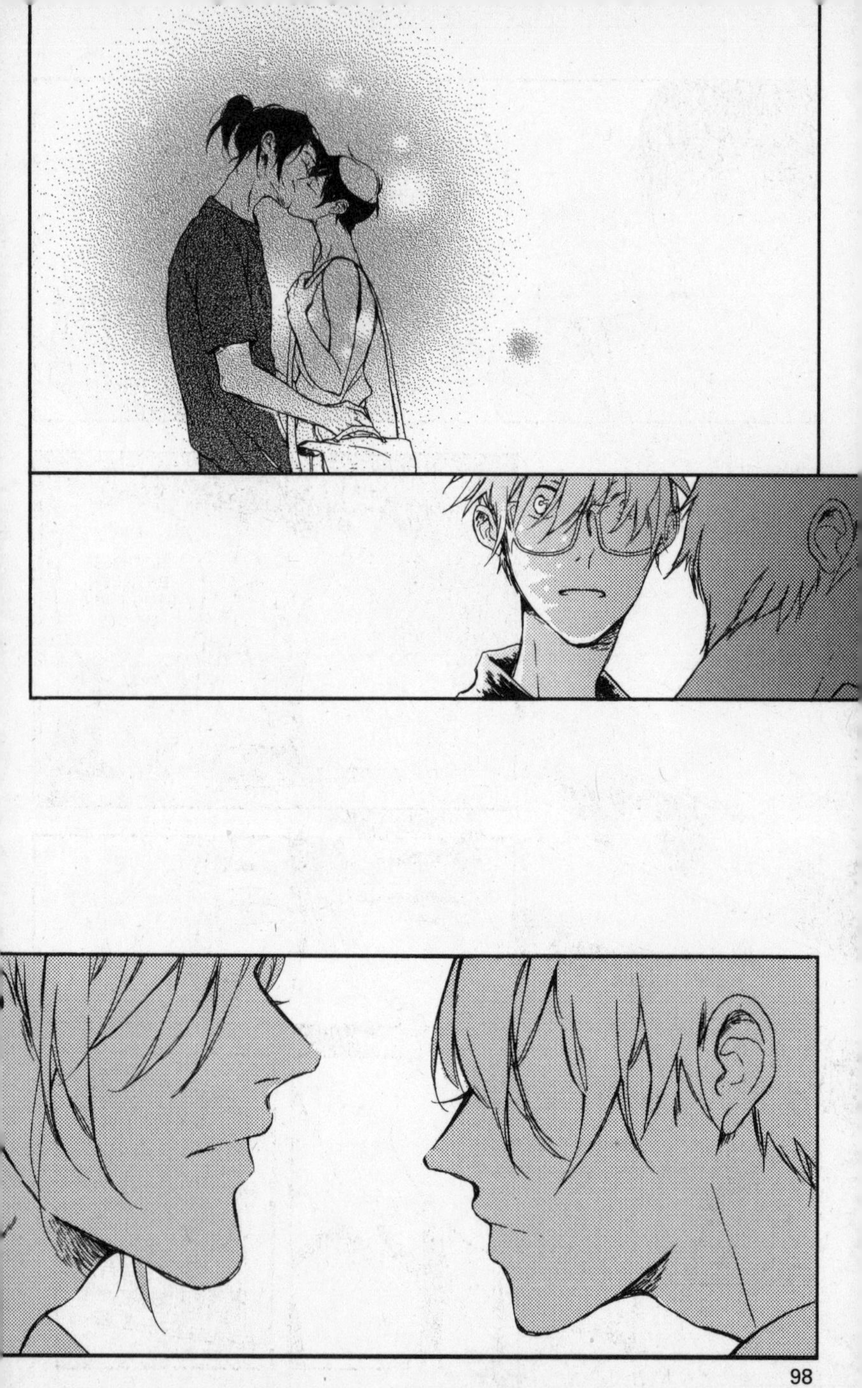

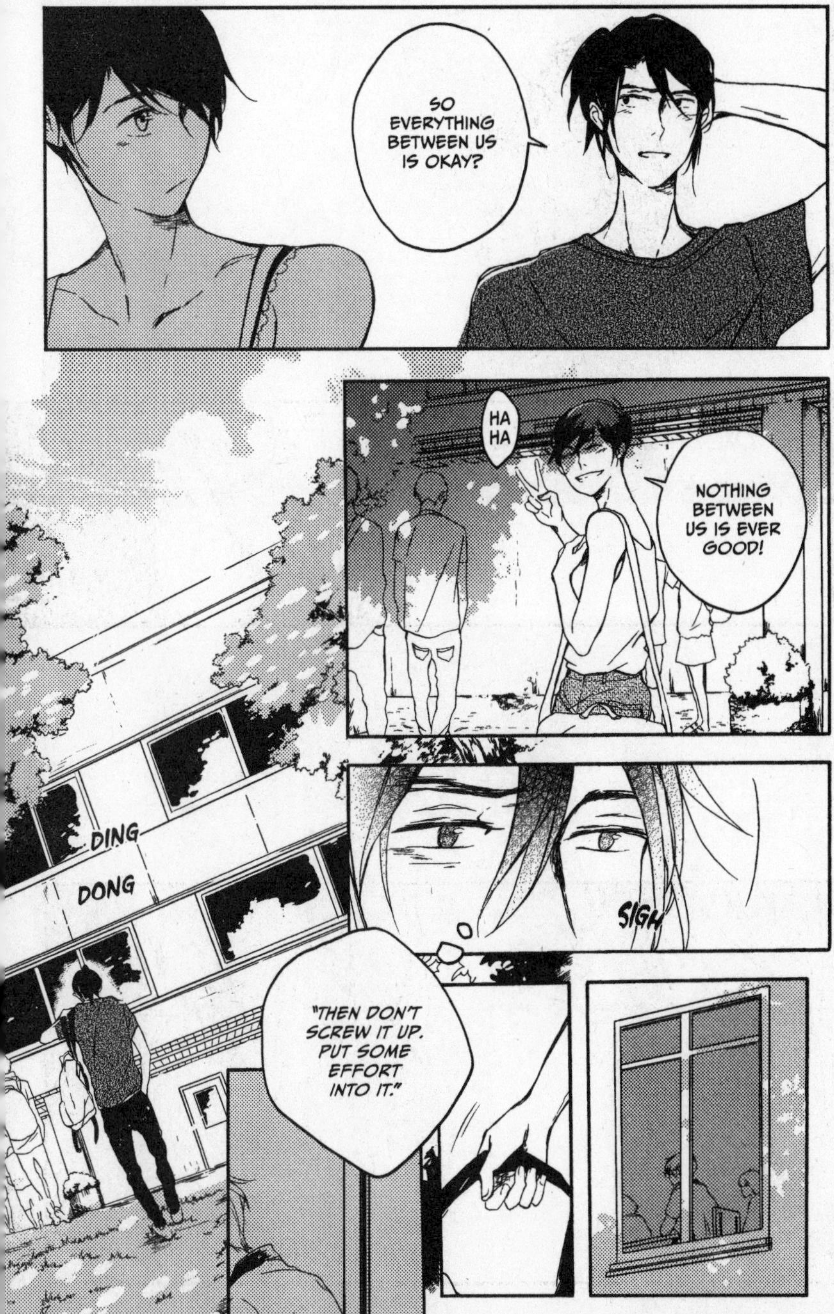
SO EVERYTHING BETWEEN US IS OKAY?
NOTHING BETWEEN US IS EVER GOOD!
HA HA
SIGH
"THEN DON'T SCREW IT UP. PUT SOME EFFORT INTO IT."
DING
DONG

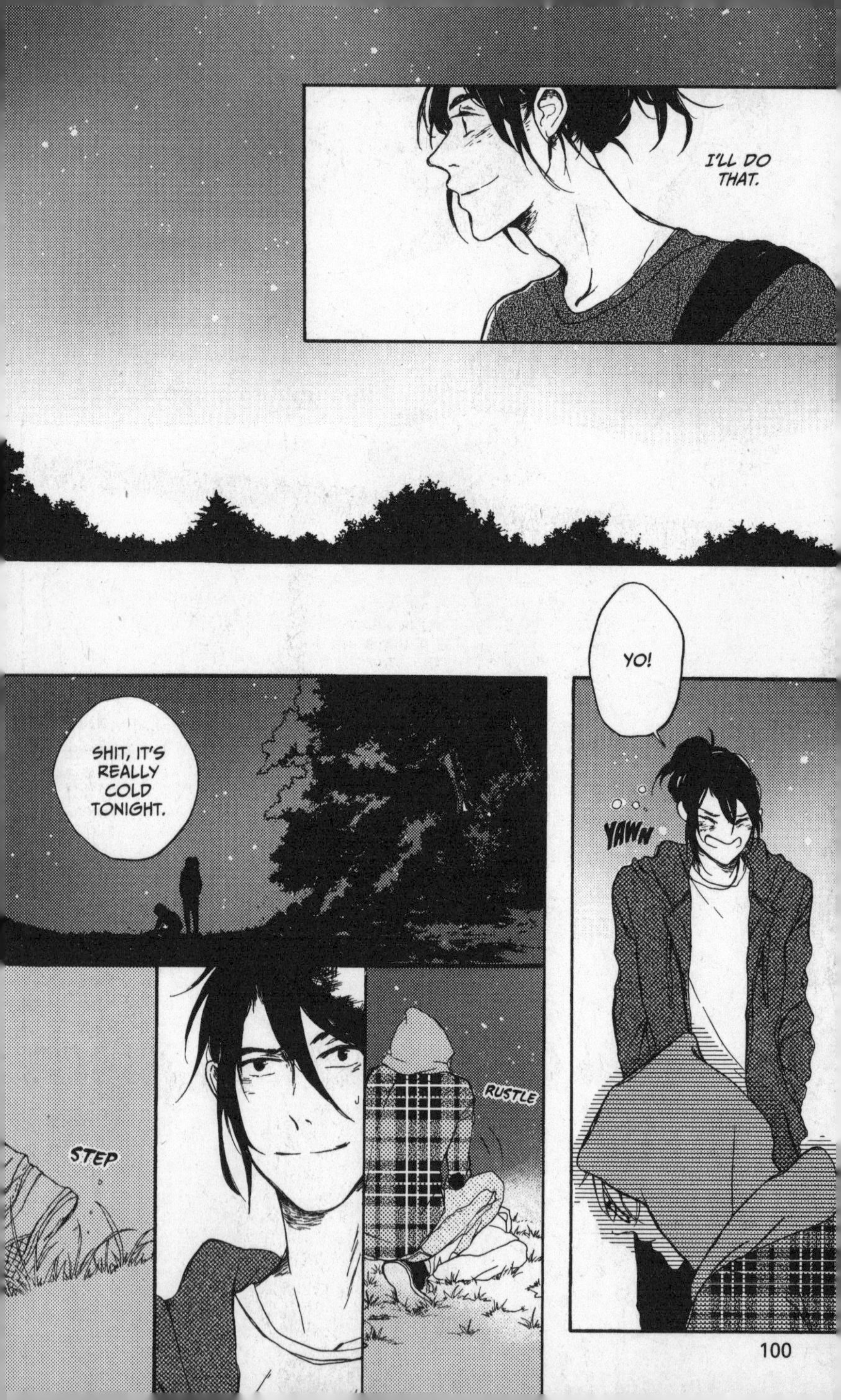
I'LL DO THAT.
YO!
YAWN
SHIT, IT'S REALLY COLD TONIGHT.
RUSTLE
STEP

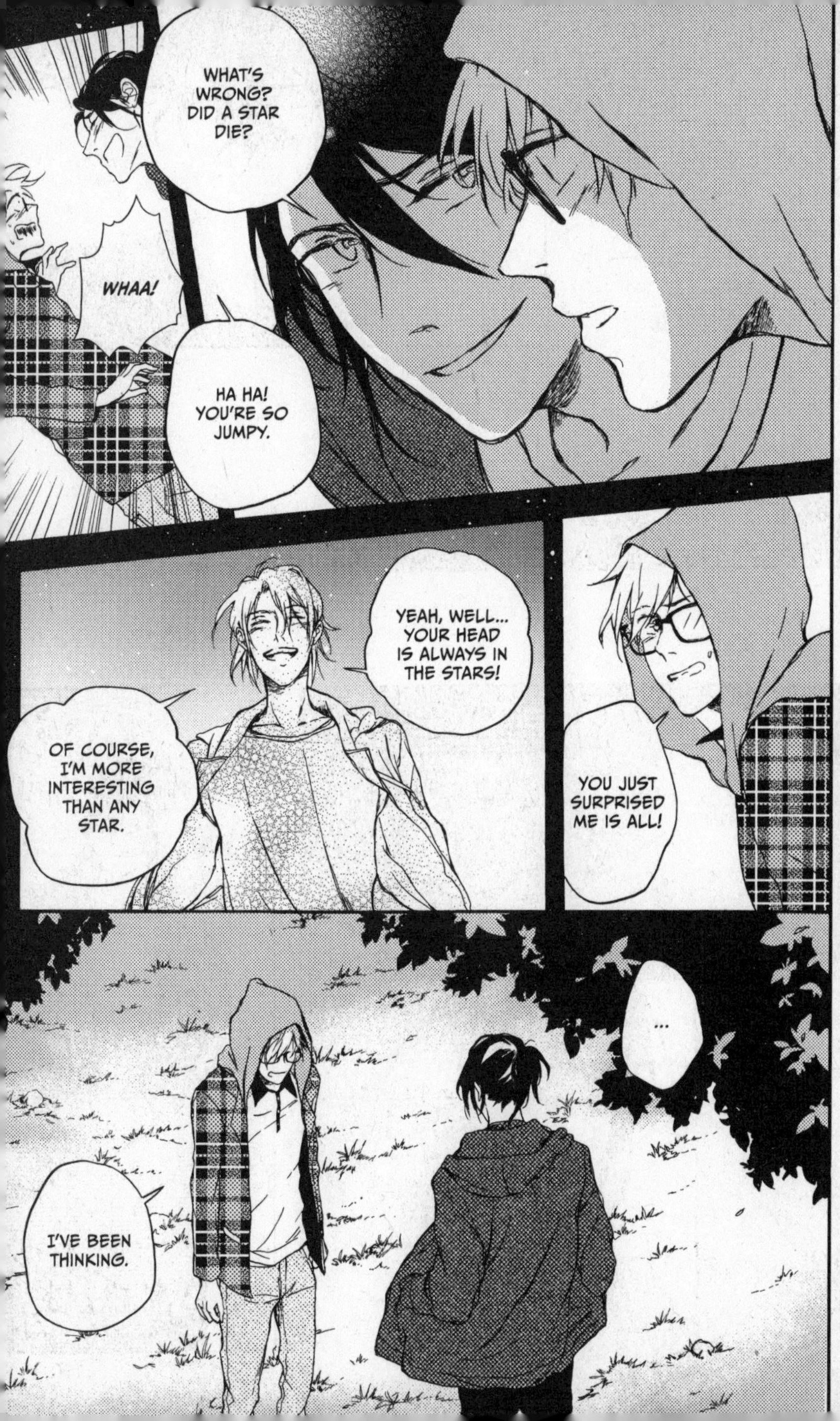
WHAT'S WRONG? DID A STAR DIE?
WHAA!
HA HA! YOU'RE SO JUMPY.
YOU JUST SURPRISED ME IS ALL!
YEAH, WELL... YOUR HEAD IS ALWAYS IN THE STARS!
OF COURSE, I'M MORE INTERESTING THAN ANY STAR.
...
I'VE BEEN THINKING.

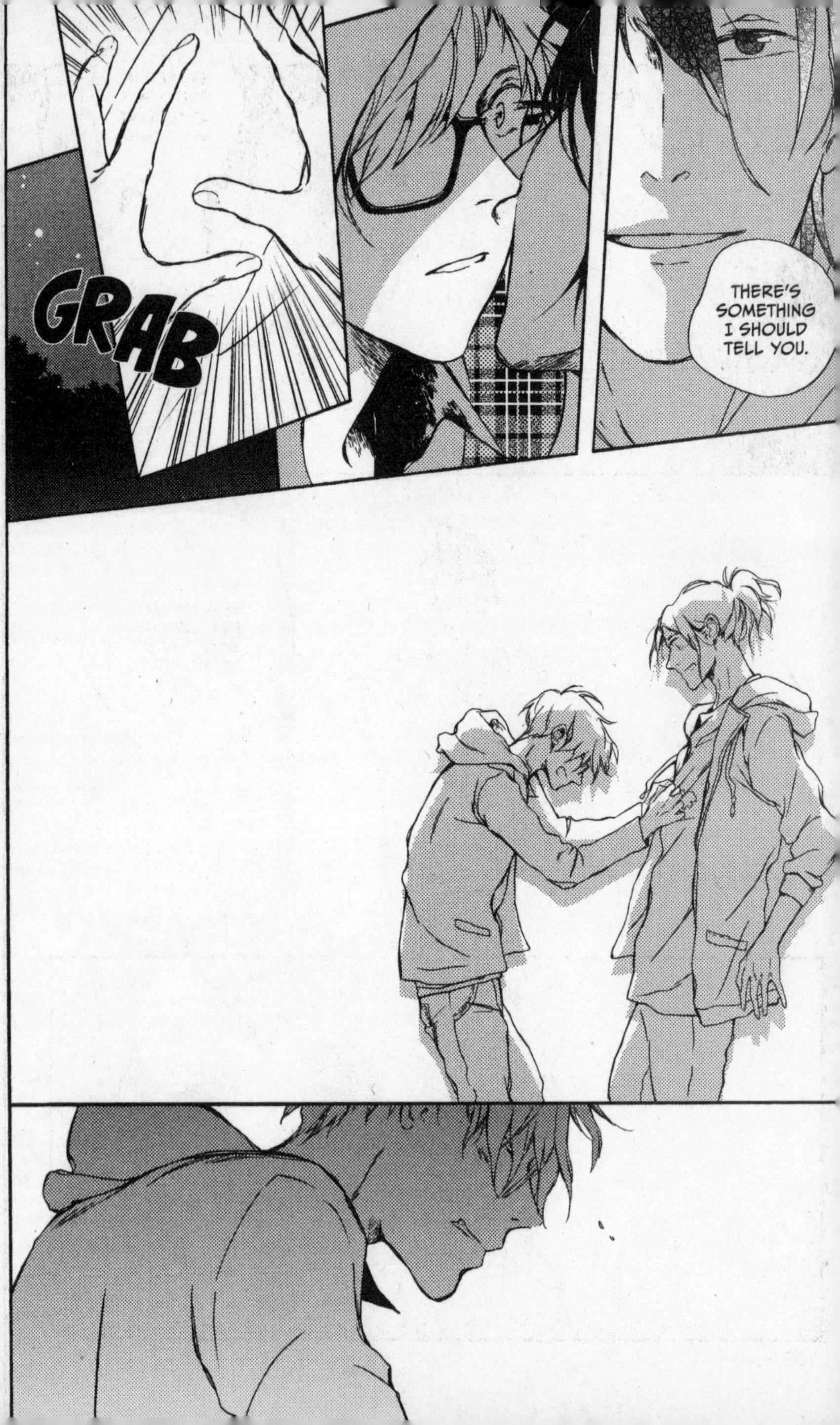
THERE'S SOMETHING I SHOULD TELL YOU.
GRAB

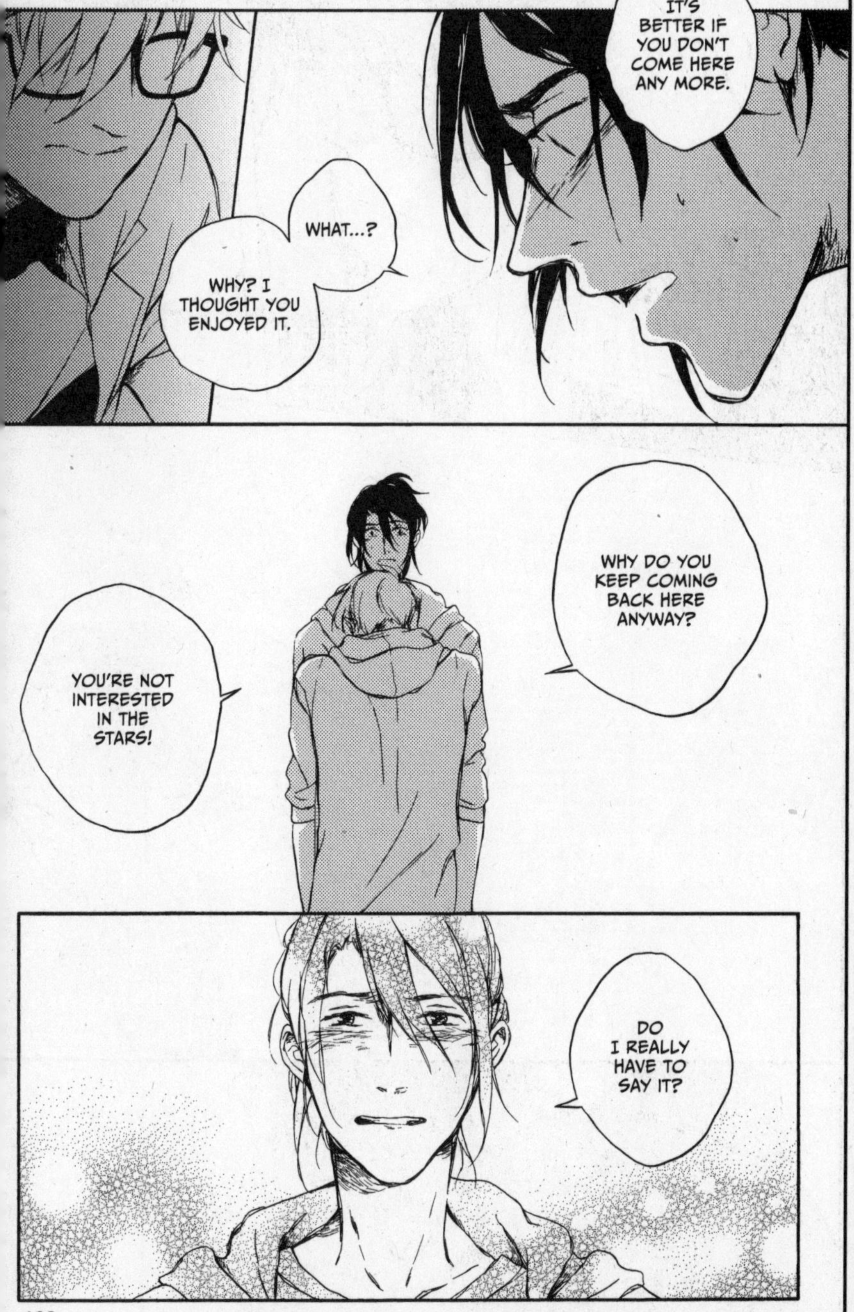
IT'S BETTER IF YOU DON'T COME HERE ANY MORE.
WHAT...?
WHY? I THOUGHT YOU ENJOYED IT.
WHY DO YOU KEEP COMING BACK HERE ANYWAY?
YOU'RE NOT INTERESTED IN THE STARS!
DO I REALLY HAVE TO SAY IT?

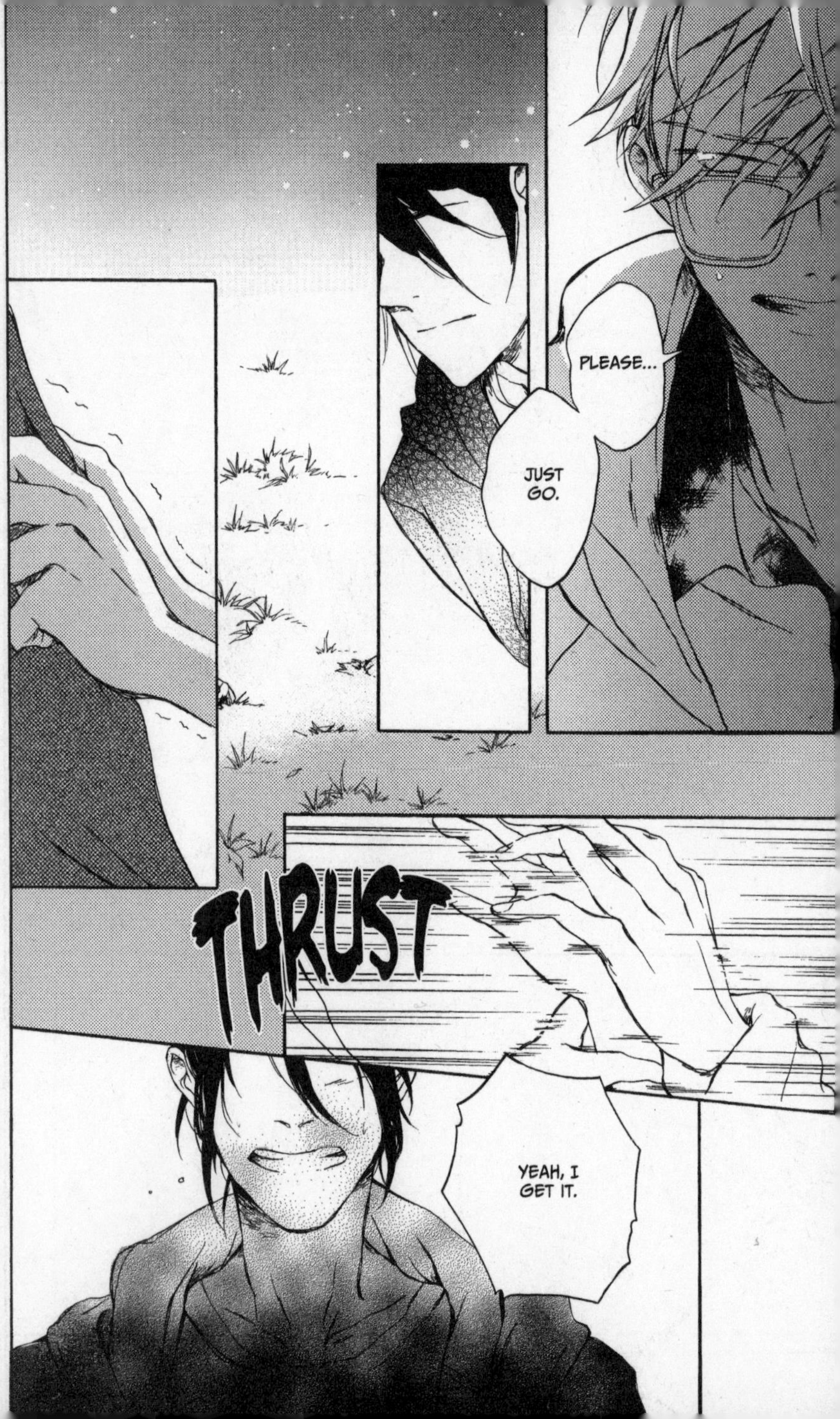
PLEASE...
JUST GO.
THRUST
YEAH, I GET IT.

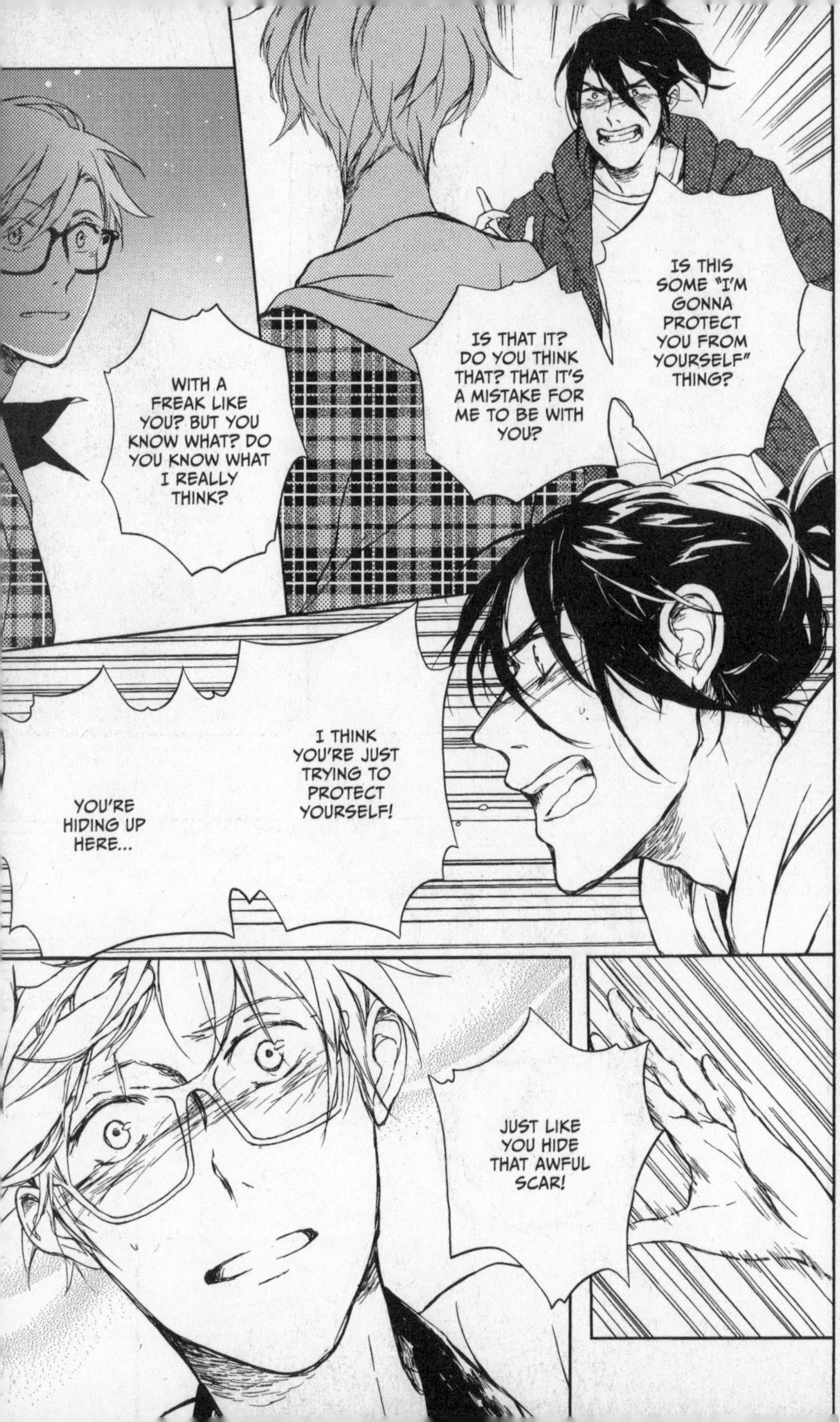
IS THIS SOME "I'M GONNA PROTECT YOU FROM YOURSELF" THING?
IS THAT IT? DO YOU THINK THAT? THAT IT'S A MISTAKE FOR ME TO BE WITH YOU?
WITH A FREAK LIKE YOU? BUT YOU KNOW WHAT? DO YOU KNOW WHAT I REALLY THINK?
I THINK YOU'RE JUST TRYING TO PROTECT YOURSELF!
YOU'RE HIDING UP HERE...
JUST LIKE YOU HIDE THAT AWFUL SCAR!

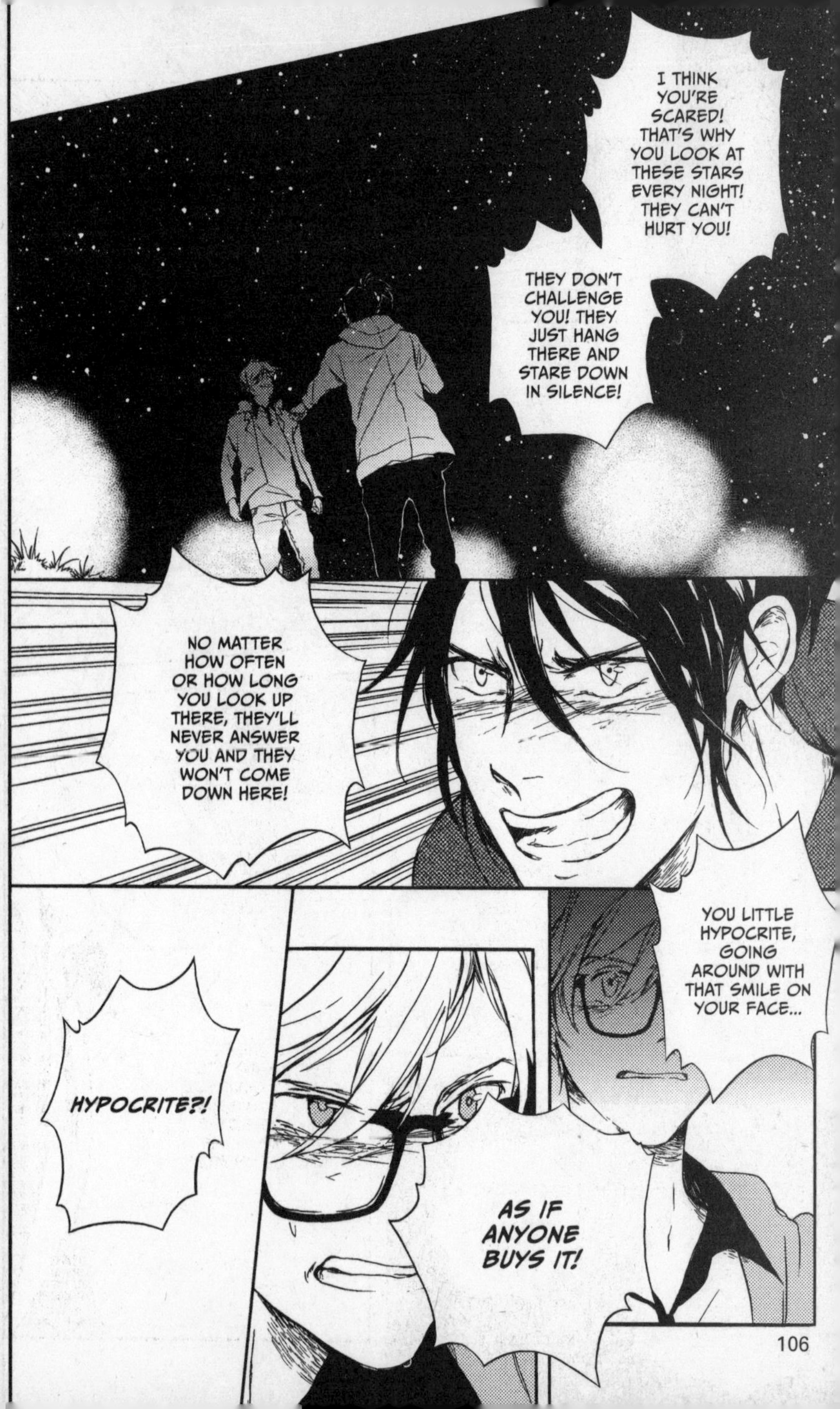
I THINK YOU'RE SCARED! THAT'S WHY YOU LOOK AT THESE STARS EVERY NIGHT! THEY CAN'T HURT YOU!
THEY DON'T CHALLENGE YOU! THEY JUST HANG THERE AND STARE DOWN IN SILENCE!
NO MATTER HOW OFTEN OR HOW LONG YOU LOOK UP THERE, THEY'LL NEVER ANSWER YOU AND THEY WON'T COME DOWN HERE!
YOU LITTLE HYPOCRITE, GOING AROUND WITH THAT SMILE ON YOUR FACE...
AS IF ANYONE BUYS IT!
HYPOCRITE?!

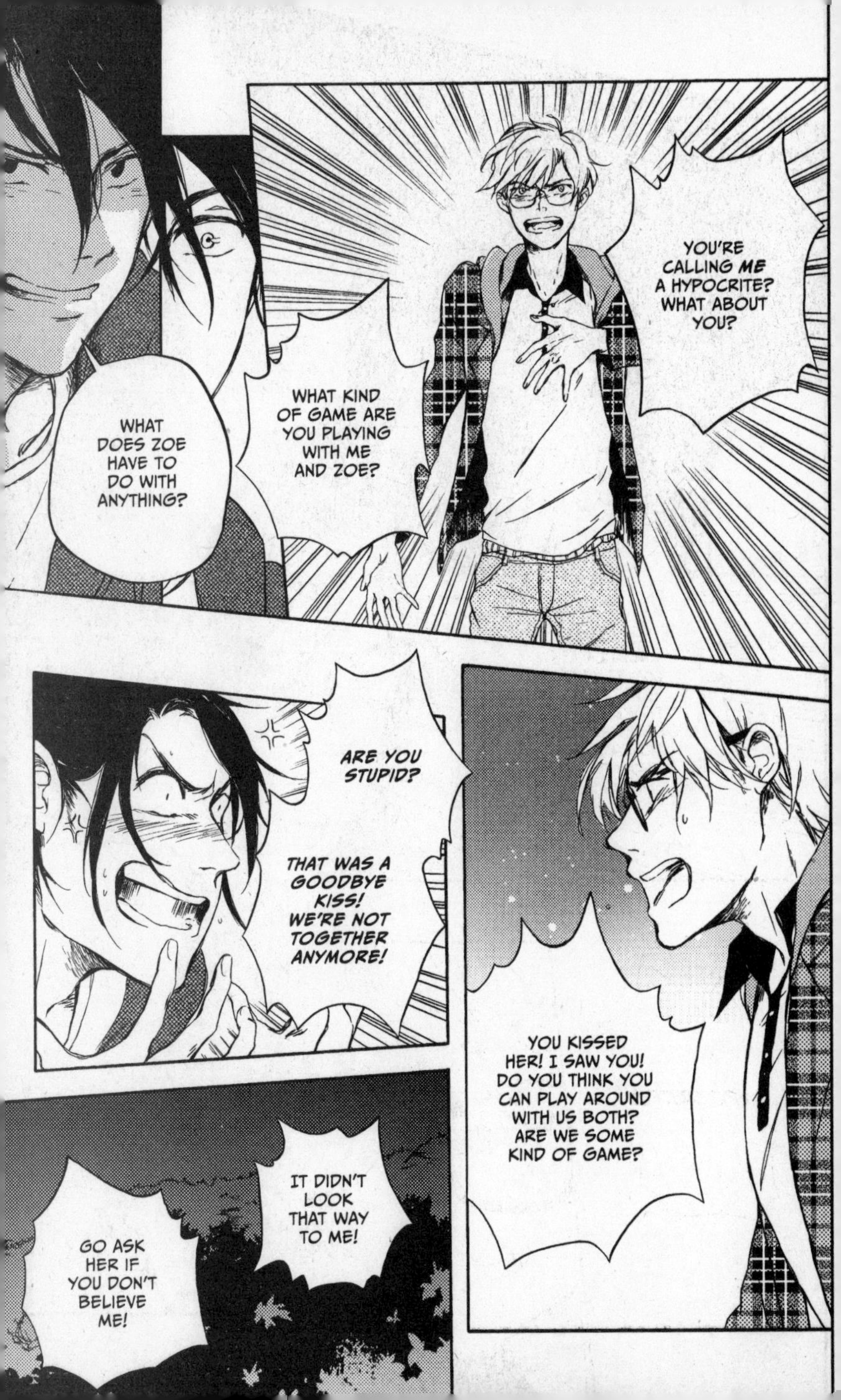
YOU'RE CALLING ME A HYPOCRITE? WHAT ABOUT YOU?
WHAT KIND OF GAME ARE YOU PLAYING WITH ME AND ZOE?
WHAT DOES ZOE HAVE TO DO WITH ANYTHING?
YOU KISSED HER! I SAW YOU! DO YOU THINK YOU CAN PLAY AROUND WITH US BOTH? ARE WE SOME KIND OF GAME?
ARE YOU STUPID?
THAT WAS A GOODBYE KISS! WE'RE NOT TOGETHER ANYMORE!
IT DIDN'T LOOK THAT WAY TO ME!
GO ASK HER IF YOU DON'T BELIEVE ME!

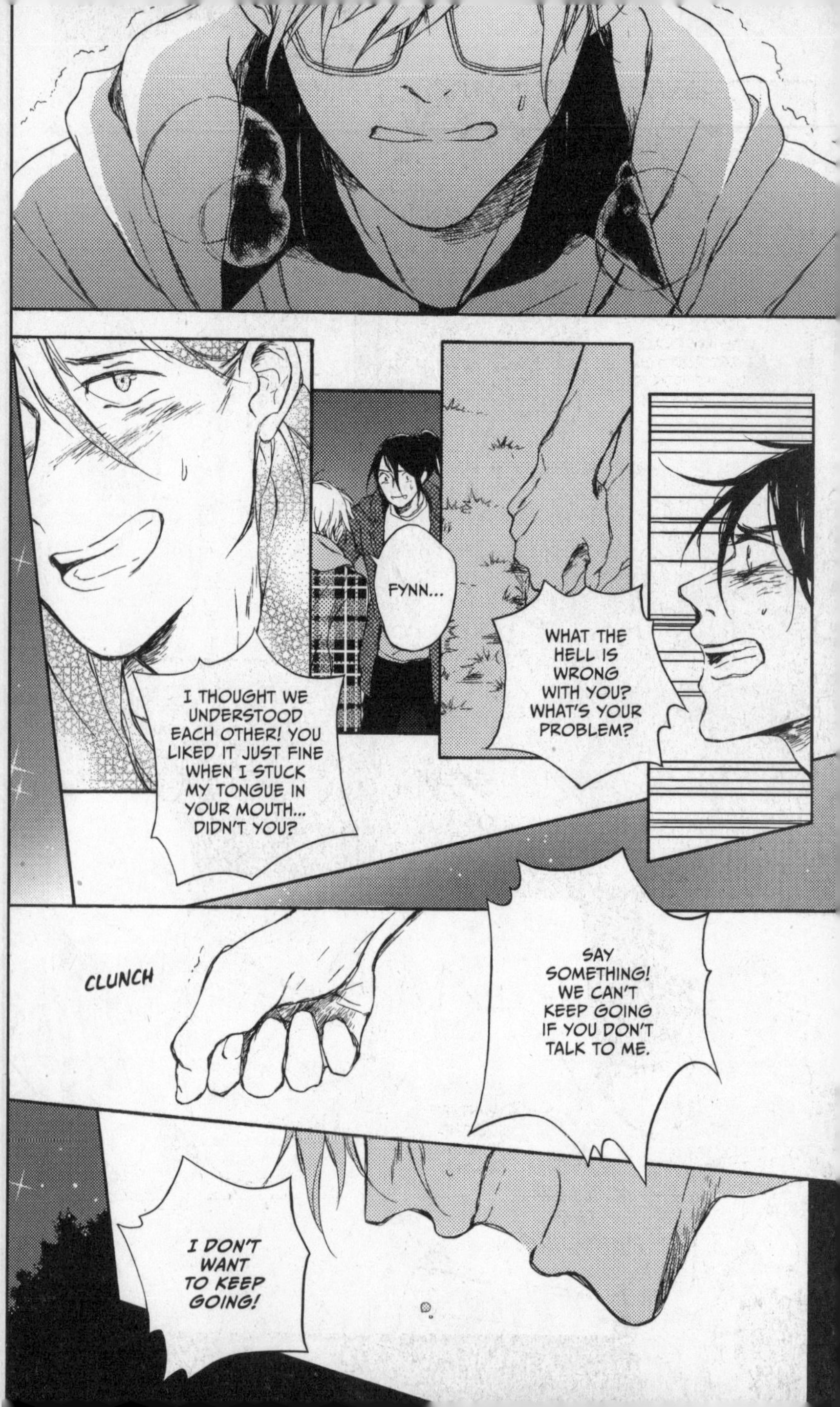
WHAT THE HELL IS WRONG WITH YOU? WHAT'S YOUR PROBLEM?
FYNN...
I THOUGHT WE UNDERSTOOD EACH OTHER! YOU LIKED IT JUST FINE WHEN I STUCK MY TONGUE IN YOUR MOUTH... DIDN'T YOU?
SAY SOMETHING! WE CAN'T KEEP GOING IF YOU DON'T TALK TO ME.
CLUNCH
I DON'T WANT TO KEEP GOING!

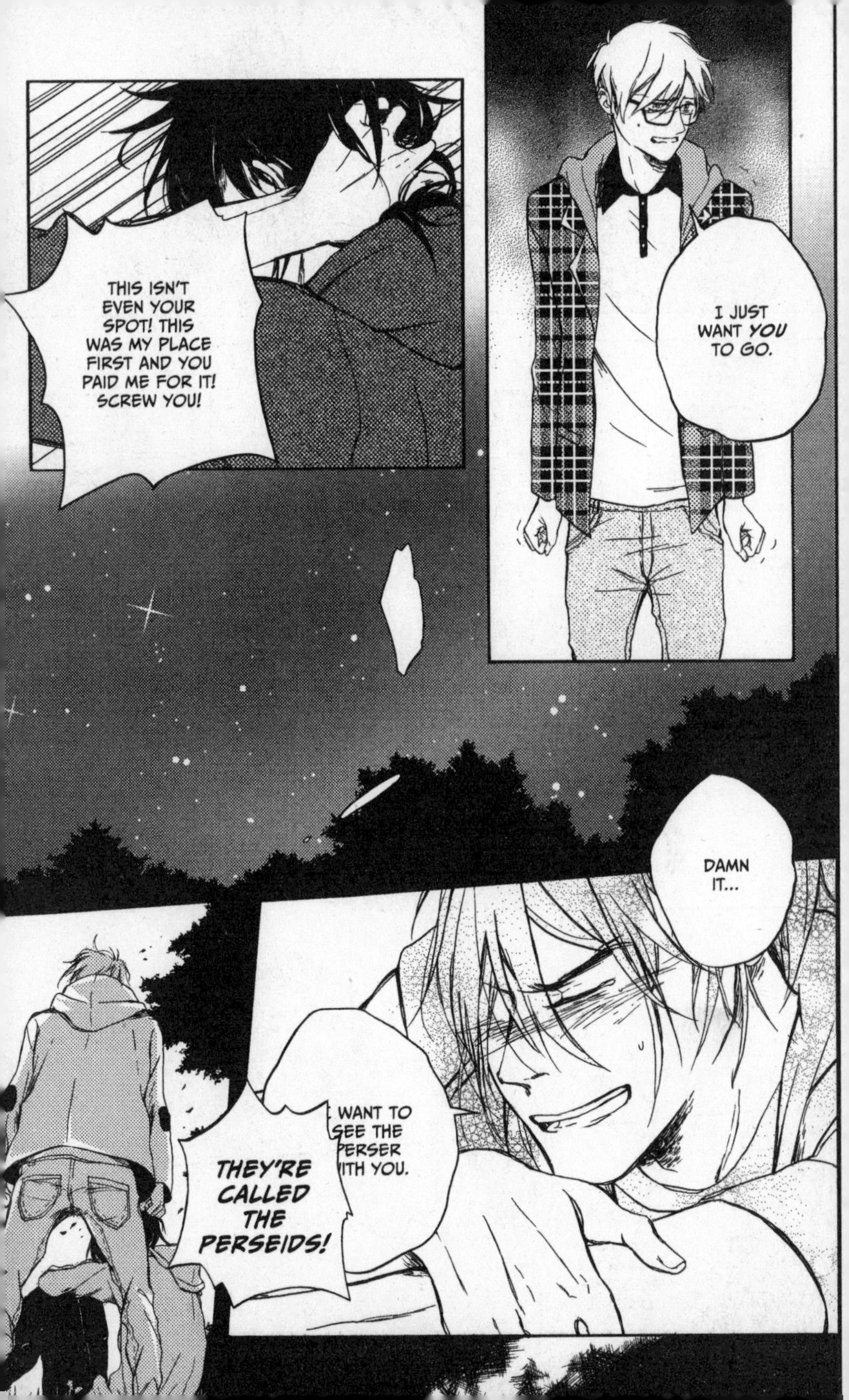
I JUST WANT *YOU* TO GO.
THIS ISN'T EVEN YOUR SPOT! THIS WAS MY PLACE FIRST AND YOU PAID ME FOR IT! SCREW YOU!
DAMN IT...
WANT TO SEE THE ERSER ITH YOU.
THEY'RE CALLED THE PERSEIDS!

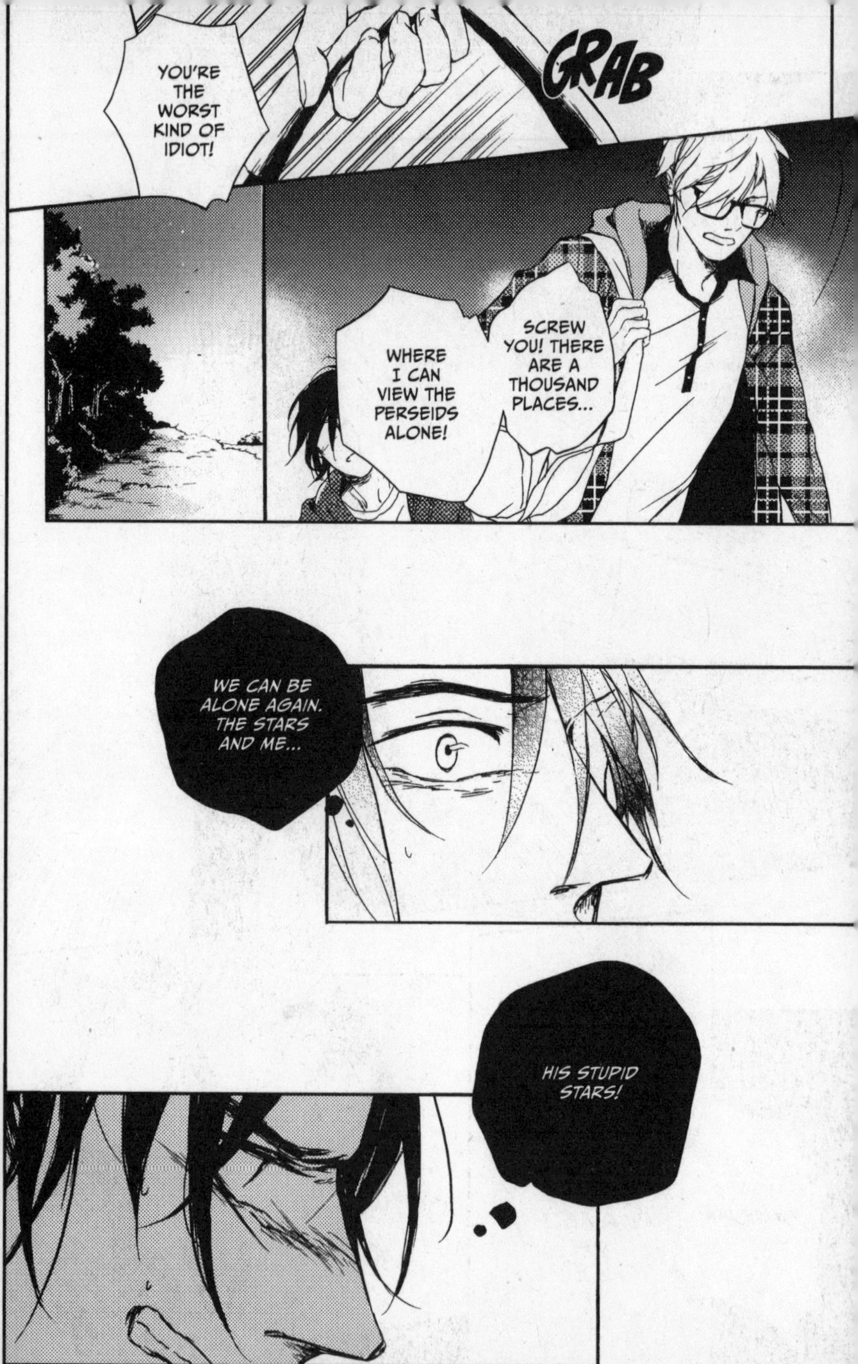
GRAB
YOU'RE THE WORST KIND OF IDIOT!
SCREW YOU! THERE ARE A THOUSAND PLACES...
WHERE I CAN VIEW THE PERSEIDS ALONE!
WE CAN BE ALONE AGAIN. THE STARS AND ME...
HIS STUPID STARS!

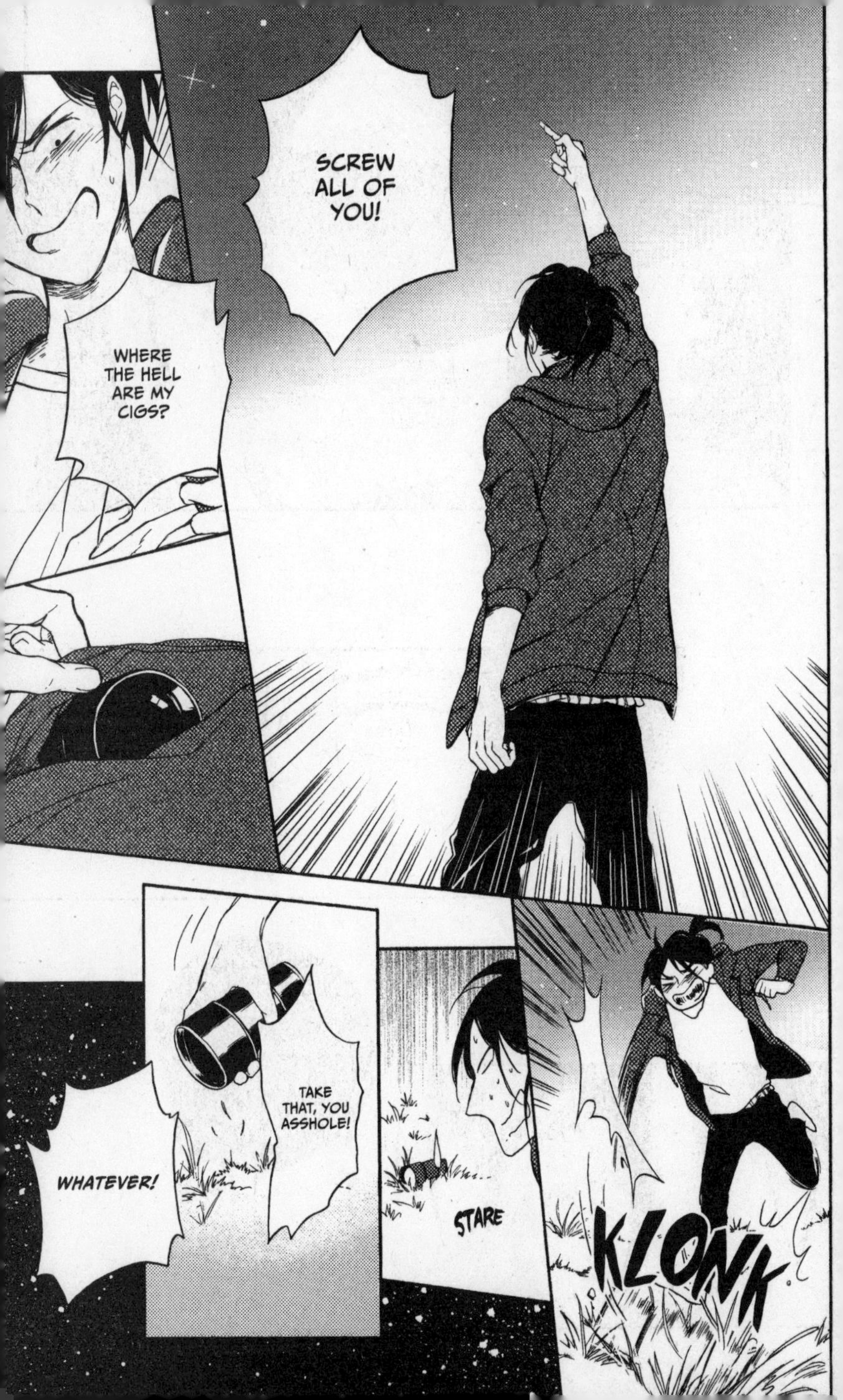
SCREW ALL OF YOU!
WHERE THE HELL ARE MY CIGS?
KLONK
STARE
TAKE THAT, YOU ASSHOLE!
WHATEVER!

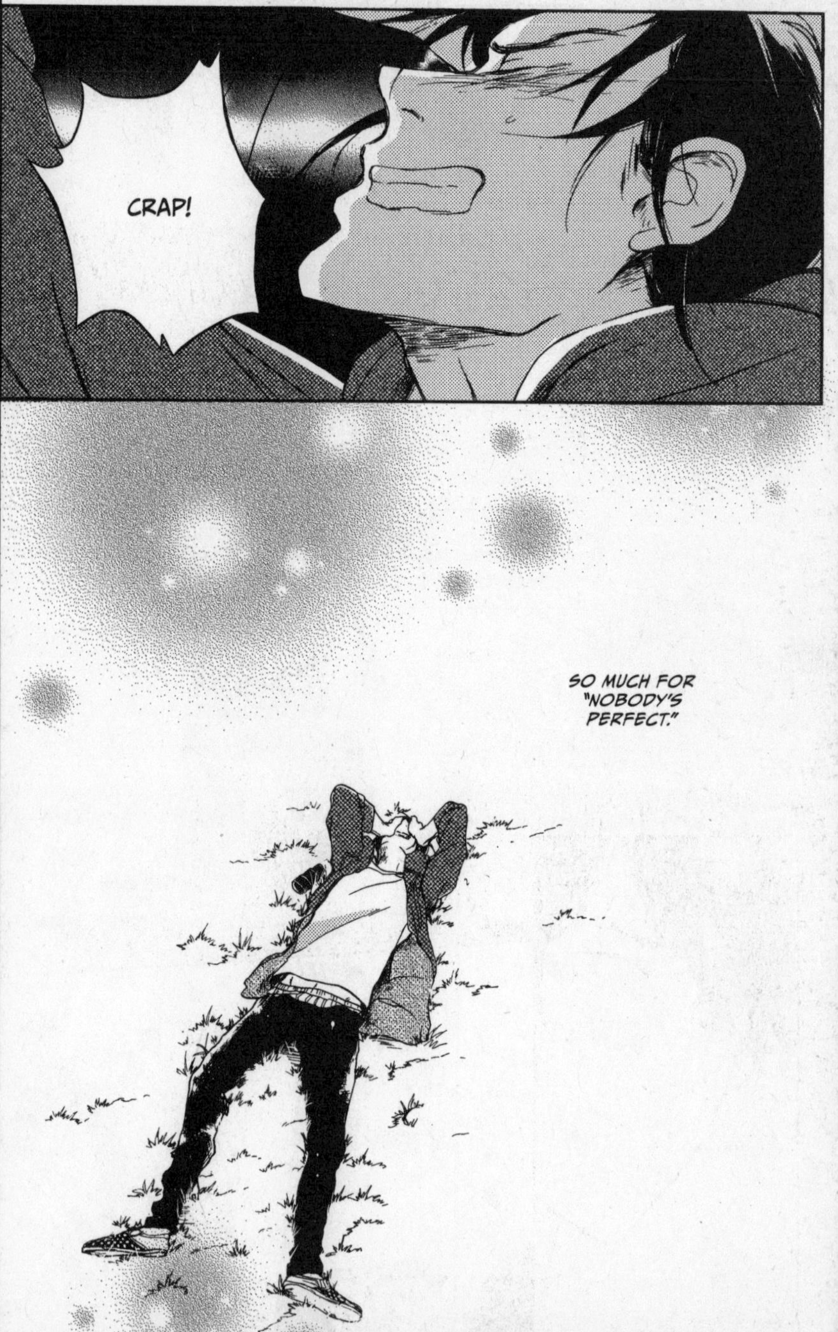
CRAP!
SO MUCH FOR "NOBODY'S PERFECT."

STAR 4

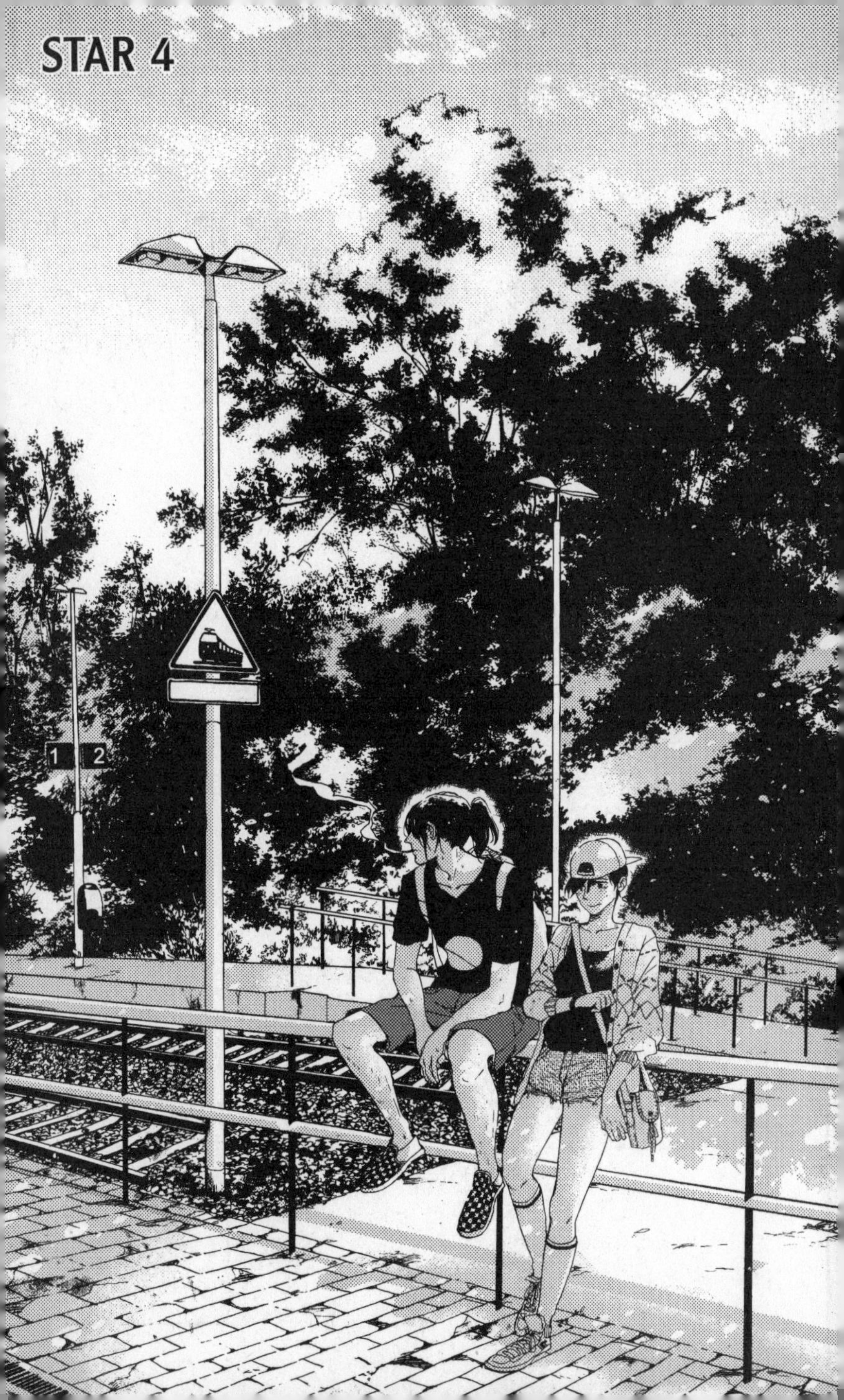
1 2

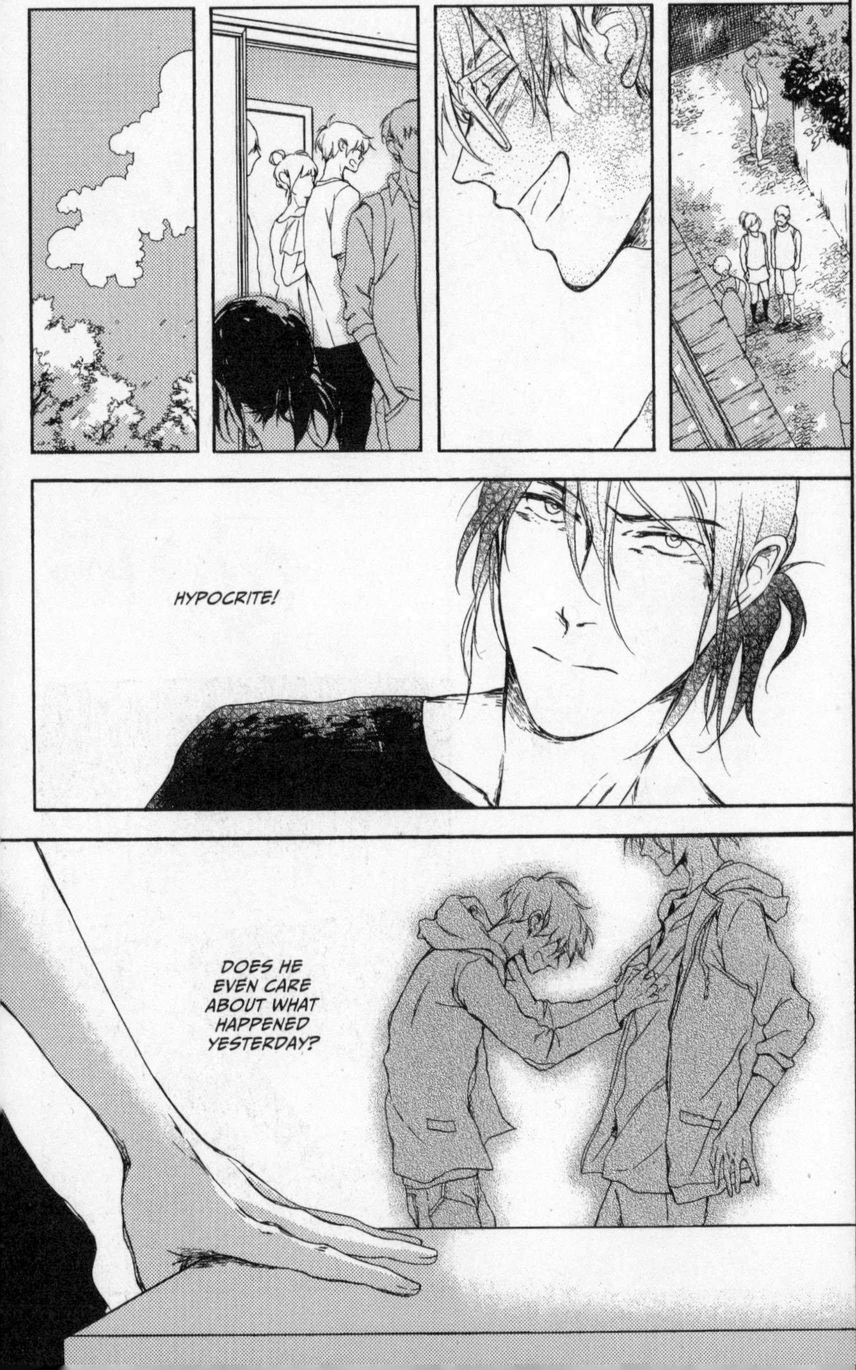
HYPOCRITE!
DOES HE EVEN CARE ABOUT WHAT HAPPENED YESTERDAY?

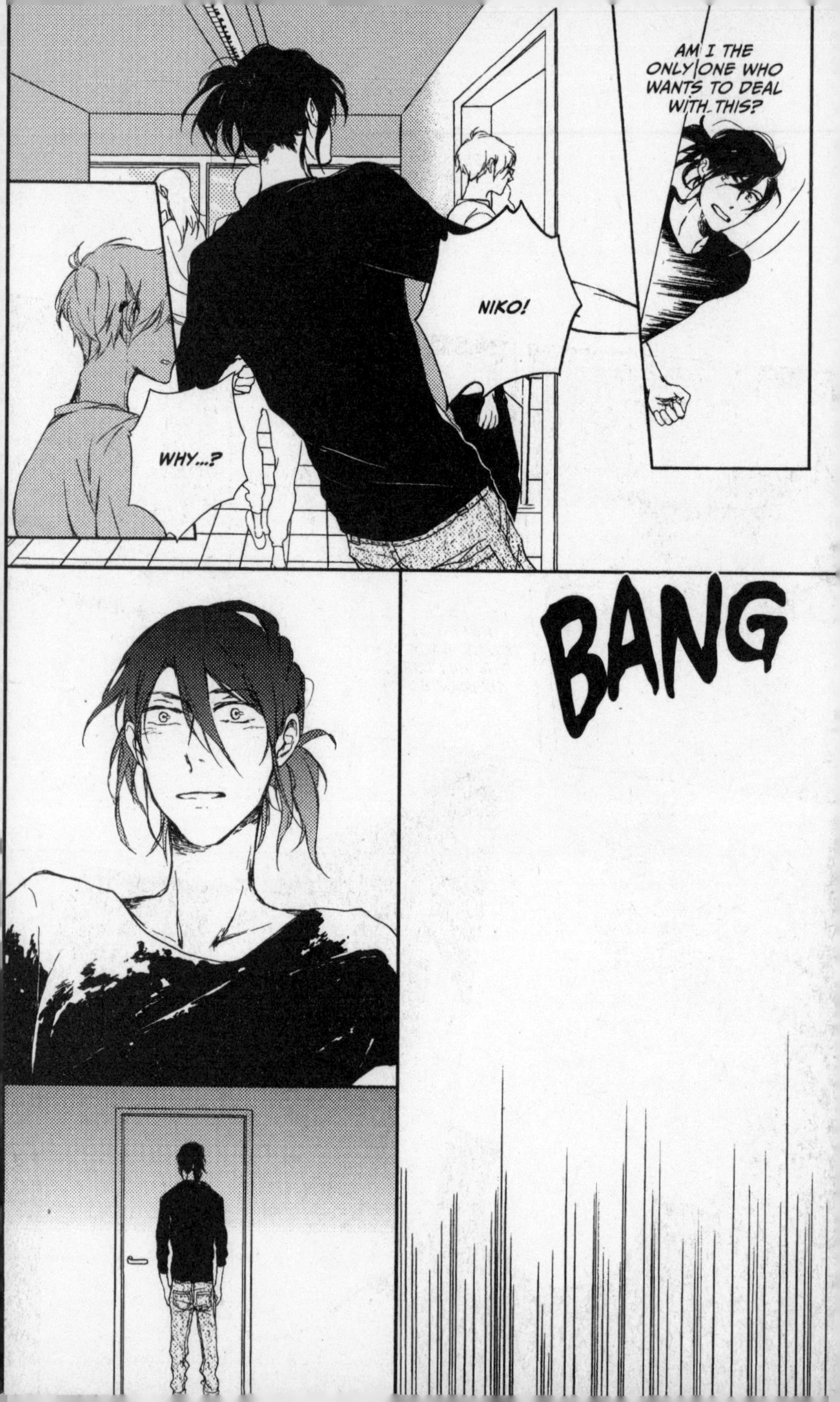
AM I THE ONLY ONE WHO WANTS TO DEAL WITH THIS?
NIKO!
WHY...?
BANG

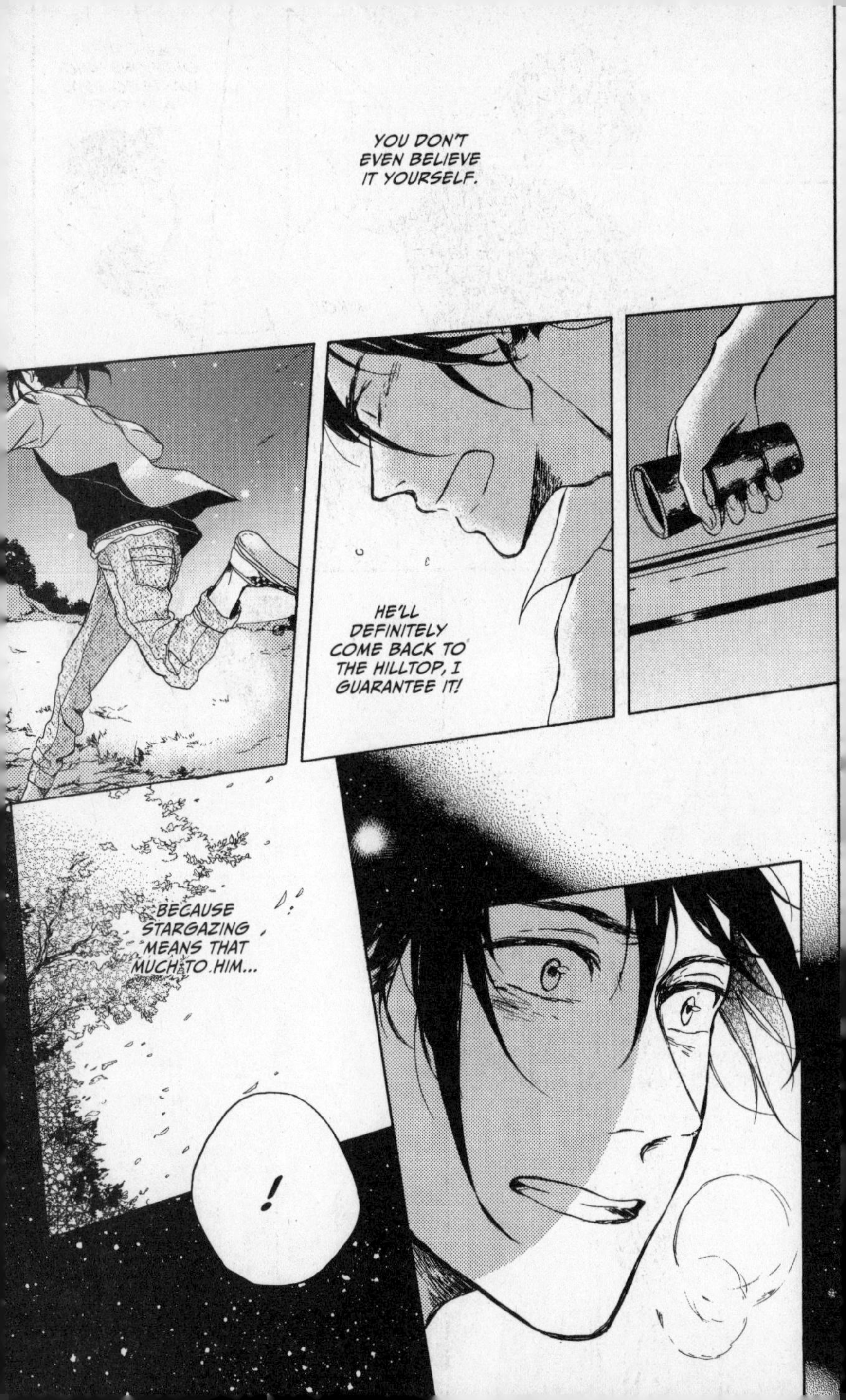
YOU DON'T EVEN BELIEVE IT YOURSELF.
HE'LL DEFINITELY COME BACK TO THE HILLTOP, I GUARANTEE IT!
BECAUSE STARGAZING MEANS THAT MUCH TO HIM...
!

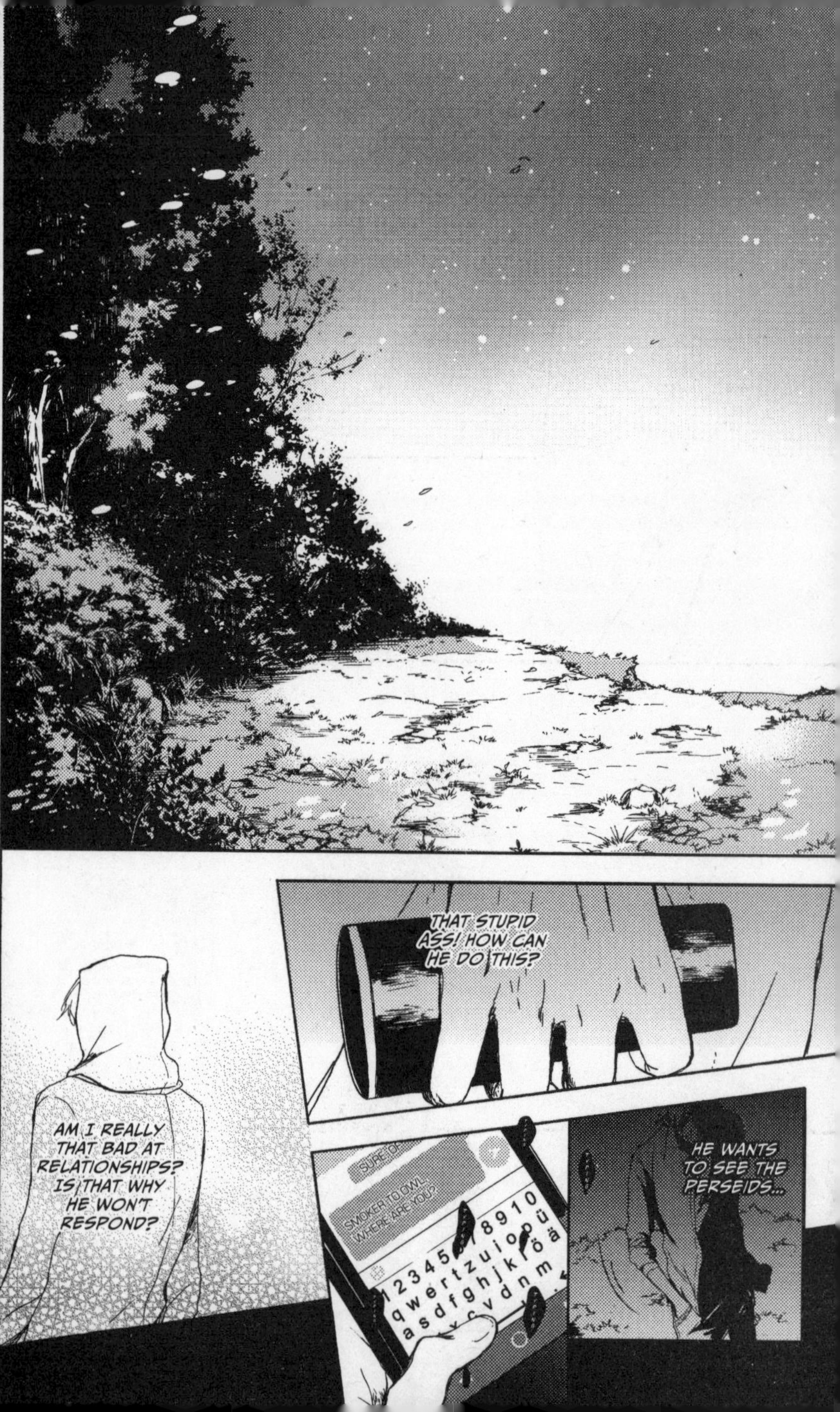
THAT STUPID ASS! HOW CAN HE DO THIS?
HE WANTS TO SEE THE PERSEIDS...
SURE OF
SMOKER TO OWL, WHERE ARE YOU?
AM I REALLY THAT BAD AT RELATIONSHIPS? IS THAT WHY HE WON'T RESPOND?

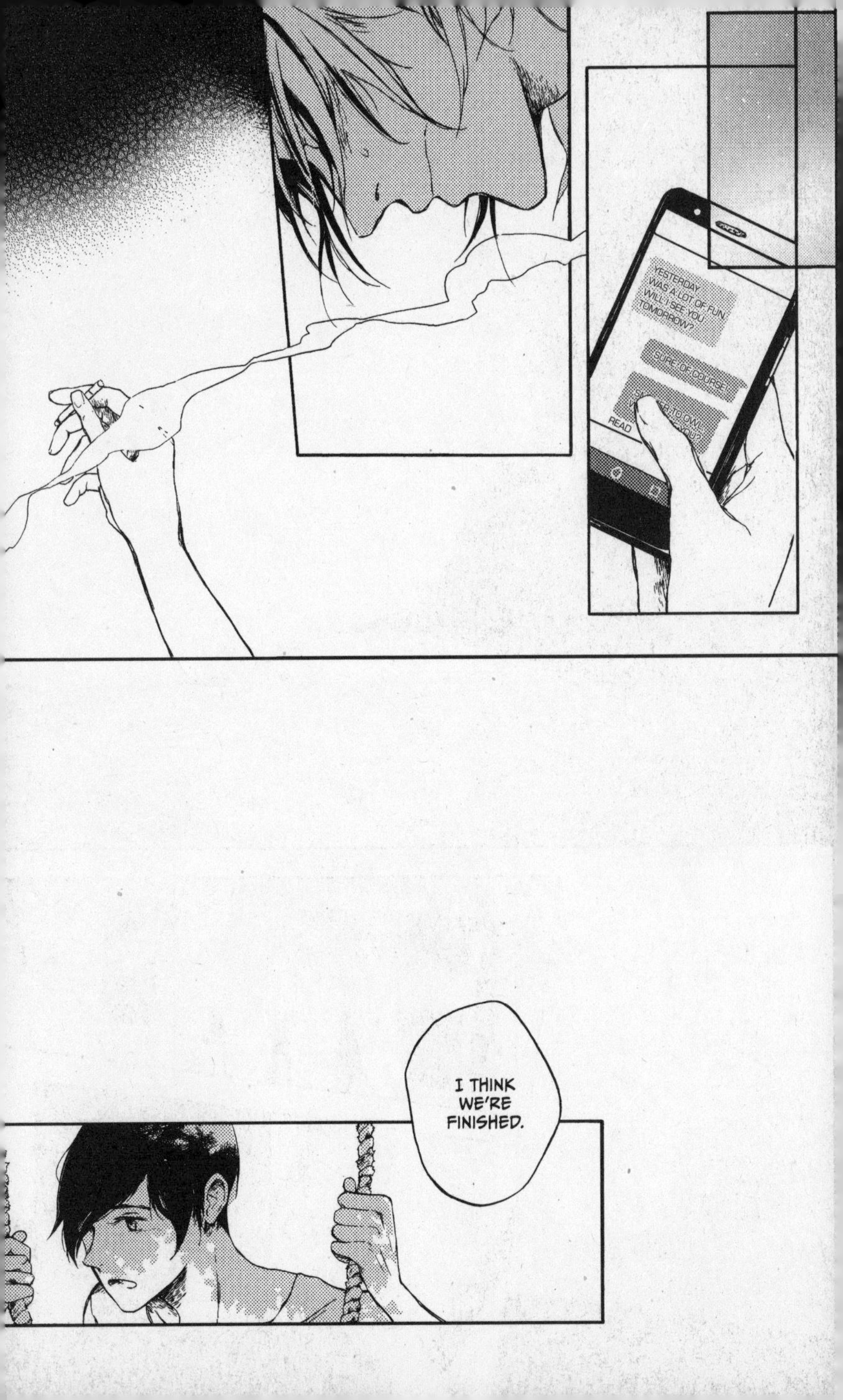
YESTERDAY WAS A LOT OF FUN. WILL I SEE YOU TOMORROW?
SURE, OF COURSE!
READ
I THINK WE'RE FINISHED.

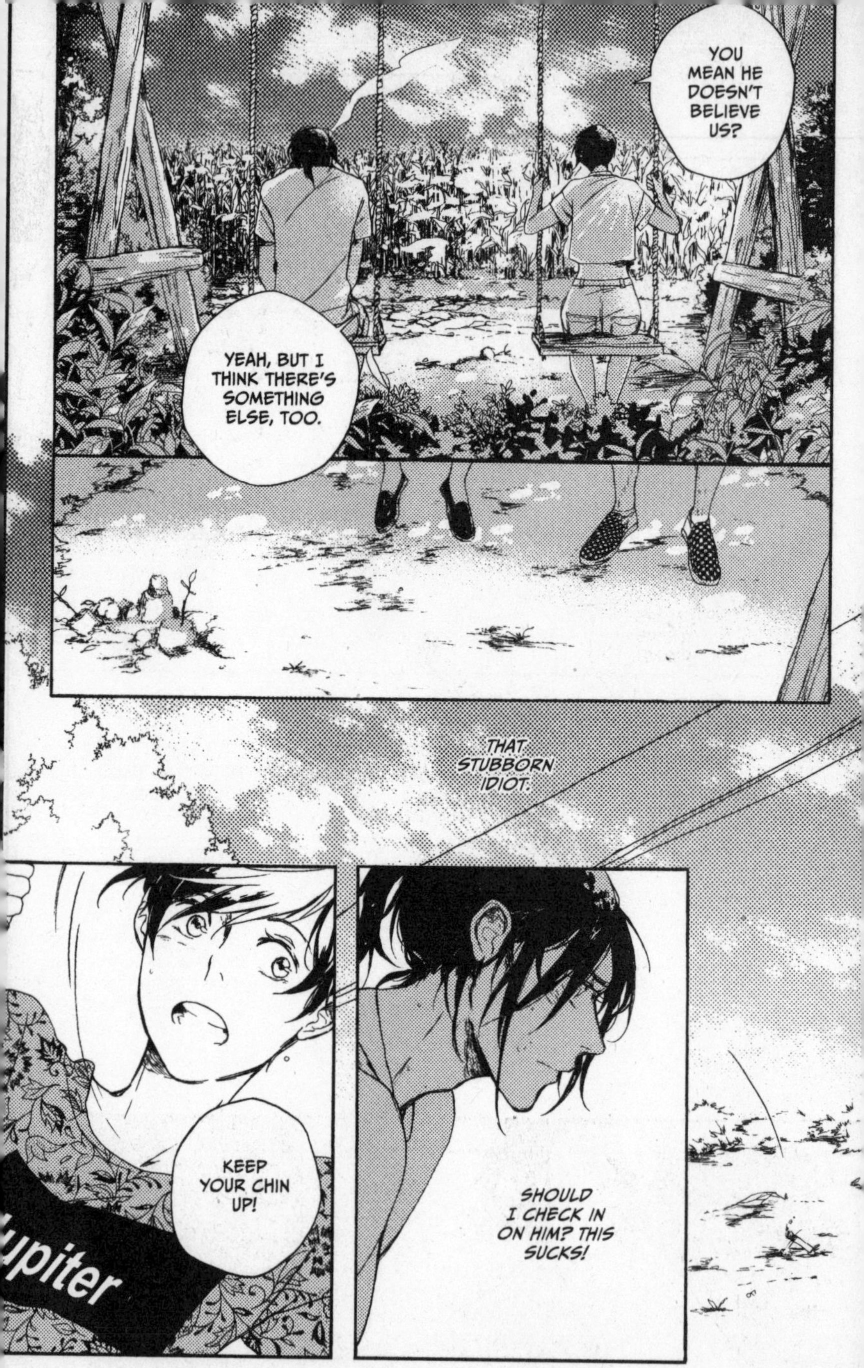
YOU MEAN HE DOESN'T BELIEVE US?
YEAH, BUT I THINK THERE'S SOMETHING ELSE, TOO.
THAT STUBBORN IDIOT.
SHOULD I CHECK IN ON HIM? THIS SUCKS!
KEEP YOUR CHIN UP!

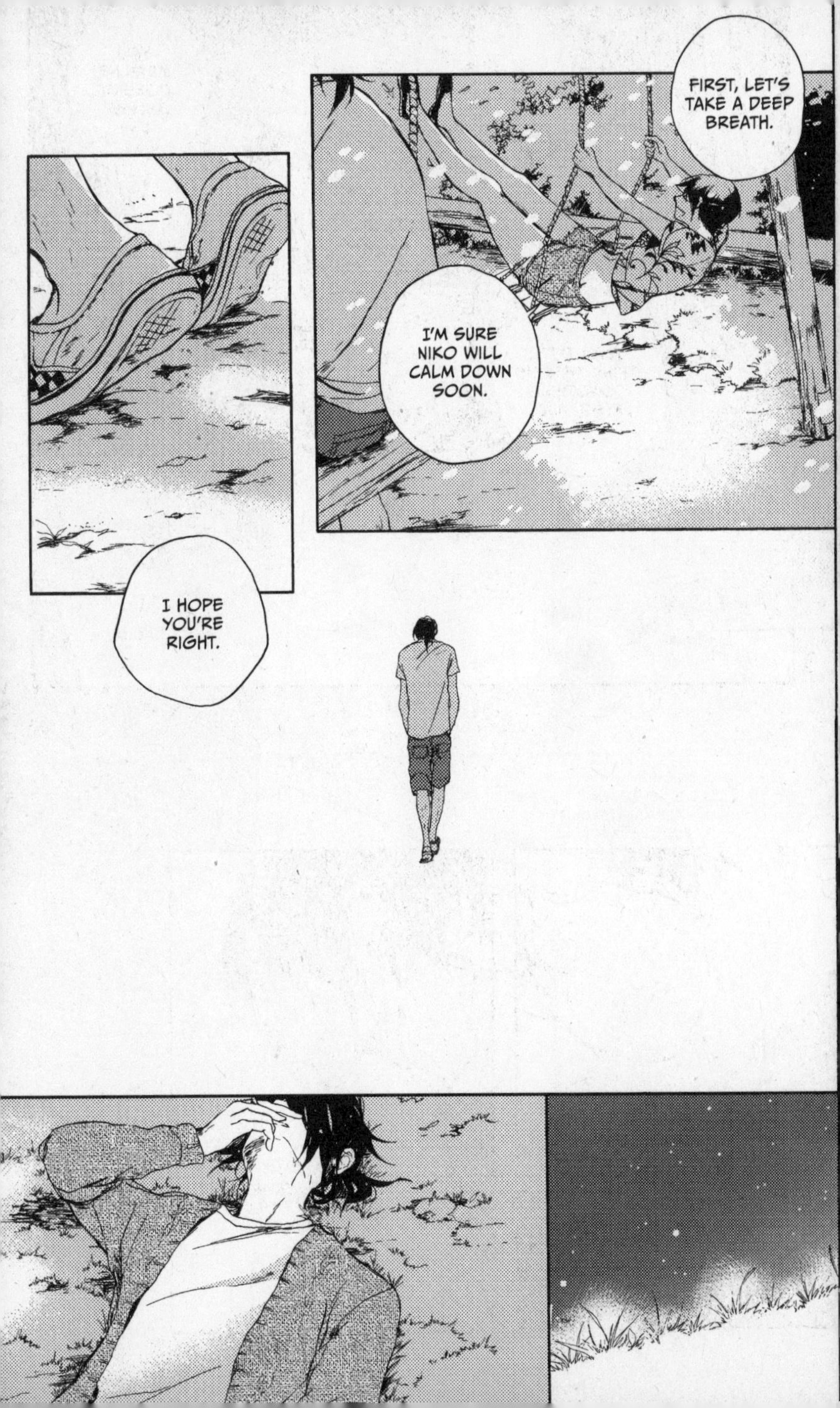
FIRST, LET'S TAKE A DEEP BREATH.
I'M SURE NIKO WILL CALM DOWN SOON.
I HOPE YOU'RE RIGHT.

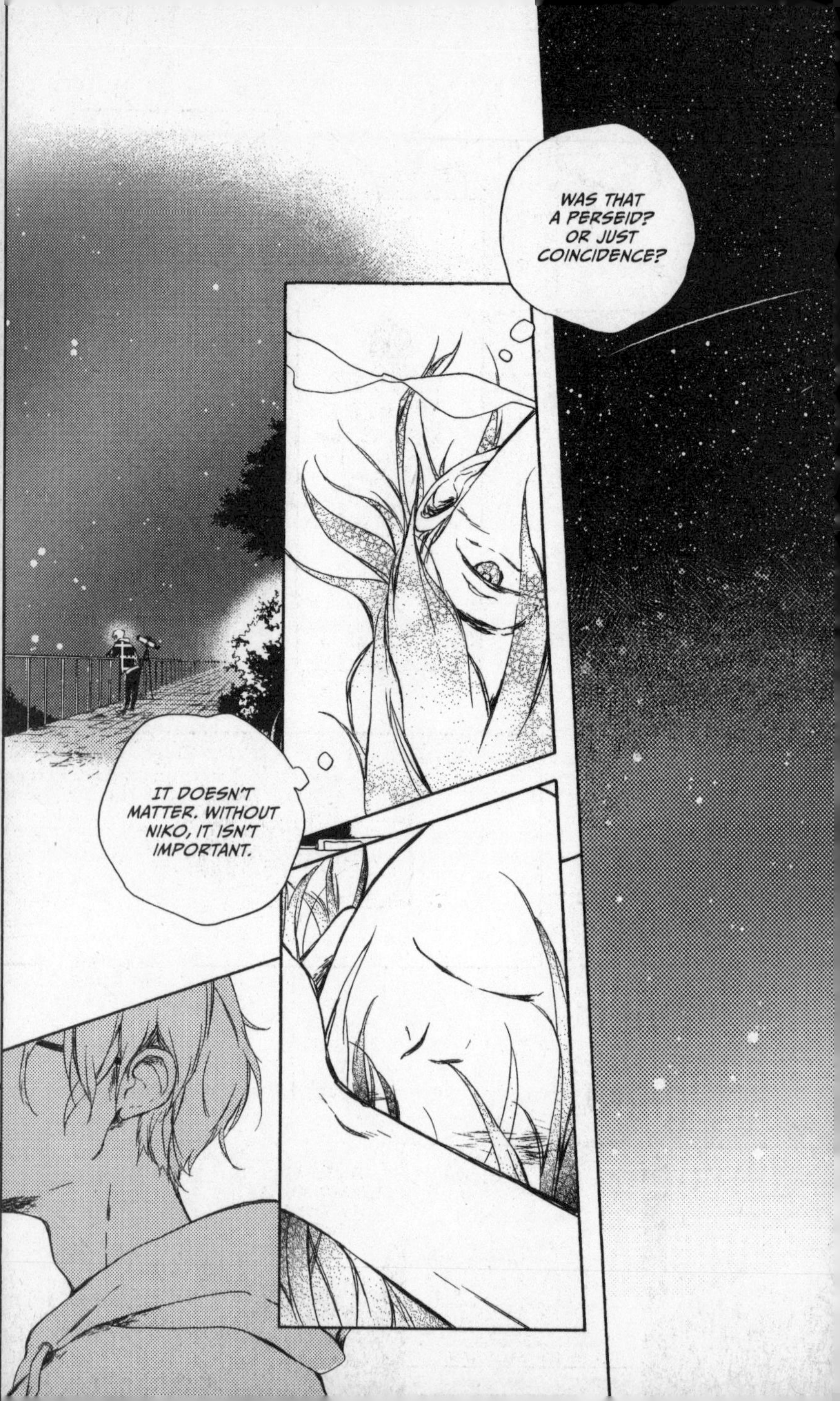
WAS THAT A PERSEID? OR JUST COINCIDENCE?
IT DOESN'T MATTER. WITHOUT NIKO, IT ISN'T IMPORTANT.

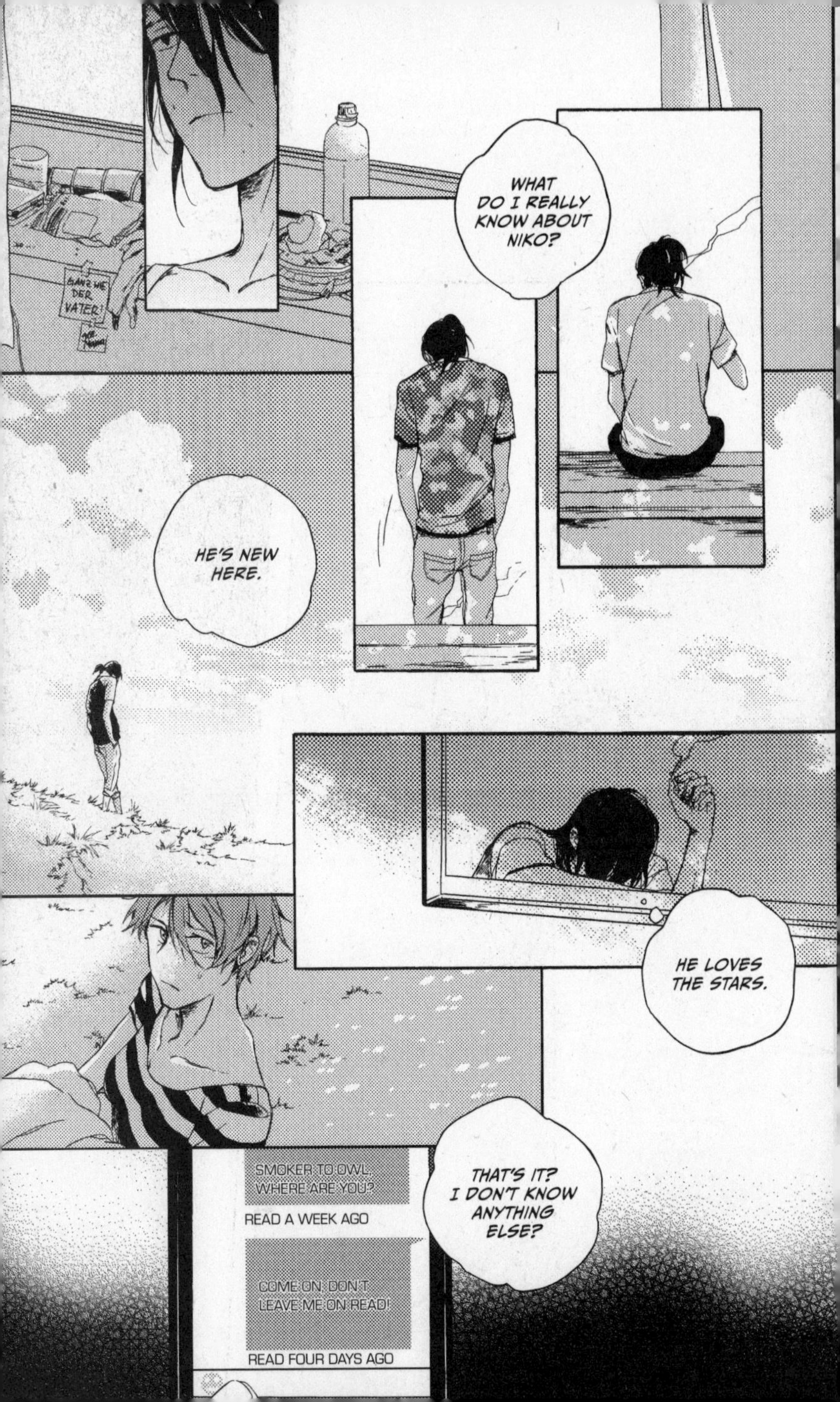
WHAT DO I REALLY KNOW ABOUT NIKO?
GANZ WIE DER VATER!
HE'S NEW HERE.
HE LOVES THE STARS.
THAT'S IT? I DON'T KNOW ANYTHING ELSE?
SMOKER TO OWL, WHERE ARE YOU?
READ A WEEK AGO
COME ON, DON'T LEAVE ME ON READ!
READ FOUR DAYS AGO

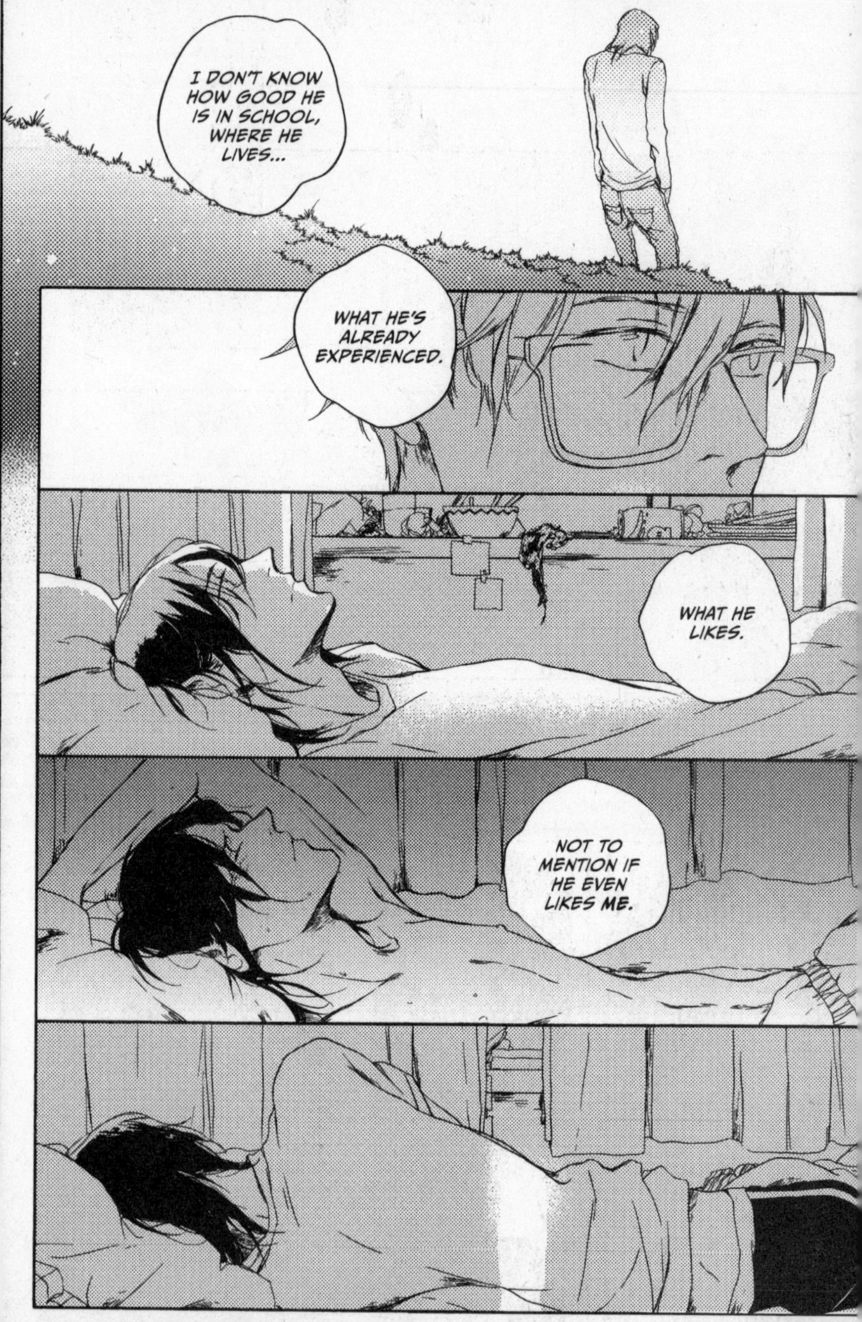
I DON'T KNOW HOW GOOD HE IS IN SCHOOL, WHERE HE LIVES...
WHAT HE'S ALREADY EXPERIENCED.
WHAT HE LIKES.
NOT TO MENTION IF HE EVEN LIKES ME.

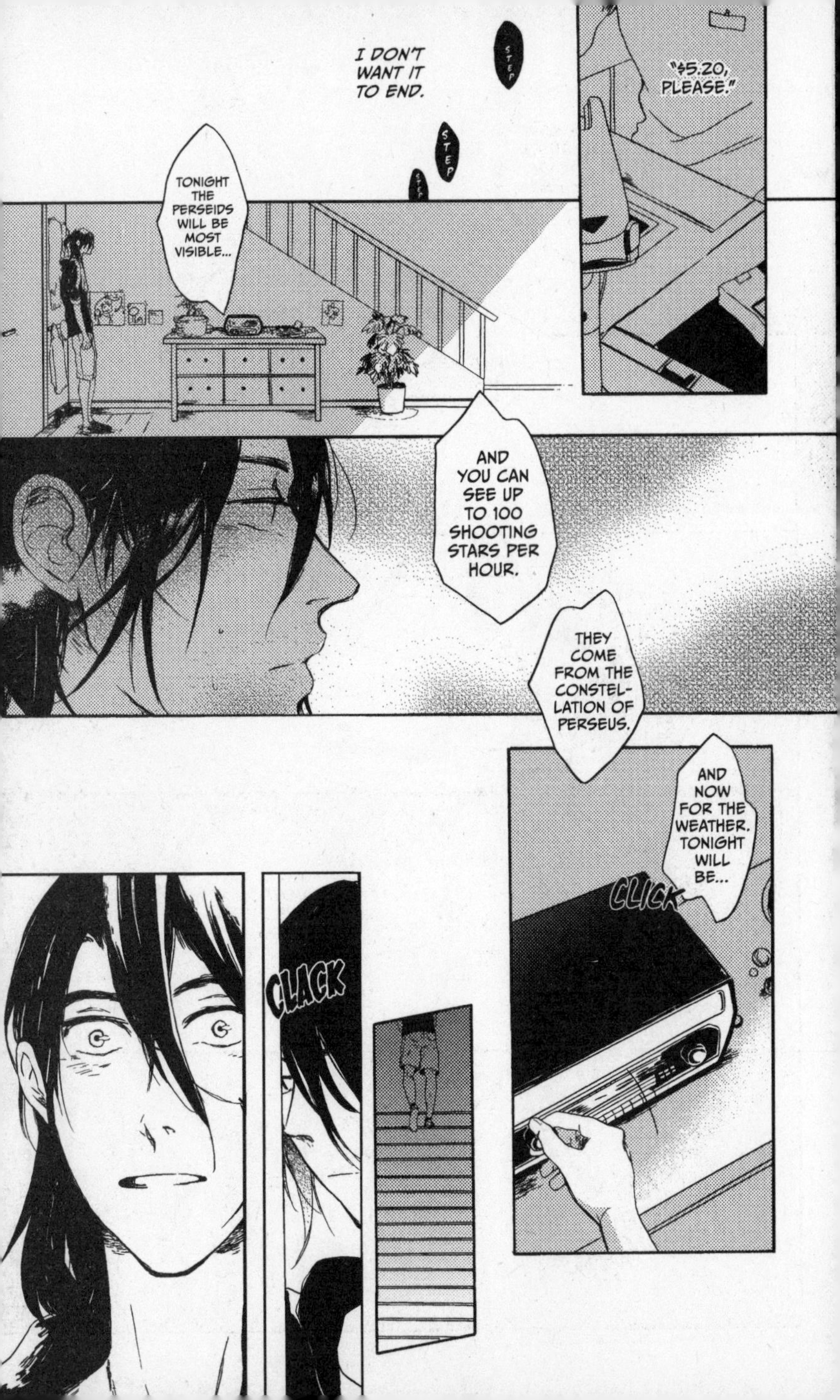
"$5.20, PLEASE."
I DON'T WANT IT TO END.
STEP
STEP
STEP
TONIGHT THE PERSEIDS WILL BE MOST VISIBLE...
AND YOU CAN SEE UP TO 100 SHOOTING STARS PER HOUR.
THEY COME FROM THE CONSTEL-LATION OF PERSEUS.
AND NOW FOR THE WEATHER. TONIGHT WILL BE...
CLICK
CLACK

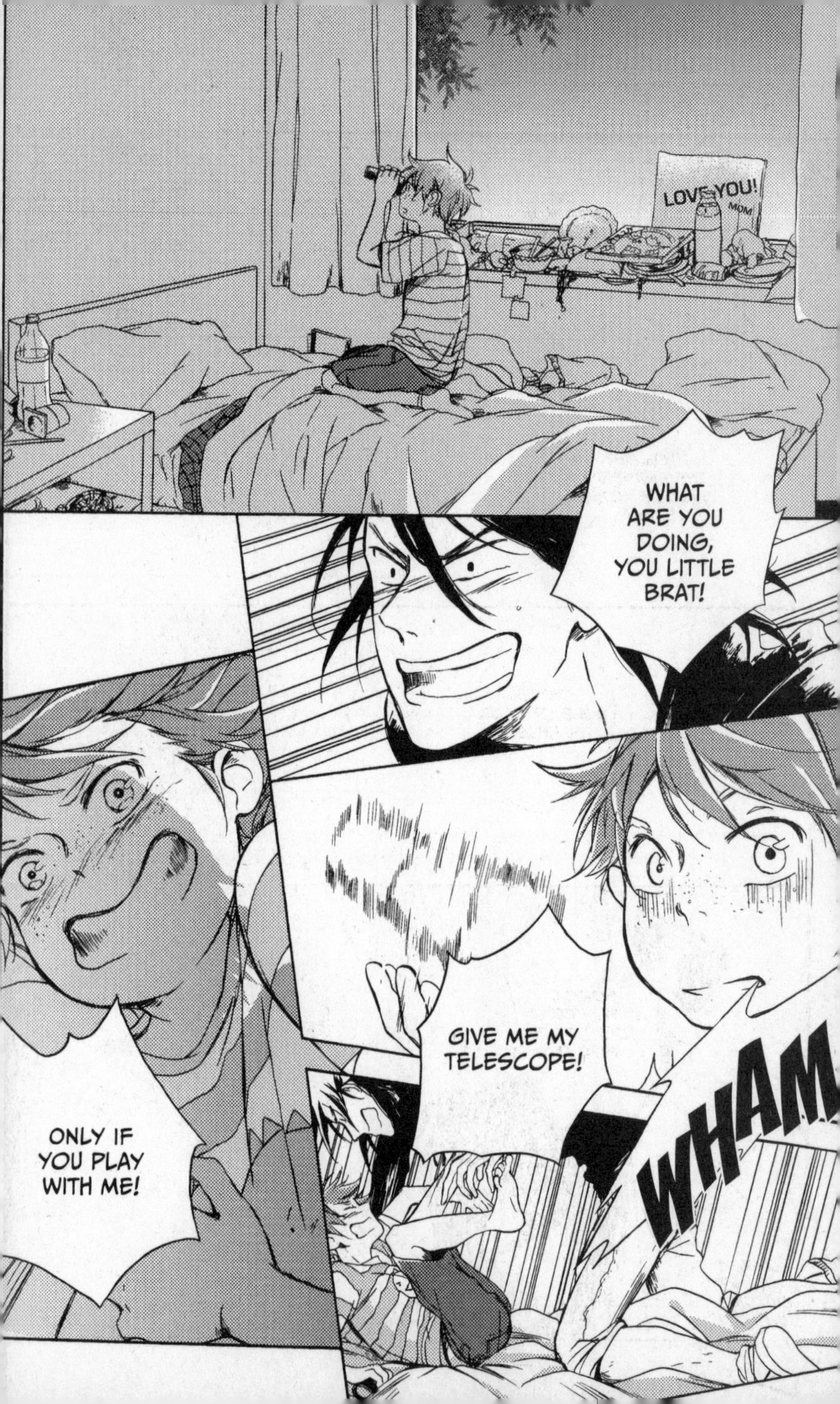
LOVE YOU!
MOM
WHAT ARE YOU DOING, YOU LITTLE BRAT!
GIVE ME MY TELESCOPE!
WHAM
ONLY IF YOU PLAY WITH ME!

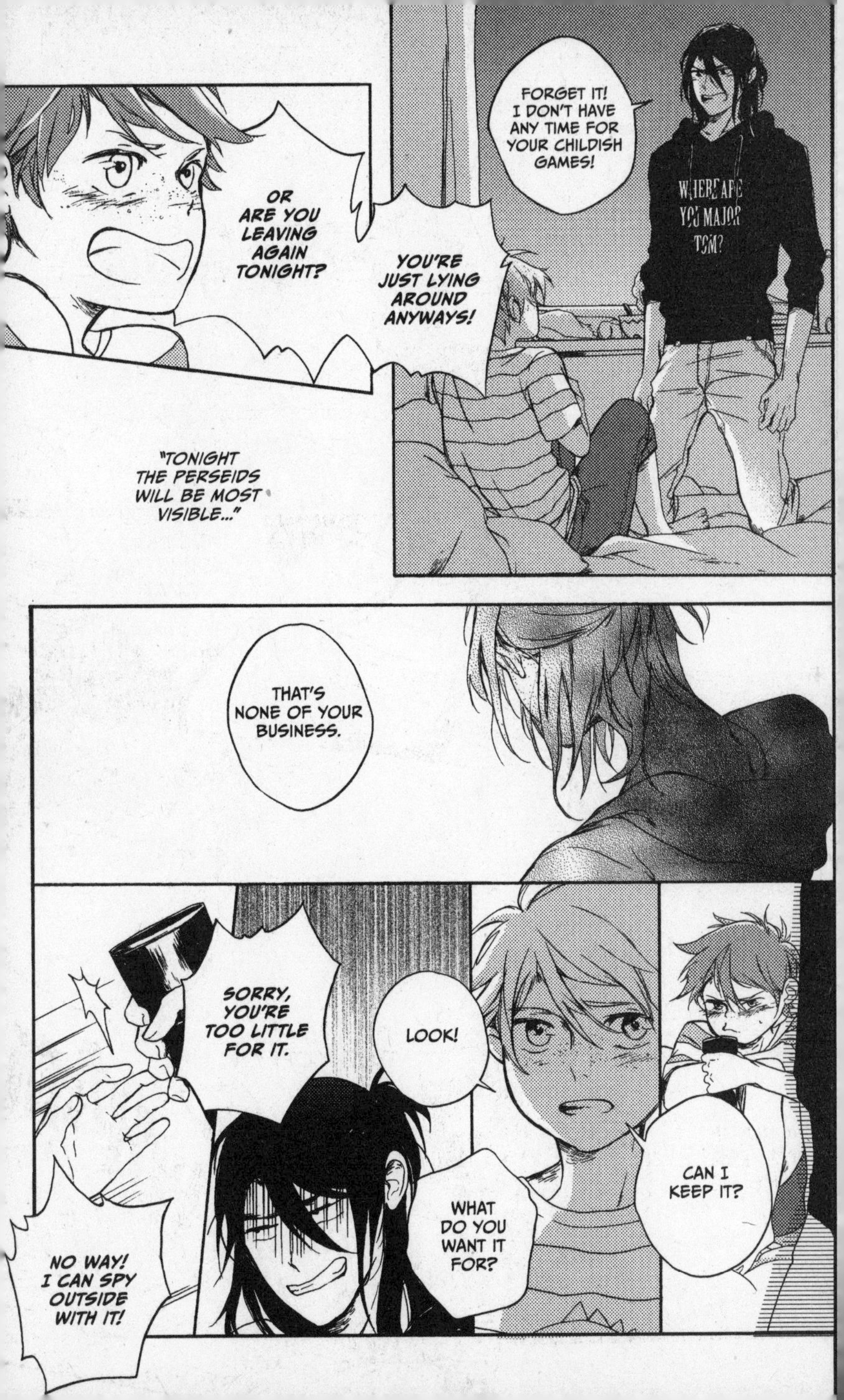
FORGET IT! I DON'T HAVE ANY TIME FOR YOUR CHILDISH GAMES!
WHERE ARE YOU MAJOR TOM?
YOU'RE JUST LYING AROUND ANYWAYS!
OR ARE YOU LEAVING AGAIN TONIGHT?
"TONIGHT THE PERSEIDS WILL BE MOST VISIBLE..."
THAT'S NONE OF YOUR BUSINESS.
CAN I KEEP IT?
LOOK!
WHAT DO YOU WANT IT FOR?
SORRY, YOU'RE TOO LITTLE FOR IT.
NO WAY! I CAN SPY OUTSIDE WITH IT!

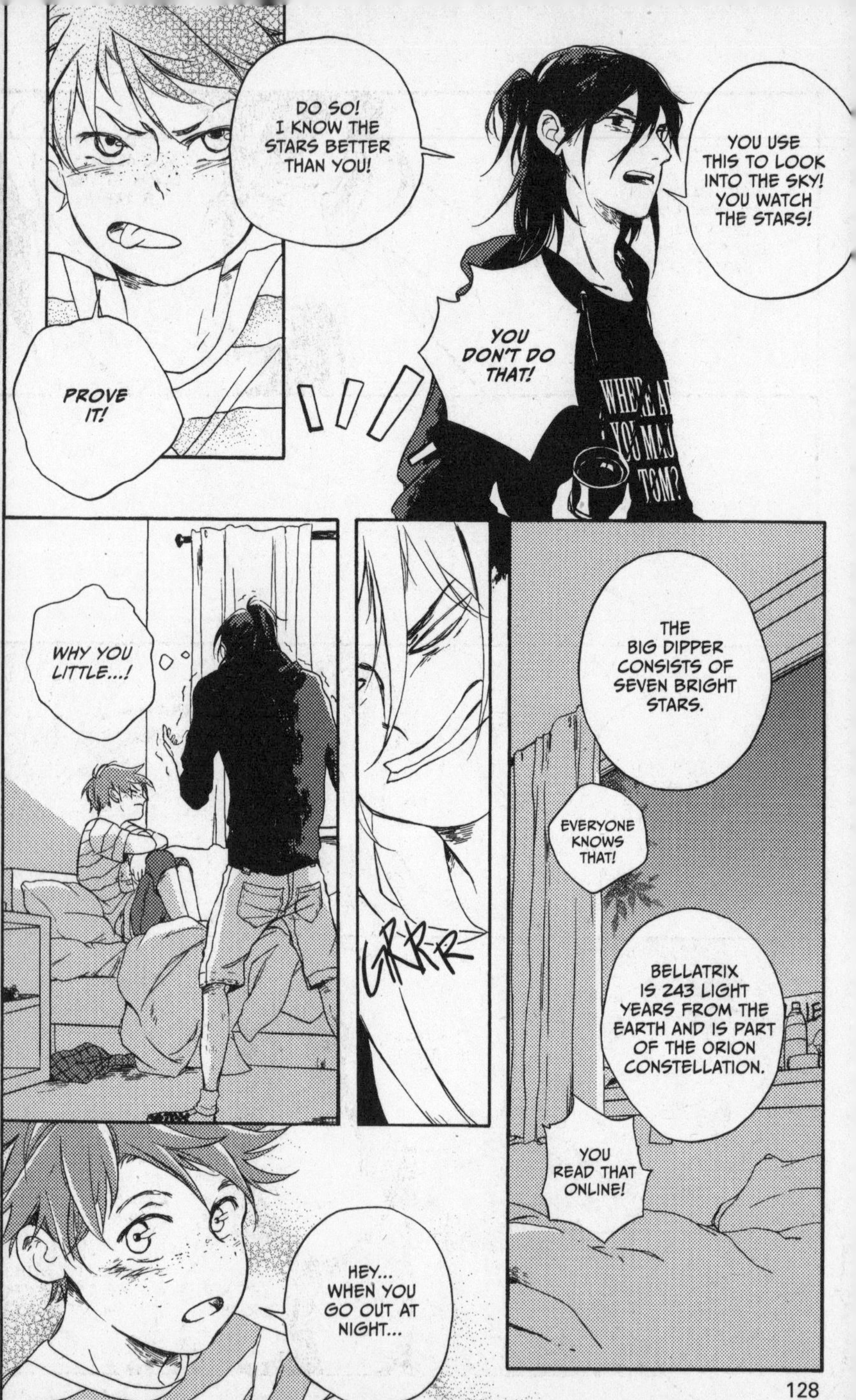
YOU USE THIS TO LOOK INTO THE SKY! YOU WATCH THE STARS!
YOU DON'T DO THAT!
DO SO! I KNOW THE STARS BETTER THAN YOU!
PROVE IT!
THE BIG DIPPER CONSISTS OF SEVEN BRIGHT STARS.
EVERYONE KNOWS THAT!
BELLATRIX IS 243 LIGHT YEARS FROM THE EARTH AND IS PART OF THE ORION CONSTELLATION.
YOU READ THAT ONLINE!
GRRR
WHY YOU LITTLE...!
HEY... WHEN YOU GO OUT AT NIGHT...

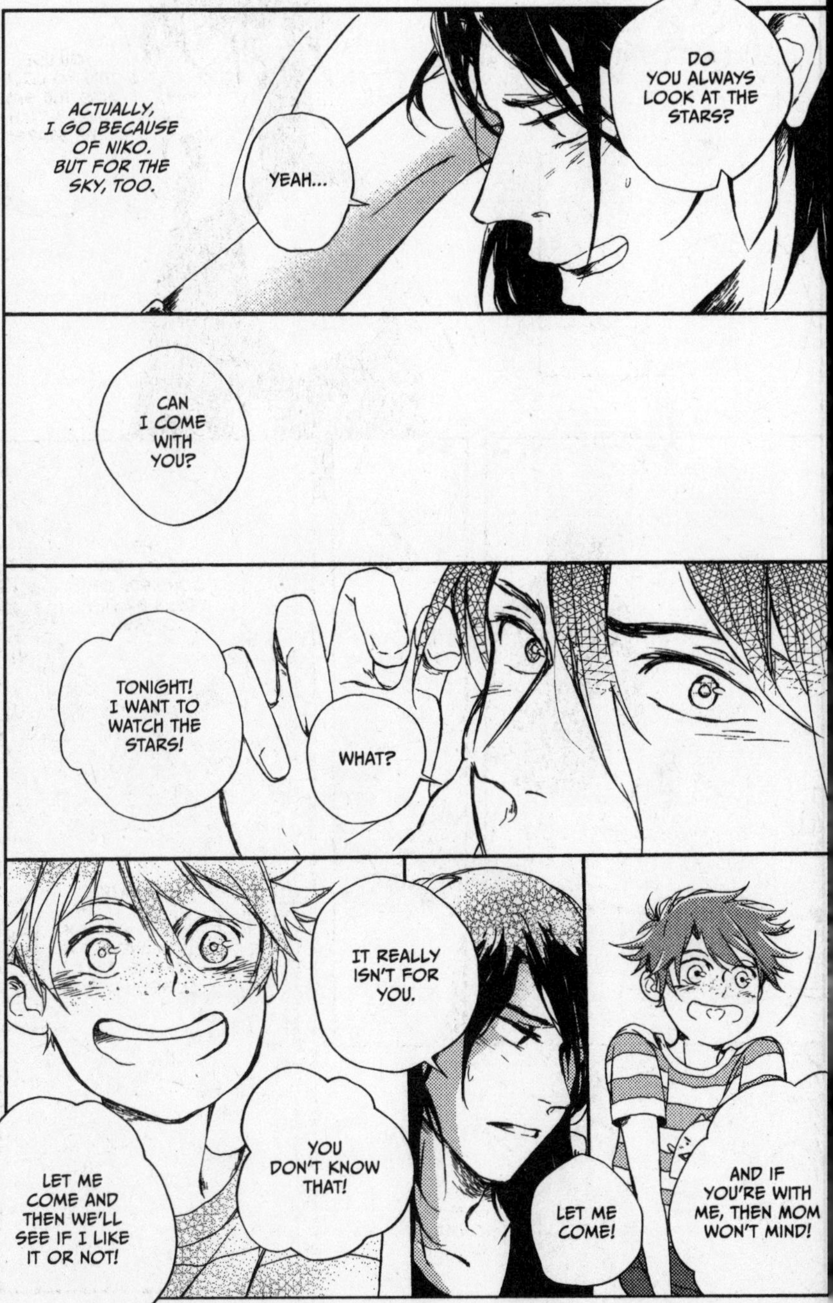
DO YOU ALWAYS LOOK AT THE STARS?
YEAH...
ACTUALLY, I GO BECAUSE OF NIKO. BUT FOR THE SKY, TOO.
CAN I COME WITH YOU?
WHAT?
TONIGHT! I WANT TO WATCH THE STARS!
AND IF YOU'RE WITH ME, THEN MOM WON'T MIND!
LET ME COME!
IT REALLY ISN'T FOR YOU.
YOU DON'T KNOW THAT!
LET ME COME AND THEN WE'LL SEE IF I LIKE IT OR NOT!

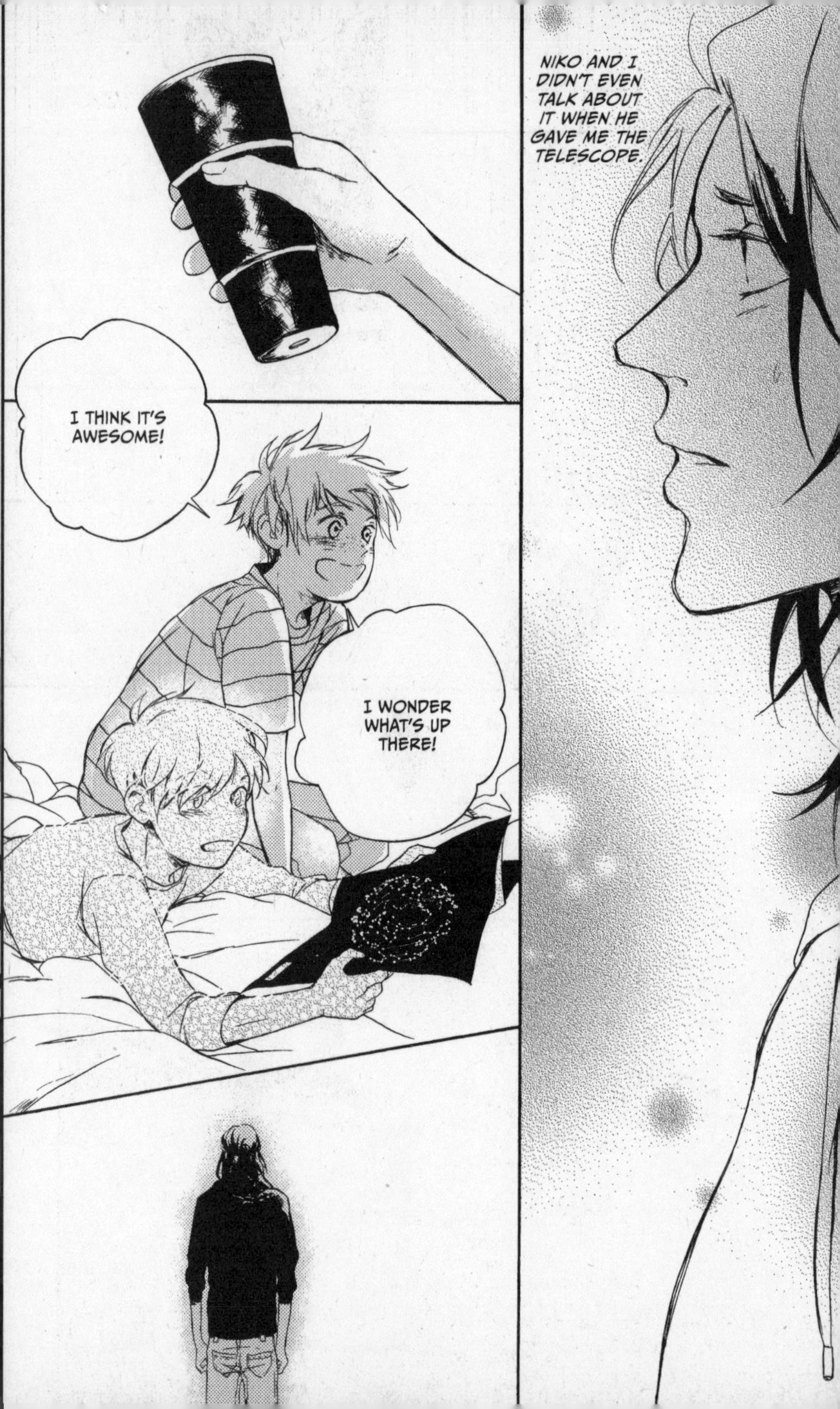
NIKO AND I DIDN'T EVEN TALK ABOUT IT WHEN HE GAVE ME THE TELESCOPE.
I THINK IT'S AWESOME!
I WONDER WHAT'S UP THERE!

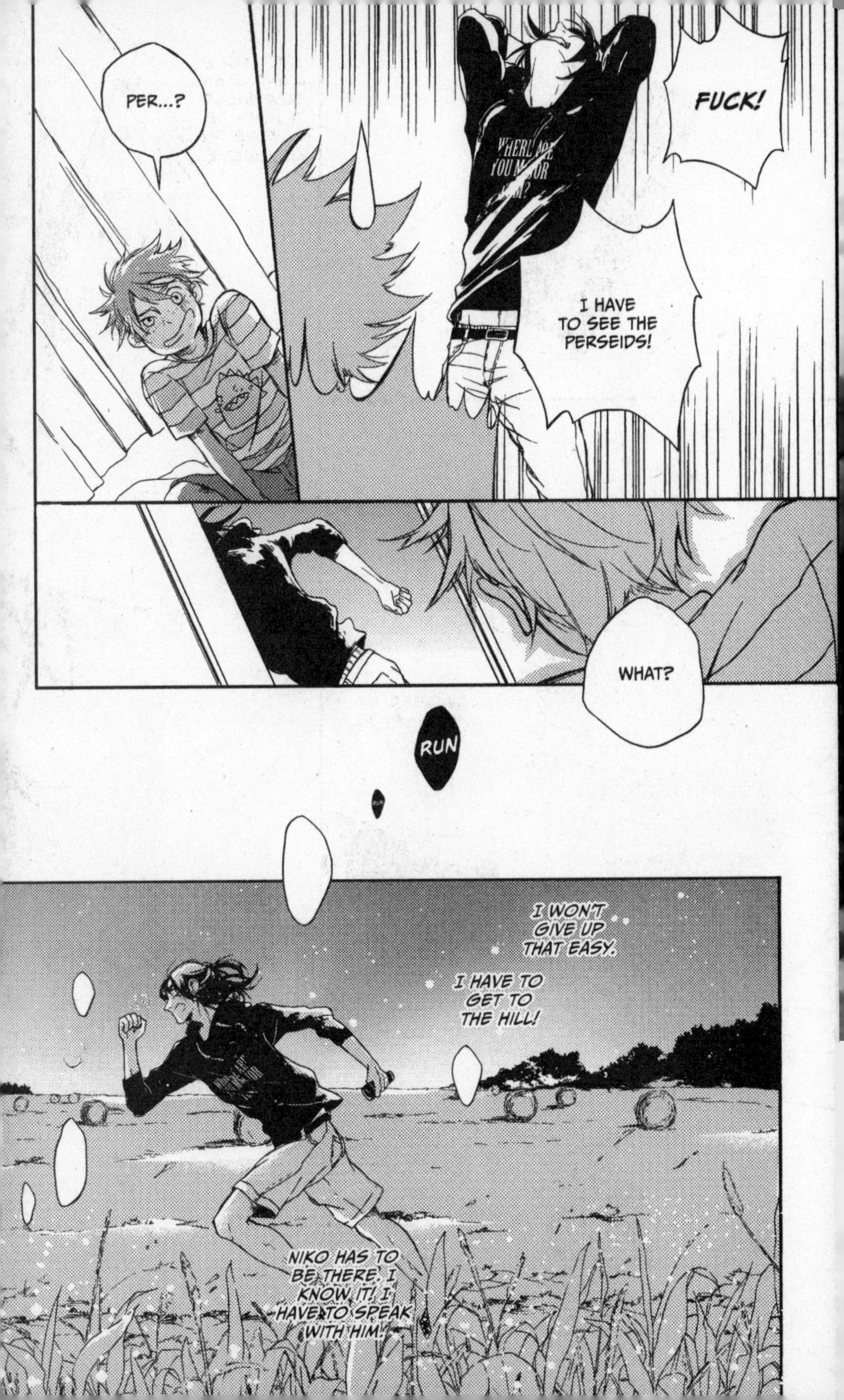
FUCK!
I HAVE TO SEE THE PERSEIDS!
PER...?
WHAT?
RUN
RUN
I WON'T GIVE UP THAT EASY.
I HAVE TO GET TO THE HILL!
NIKO HAS TO BE THERE. I KNOW IT! I HAVE TO SPEAK WITH HIM!

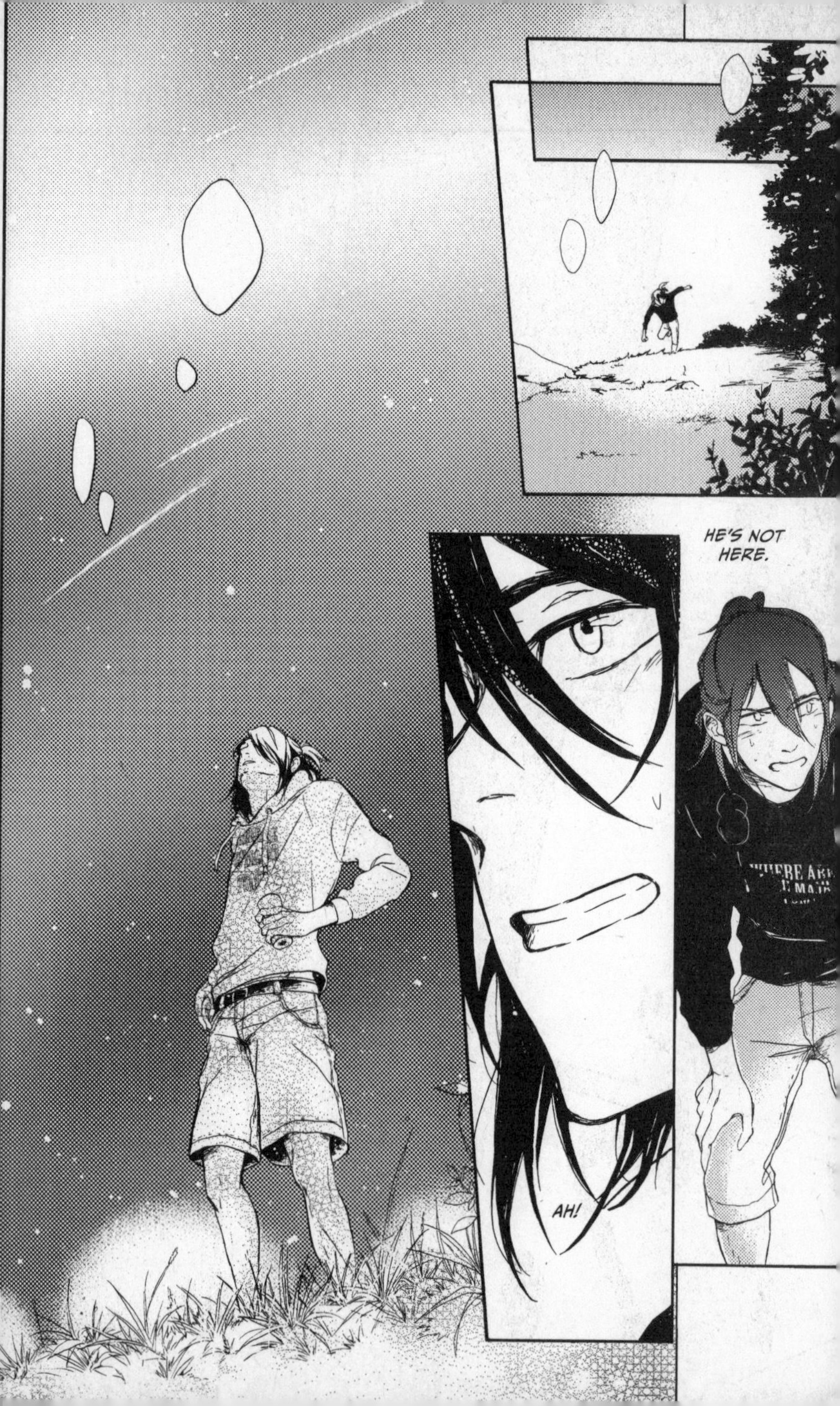
HE'S NOT HERE.
AH!

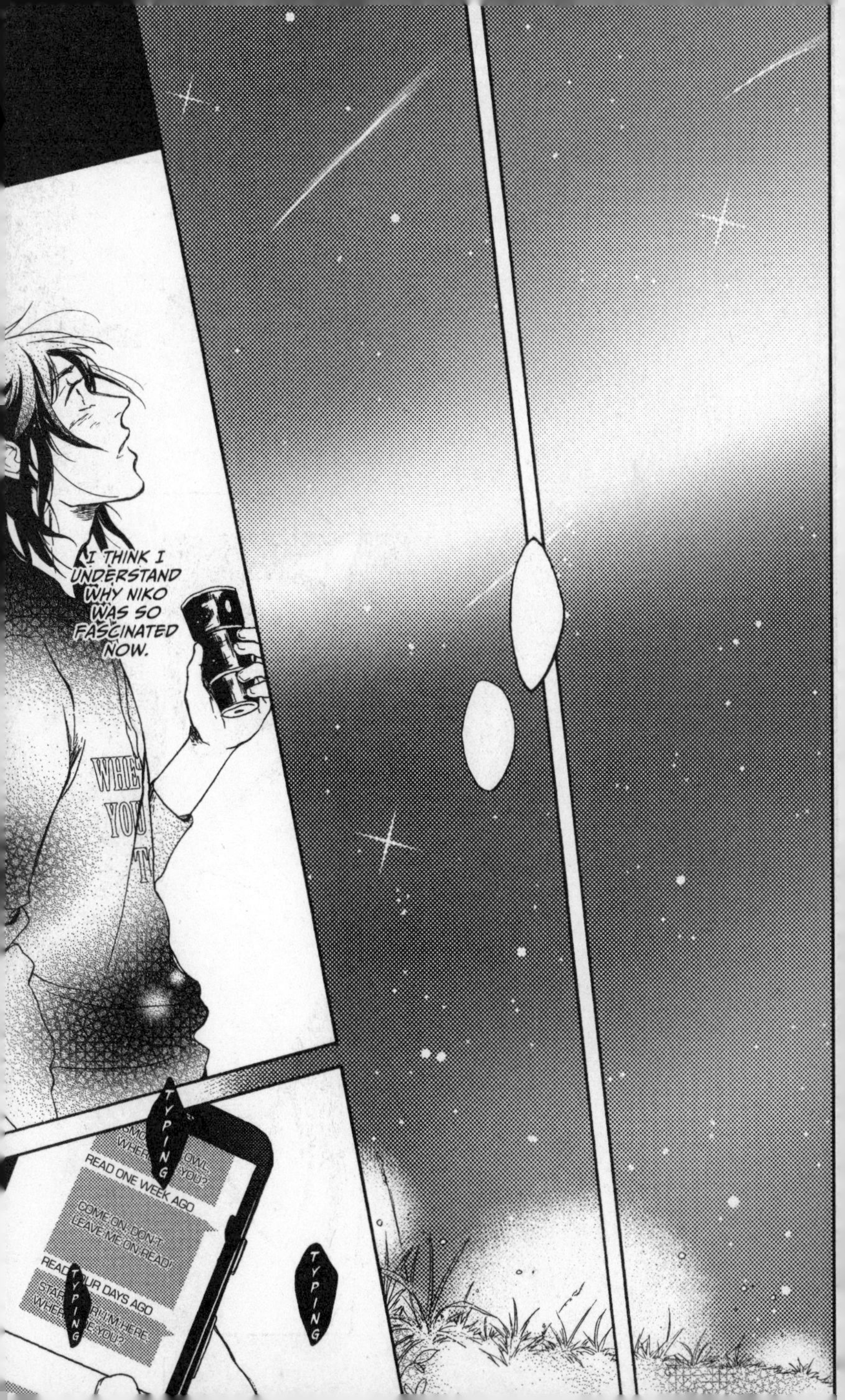
I THINK I UNDERSTAND WHY NIKO WAS SO FASCINATED NOW.
TYPING
READ ONE WEEK AGO
COME ON. DON'T LEAVE ME ON READ!
TYPING
TYPING

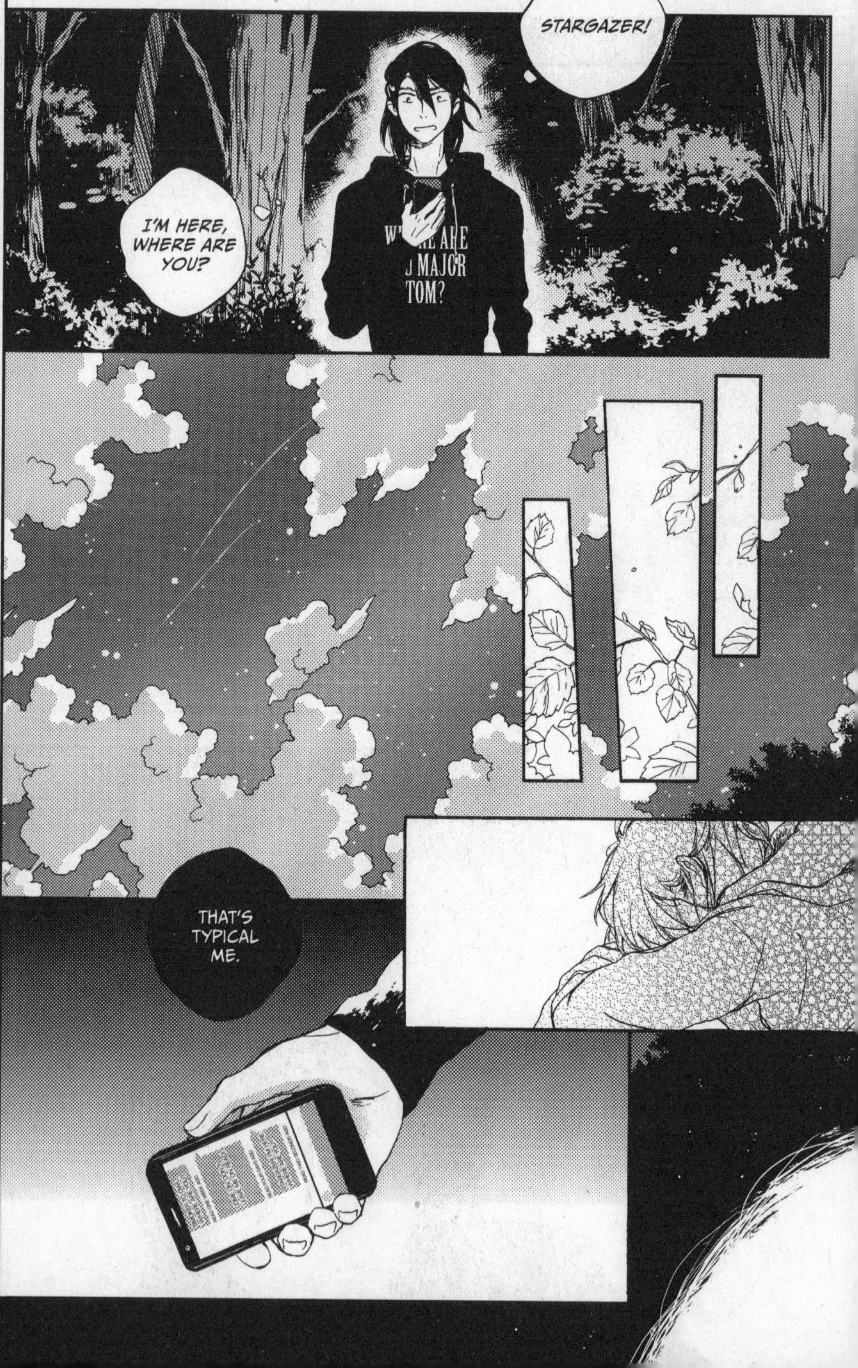
STARGAZER!
I'M HERE, WHERE ARE YOU?
THAT'S TYPICAL ME.

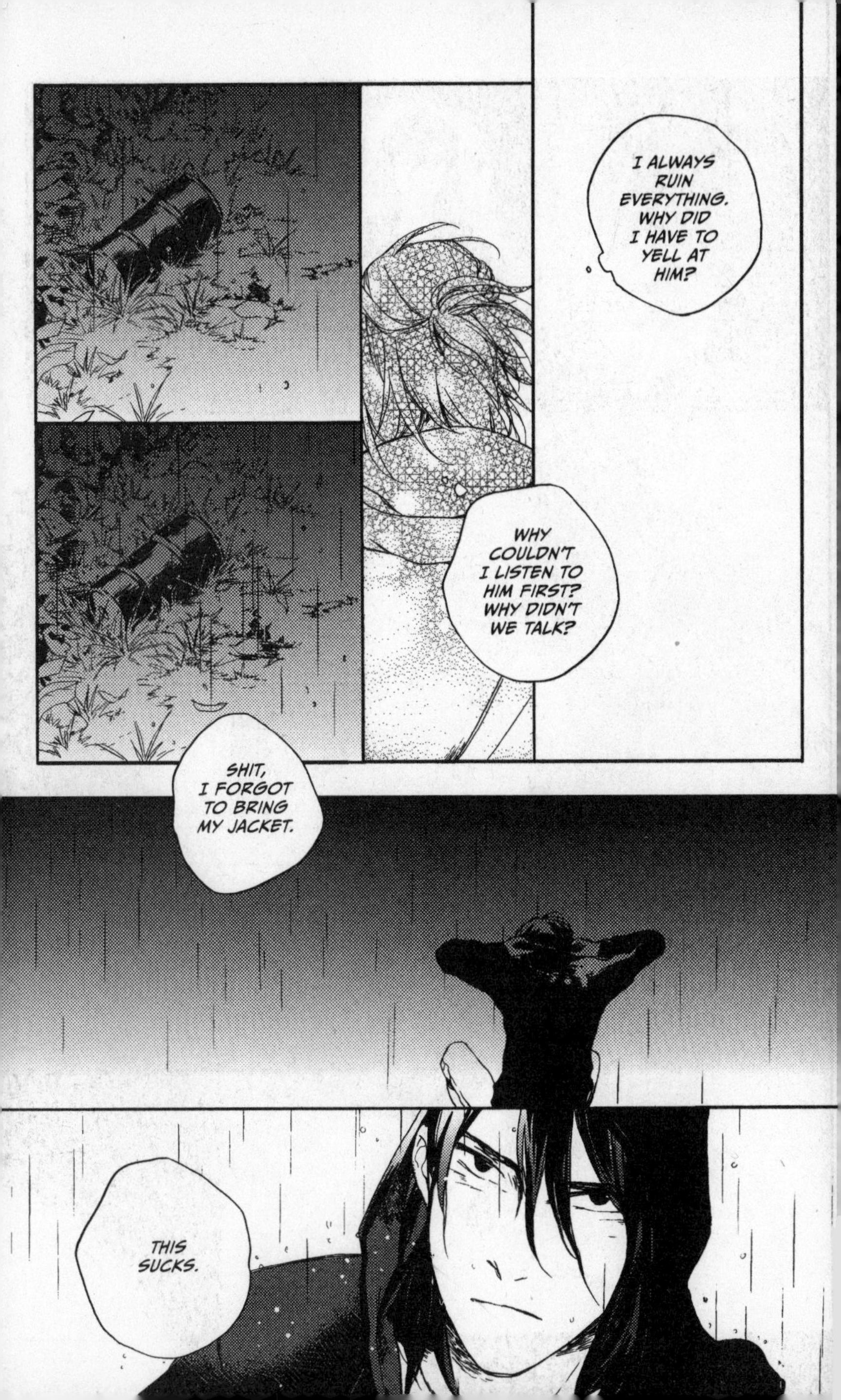
I ALWAYS RUIN EVERYTHING. WHY DID I HAVE TO YELL AT HIM?
WHY COULDN'T I LISTEN TO HIM FIRST? WHY DIDN'T WE TALK?
SHIT, I FORGOT TO BRING MY JACKET.
THIS SUCKS.

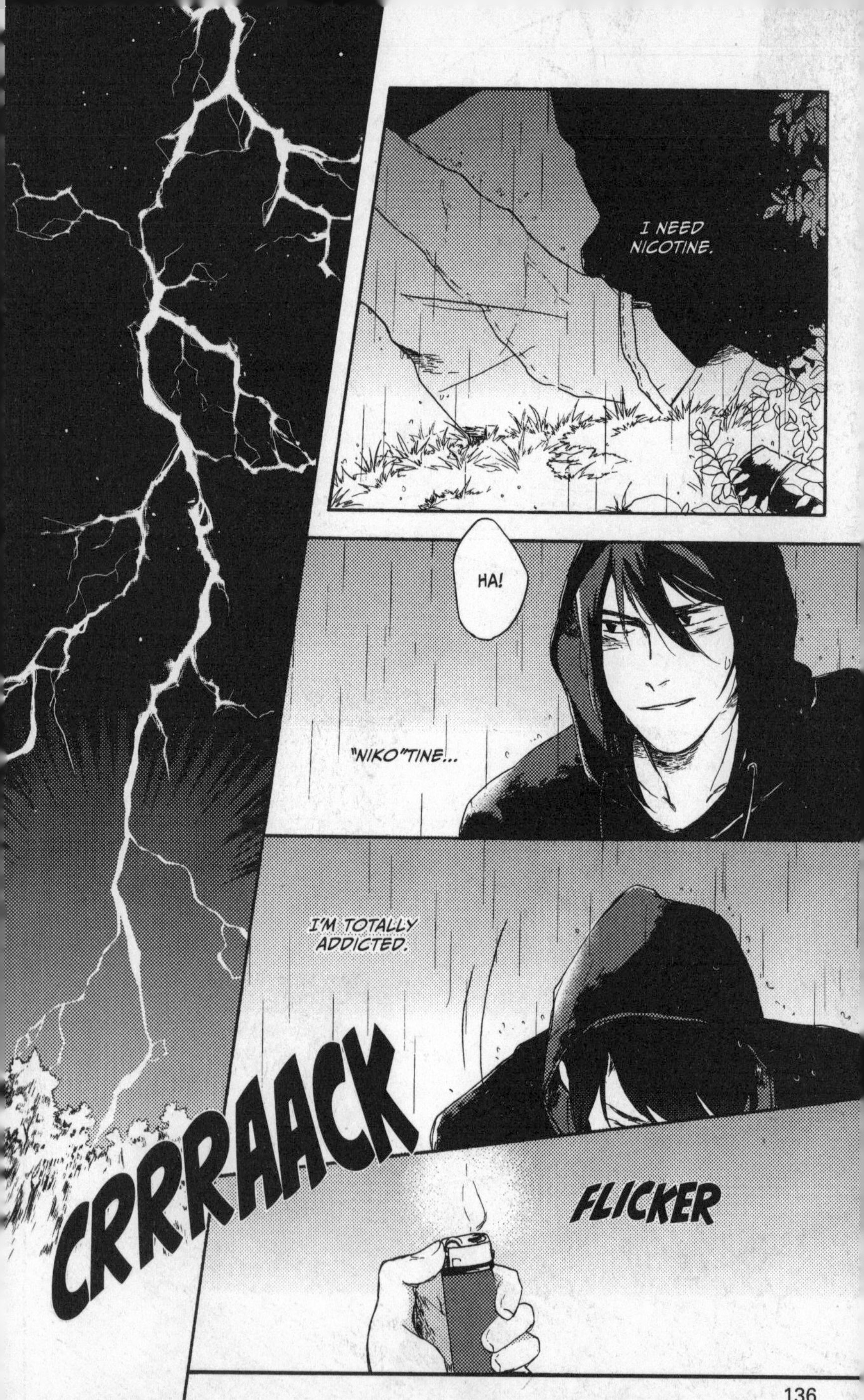
I NEED NICOTINE.
HA!
"NIKO"TINE...
I'M TOTALLY ADDICTED.
FLICKER
CRRRAACK

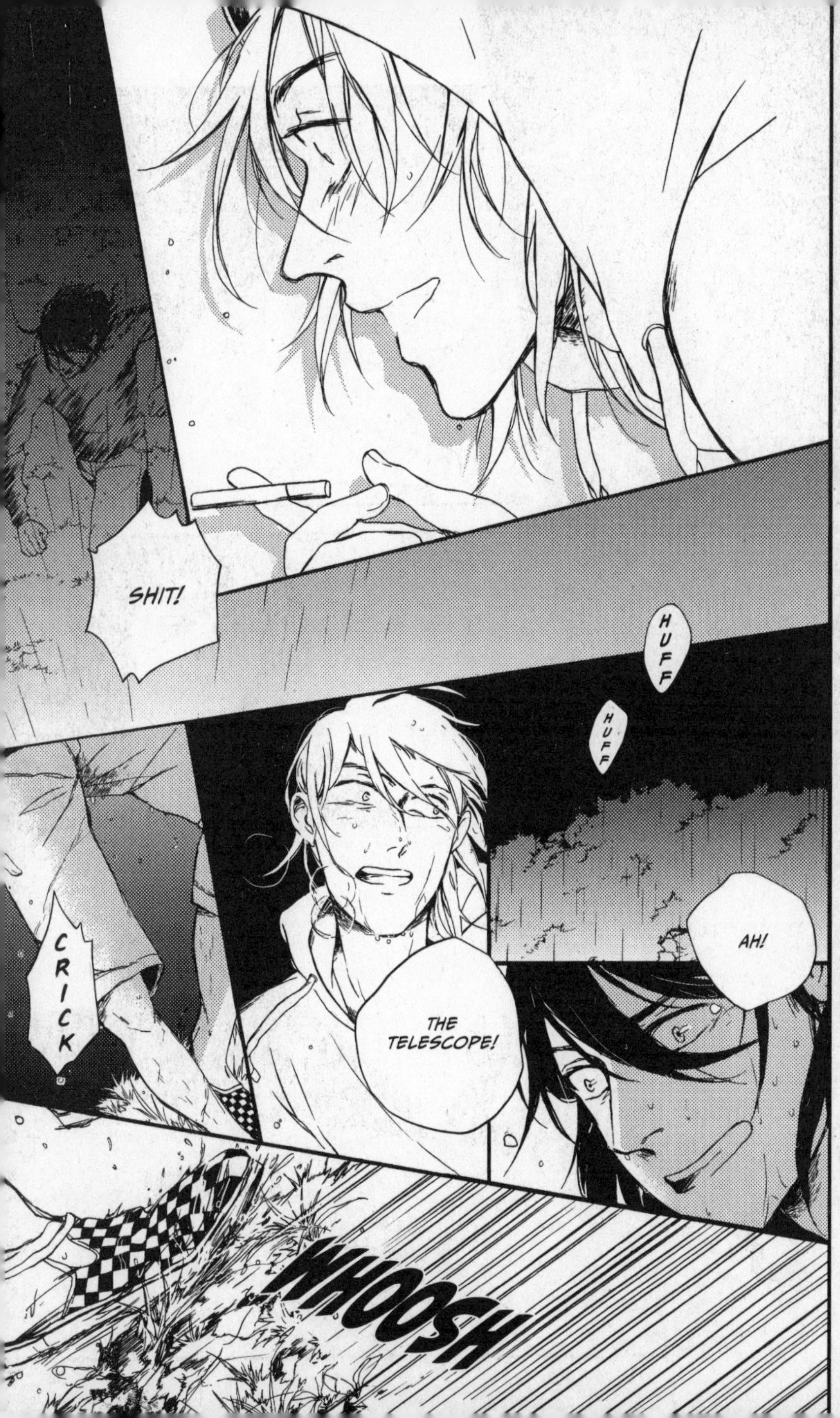
SHIT!
HUFF
HUFF
AH!
THE TELESCOPE!
CRICK
WHOOSH

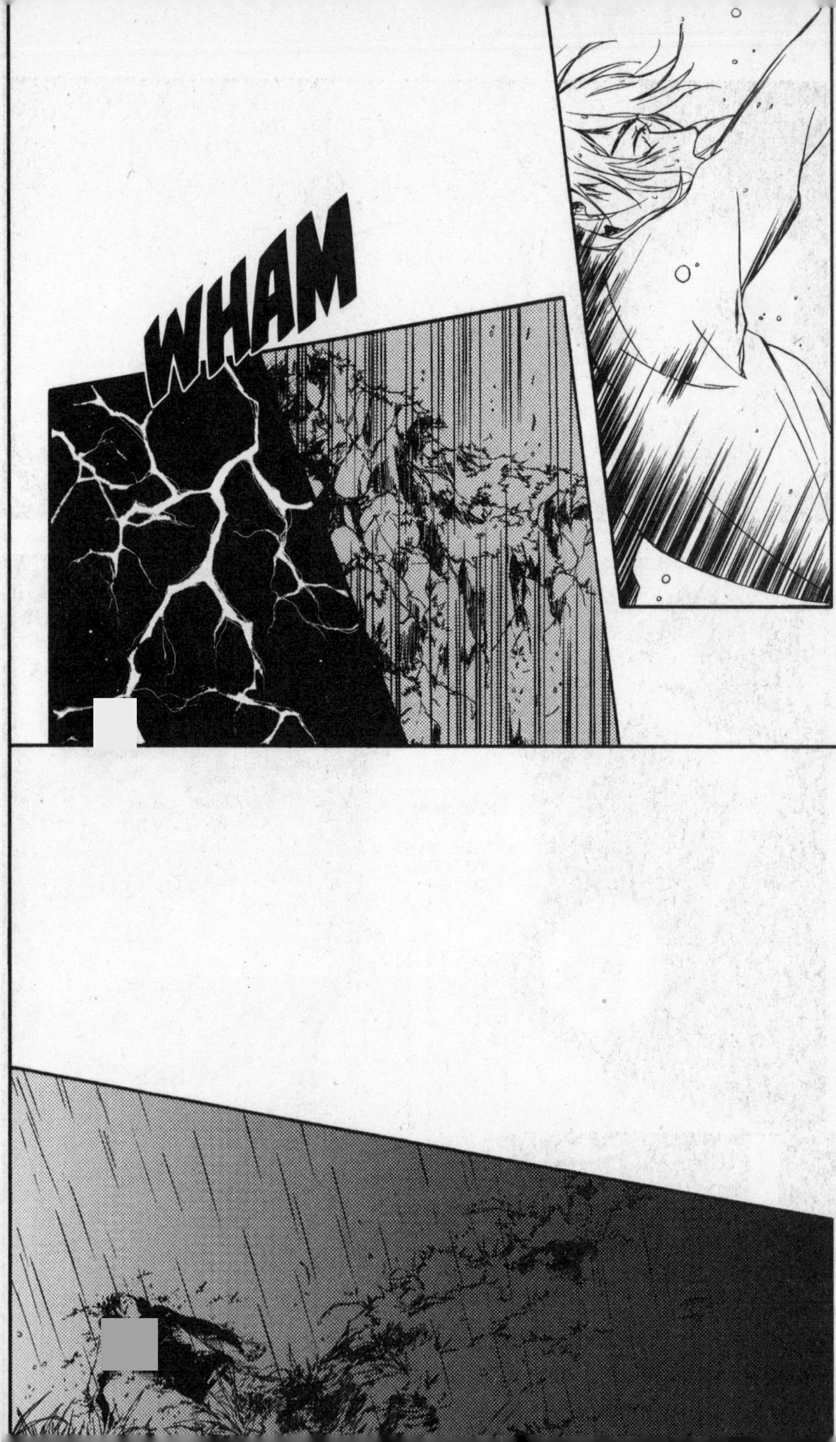
WHAM

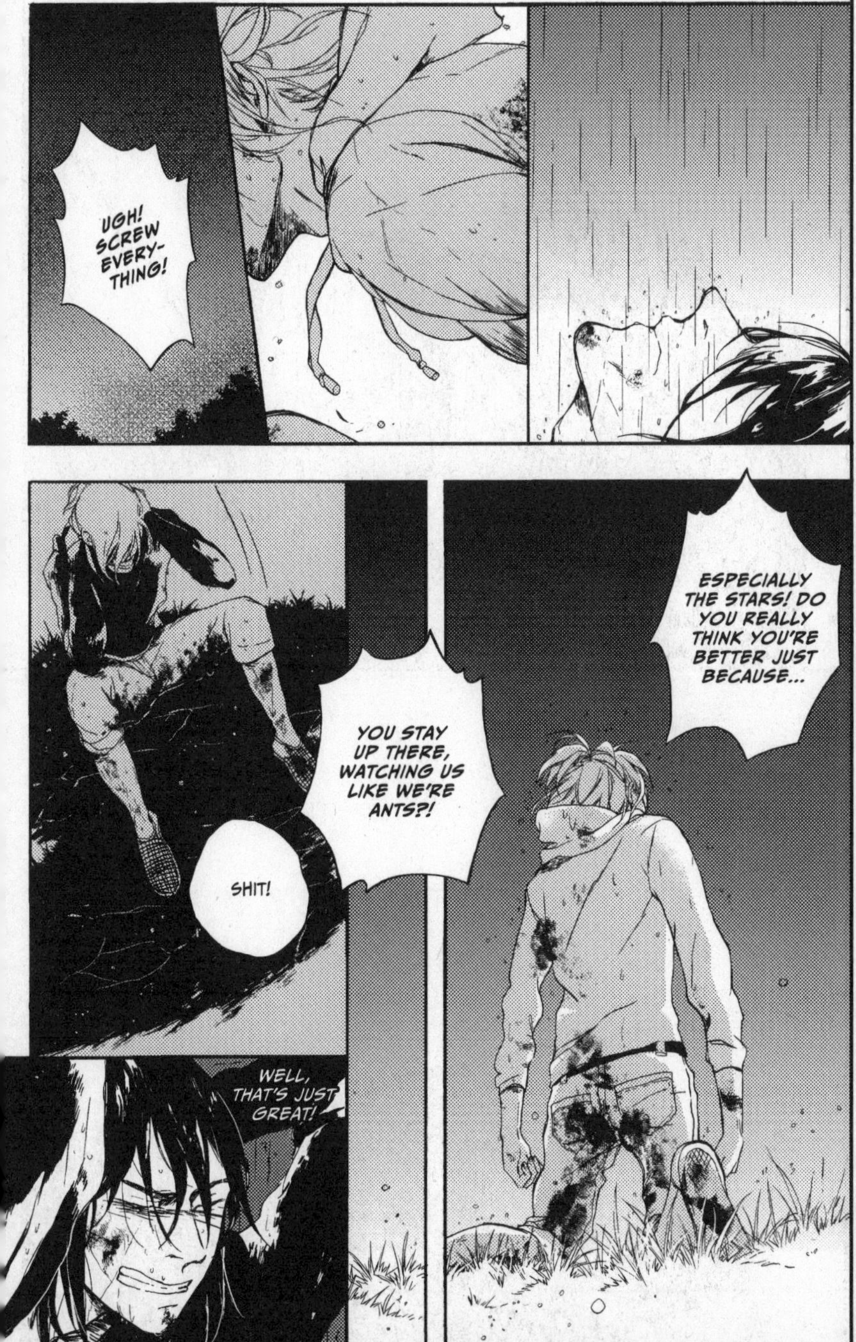
UGH! SCREW EVERY-THING!
ESPECIALLY THE STARS! DO YOU REALLY THINK YOU'RE BETTER JUST BECAUSE...
YOU STAY UP THERE, WATCHING US LIKE WE'RE ANTS?!
SHIT!
WELL, THAT'S JUST GREAT!

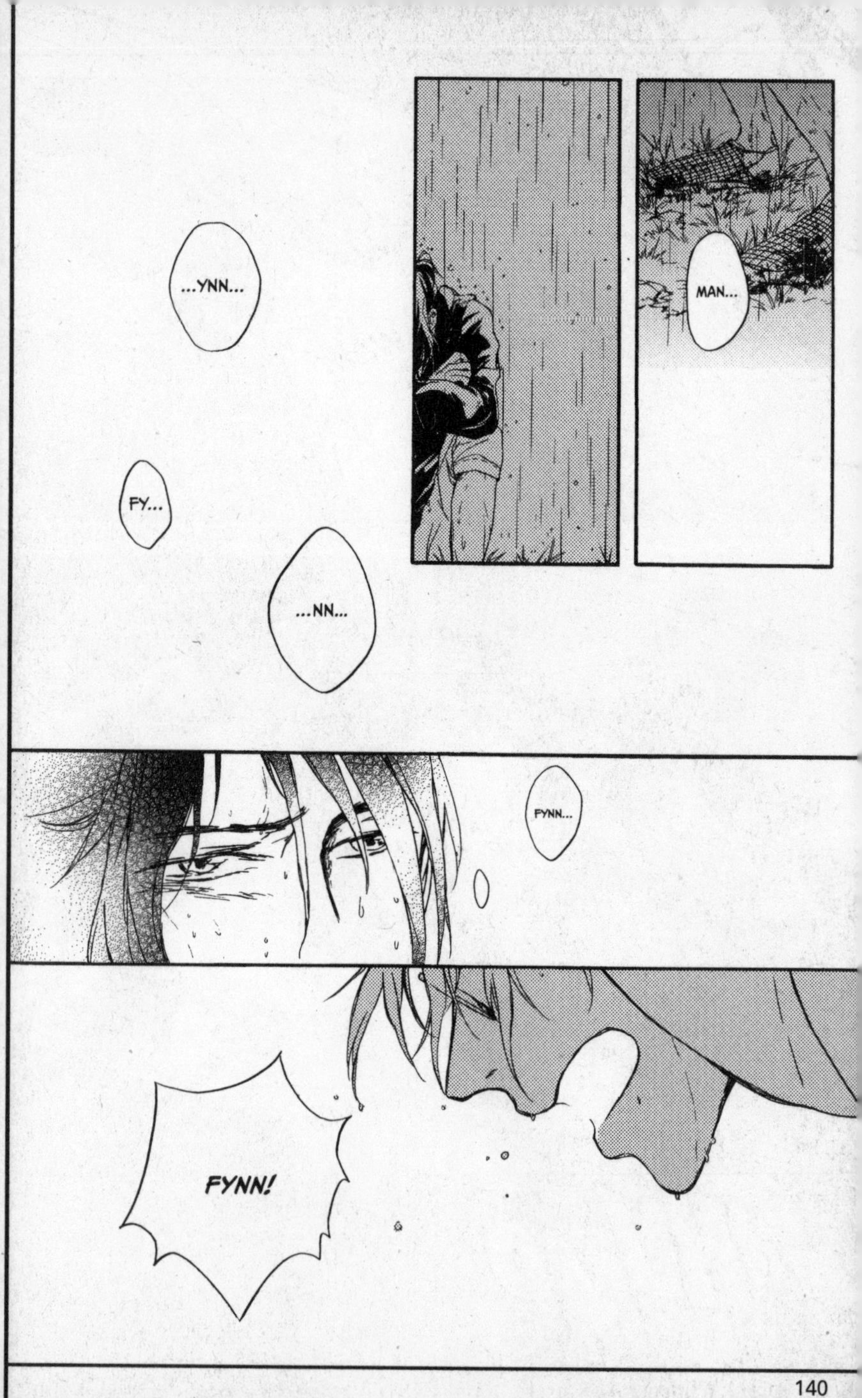
MAN...
...YNN...
FY...
...NN...
FYNN...
FYNN!

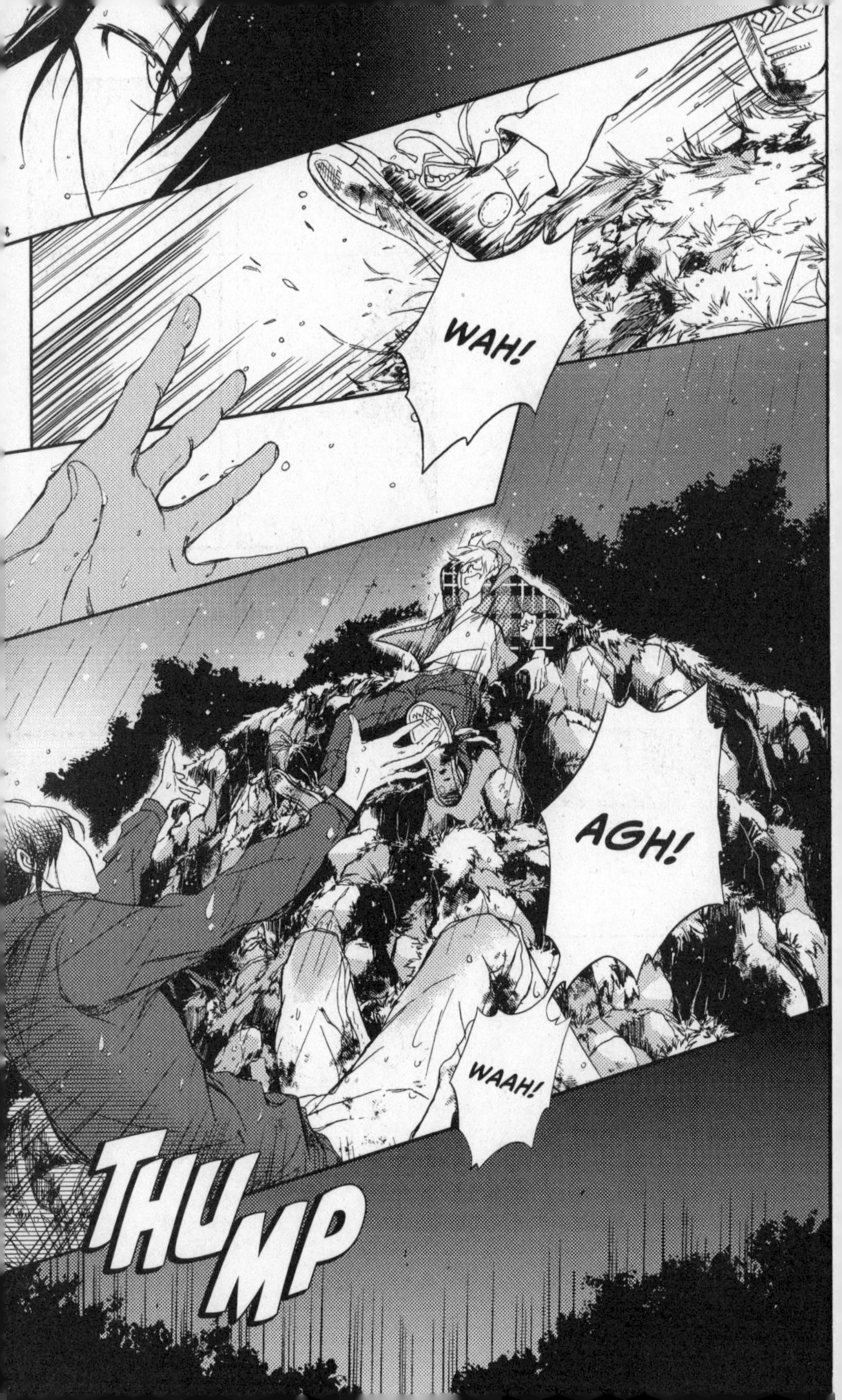
WAH!
AGH!
WAAH!
THUMP

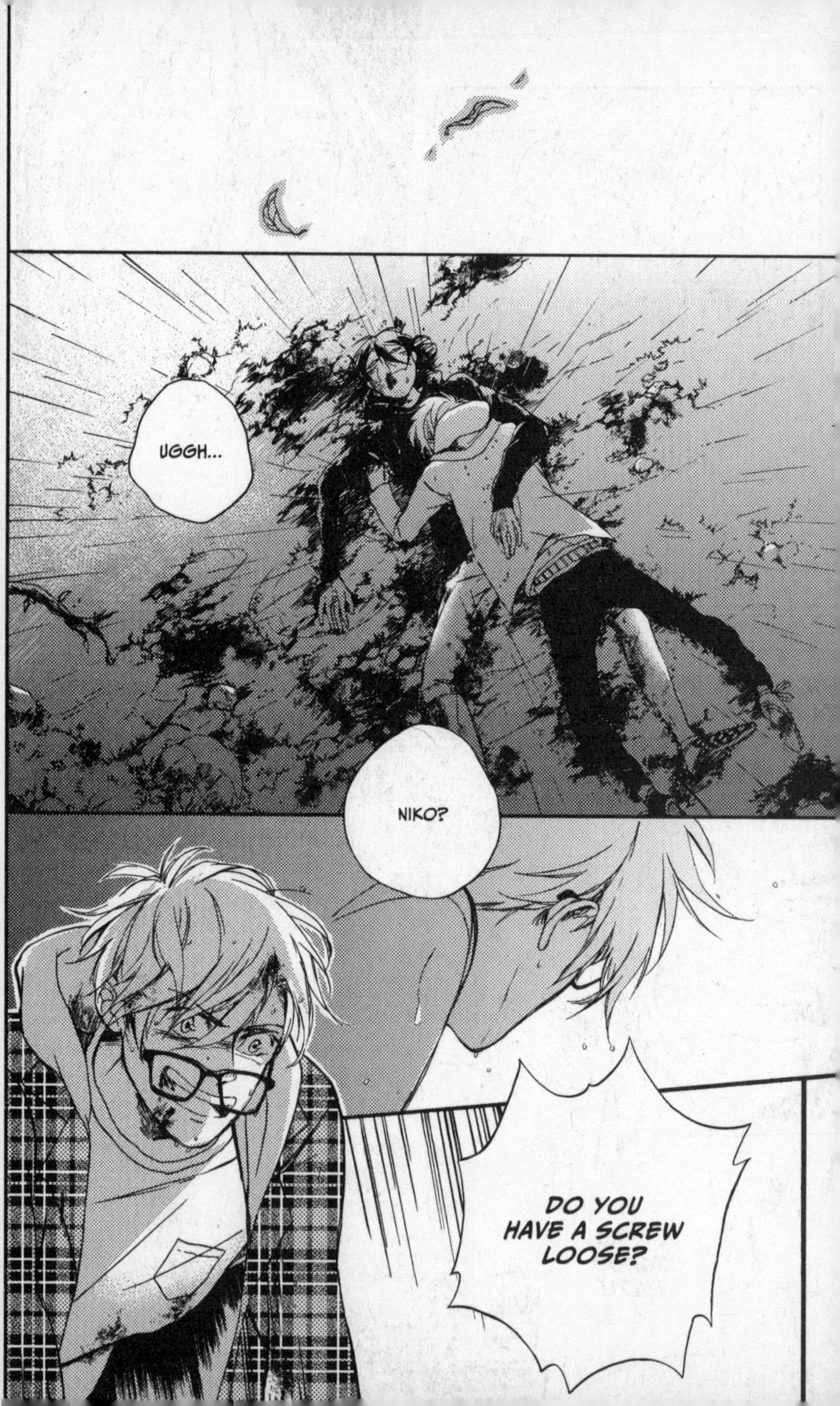
UGGH...
NIKO?
DO YOU HAVE A SCREW LOOSE?

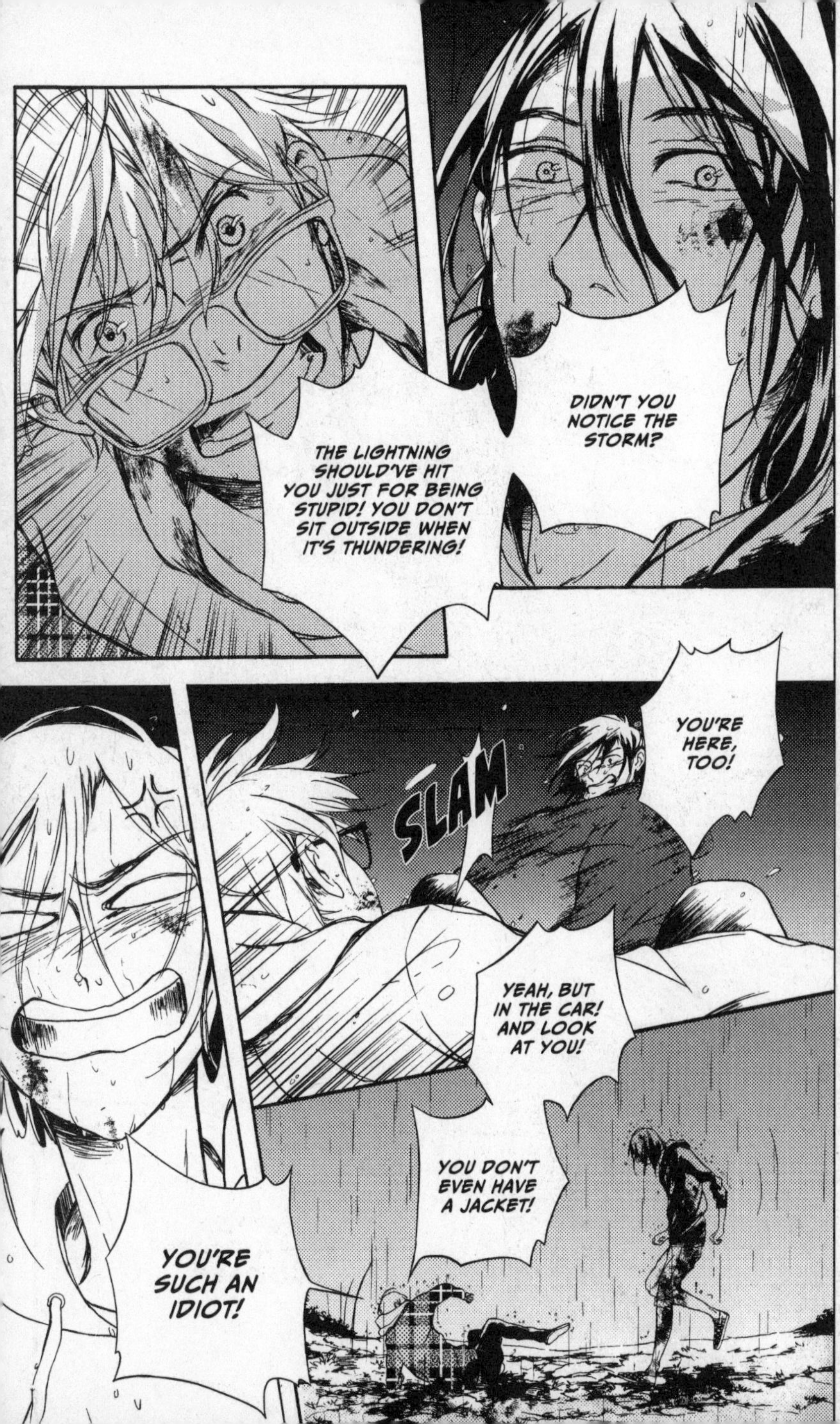
DIDN'T YOU NOTICE THE STORM?
THE LIGHTNING SHOULD'VE HIT YOU JUST FOR BEING STUPID! YOU DON'T SIT OUTSIDE WHEN IT'S THUNDERING!
YOU'RE HERE, TOO!
SLAM
YEAH, BUT IN THE CAR! AND LOOK AT YOU!
YOU DON'T EVEN HAVE A JACKET!
YOU'RE SUCH AN IDIOT!

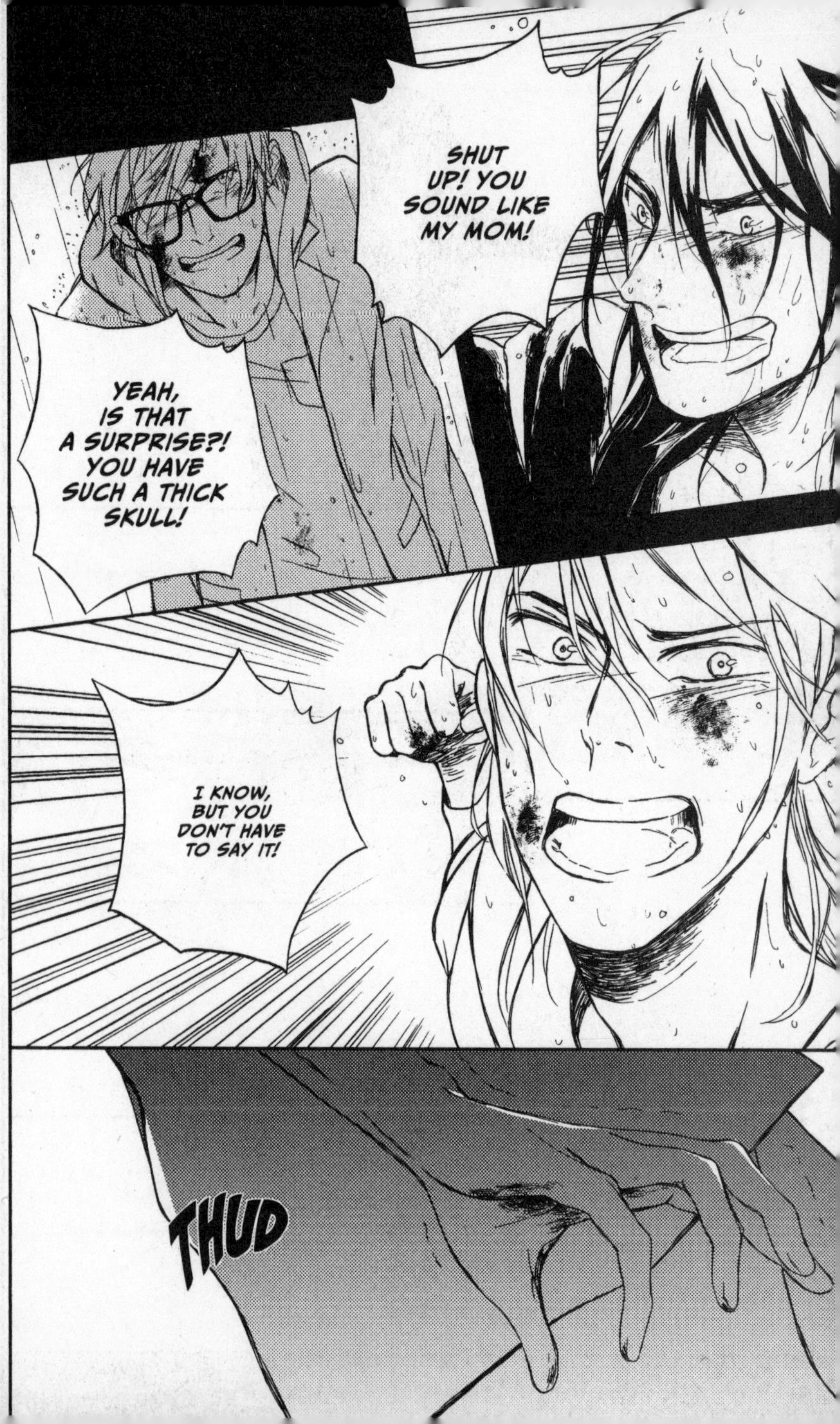
SHUT UP! YOU SOUND LIKE MY MOM!
YEAH, IS THAT A SURPRISE?! YOU HAVE SUCH A THICK SKULL!
I KNOW, BUT YOU DON'T HAVE TO SAY IT!
THUD

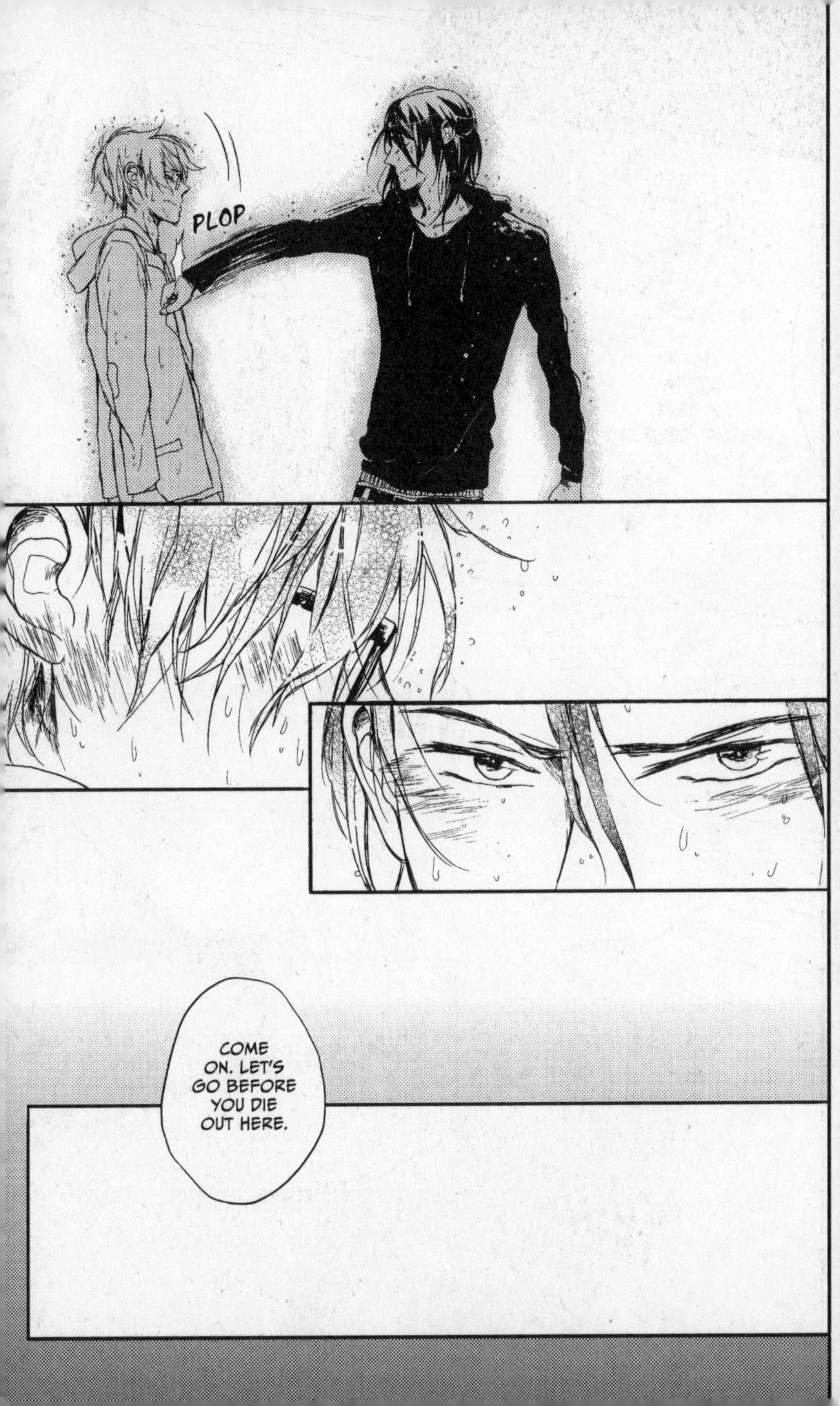
PLOP
COME ON. LET'S GO BEFORE YOU DIE OUT HERE.

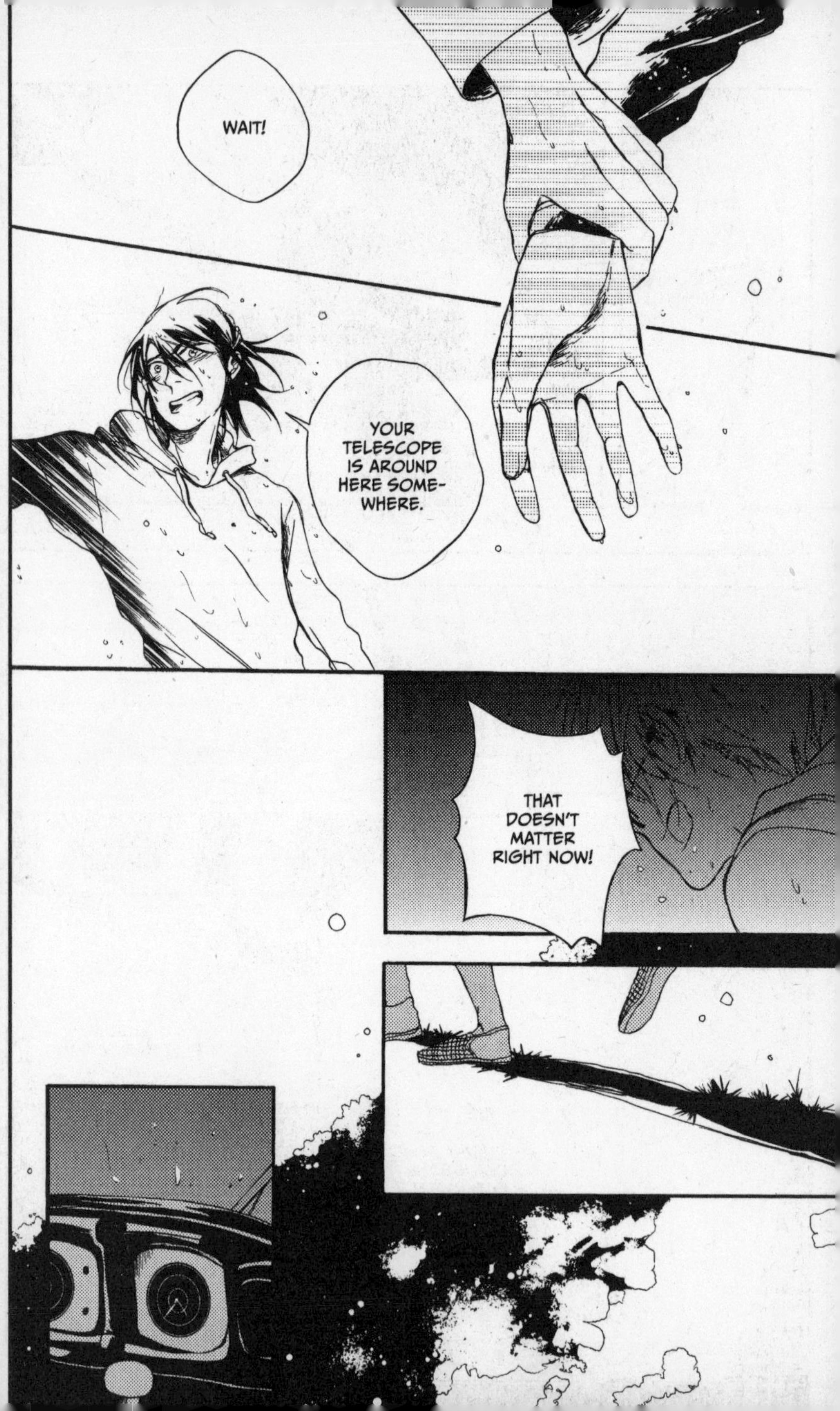
WAIT!
YOUR TELESCOPE IS AROUND HERE SOME-WHERE.
THAT DOESN'T MATTER RIGHT NOW!

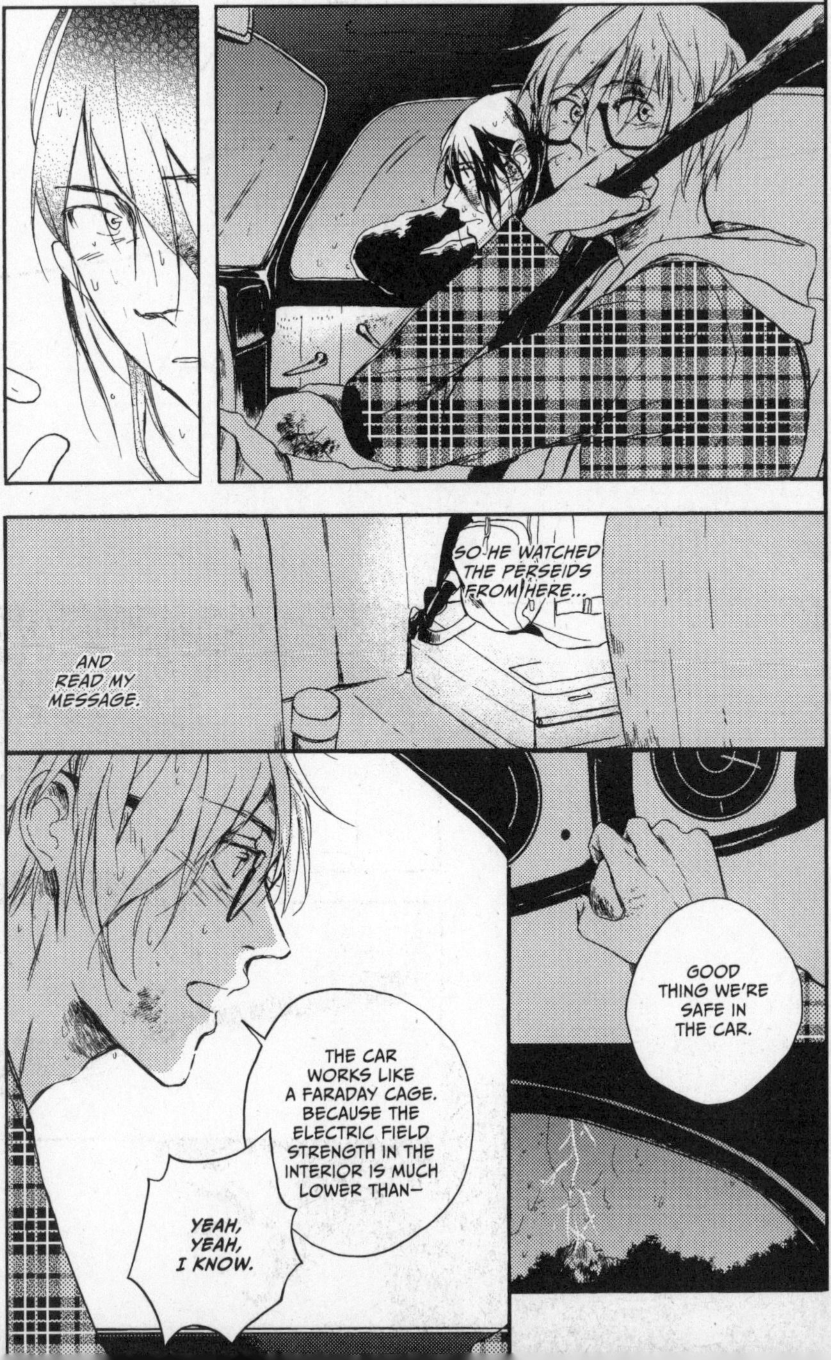
SO HE WATCHED THE PERSEIDS FROM HERE...
AND READ MY MESSAGE.
GOOD THING WE'RE SAFE IN THE CAR.
THE CAR WORKS LIKE A FARADAY CAGE. BECAUSE THE ELECTRIC FIELD STRENGTH IN THE INTERIOR IS MUCH LOWER THAN—
YEAH, YEAH, I KNOW.

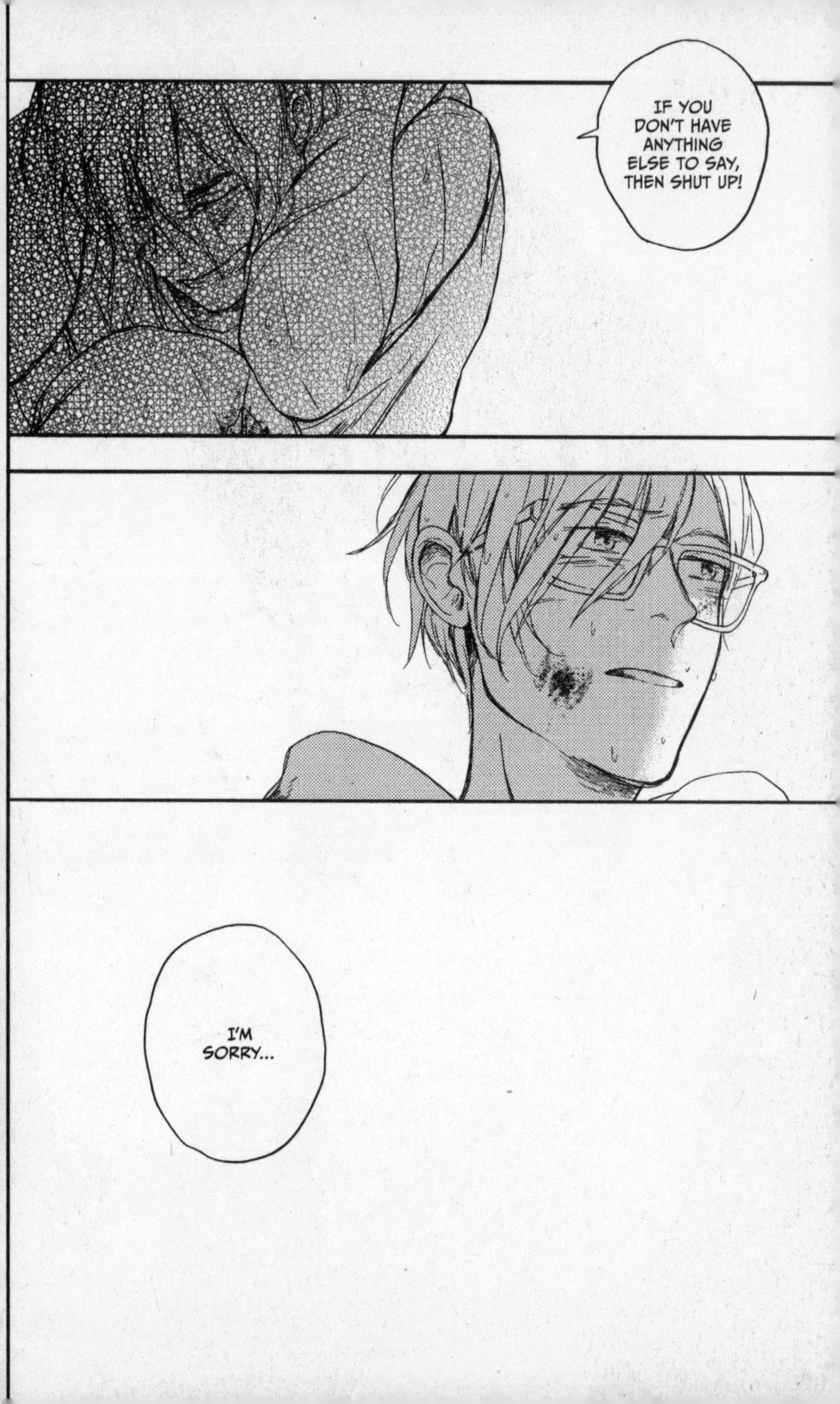
IF YOU DON'T HAVE ANYTHING ELSE TO SAY, THEN SHUT UP!
I'M SORRY...

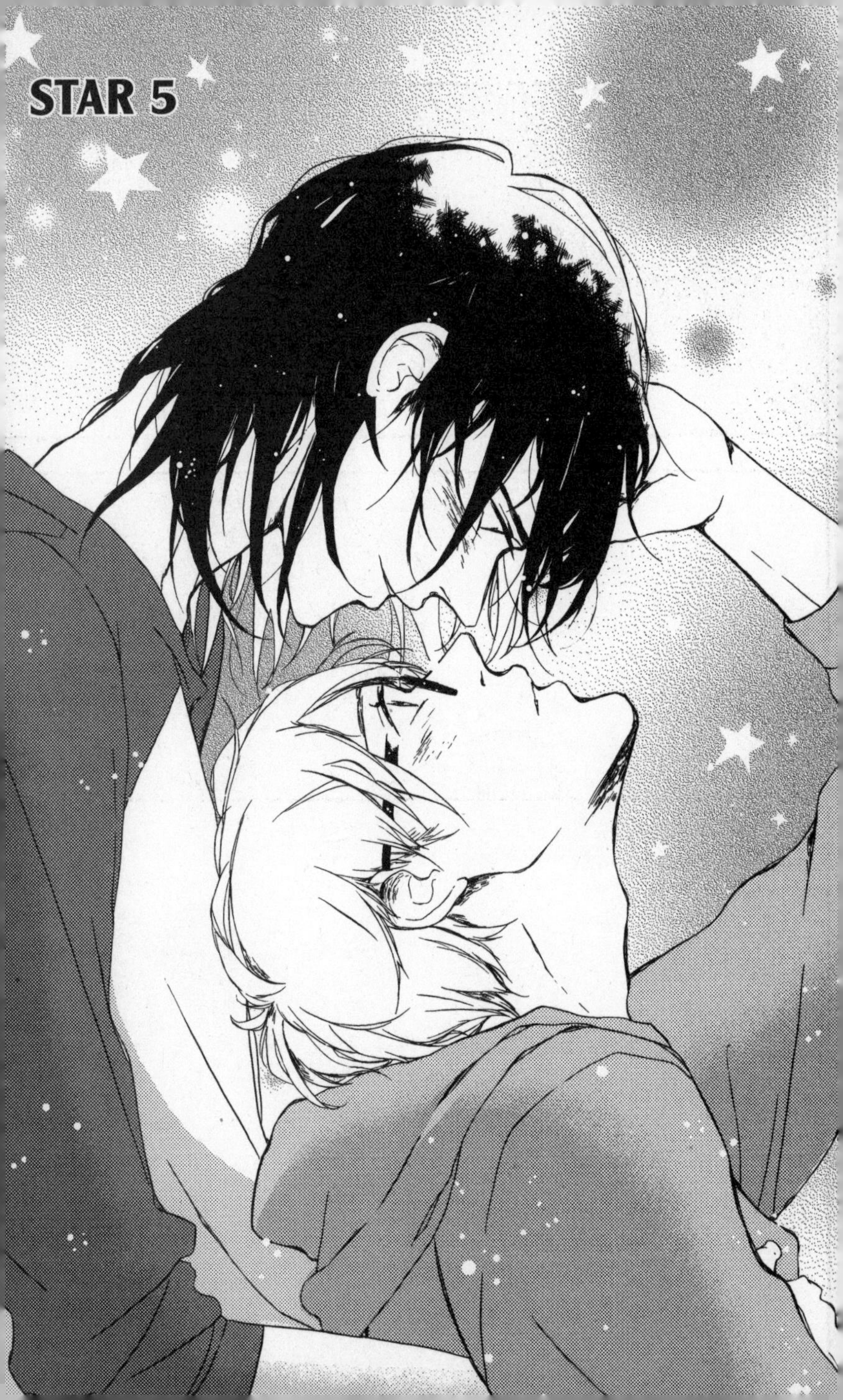
STAR 5

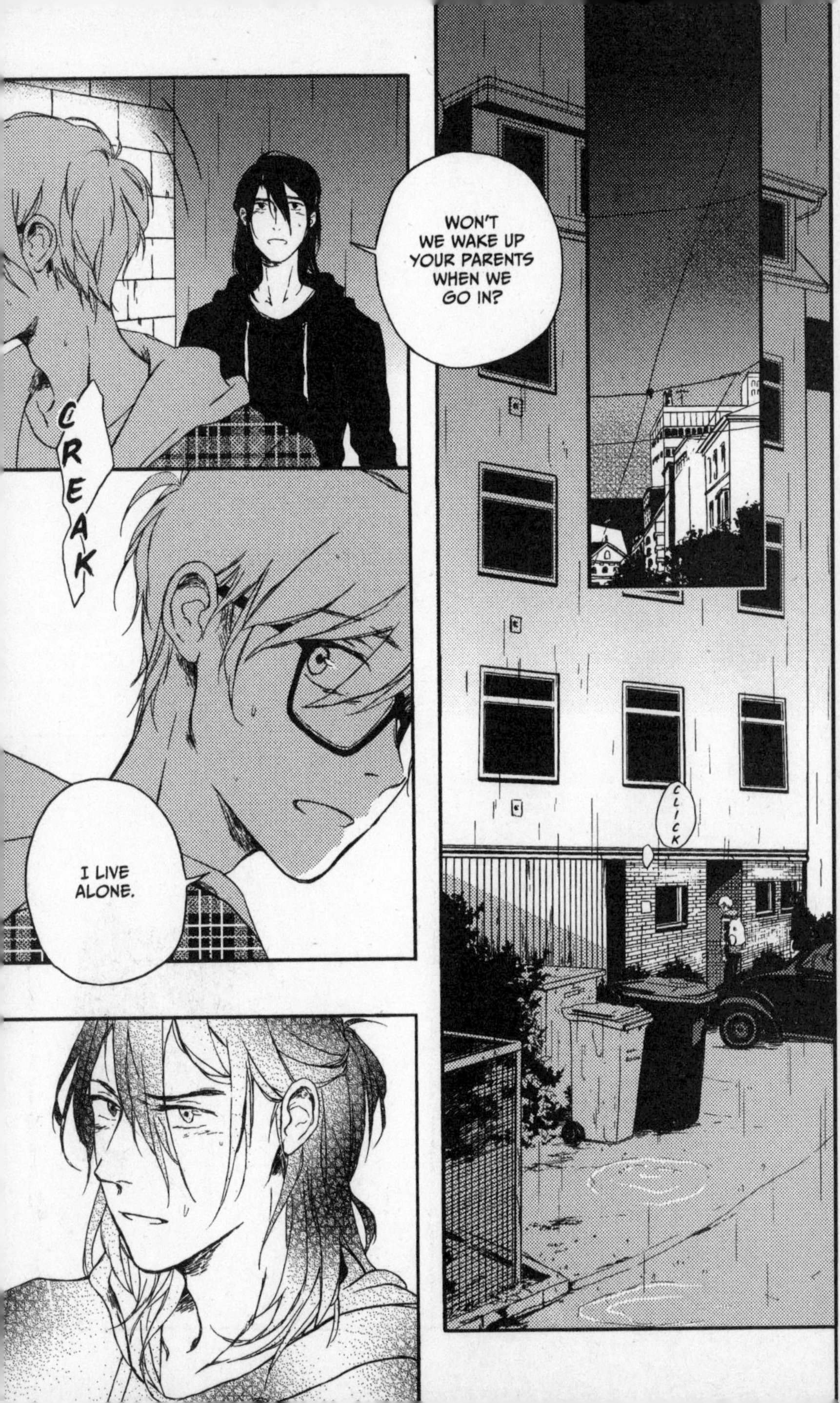
CLICK
WON'T WE WAKE UP YOUR PARENTS WHEN WE GO IN?
CREAK
I LIVE ALONE.

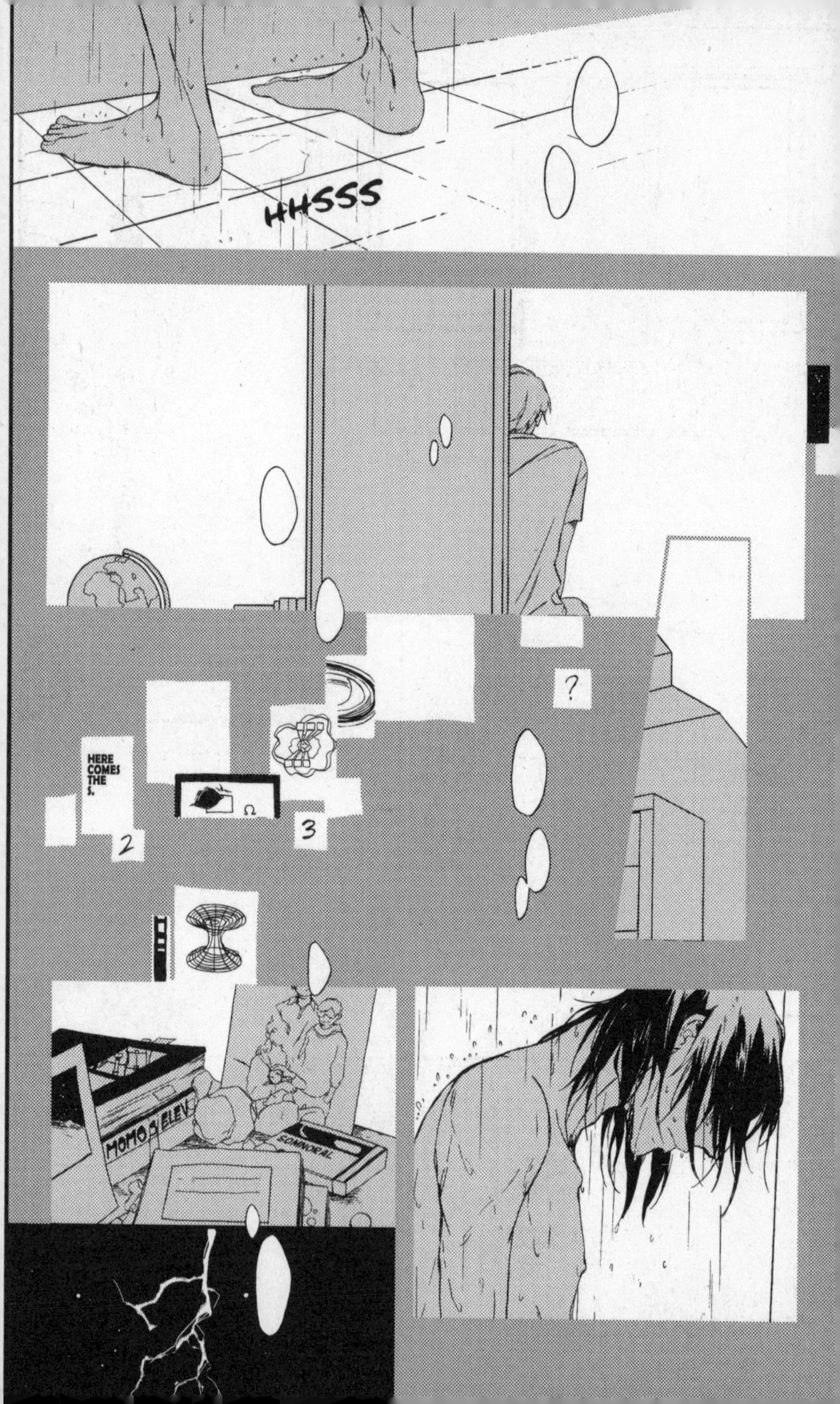

HHSSS
?
HERE COMES THE S.
2
3
MOMO'S ELEV
SOMNORAL

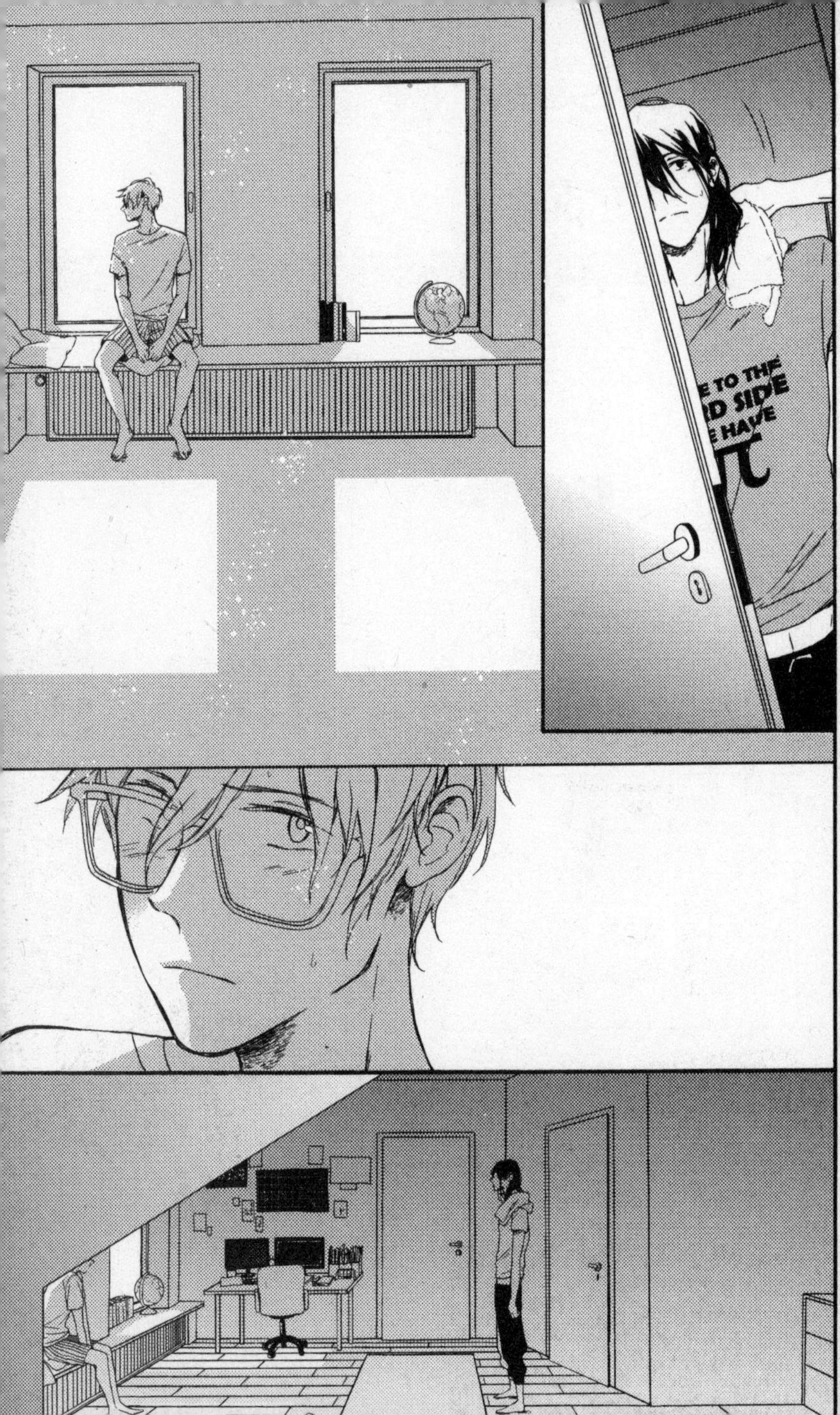
E TO THE
RD SIDE
E HAVE
π

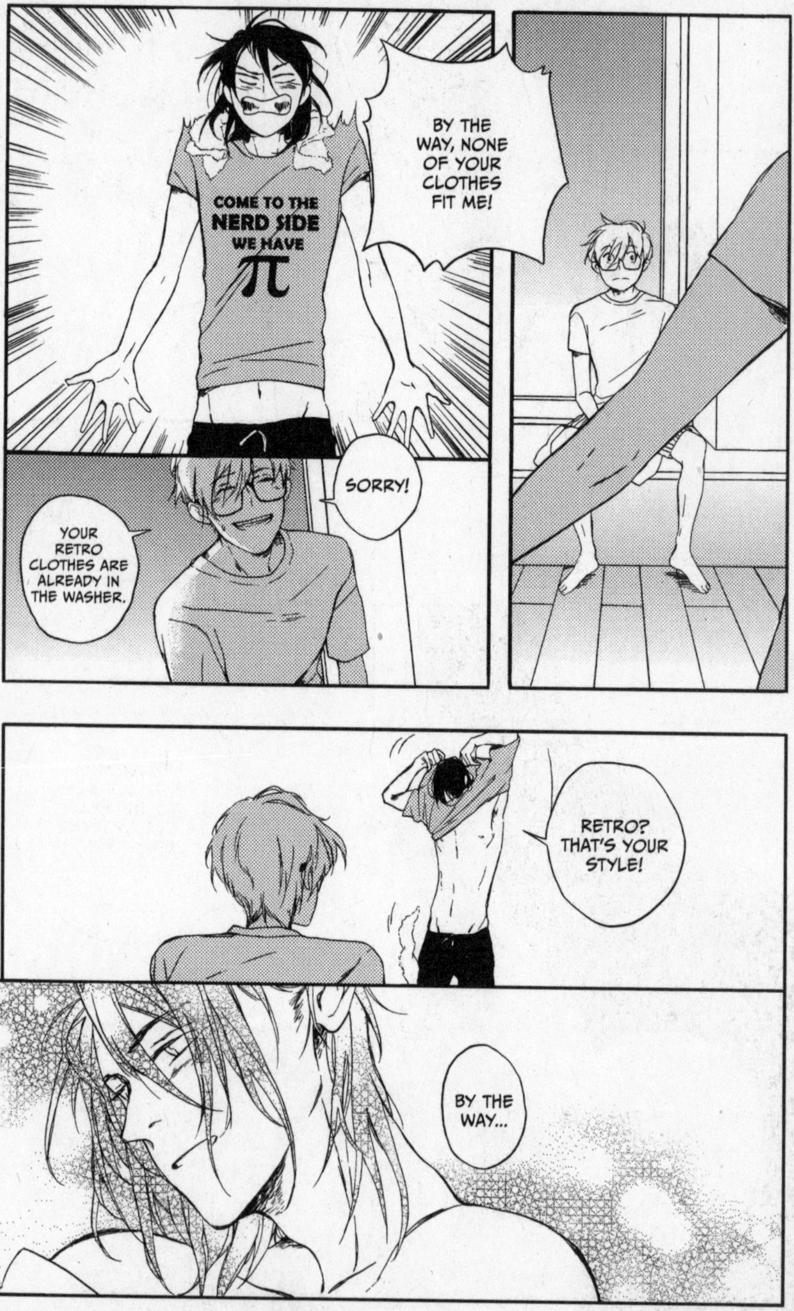
BY THE WAY, NONE OF YOUR CLOTHES FIT ME!
COME TO THE NERD SIDE WE HAVE π
SORRY!
YOUR RETRO CLOTHES ARE ALREADY IN THE WASHER.
RETRO? THAT'S YOUR STYLE!
BY THE WAY...

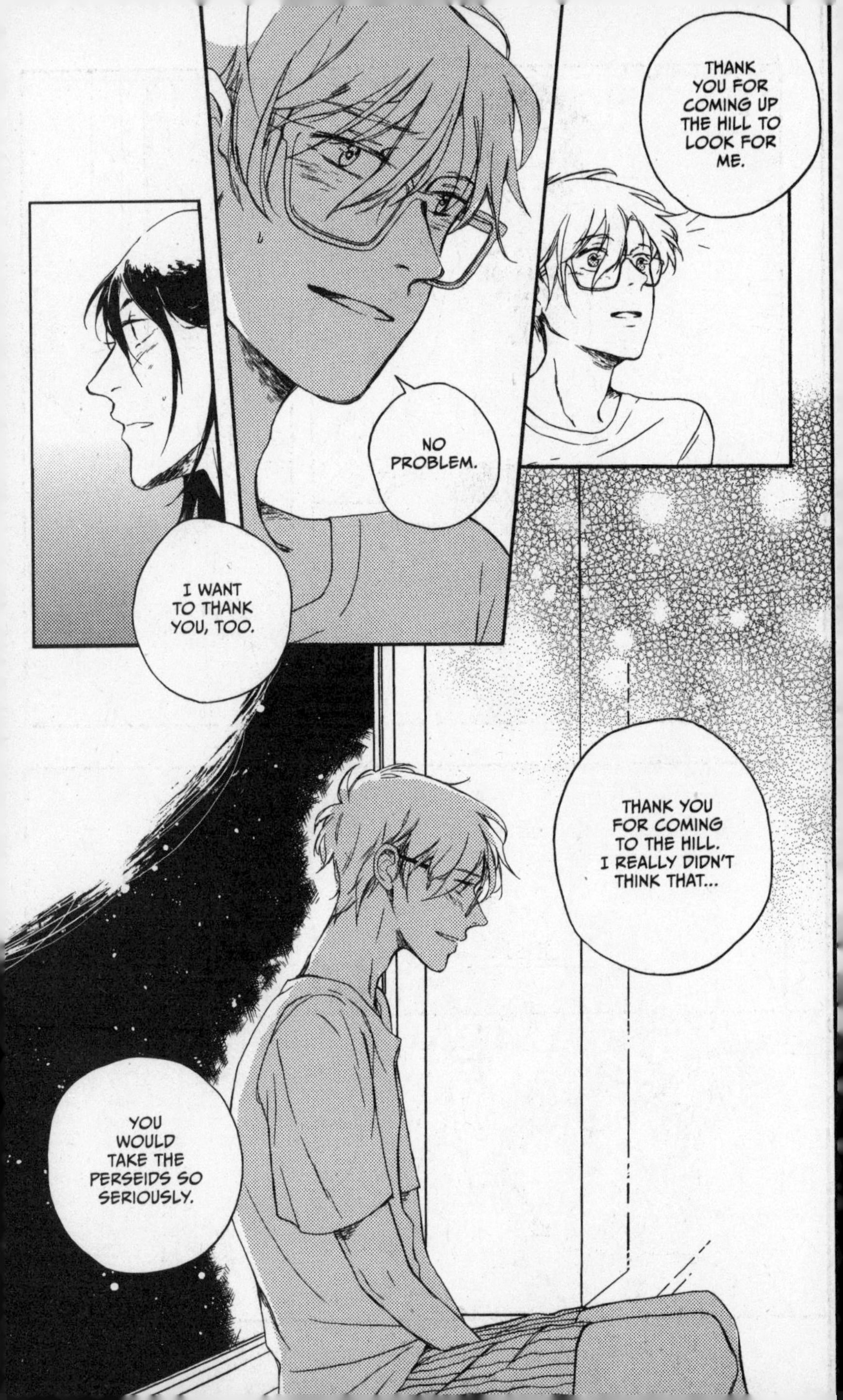
THANK YOU FOR COMING UP THE HILL TO LOOK FOR ME.
NO PROBLEM.
I WANT TO THANK YOU, TOO.
THANK YOU FOR COMING TO THE HILL. I REALLY DIDN'T THINK THAT...
YOU WOULD TAKE THE PERSEIDS SO SERIOUSLY.

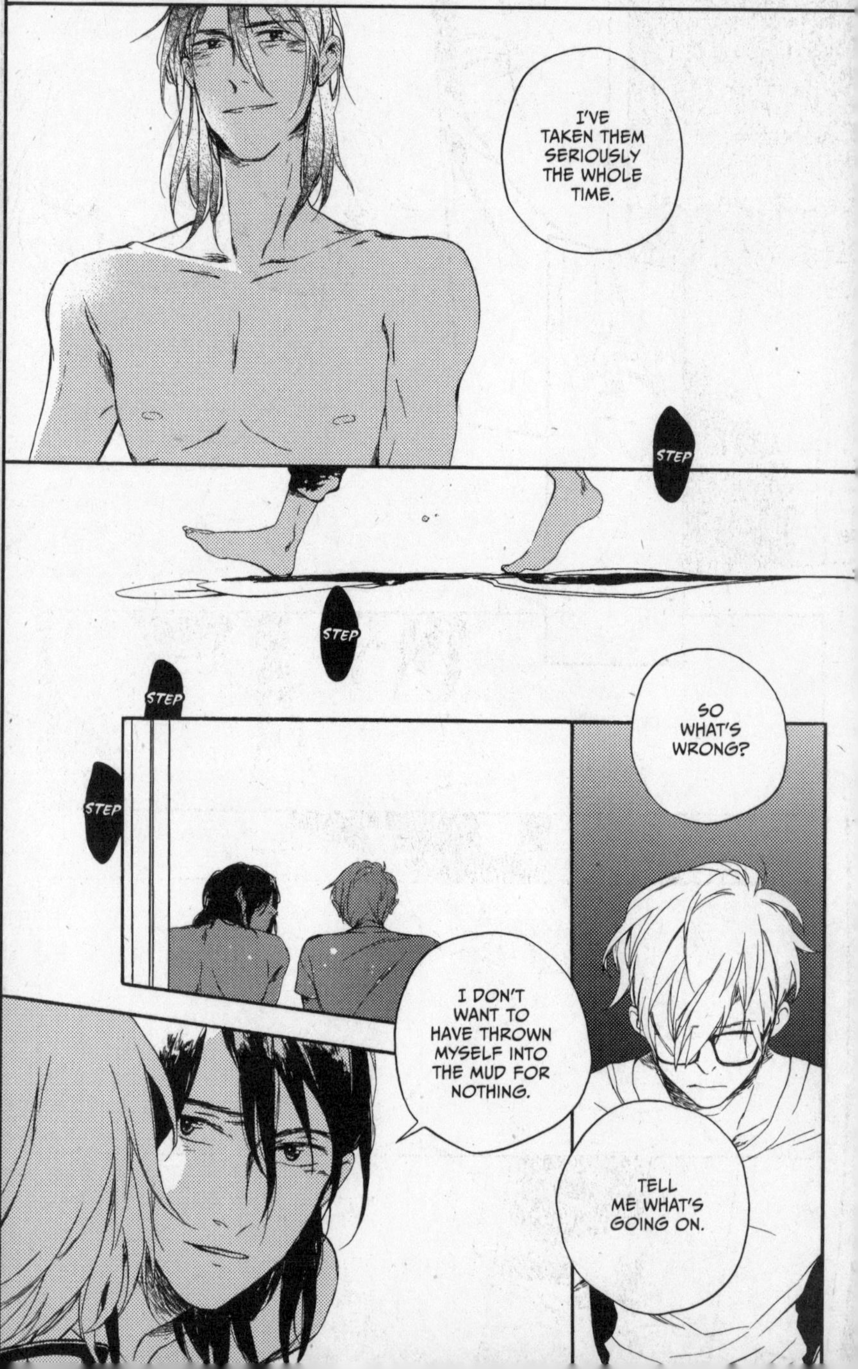
I'VE TAKEN THEM SERIOUSLY THE WHOLE TIME.
STEP
STEP
STEP
STEP
SO WHAT'S WRONG?
TELL ME WHAT'S GOING ON.
I DON'T WANT TO HAVE THROWN MYSELF INTO THE MUD FOR NOTHING.

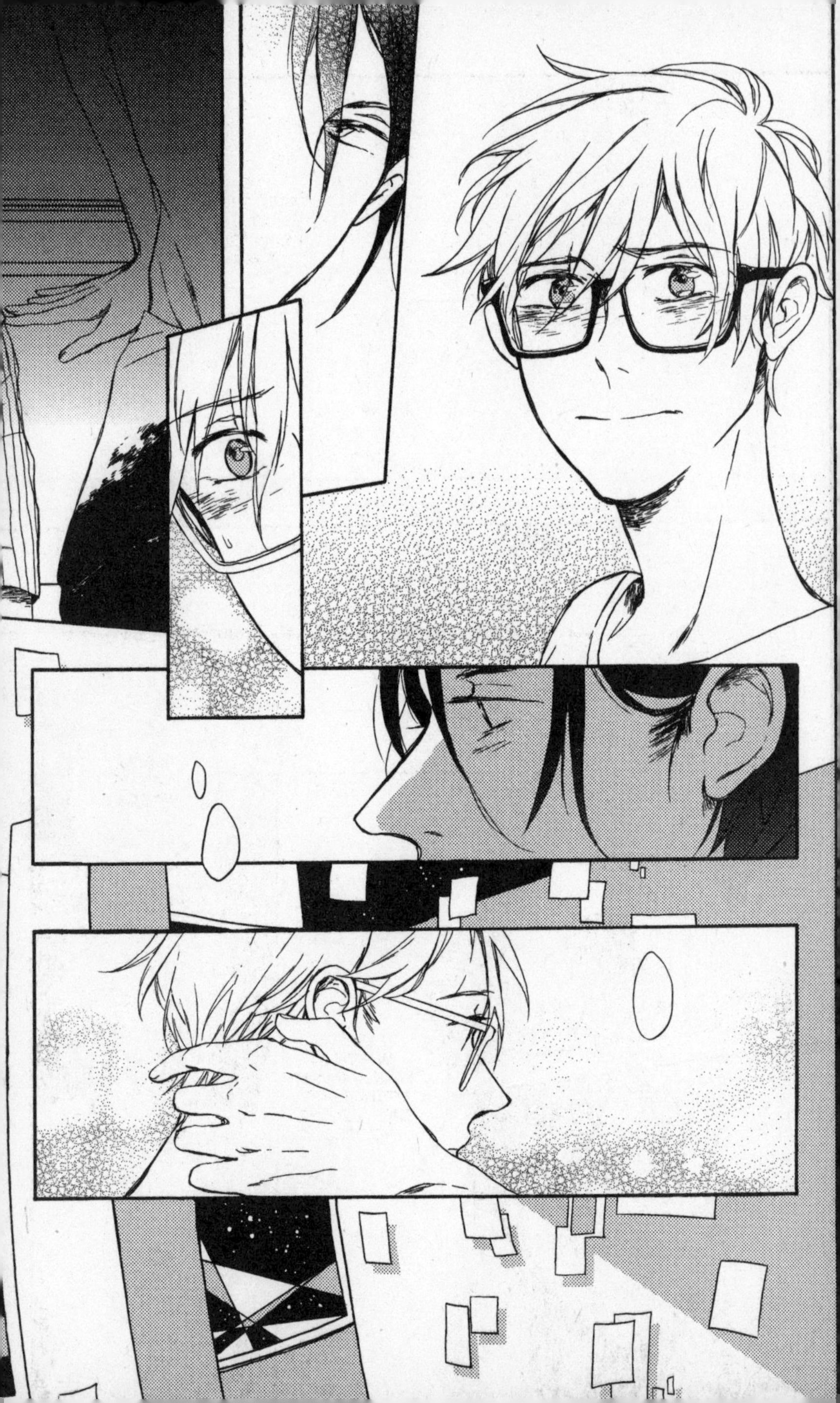

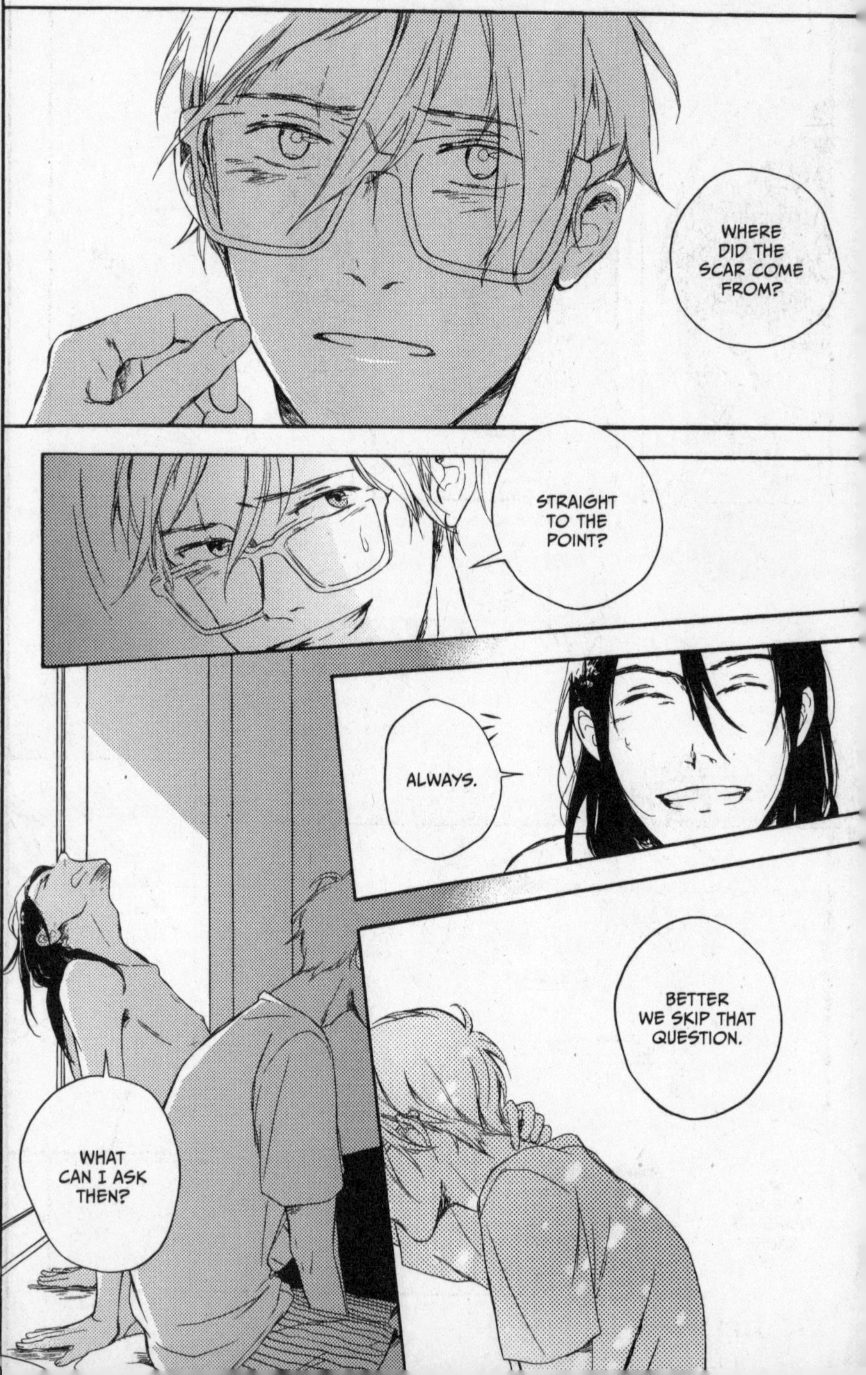
WHERE DID THE SCAR COME FROM?
STRAIGHT TO THE POINT?
ALWAYS.
BETTER WE SKIP THAT QUESTION.
WHAT CAN I ASK THEN?

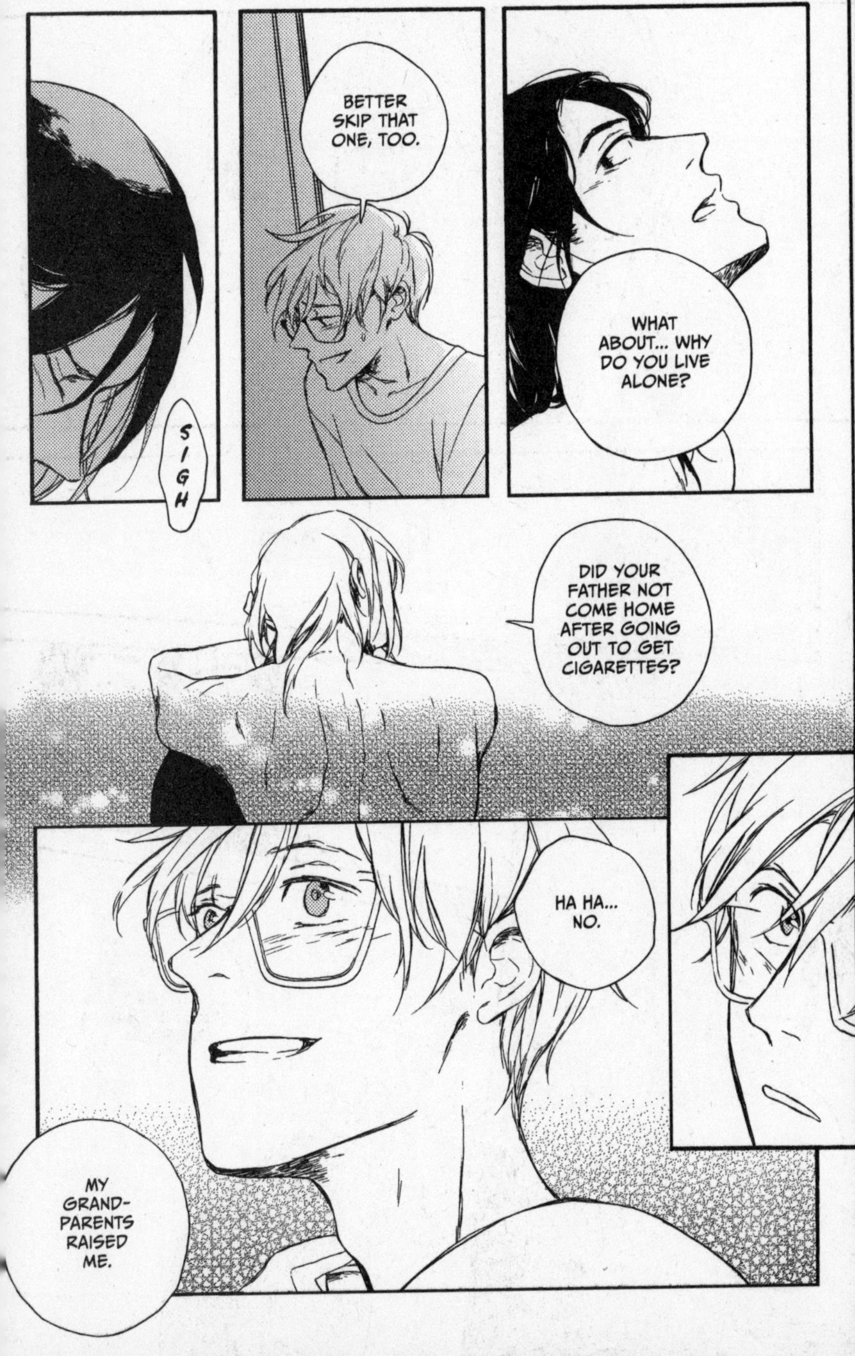
WHAT ABOUT... WHY DO YOU LIVE ALONE?
BETTER SKIP THAT ONE, TOO.
SIGH
DID YOUR FATHER NOT COME HOME AFTER GOING OUT TO GET CIGARETTES?
HA HA... NO.
MY GRAND-PARENTS RAISED ME.

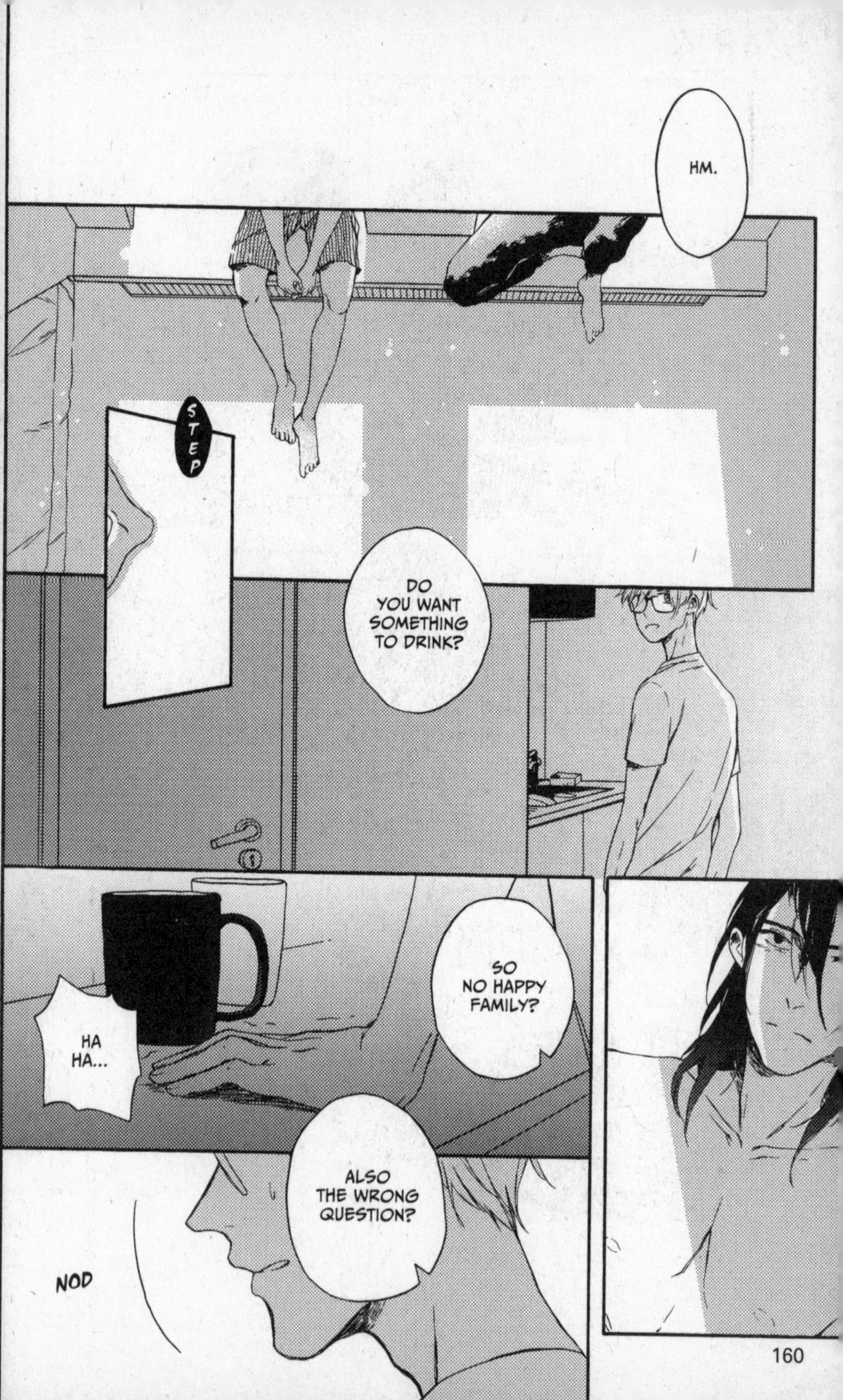
HM.
STEP
DO YOU WANT SOMETHING TO DRINK?
SO NO HAPPY FAMILY?
HA HA...
ALSO THE WRONG QUESTION?
NOD

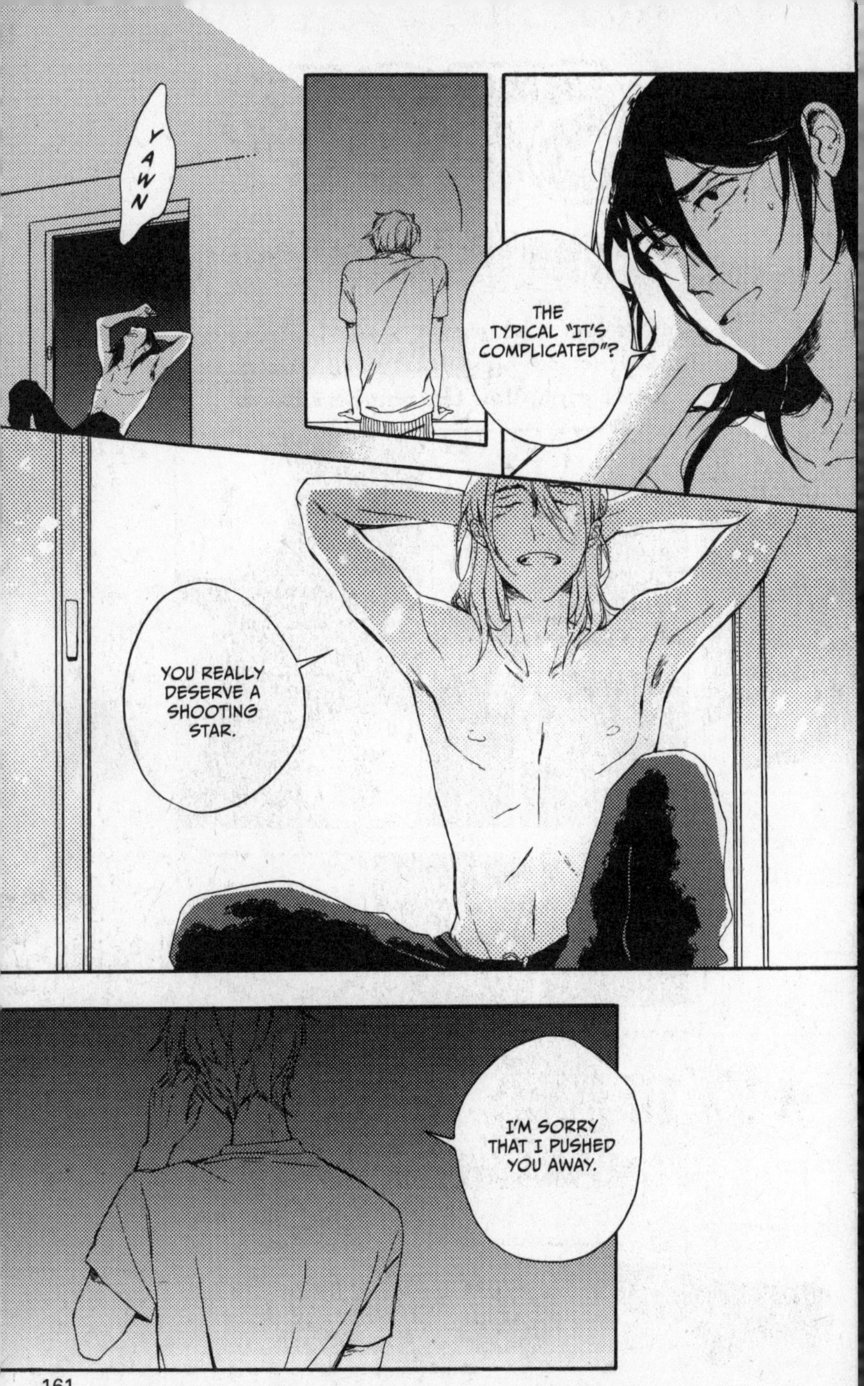
THE TYPICAL "IT'S COMPLICATED"?
YAWN
YOU REALLY DESERVE A SHOOTING STAR.
I'M SORRY THAT I PUSHED YOU AWAY.

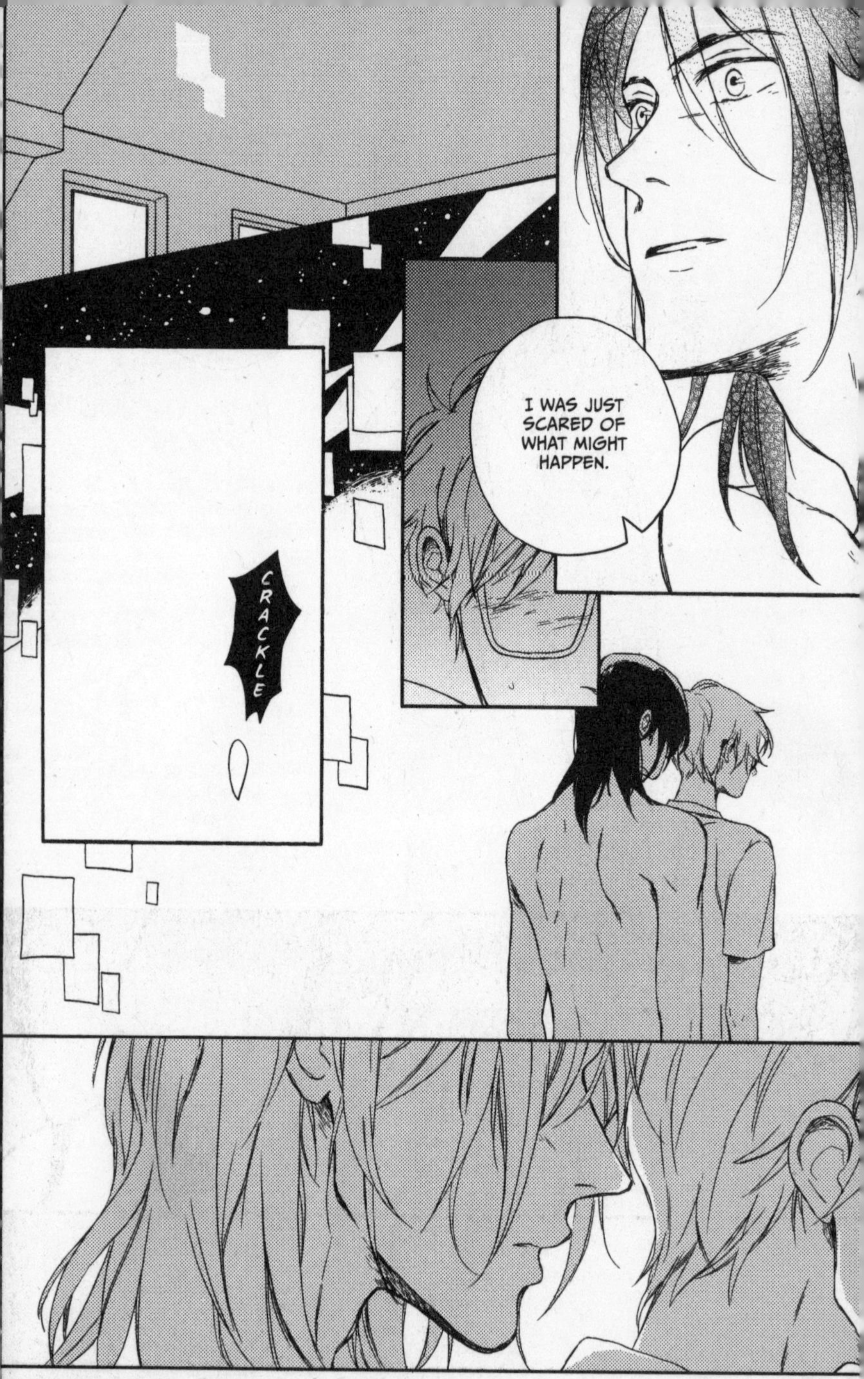
I WAS JUST SCARED OF WHAT MIGHT HAPPEN.
CRACKLE

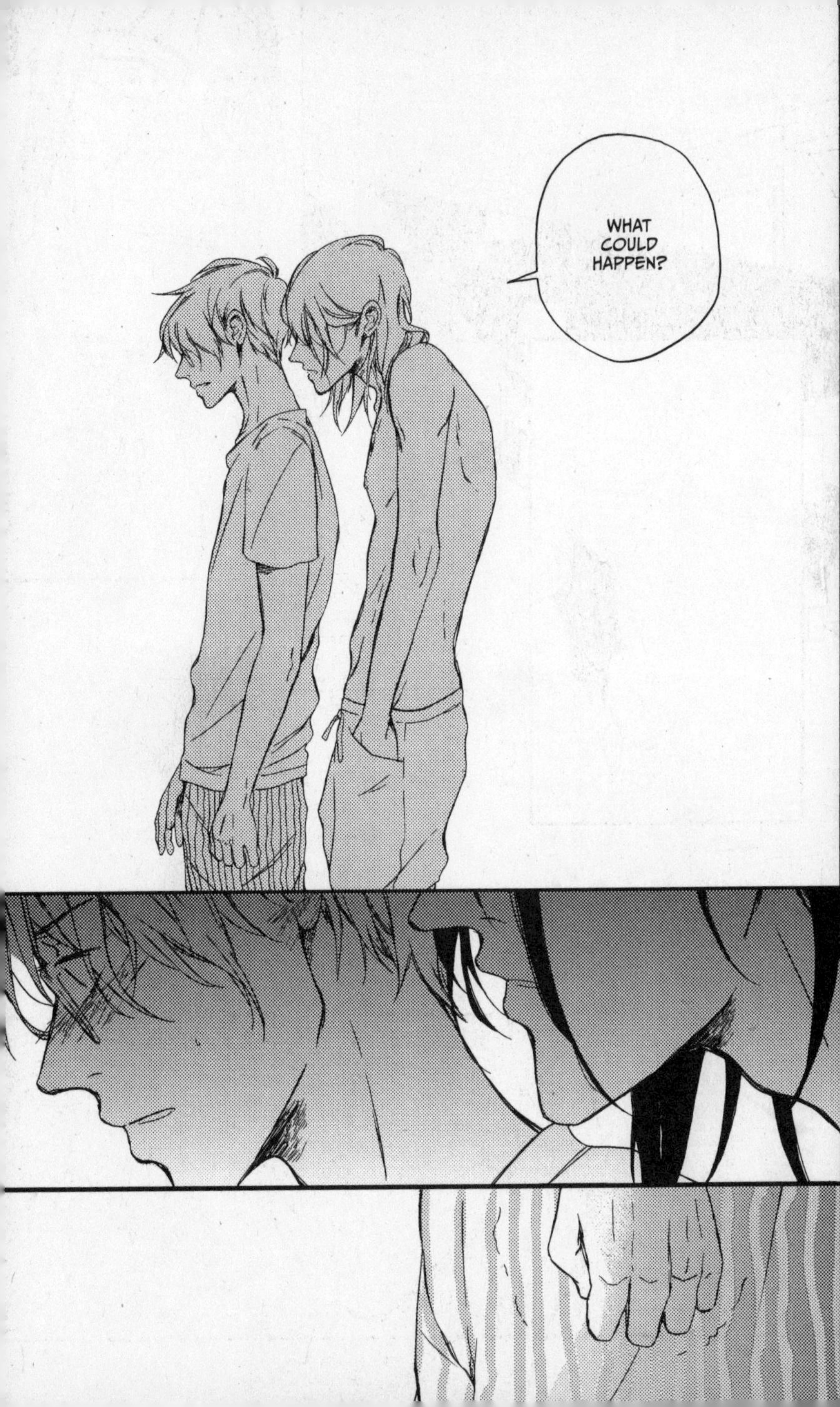
WHAT COULD HAPPEN?

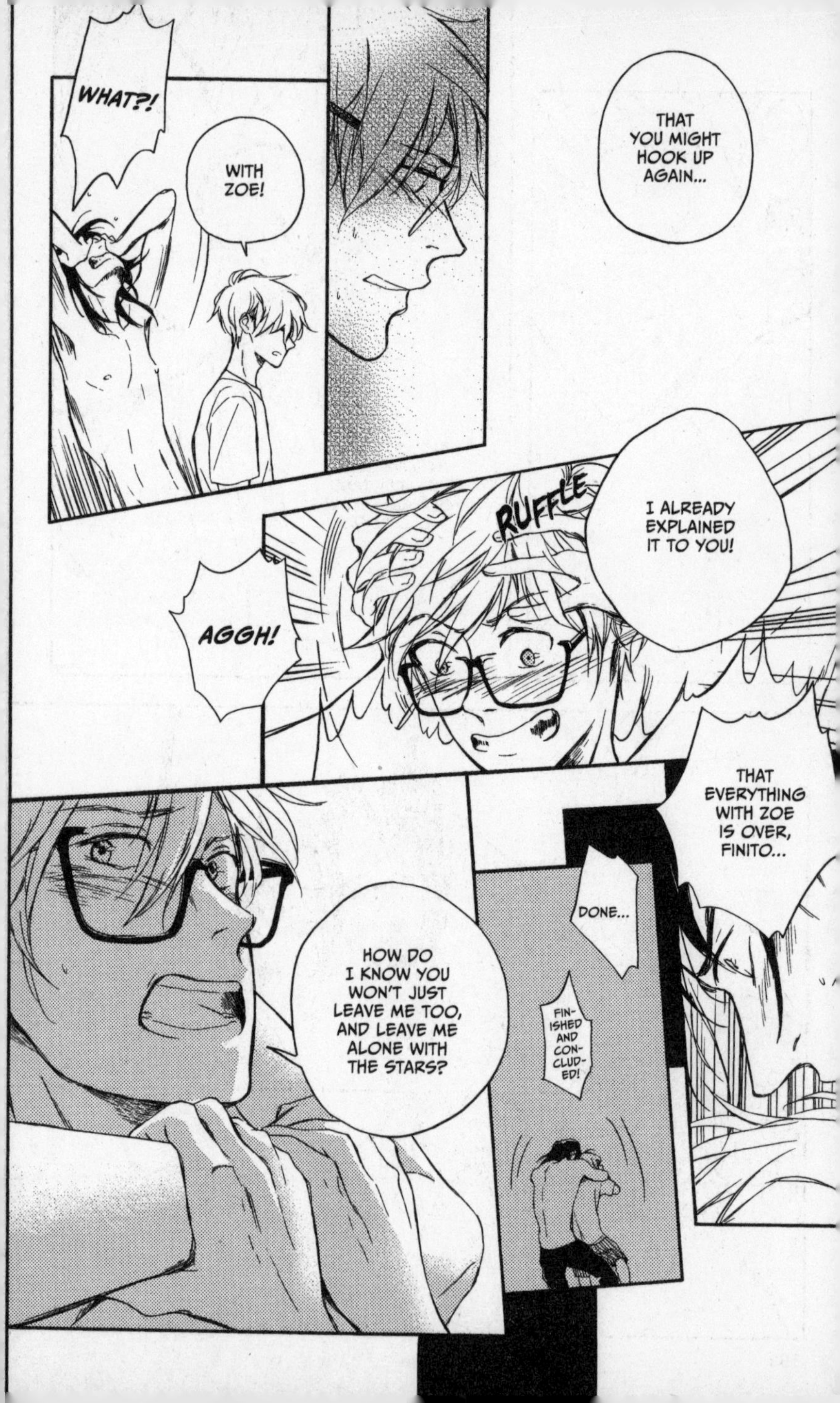
THAT YOU MIGHT HOOK UP AGAIN...
WITH ZOE!
WHAT?!
I ALREADY EXPLAINED IT TO YOU!
RUFFLE
AGGH!
THAT EVERYTHING WITH ZOE IS OVER, FINITO...
DONE...
FIN-ISHED AND CON-CLUD-ED!
HOW DO I KNOW YOU WON'T JUST LEAVE ME TOO, AND LEAVE ME ALONE WITH THE STARS?

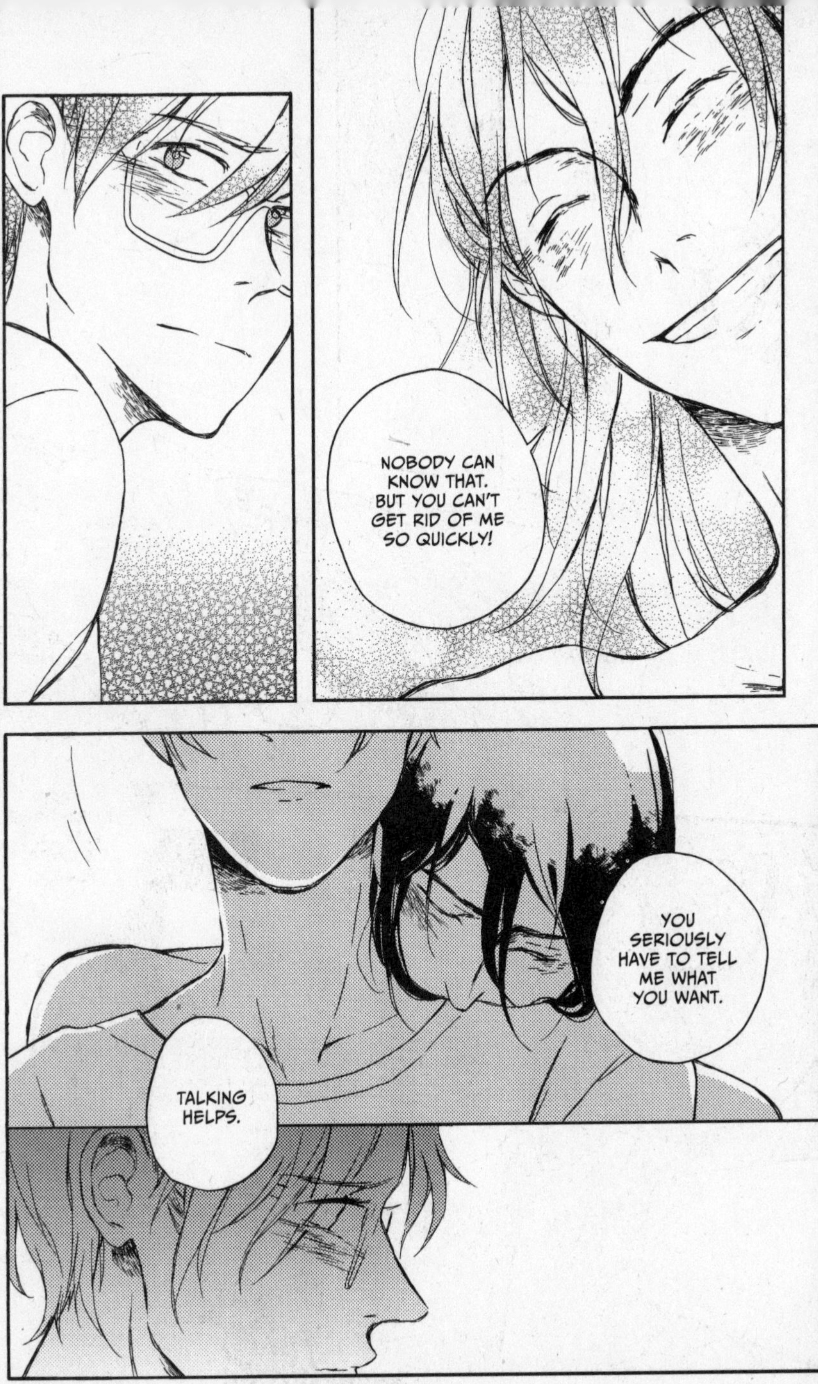
NOBODY CAN KNOW THAT. BUT YOU CAN'T GET RID OF ME SO QUICKLY!
YOU SERIOUSLY HAVE TO TELL ME WHAT YOU WANT.
TALKING HELPS.

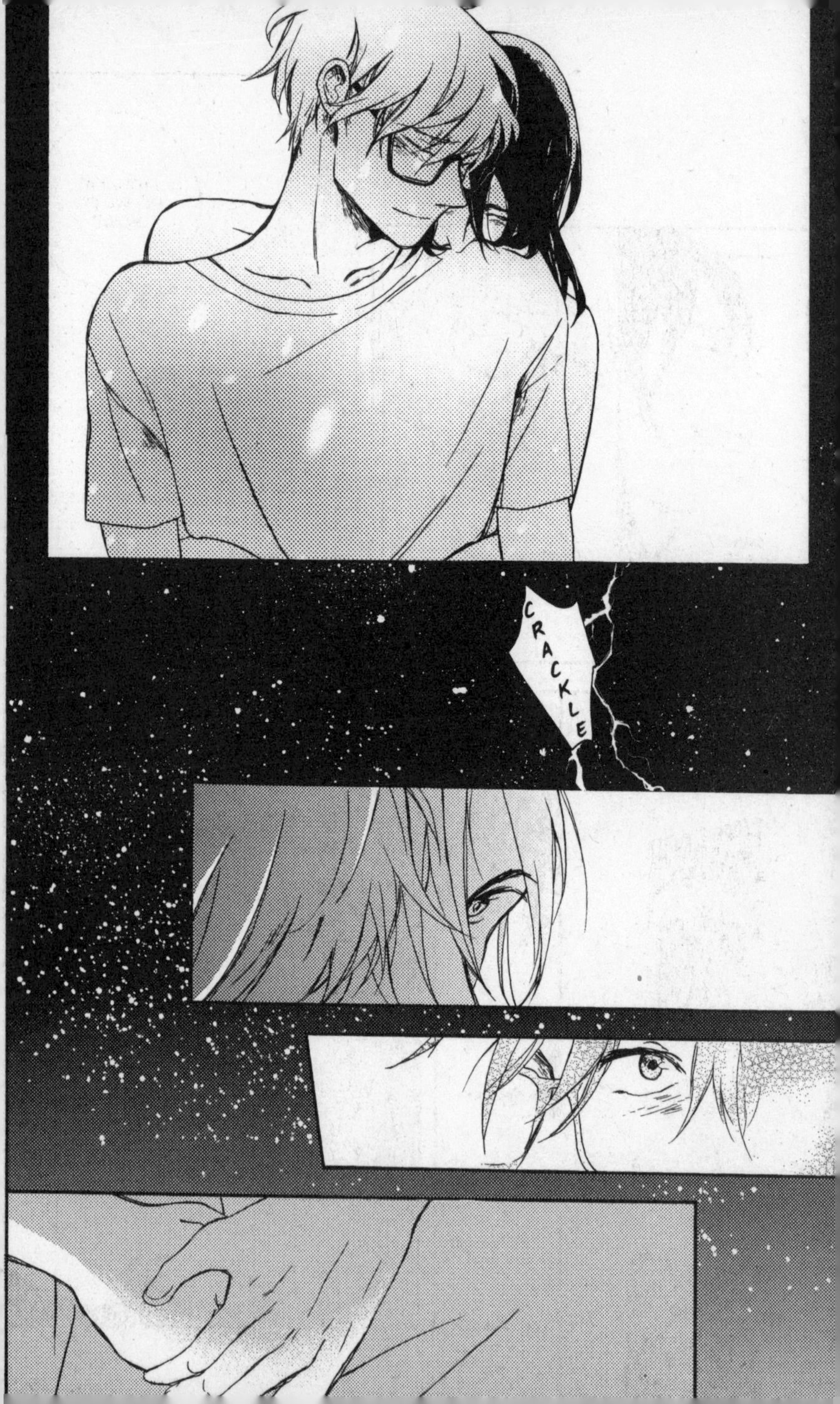
CRACKLE

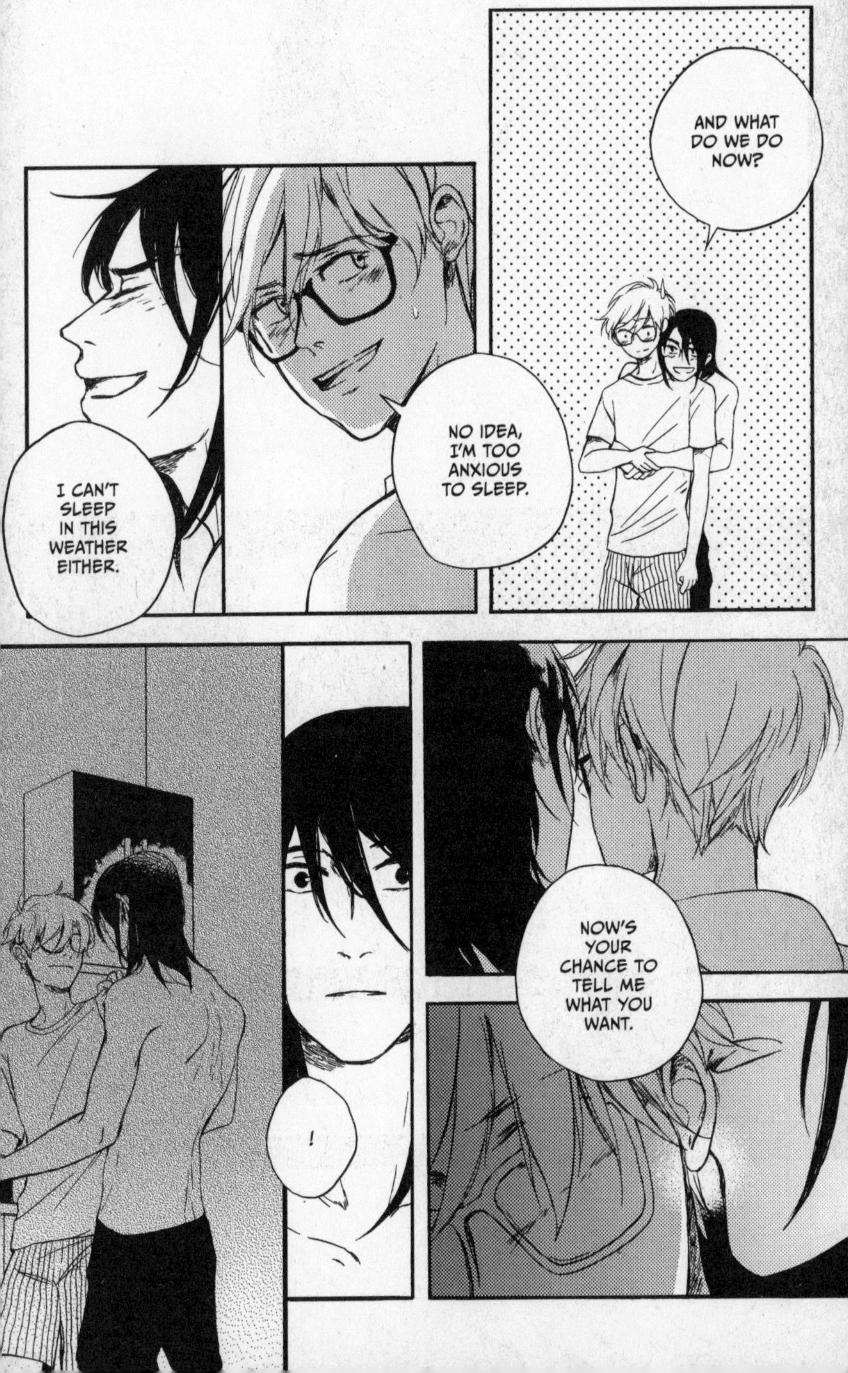
AND WHAT DO WE DO NOW?
NO IDEA, I'M TOO ANXIOUS TO SLEEP.
I CAN'T SLEEP IN THIS WEATHER EITHER.
NOW'S YOUR CHANCE TO TELL ME WHAT YOU WANT.
!

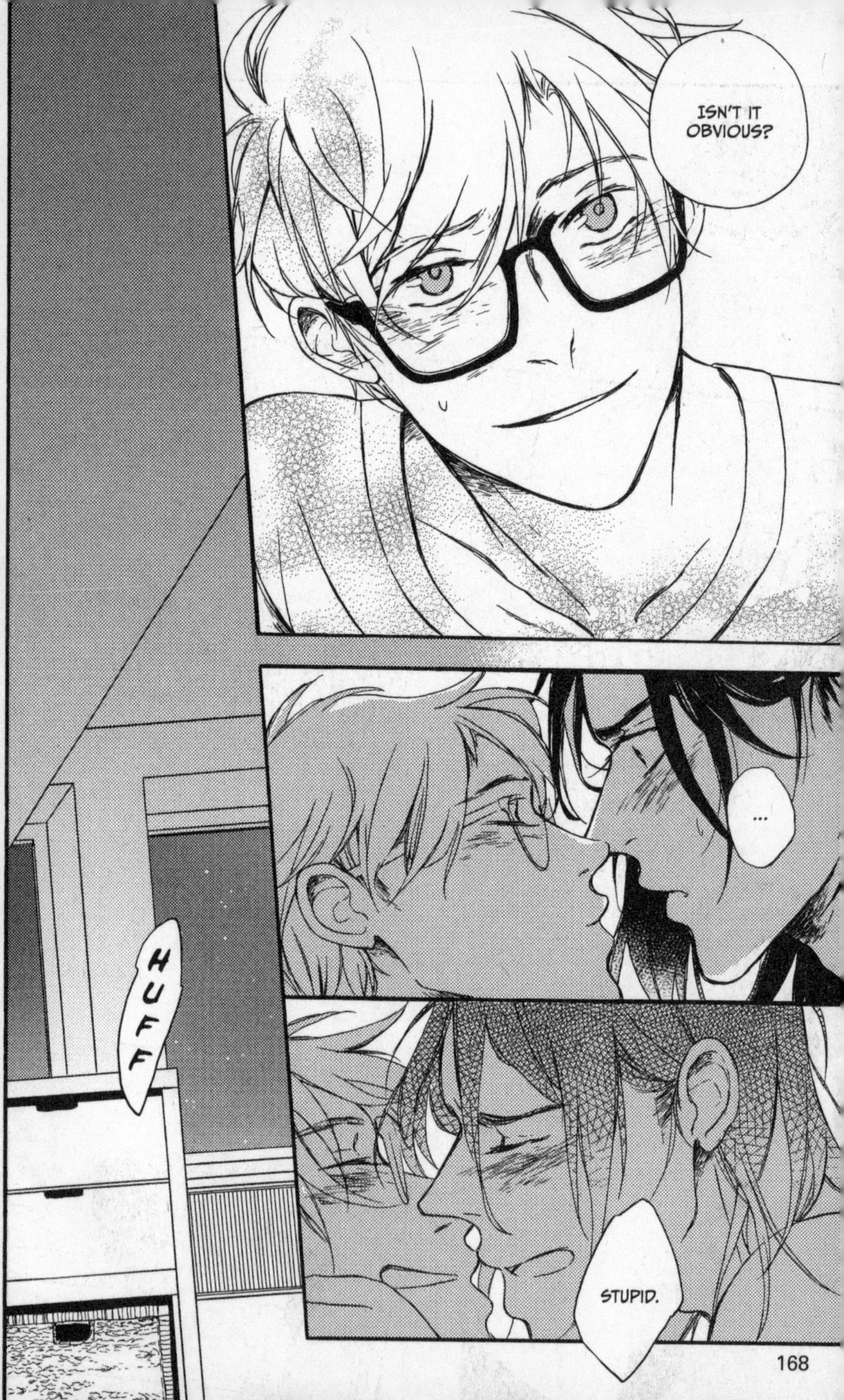

ISN'T IT OBVIOUS?
...
HUFF
STUPID.

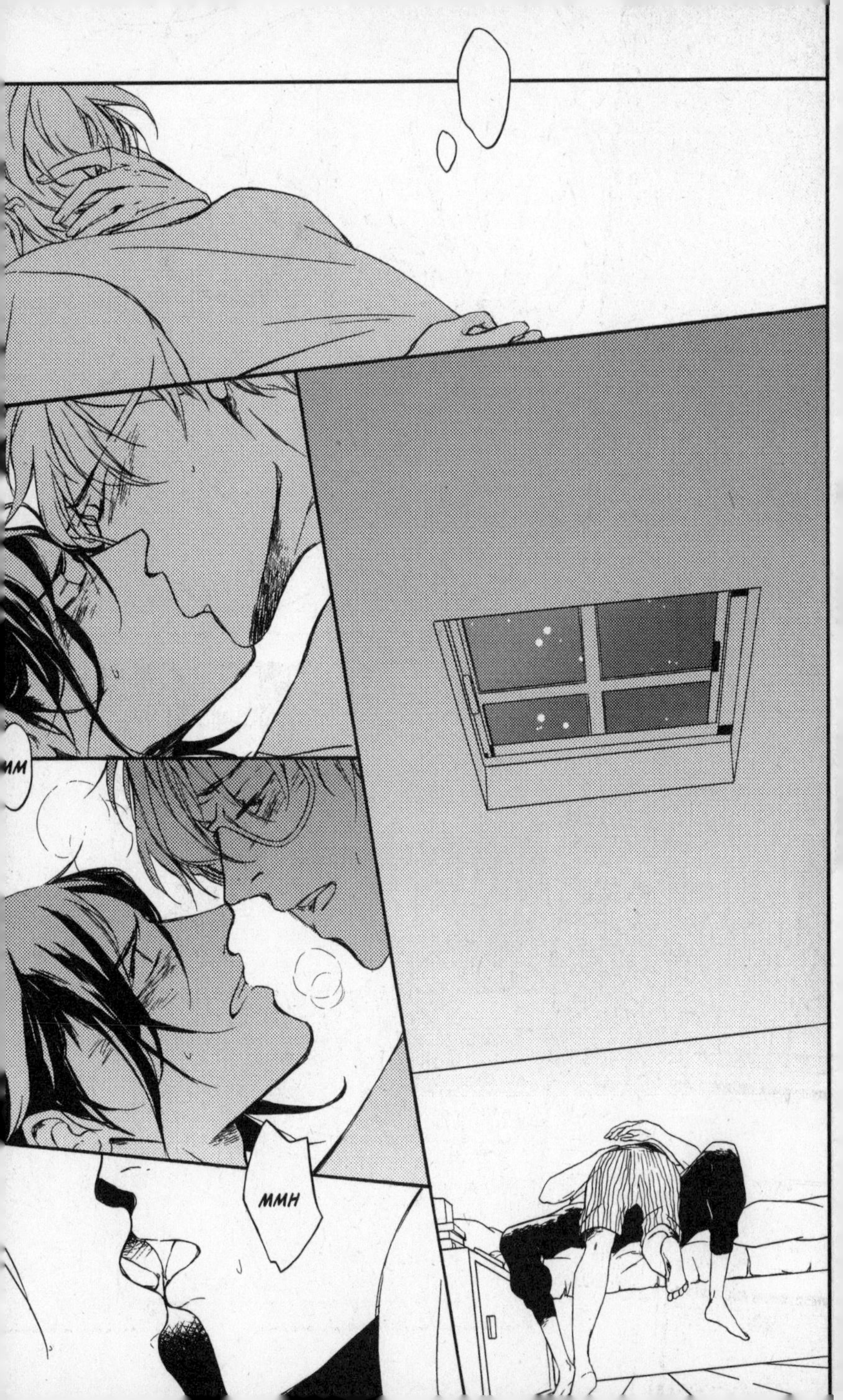
MMH
MM

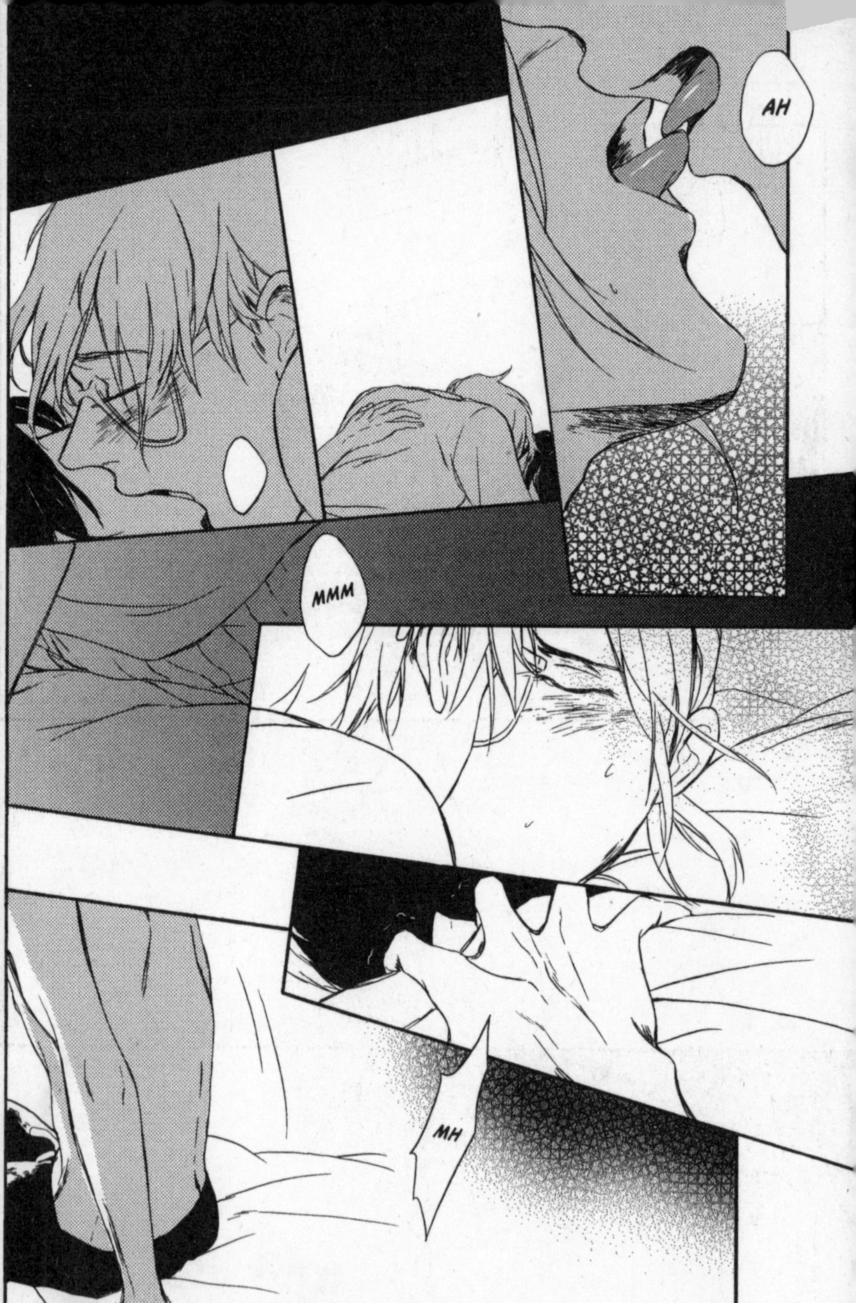
AH
MMM
MH

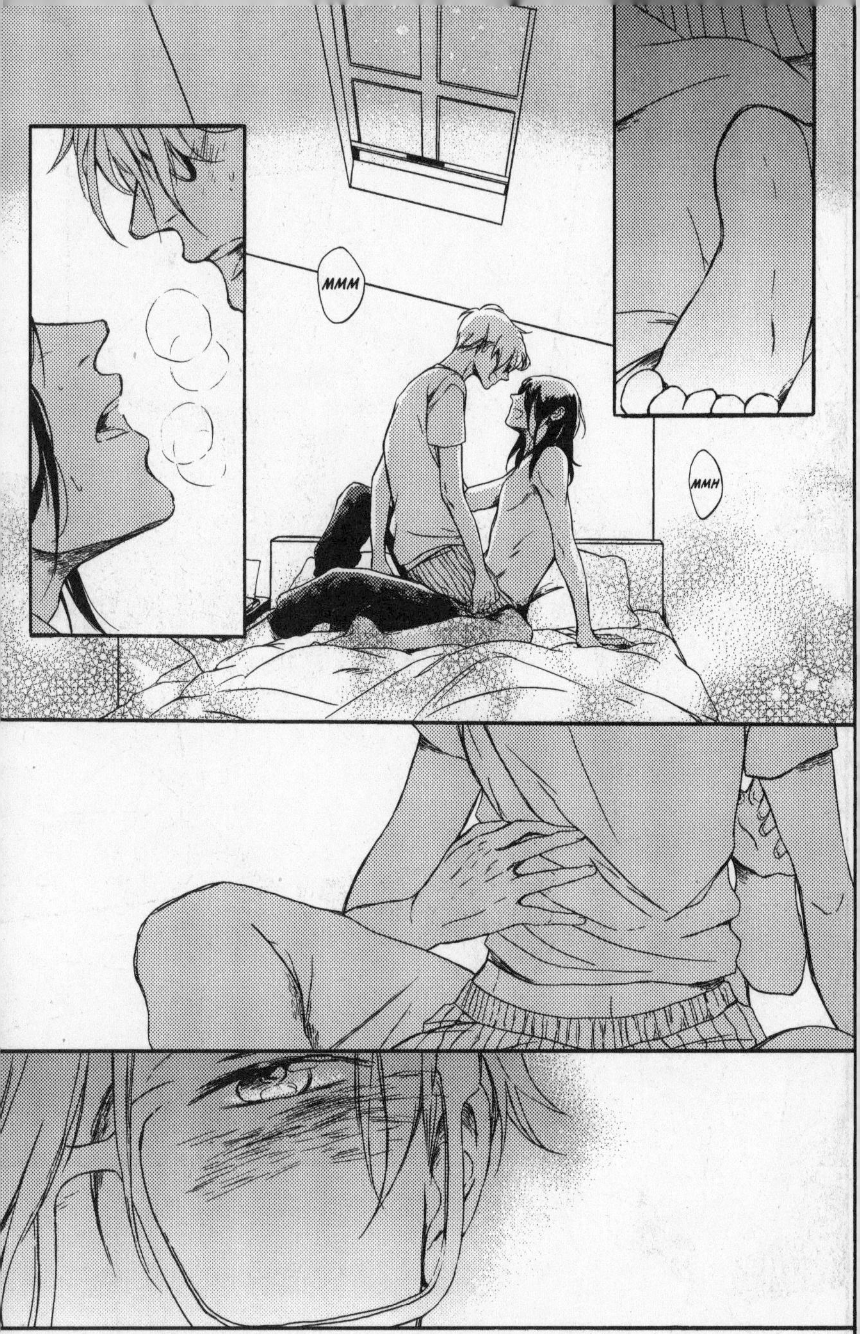
MMM
MMH

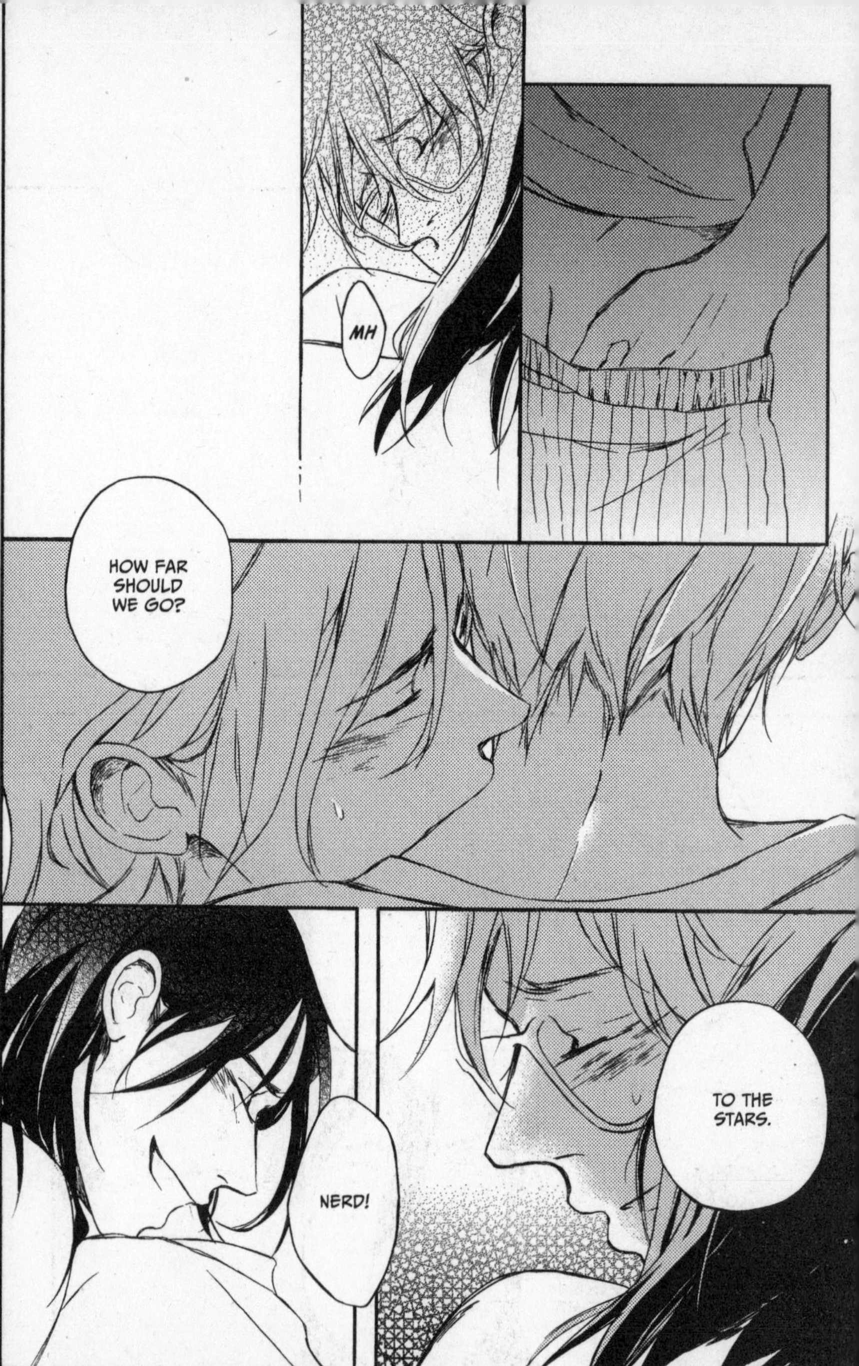
MH
HOW FAR SHOULD WE GO?
TO THE STARS.
NERD!

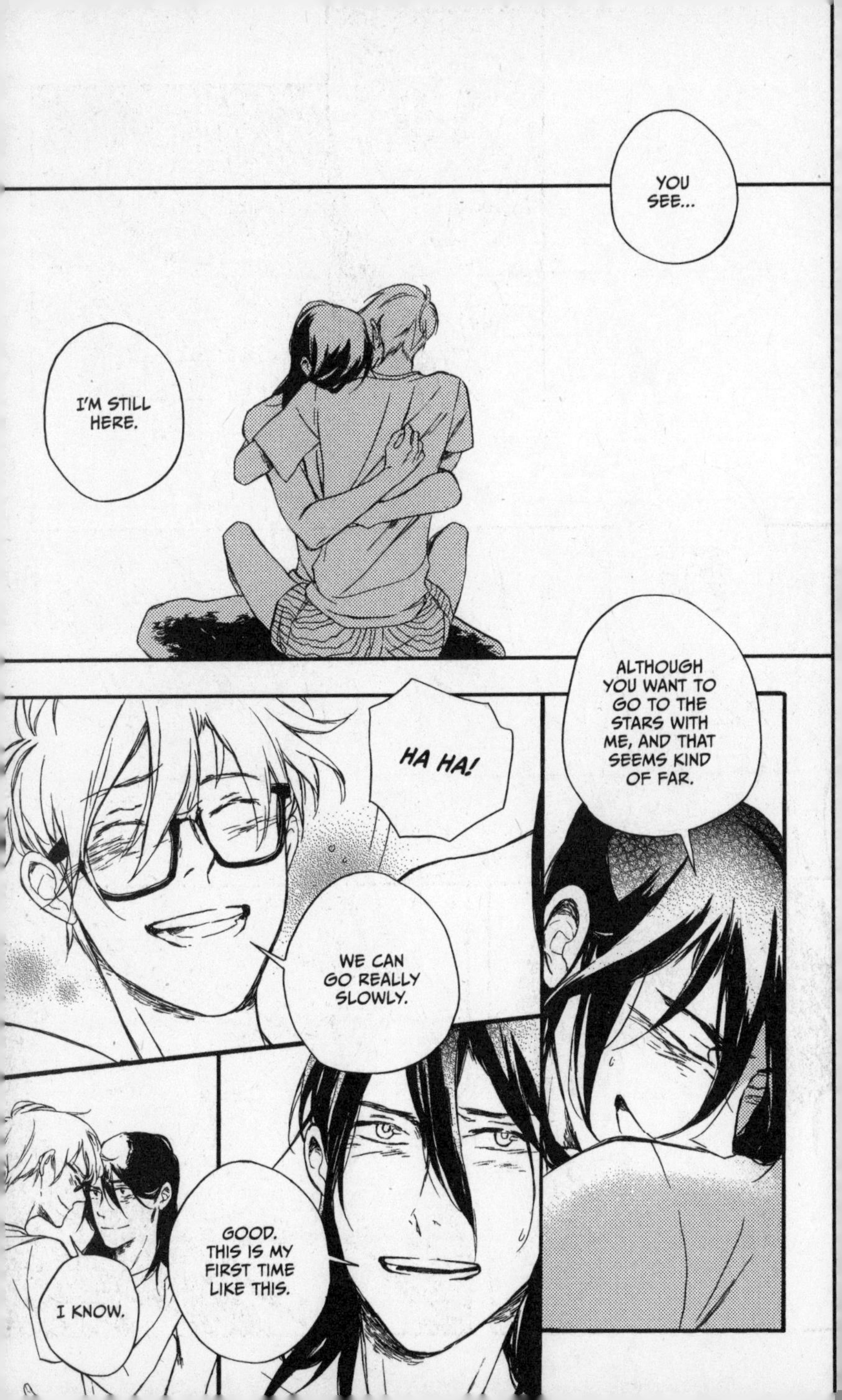
YOU SEE...
I'M STILL HERE.
ALTHOUGH YOU WANT TO GO TO THE STARS WITH ME, AND THAT SEEMS KIND OF FAR.
HA HA!
WE CAN GO REALLY SLOWLY.
GOOD. THIS IS MY FIRST TIME LIKE THIS.
I KNOW.

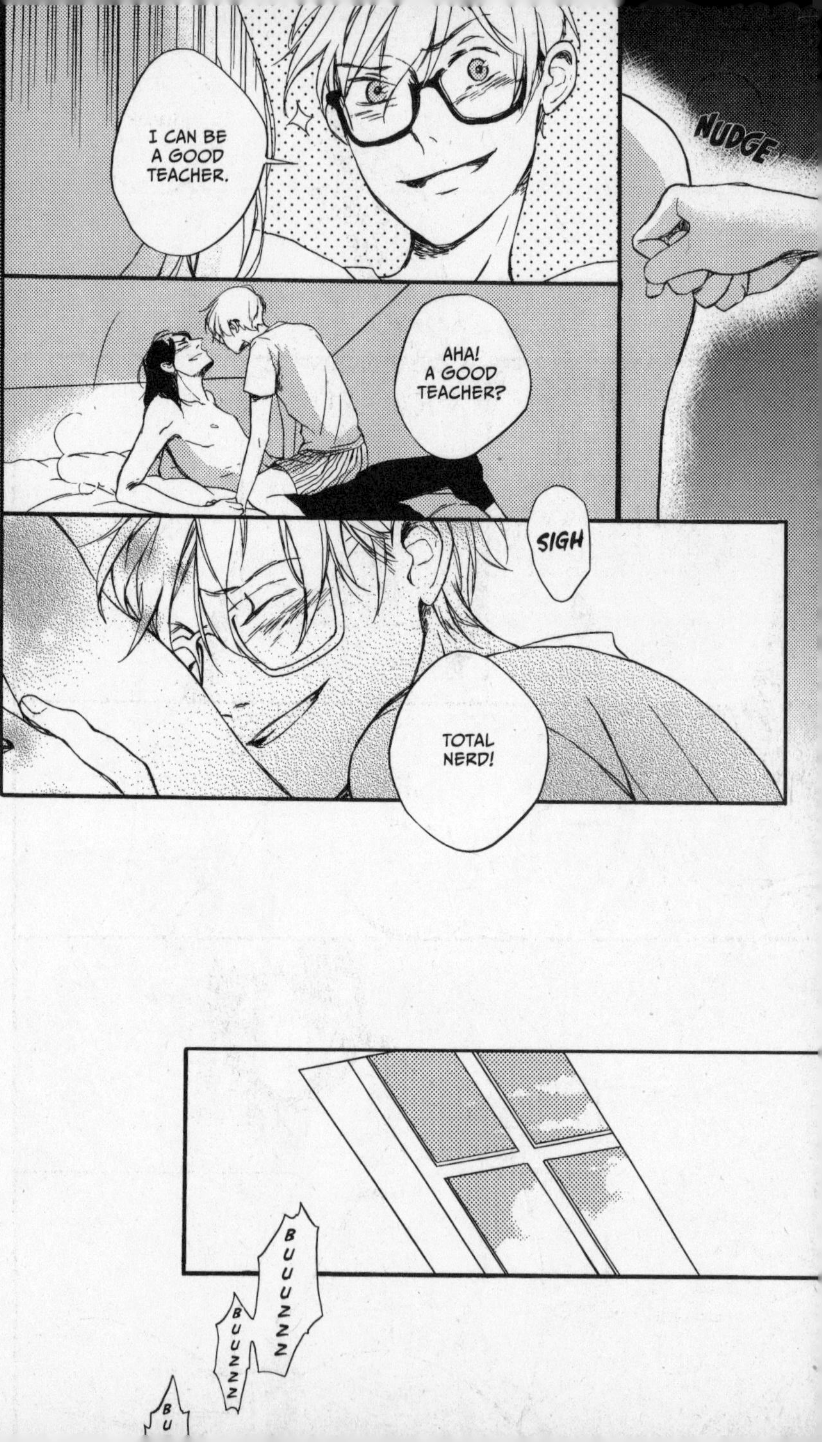
NUDGE
I CAN BE A GOOD TEACHER.
AHA! A GOOD TEACHER?
SIGH
TOTAL NERD!
BUUUZZZ
BUUZZZ
BUU

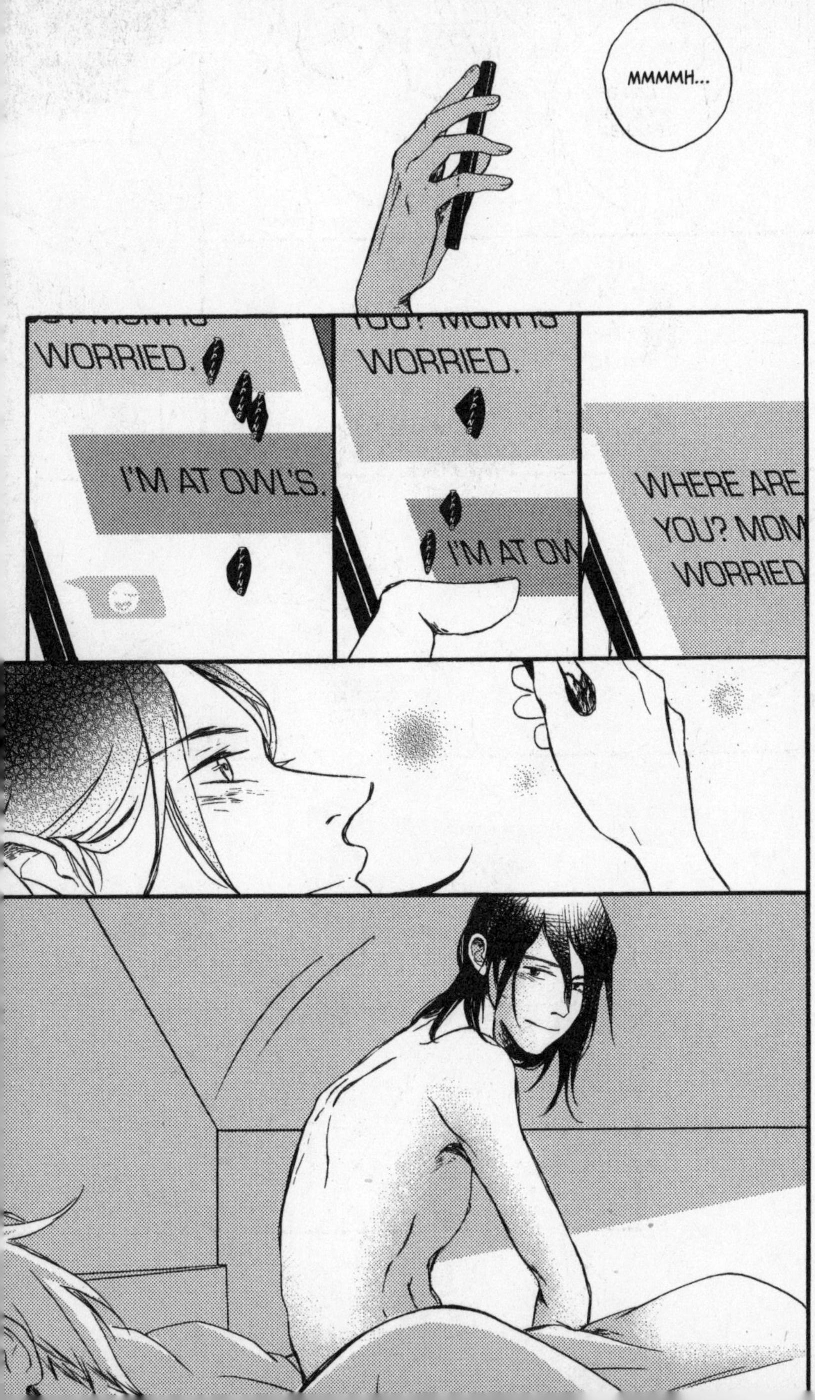
MMMMH...
WHERE ARE
YOU? MOM
WORRIED
WORRIED.
I'M AT OW
WORRIED.
I'M AT OWL'S.

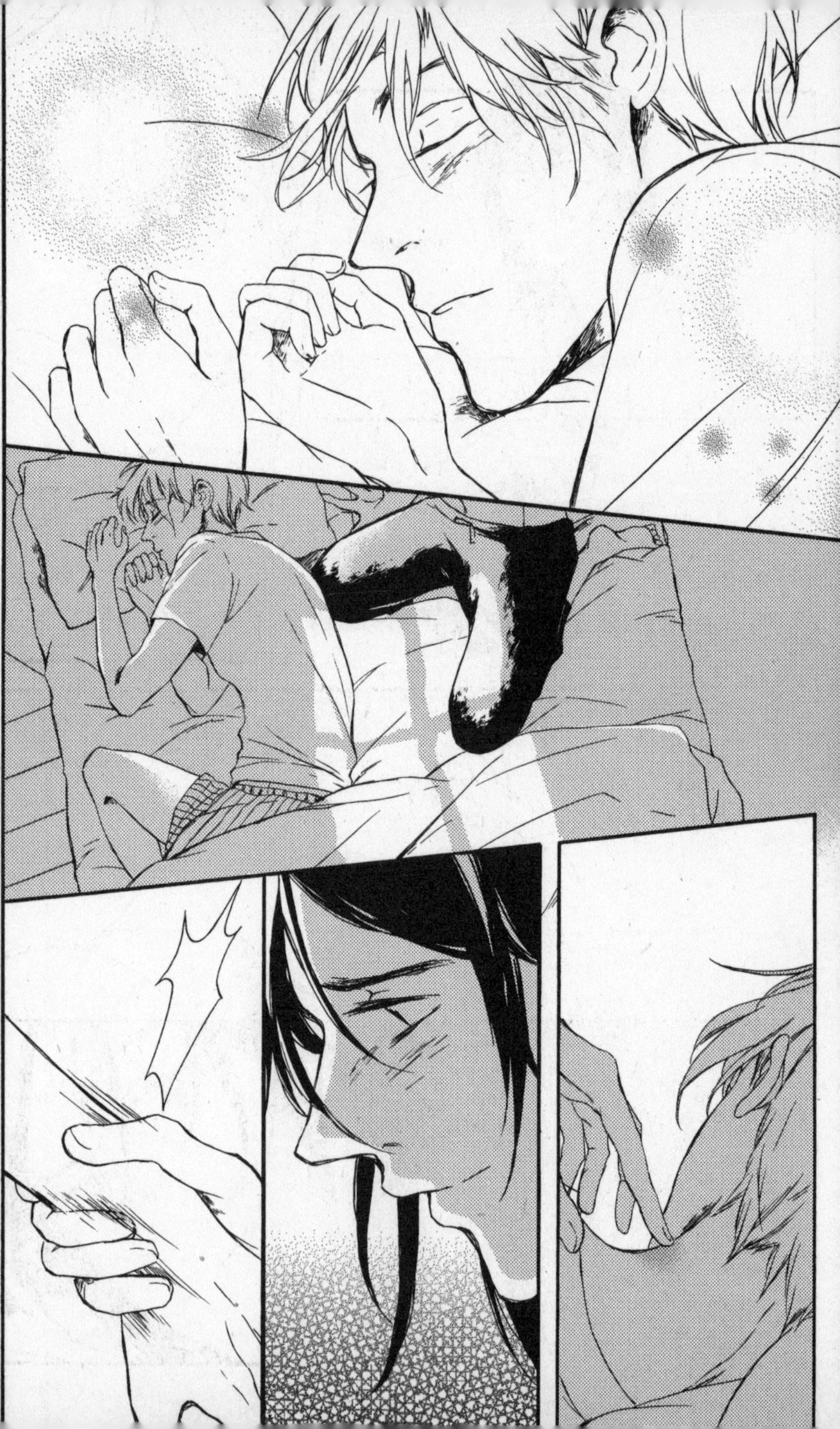

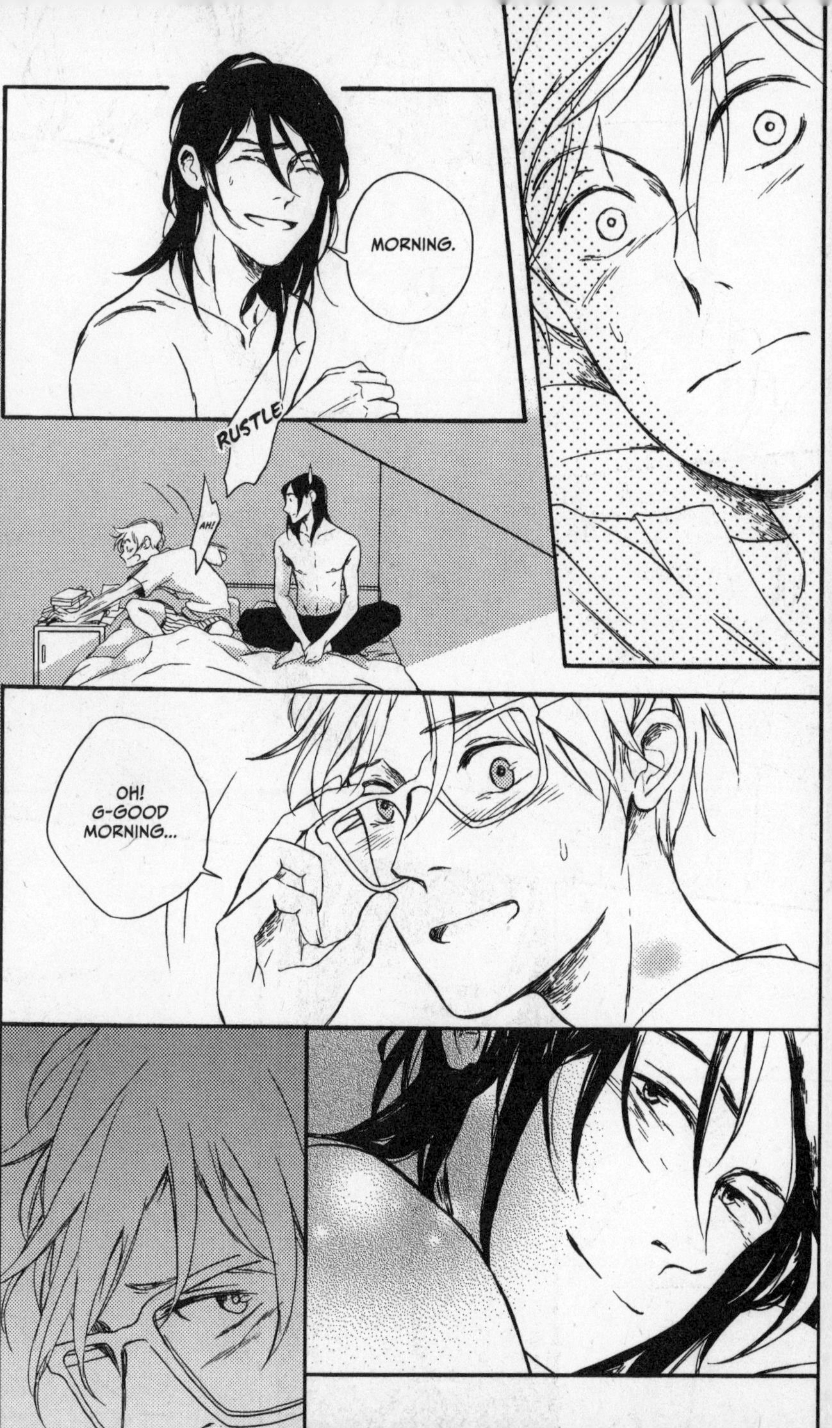
MORNING.
RUSTLE
AH!
OH! G-GOOD MORNING...

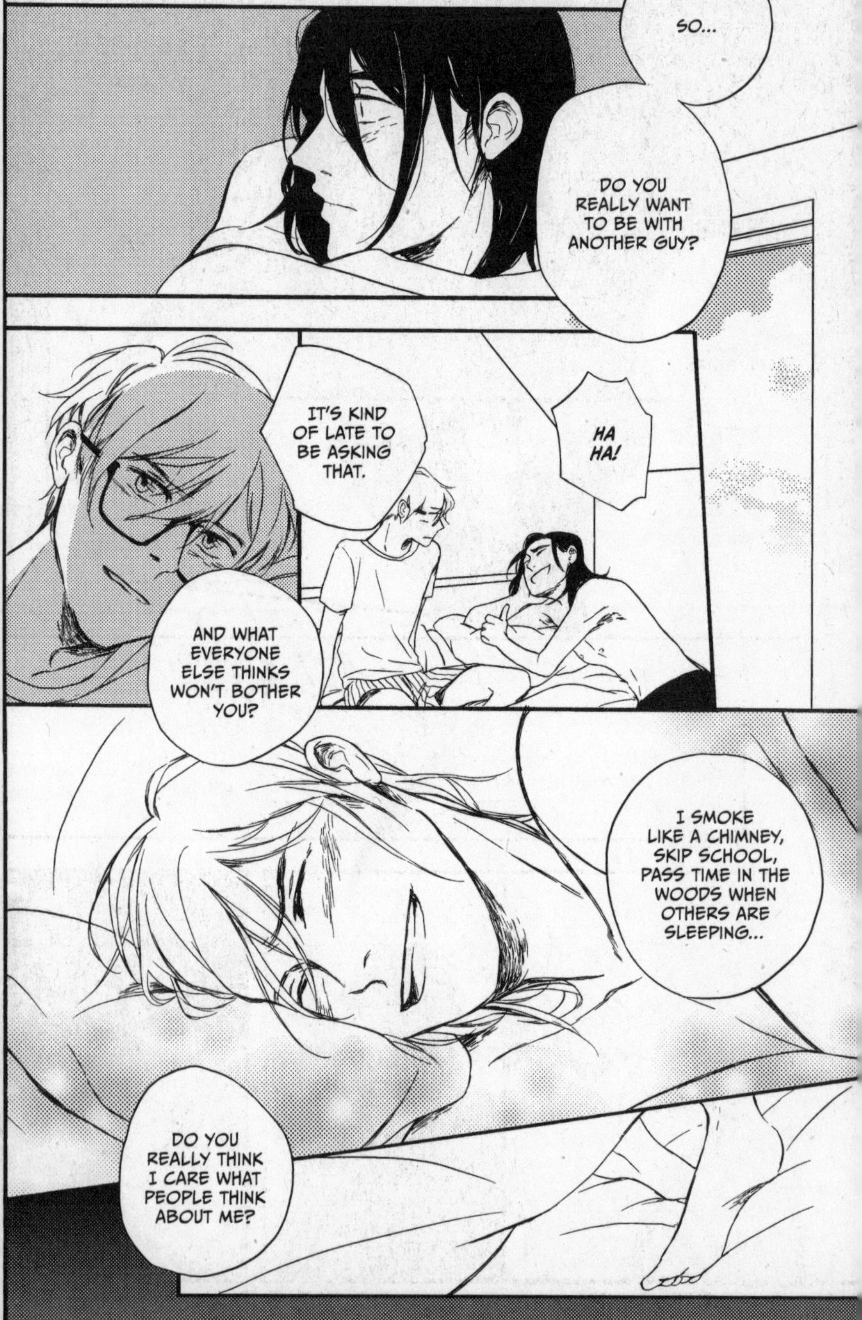
SO...
DO YOU REALLY WANT TO BE WITH ANOTHER GUY?
IT'S KIND OF LATE TO BE ASKING THAT.
HA HA!
AND WHAT EVERYONE ELSE THINKS WON'T BOTHER YOU?
I SMOKE LIKE A CHIMNEY, SKIP SCHOOL, PASS TIME IN THE WOODS WHEN OTHERS ARE SLEEPING...
DO YOU REALLY THINK I CARE WHAT PEOPLE THINK ABOUT ME?

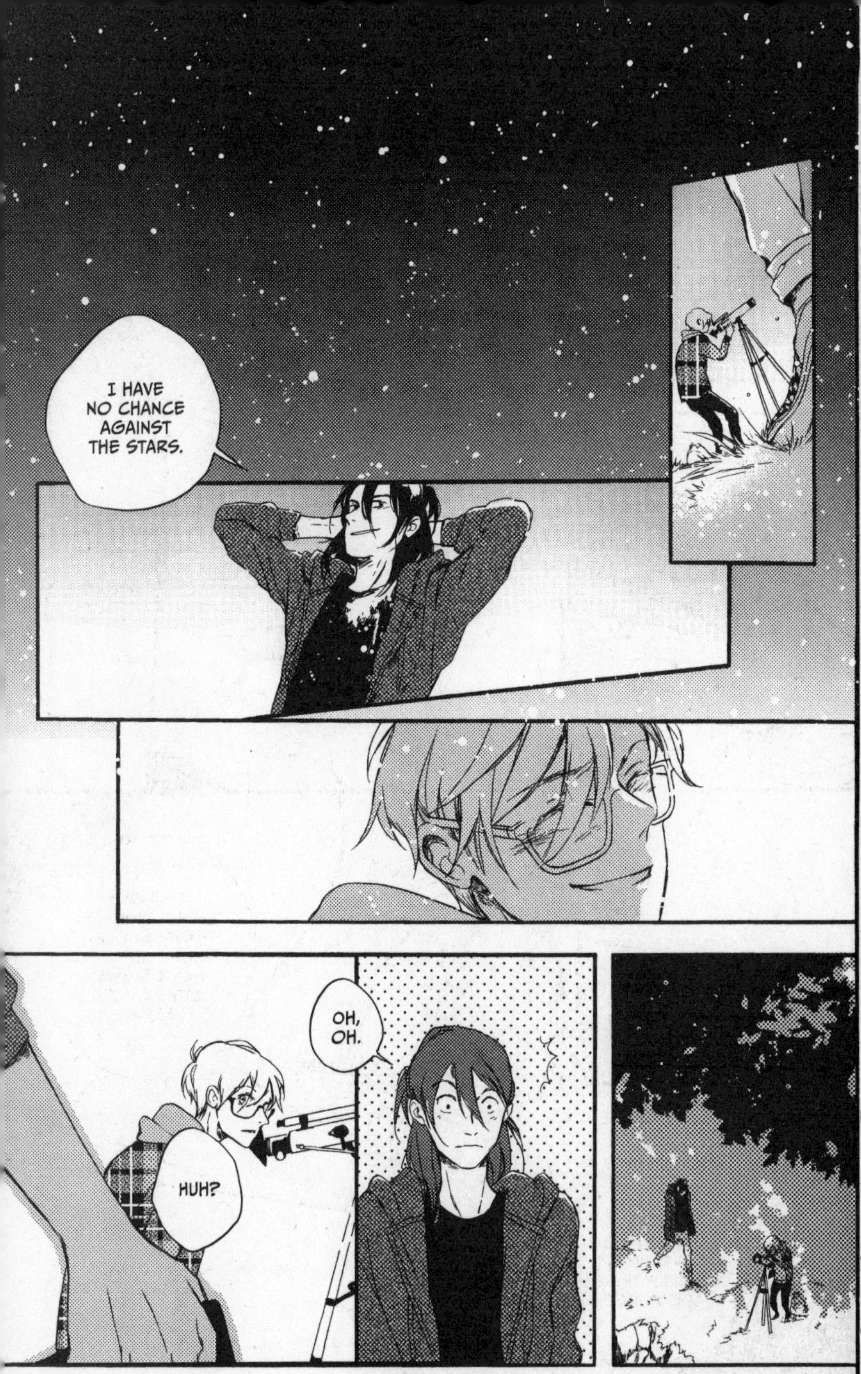
I HAVE NO CHANCE AGAINST THE STARS.
OH, OH.
HUH?

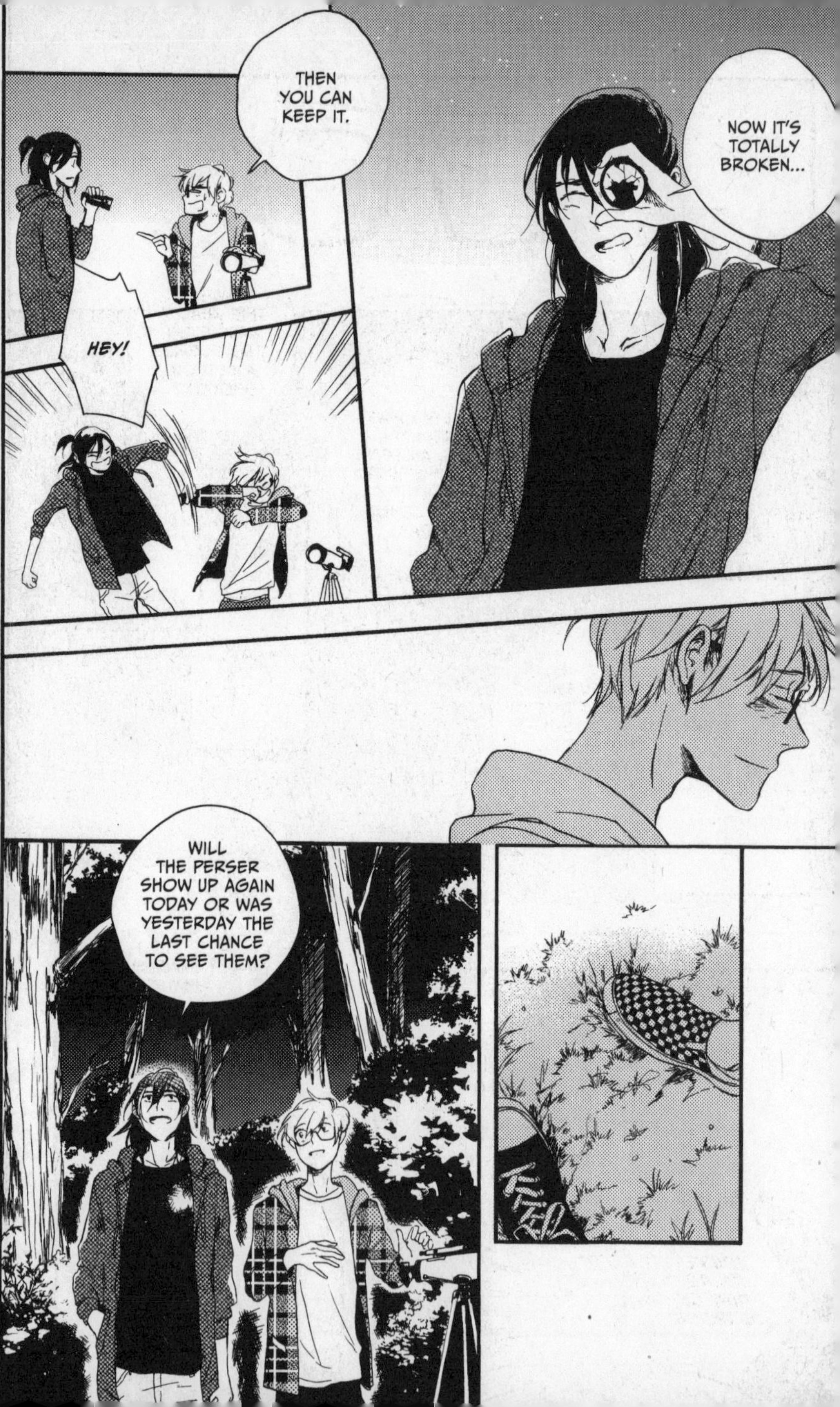
NOW IT'S TOTALLY BROKEN...
THEN YOU CAN KEEP IT.
HEY!
WILL THE PERSER SHOW UP AGAIN TODAY OR WAS YESTERDAY THE LAST CHANCE TO SEE THEM?

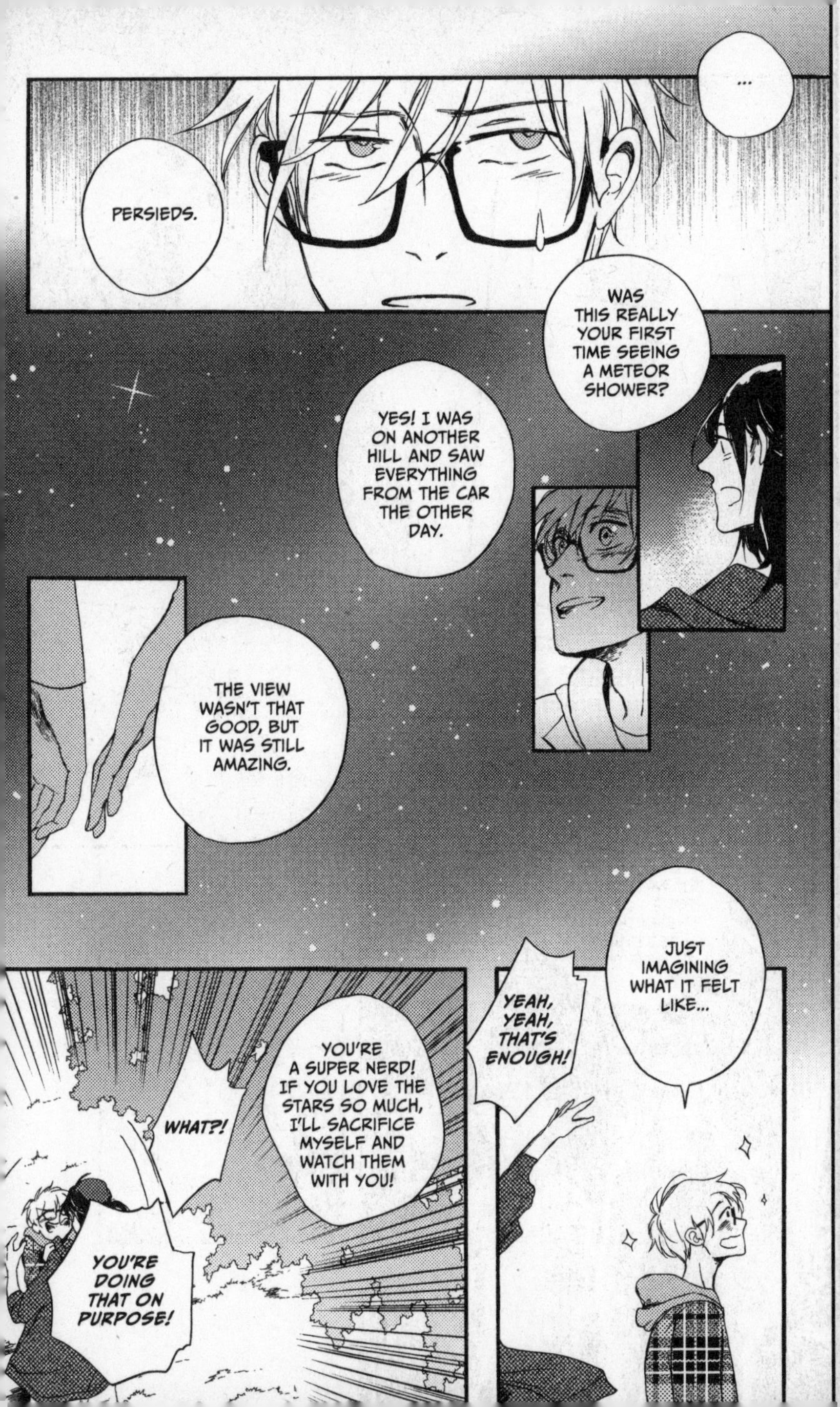
...
PERSIEDS.
WAS THIS REALLY YOUR FIRST TIME SEEING A METEOR SHOWER?
YES! I WAS ON ANOTHER HILL AND SAW EVERYTHING FROM THE CAR THE OTHER DAY.
THE VIEW WASN'T THAT GOOD, BUT IT WAS STILL AMAZING.
JUST IMAGINING WHAT IT FELT LIKE...
YEAH, YEAH, THAT'S ENOUGH!
YOU'RE A SUPER NERD! IF YOU LOVE THE STARS SO MUCH, I'LL SACRIFICE MYSELF AND WATCH THEM WITH YOU!
WHAT?!
YOU'RE DOING THAT ON PURPOSE!

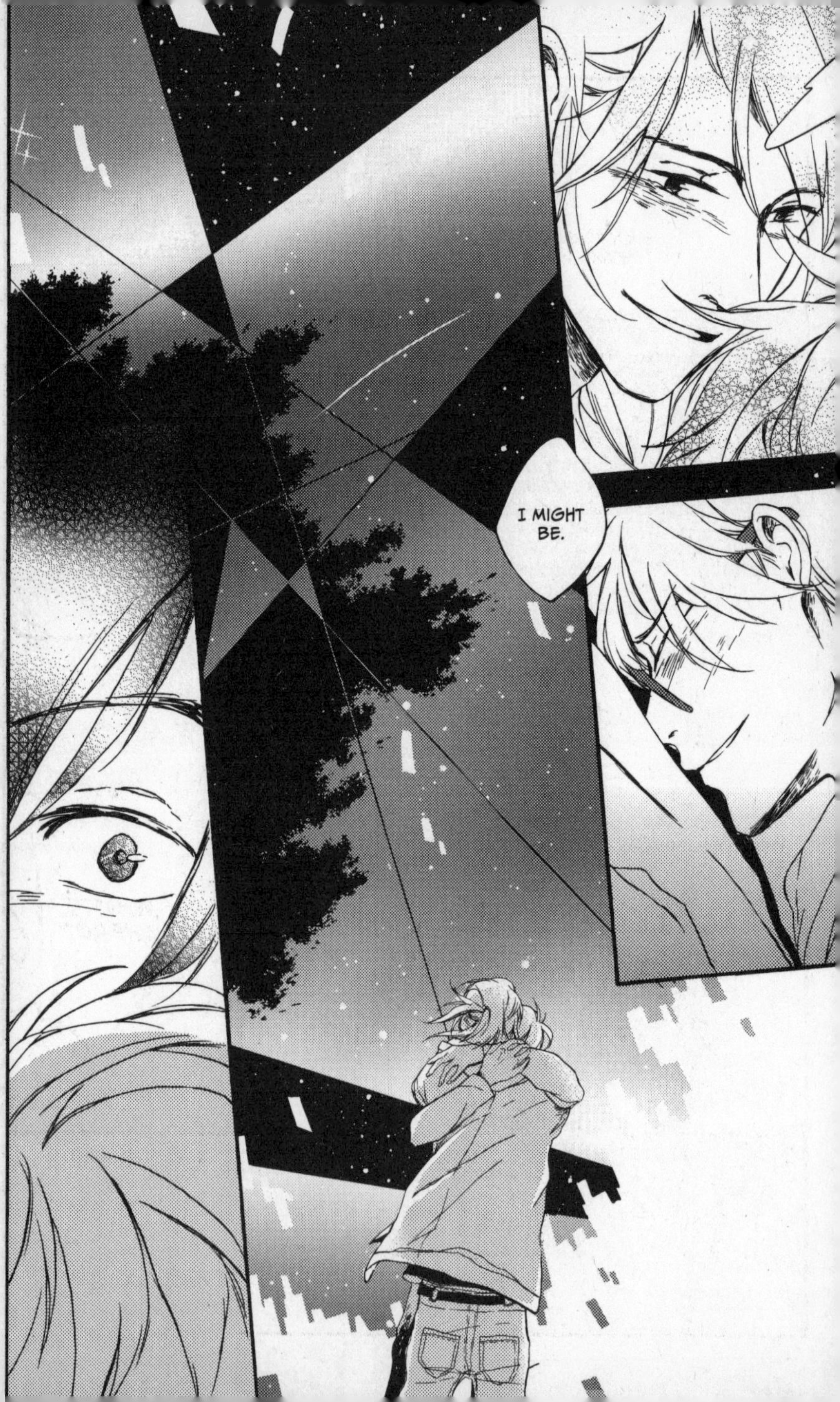
I MIGHT BE.

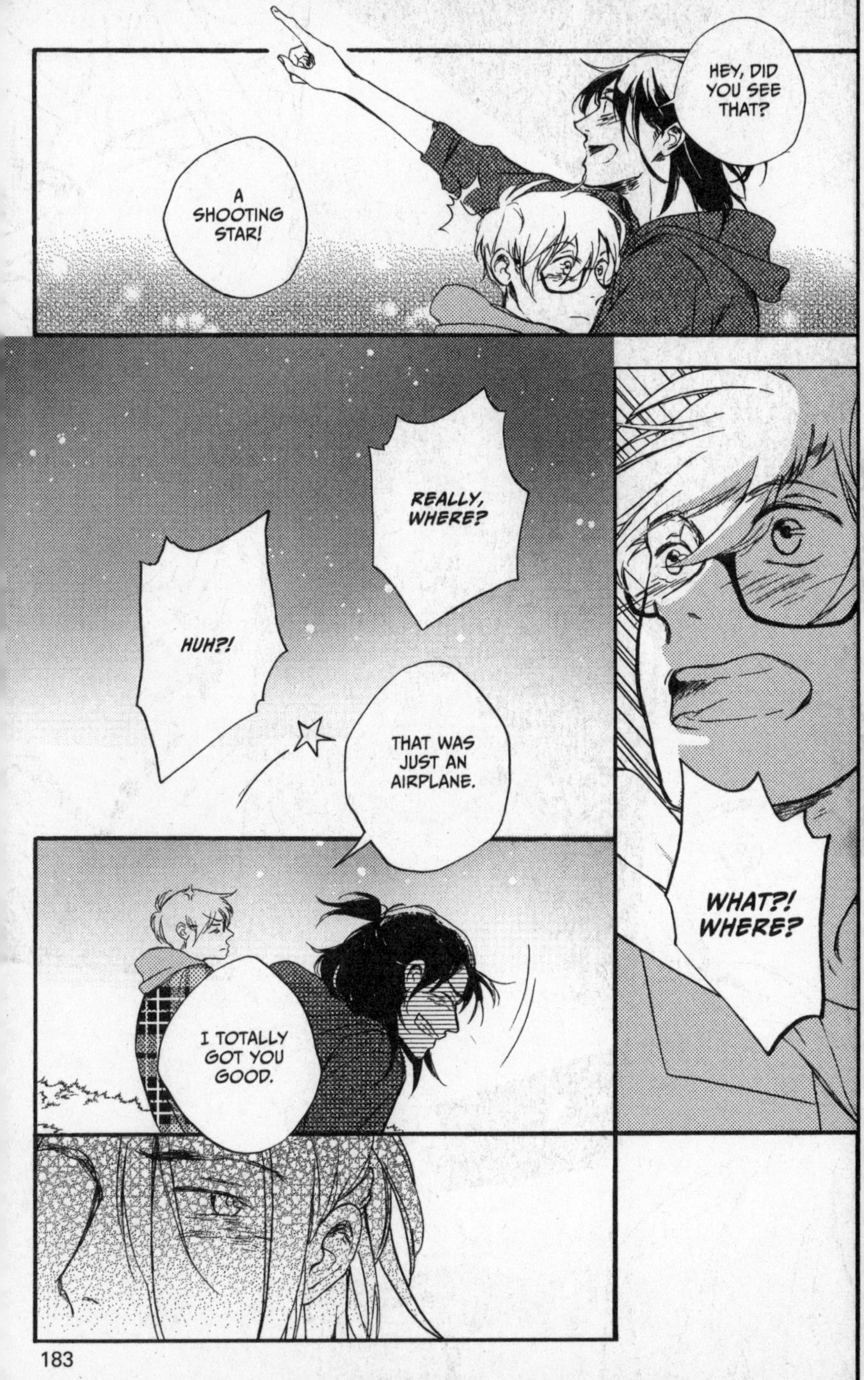
HEY, DID YOU SEE THAT?
A SHOOTING STAR!
WHAT?! WHERE?
REALLY, WHERE?
HUH?!
THAT WAS JUST AN AIRPLANE.
I TOTALLY GOT YOU GOOD.

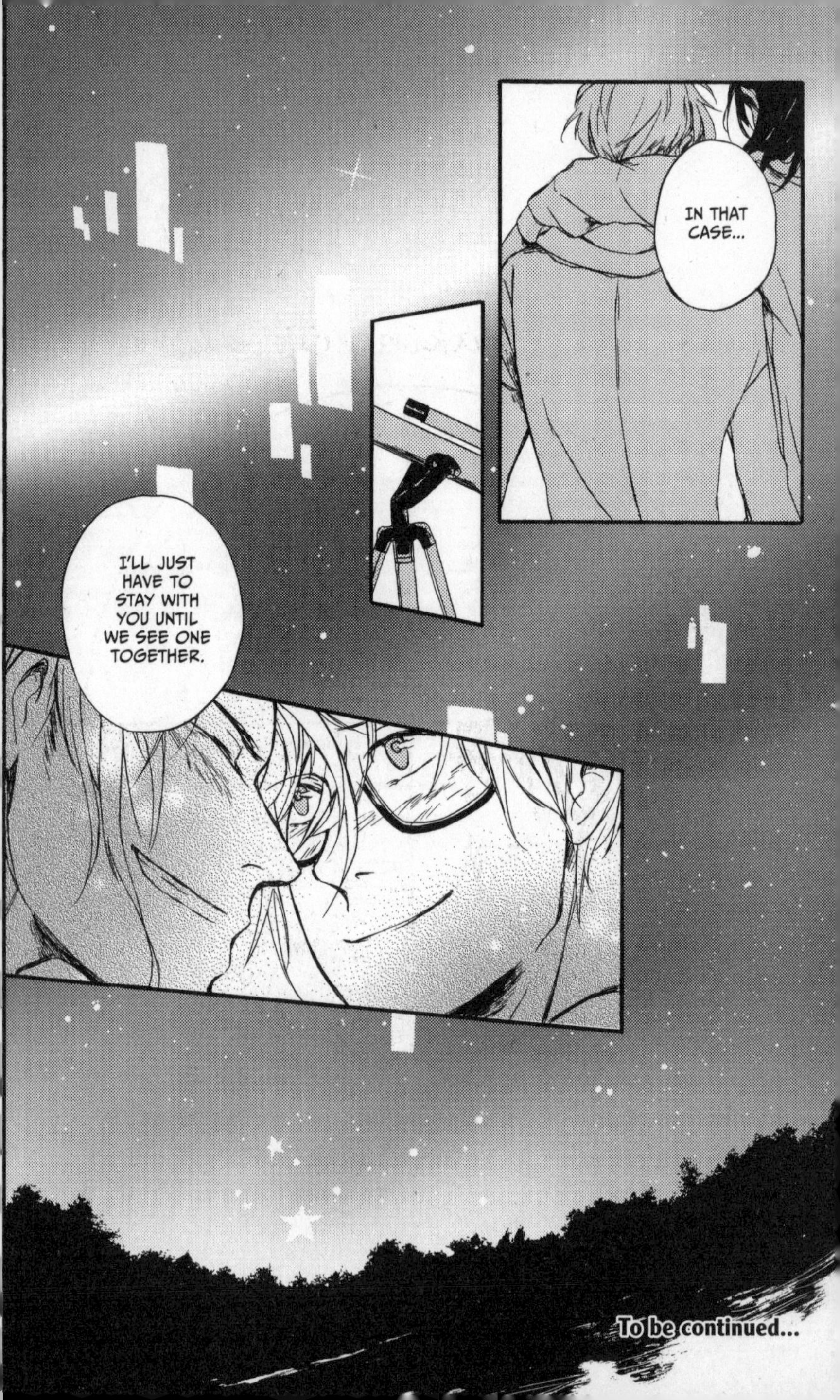
IN THAT CASE...
I'LL JUST HAVE TO STAY WITH YOU UNTIL WE SEE ONE TOGETHER.
To be continued...

Making Of

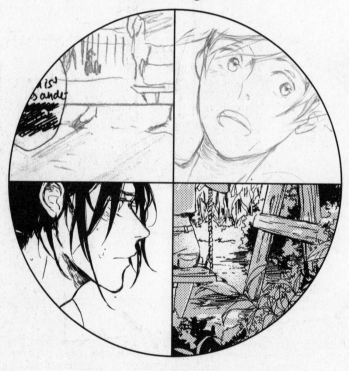

Sophie: First of all, we write the plot of the story. Anna and I lay out all of our ideas and then I put it all together. When we're satisfied, we hand it over to our editor Bea, who then looks over it. Once we're all ready to move forward, Anna continues with the storyboard. :D

Storyboard

You mean he doesn't believe us?
Yeah, but I think there's something else, too.
Dawn
That stubborn idiot.
Should I check in on him? This sucks!
Keep your chin up!
First, let's take a deep breath.
I'm sure Niko will calm down soon.
I hope you're right.

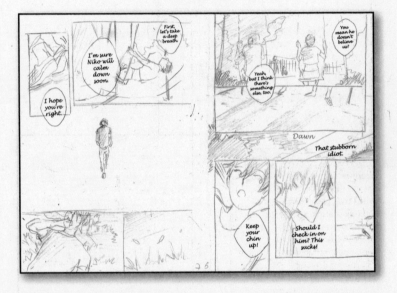

Anna: Wherever conversations take place, sometimes the dialogue is decided during the storyboard phase because Sophie leaves room for changes in the plot. During paneling, I take into account that there are two sides facing each other and the black and white parts are consistent.

Sophie: After we clarify which elements of the story are important and Anna has given me the storyboard, I look over it and sometimes correct the dialogue or make comments regarding the paneling, flow of reading, etc. After that, we pass everything on to Bea in the editorial office. :)

Sketches

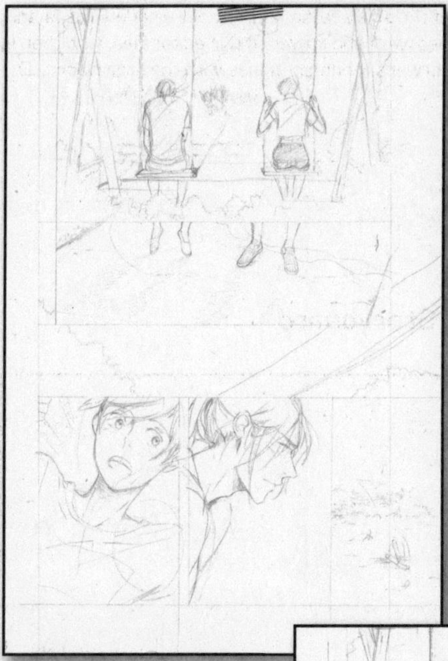

Anna: The sketches are done in pencil, so it literally takes a lot of physical effort. :D

Imagine 'blue lines' here! :'D

Sophie: The next step would be the "Blue Lines" (because I like blue better than red ;D). Unfortunately, you can't see this here as the page is shown here in black and white. If I notice something, I will scribble on Anna's drawings. Sometimes she asks what I meant... :'D The things that I like most get a heart! <3

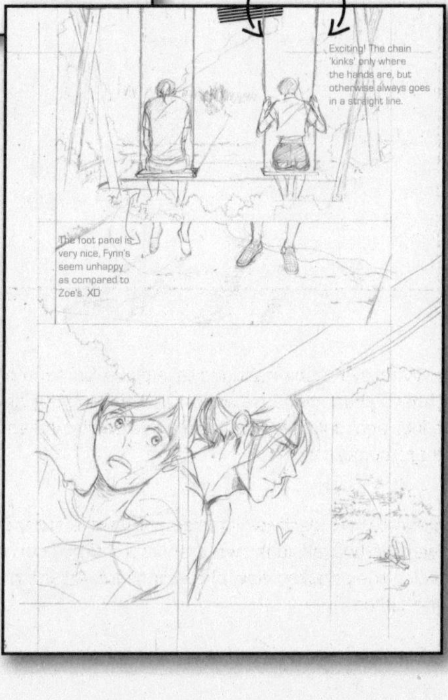
Exciting! The chain 'kinks' only where the hands are, but otherwise always goes in a straight line.
The foot panel is very nice, Fynn's seem unhappy as compared to Zoe's. XD

Lines

Anna: On the same sheet, the outlines are created with pen and ink. Usually, I draw the backgrounds in this step. I'm very glad that Bea trusts my judgment. (: Unfortunately, I still make smears, which gets me in trouble... but can be corrected on the PC! This saves my hands! ;D

Sophie: After scanning, I clean up the artwork: I remove lint and dust particles, and I try to get the pages and speech bubbles looking as clean as possible. :D Depending on the artwork, this can be done quickly, but other times it takes a long while.

Raster

Sophie: Again, scanning is my job and I put the digital raster on the pages. :) Sometimes this is one of my favorite tasks. Anna tells me what she thinks and then I try to work it out. :) Meanwhile, we have a couple "code words" that we both understand. XD

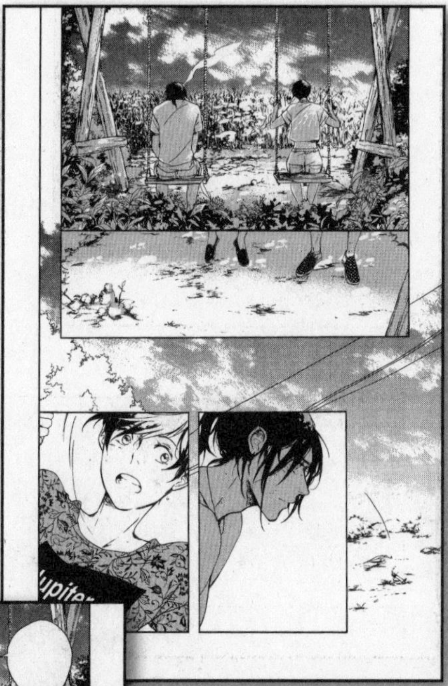

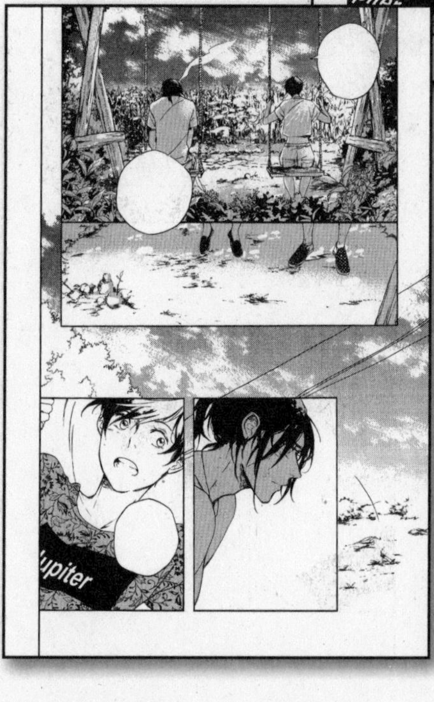

Speech Bubbles and Sound Effects Words

Anna: The speech bubbles and sound effects are created separately in a new layer. This makes it possible to edit the speech bubbles without affecting the illustration.

PSD - Data

Sophie: Last but not least, in the PSD files where Anna placed the speech bubbles and special effects words, I swap the line art with the fully rendered pages. Then we send them to TOKYOPOP. We then receive an email with corrections and questions that need to be clarified. In the end, everything then is sent to the printing house. :D

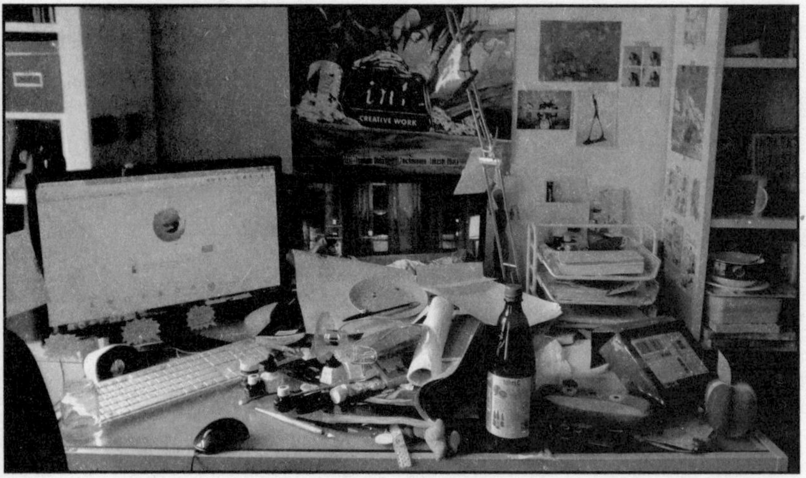
CREATIVE WORK

Anna's work space.

Character Study

Niko

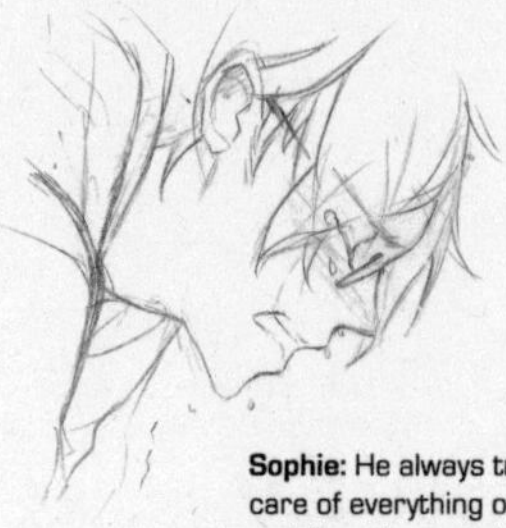

Sophie: He always tries to take care of everything on his own and doesn't want others to see him like this...

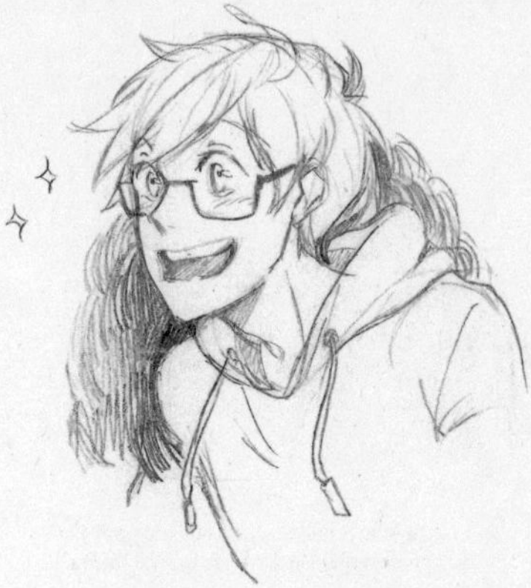

Sophie: From the beginning, Niko was a character who smiles a lot.

Anna: Niko's spirit animal? Definitely a dog!

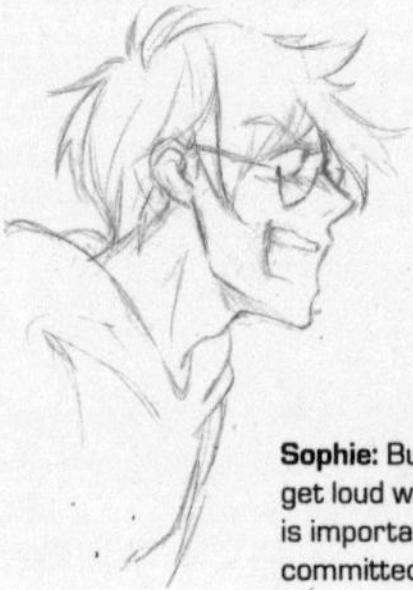

Sophie: But he doesn't hesitate to get loud when necessary. If something is important to him, then he's committed to it.

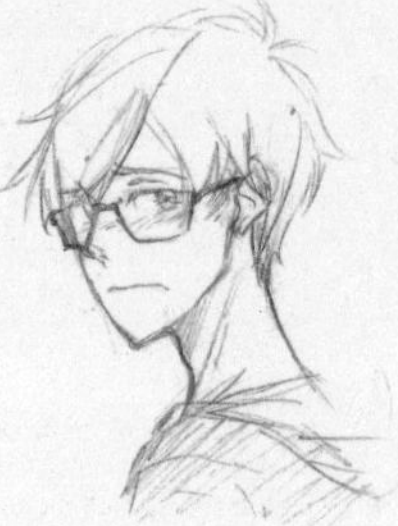

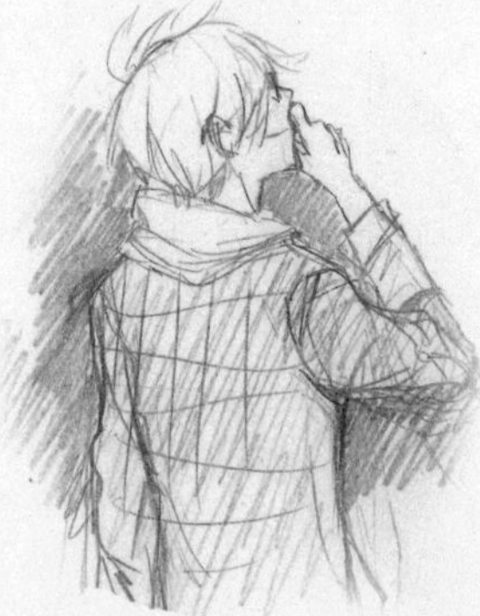

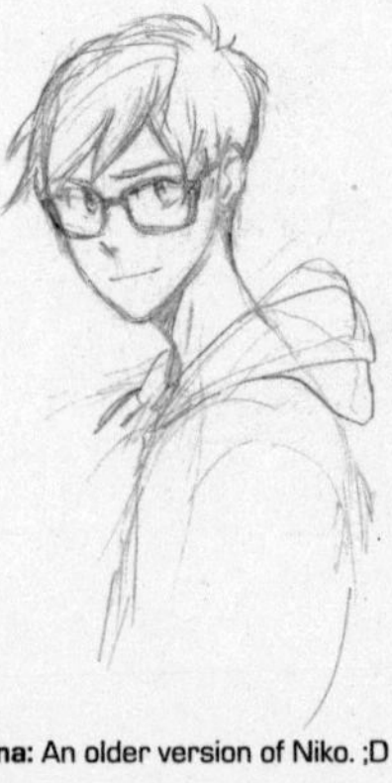

Anna: An older version of Niko. ;D

Sophie: Basically, Niko is a very positive person and always tries to look forward.

Anna: Niko is easy to draw. His fluffy hair is fun to draw!

Anna: One of the first sketches I made for *Star Collector*. Right after, we got the idea for the story! I still like this picture a lot!

Sophie: He didn't get suspenders after all... Maybe in the next volume. :'D

Anna: *Hopefully* in the next volume, Sophie!

Fynn

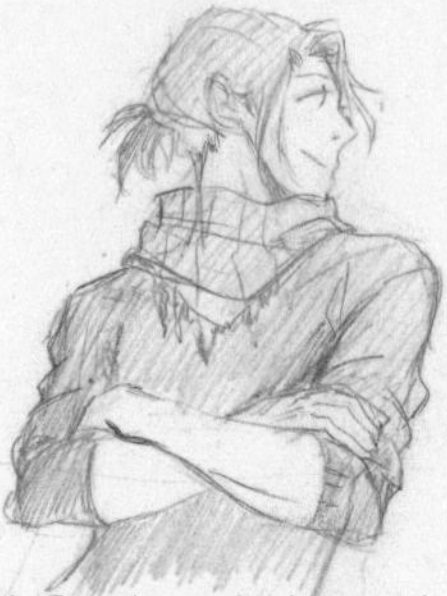

Sophie: Fynn always takes it easy and rarely notices problems. When he does, he just shrugs his shoulders.

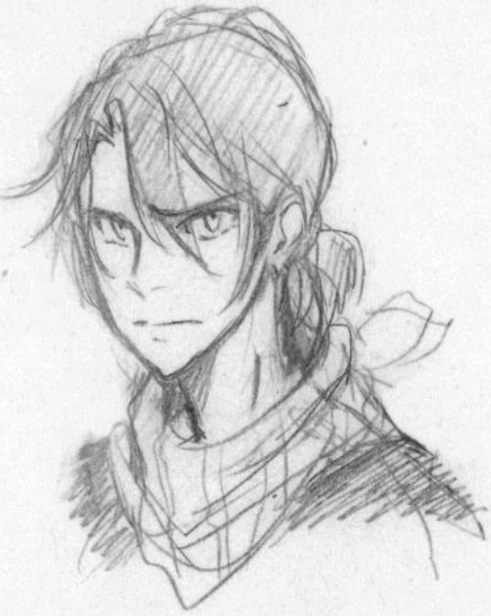

Sophie: Ha ha. Fynn looks very young here! :D And it ended up being too warm for the scarf. XD

Anna: I think Fynn has changed the most during the creation process. Cute characters easily become cooler. Well, Fynn isn't really cool and I had to get used to him at first. (:

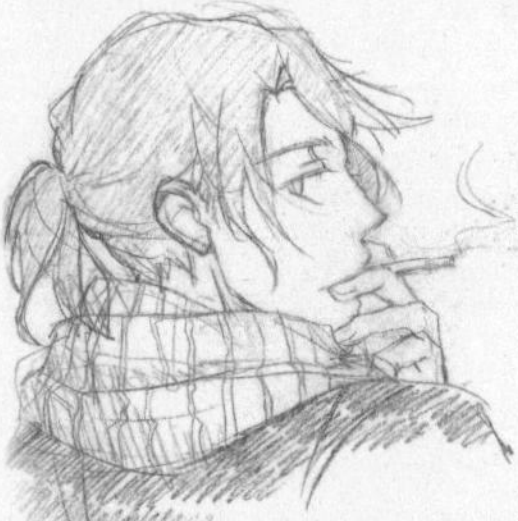

Anna: Drawing Fynn smoking was difficult for me as a nonsmoker. I felt that I couldn't draw it authentically.

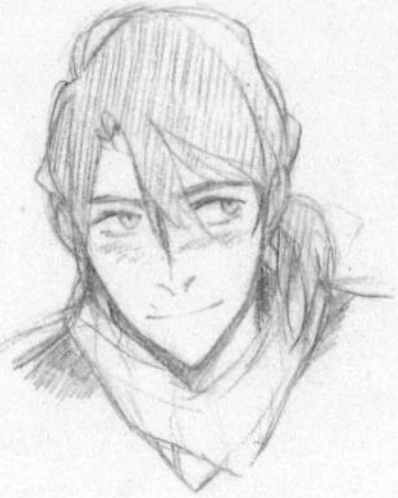

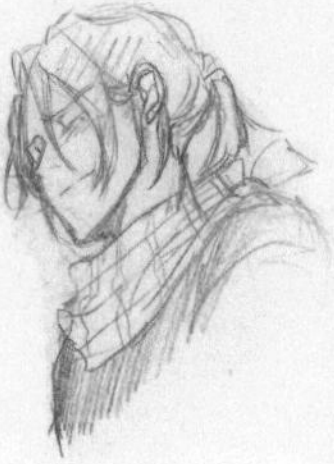

Anna: Fynn was actually the first longhaired boy that I've drawn.

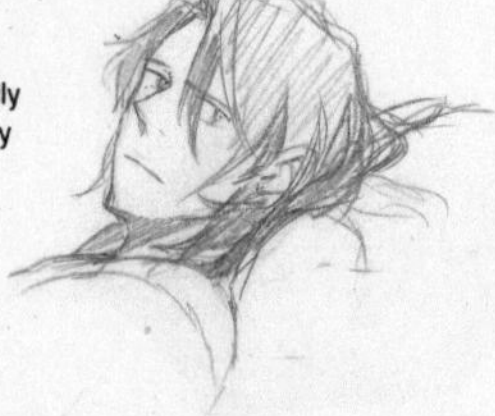

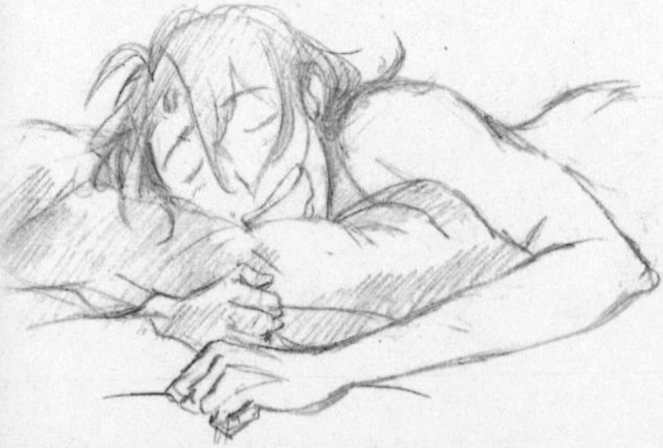

Sophie: Fynn has always been great at sleeping XD

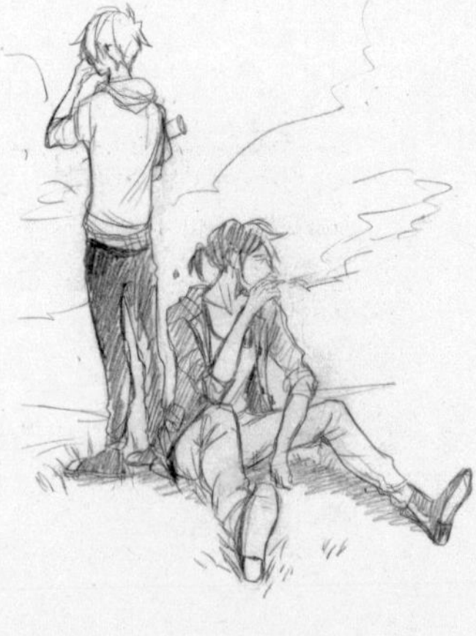

Sophie: The two boys doing what they each do best.

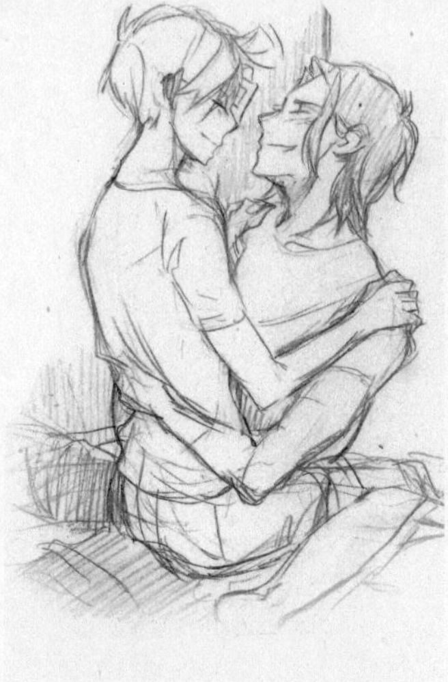

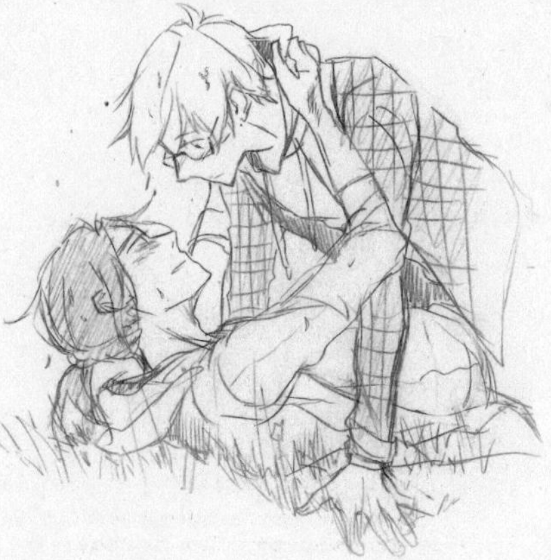

Anna: This sketch is similar to what took place in Chapter 5, I noticed that after the drawing phase! :D

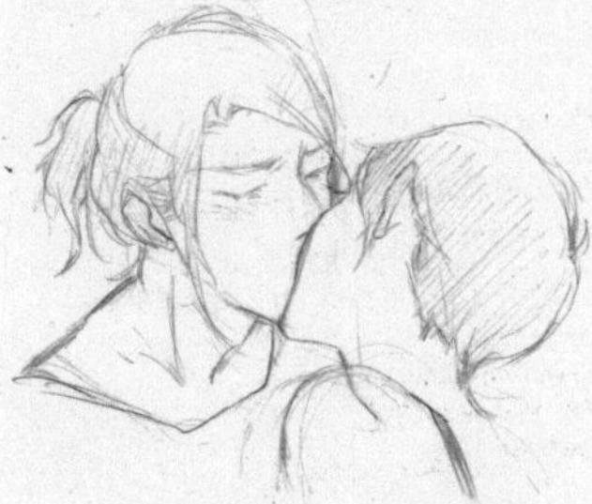

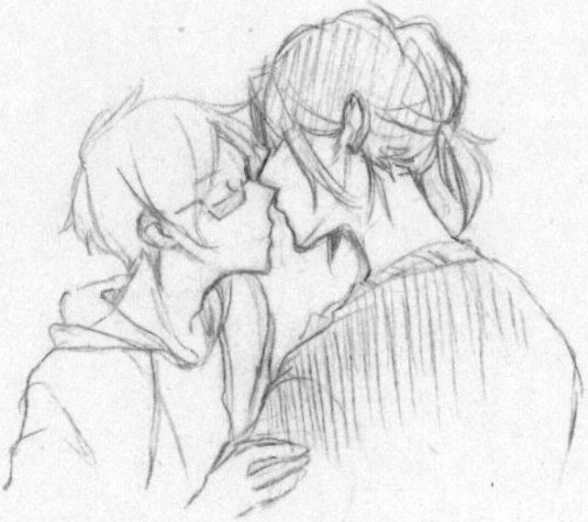

Anna: The scenery for Fynn and Zoe's discussion came to mind early on.

Sophie: I really like the relationship between Fynn and Zoe. :) You can feel the deep bond between the two somehow. Poor Zoe...

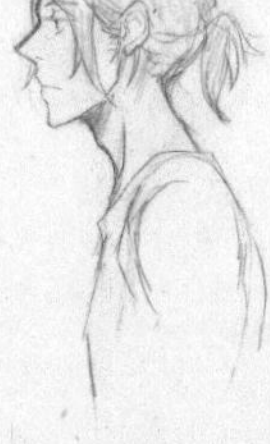

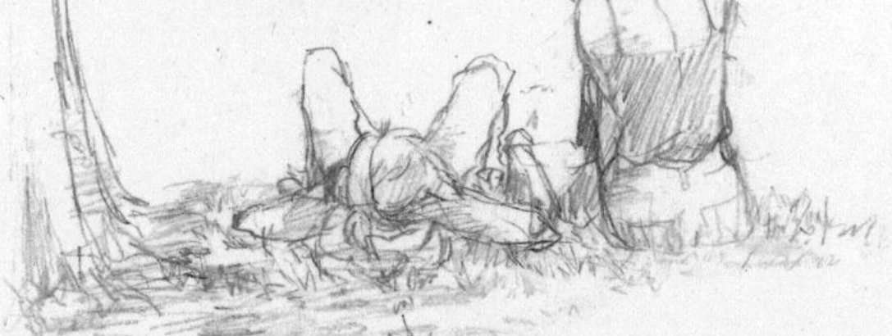

Zoe

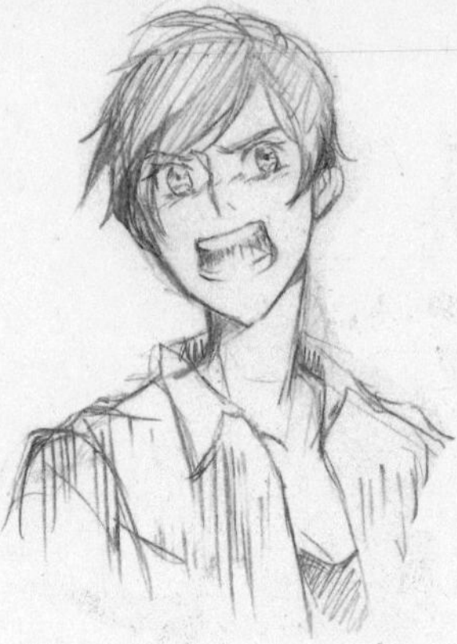

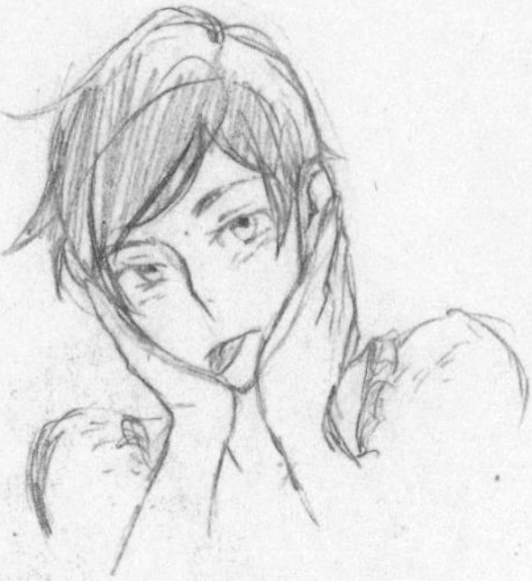

Anna: With Zoe, I could pursue my love for Pixie hairstyles! :D

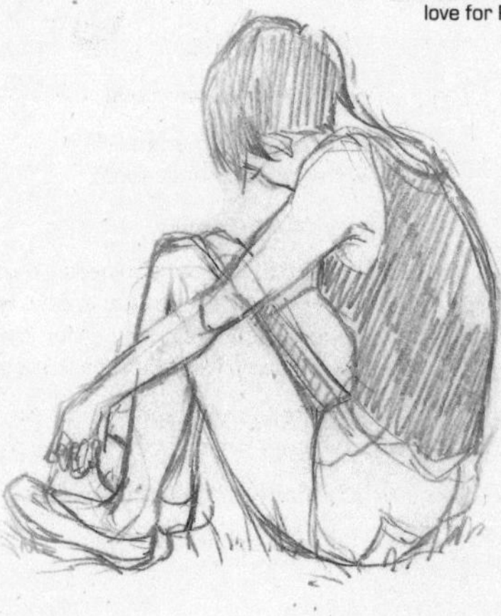

Sophie: Even though Zoe tries to hide it, she's very distressed about breaking up with Fynn.

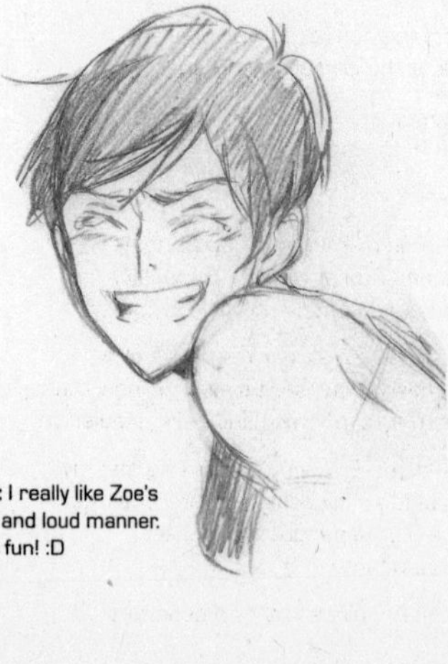

Sophie: I really like Zoe's cheeky and loud manner. It's just fun! :D

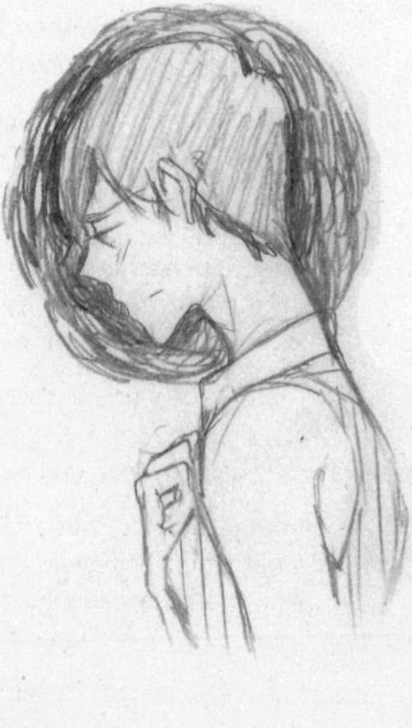

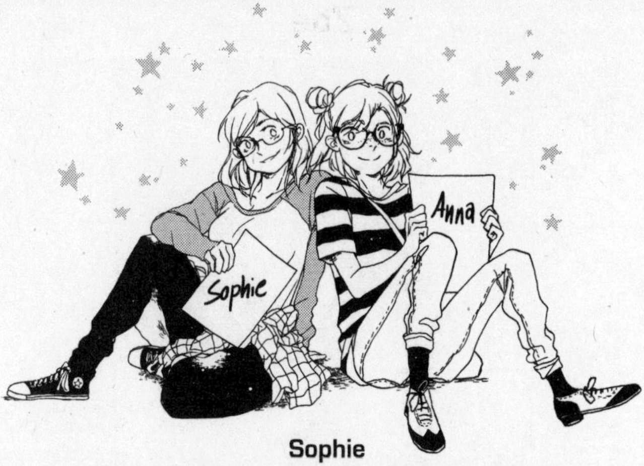
Anna
Sophie

Sophie

...was born in 1991, currently lives in Bavaria and works in debt collection.

Facebook: @Salamandra91
Twitter: @SalamandraSan

Hello everyone!

In Star Collector, not only did Niko and Fynn find happiness, I also gained a lot of new experiences and started a little journey. Together with Anna, Bea, Hanna and Ma, it was an exciting adventure that I definitely will cherish. Thank you all for joining me! First of all you, Anna. If not for you, there would be no Niko, Fynn or this exciting journey. :)

In the end, Niko unfortunately did not see a single shooting star.
But if it's any consolation, we haven't seen any on starry nights either! XD

I hope that you have more luck than Niko and fulfill your wishes! See you soon!

Sophie

Anna

...was born in 1995 and has been drawing comics for ten years.
She currently is studying Social Work at the University of Kassel.

Facebook: @Holzesserin
Twitter: @Traumholz

Dear Reader!

The first release from a major publisher is tremendously exciting. I'm glad that I have Sala, Bea, Fynn, Niko and Zoe at my side. Especially without you, Sala, it certainly would not have been possible. (:

Ultimately, the work on this volume was neither lonely nor chaotic. Not a simple flower for the picking, but demanding a positive sense. It's nice to know that there is more going on, as long as you continue moving forward and being inquisitive.

I would like to thank all those who take what I do seriously by supporting me: my family and friends; especially Jonas and my rapidly increasing number of aunts. And you, dear reader, because you are truly a part of this project. I hope that you liked this volume. (:

I hope to see you soon! I want to give Fynn the happiness that he deserves! ;D

Anna

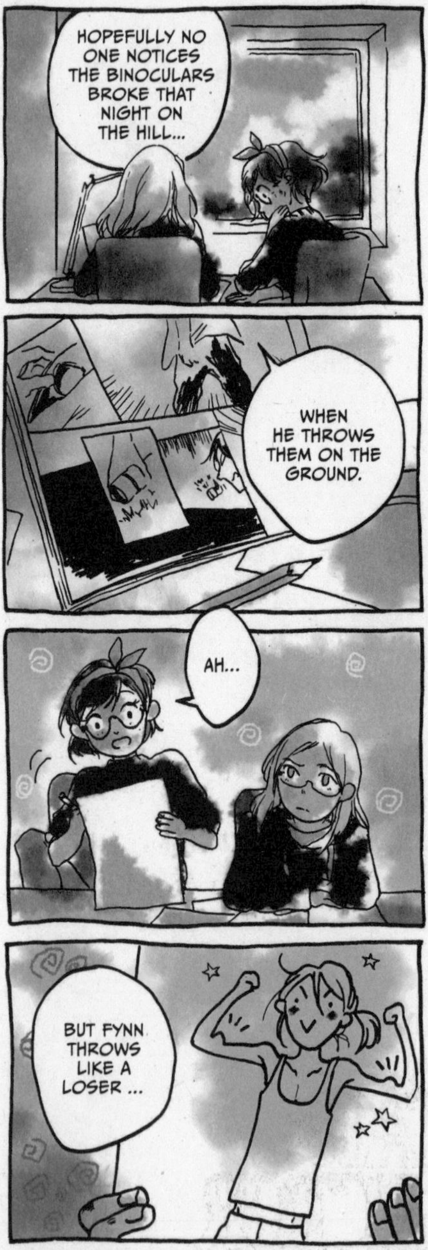
HOPEFULLY NO ONE NOTICES THE BINOCULARS BROKE THAT NIGHT ON THE HILL...
WHEN HE THROWS THEM ON THE GROUND.
AH...
BUT FYNN THROWS LIKE A LOSER ...

STAR COLLECTOR

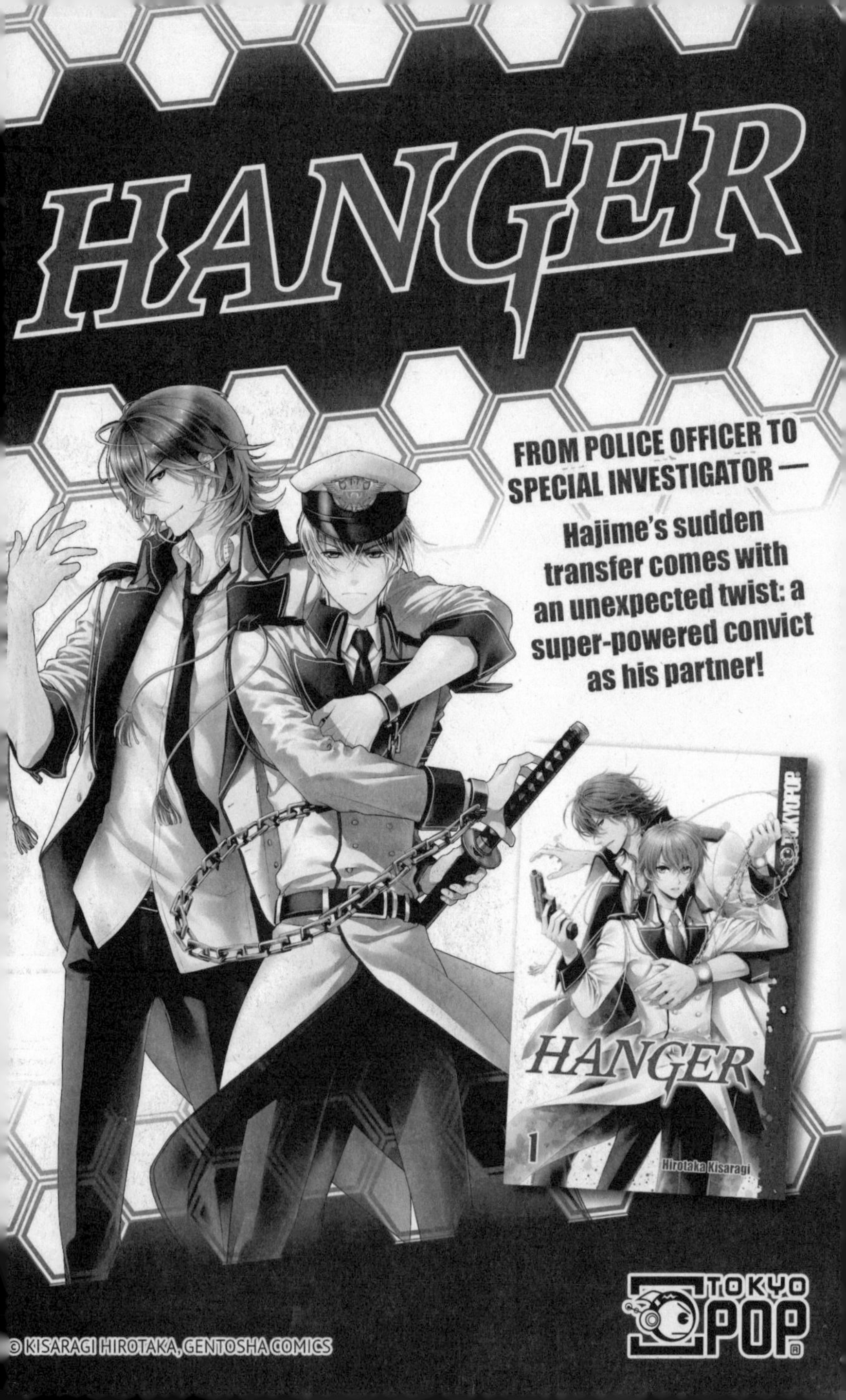
HANGER
FROM POLICE OFFICER TO SPECIAL INVESTIGATOR —
Hajime's sudden transfer comes with an unexpected twist: a super-powered convict as his partner!
HANGER
1
Hirotaka Kisaragi
TOKYOPOP
© KISARAGI HIROTAKA, GENTOSHA COMICS
TOKYO POP

Servant & Lord

YEARS
AGO, MUSIC
BROUGHT THEM
TOGETHER...

AND THEN,
EVERYTHING
CHANGED.

INTERNATIONAL
WOMEN of MANGA

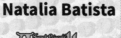

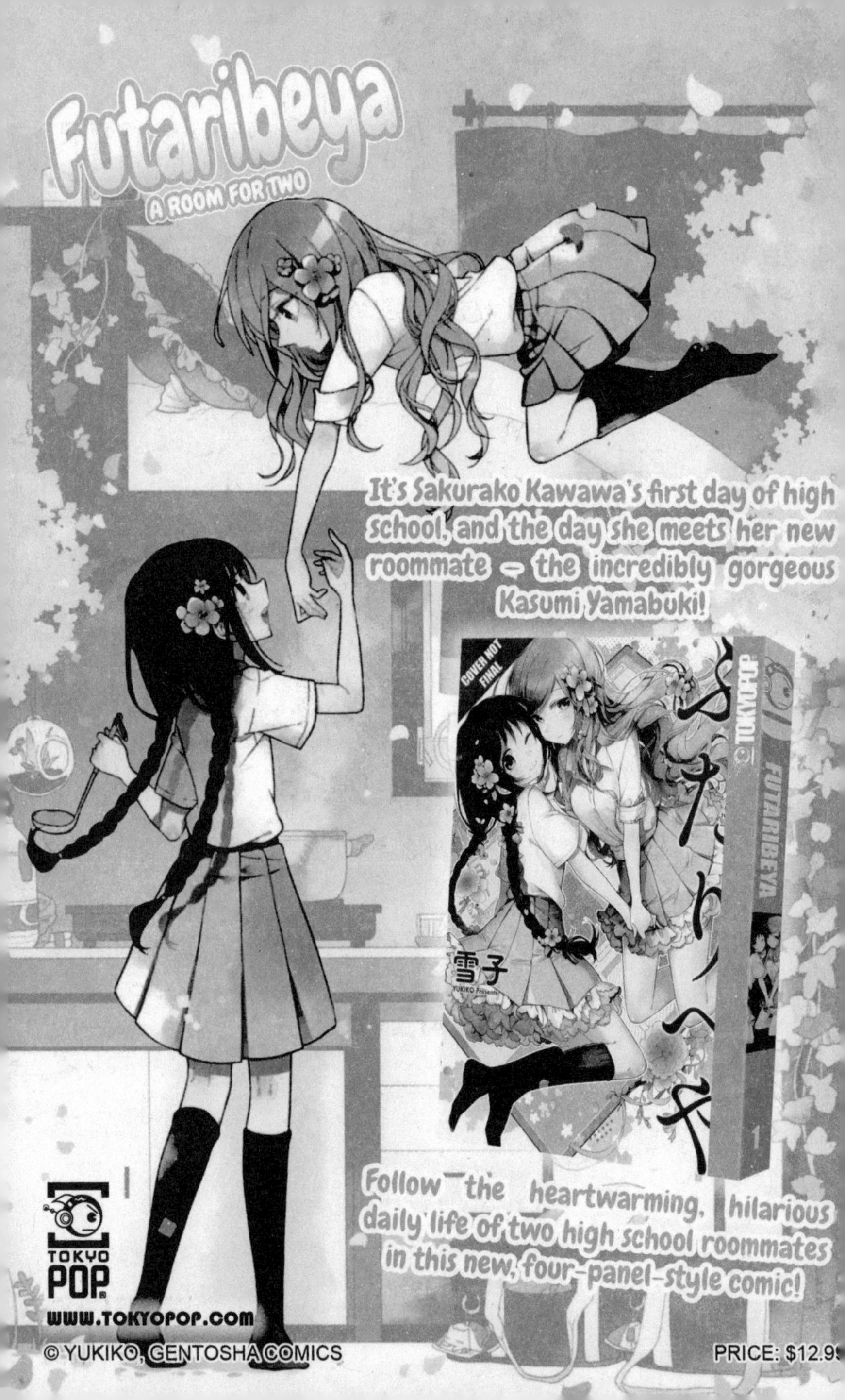

Futaribeya
A ROOM FOR TWO
It's Sakurako Kawawa's first day of high school, and the day she meets her new roommate – the incredibly gorgeous Kasumi Yamabuki!
COVER NOT FINAL
雪子
YUKIKO Presents
TOKYOPOP
FUTARIBEYA
1
Follow the heartwarming, hilarious daily life of two high school roommates in this new, four-panel-style comic!
TOKYO POP
WWW.TOKYOPOP.COM
© YUKIKO, GENTOSHA COMICS
PRICE: $12.9

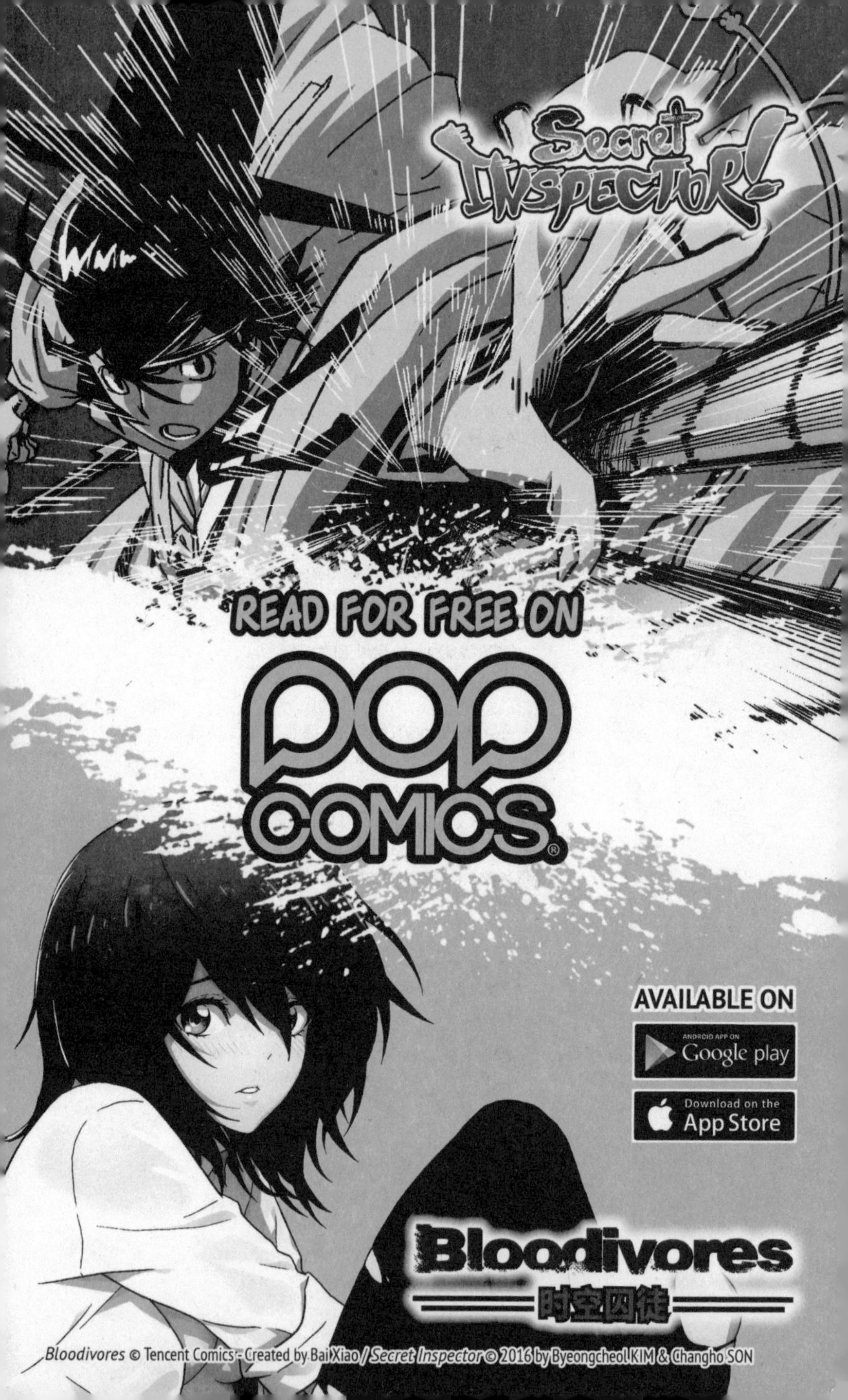
Secret INSPECTOR!
READ FOR FREE ON
POP COMICS®
AVAILABLE ON
ANDROID APP ON Google play
Download on the App Store
Bloodivores
时空囚徒
Bloodivores © Tencent Comics - Created by Bai Xiao / Secret Inspector © 2016 by Byeongcheol KIM & Changho SON

Star Collector, Volume 1
Manga by Anna B. & Sophie Schönhammer

Editor - Lena Atanassova
Marketing Associate - Kae Winters
Technology and Digital Media Assistant - Phillip Hong
Translator - Kenneth Shinabery
Graphic Designer - Phillip Hong
Retouching and Lettering - Vibrraant Publishing Studio
Editor-in-Chief & Publisher - Stu Levy

A  Manga

TOKYOPOP and 🐸 are trademarks or registered trademarks of TOKYOPOP Inc.

TOKYOPOP Inc.
5200 W. Century Blvd. Suite 705
Los Angeles, 90045

E-mail: info@TOKYOPOP.com
Come visit us online at www.TOKYOPOP.com

f www.facebook.com/TOKYOPOP
🐦 www.twitter.com/TOKYOPOP
p www.pinterest.com/TOKYOPOP
📷 www.instagram.com/TOKYOPOP

ISBN: 978-1-4278-6020-0
First TOKYOPOP Printing: February 2019
10 9 8 7 6 5 4 3 2 1
Printed in CANADA

S…

THIS IS THE … BOOK!

How do you read manga-style? It's simple! Let's practice -- just start in the top right panel and follow the numbers below!

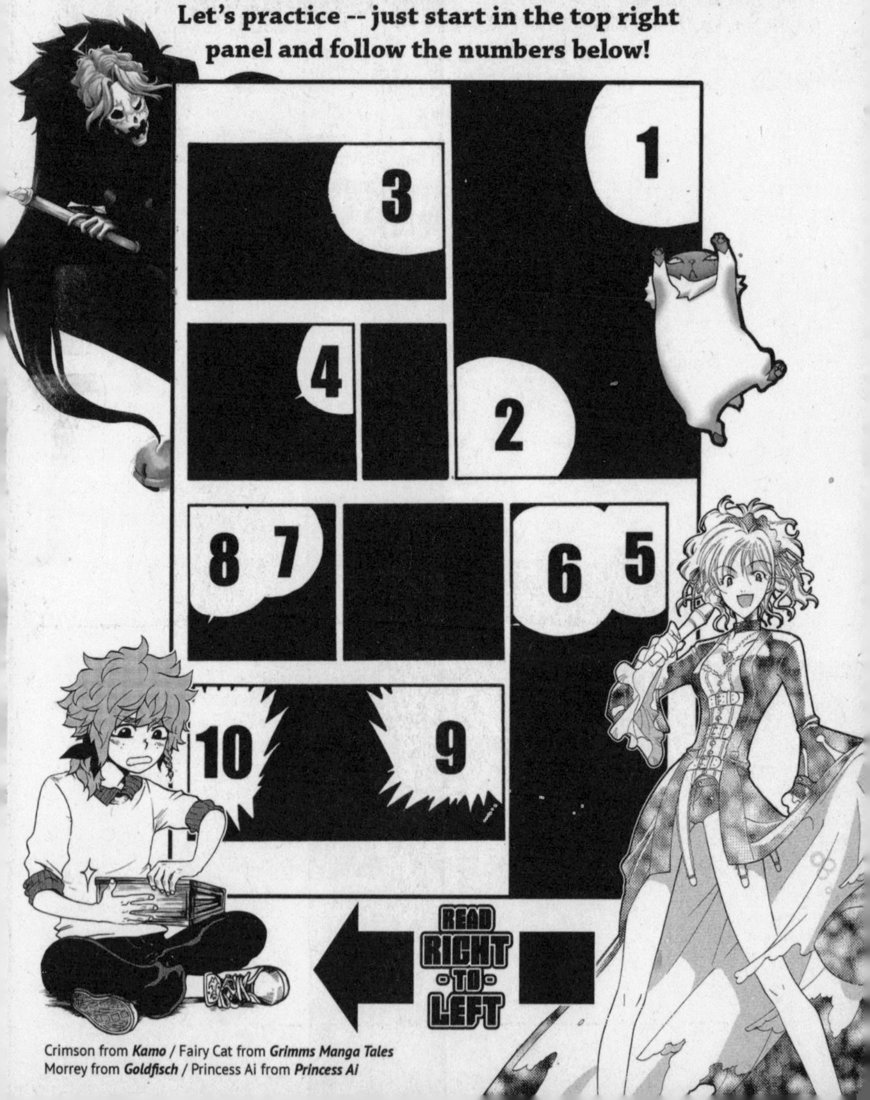
1
2
3
4
5
6
7
8
9
10
READ RIGHT -TO- LEFT

Crimson from ***Kamo*** / Fairy Cat from ***Grimms Manga Tales***
Morrey from ***Goldfisch*** / Princess Ai from ***Princess Ai***